The Politics of the Extreme Right

The Politics of the Extreme Right

From the margins to the mainstream

Edited by Paul Hainsworth

PINTER

London and New York

Pinter
A Continuum Imprint
Wellington House, 125 Strand, London WC2R OBB
370 Lexington Avenue, New York, NY 10017–6550

First published 2000

British Library Cataloguing in Publication Data
A catalogue record for this book is available from the British Library.

ISBN 1–85567–458–0 (hardback)
   1–85567–459–9 (paperback)

Library of Congress Cataloging-in-Publication Data
The politics of the extreme right: from the margins to the mainstream / edited by Paul Hainsworth.
      p. cm.
   Includes bibliographical references and index.
   ISBN 1-85567-458-0 (hb) — ISBN 1-85567-459-9 (pb)
      1. Conservatism—Europe. 2. Conservatism—United States. 3. Right-wing extremists—Europe. 4. Right-wing extremists—United States. I. Hainsworth, Paul, 1950–

JC573.2.E85 P65 2000
320.53'3'09409049 21—dc21
                                                                99-044977

Typeset by York House Typographic Ltd
Printed and bound in Great Britain by Biddles Ltd, Guildford and King's Lynn

Contents

Contributors

Jørgen Goul Andersen is Professor of Political Sociology at the University of Aalborg.

Susann Backer is a Lecturer in European Politics at the University of Bradford.

Tor Bjørklund is Associate Professor of Politics at the University of Oslo.

Michael Cox is Professor of Politics at the University of Aberystwyth.

Martin Durham is a Senior Lecturer in Politics at the University of Wolverhampton.

Roger Eatwell is Professor of European Politics at the University of Bath.

Tom Gallagher is Professor of European Peace Studies at the University of Bradford.

Paul Hainsworth is a Senior Lecturer in Politics at the University of Ulster.

Joop Van Holsteyn is a Lecturer in Politics at Leiden University.

Stan Markotich is a Lecturer in Balkan Studies at Middlebury College.

Duncan Morrow is a Lecturer in Politics at the University of Ulster.

Cas Mudde is a Lecturer in Politics at the University of Edinburgh.

Michael Shafir is Senior Area Specialist for Radio Free Europe and editor of RFE/RL's *East European Perspective*.

Peter Shearman is a Senior Lecturer in Politics at the University of Melbourne.

Marc Swyngedouw is an Associate Professor in the Faculty of Political and Social Sciences at the Catholic University of Brussels and Research Director of the Interuniversity Centre for Political Opinion Research, at the Catholic University of Leuven.

Acknowledgements

In compiling this volume, a number of debts have been incurred and I would like to acknowledge these. Several individuals have been generous with their time and expertise, and have read and made helpful, constructive comments on the various chapters. My thanks, therefore, go to David Arter, Nigel Copsey, Mark Donovan, Roger Eatwell (who is also a contributor to the book), Peter Emerson, John Fitzmaurice, Tom Gallagher (another contributor), Kate Hudson, Chris Husbands, Robert Knight, Eva Kolinsky, Klaus Larres, Richard Luther, Paul Mitchell, Guy Peters, Bill Riches, Geoffrey Roberts, Jim Shields and Ztlatko Skribis (apologies for any omissions).

At Continuum, my appreciation goes especially to Caroline Wintersgill (Senior Commissioning Editor) for her patience, prompting and facilitating; to her predecessors, Petra Recter and Nicola Viinikka; and to Dominic Shryane (Editor) for his efficient and friendly work. My thanks too to Peter Harrison for his meticulous copy-editing. Elsewhere, Mick Cox was very supportive at a time when the project was not moving as quickly as I would have liked it to.

At my home institution, I would like to acknowledge the ongoing support and encouragement of Henry Patterson, Alan Sharp and Tom Fraser, as well as the financial backing of the Politics Unit and the Faculty of Humanities (University of Ulster) Research Committee. The library staff of the University of Ulster also deserve my gratitude.

Finally, all the contributors were very professional and co-operative to work with. It goes without saying that only the editor, in particular, and the respective authors are responsible for any failings of the book.

Paul Hainsworth
University of Ulster at Jordanstown
November 1999

CHAPTER ONE

Introduction: the extreme right

Paul Hainsworth

Introduction

As the millennium dawns, historians and political commentators will look back upon a century of extremism, in which fascism and intolerance figured prominently, and to devastating effect. Total war, Holocaust, ethnic cleansing and scapegoating of 'the Other' have marked the past hundred years of Western 'civilization'. The mid-point of the century, of course, witnessed the defeat of Nazi and fascist forces and signalled – in the West – the victory of liberal democratic ideas, rooted in pluralism, multi-partyism, a renewed assertion of the dignity of the individual and a respect for human rights. While undoubtedly the end of World War II served as a watershed in this context, the last decades of the century witnessed some rapid and deep changes that culminated in such developments as 'the fall of the wall' and communism in Eastern and Central Europe, accelerated European integration in Western Europe, German reunification and a trend towards globalization and a new world order. These changes carried sweeping implications for the nation-states, economies and cultures of the late twentieth and the twenty-first centuries.

Another striking feature of post-war, pre-millennium European politics has been the emergence or resurgence of extreme right-wing or neo-populist politics and parties that, to some extent, have revived fears of a return to the dark past, but which, in other ways, are very much the products of more contemporary developments. Indeed, the contemporary extreme right has been more successful electorally in Western Europe when it has been able to mark its distance from past extremist forms, such as Nazism and fascism, and appear as a populist response to current anxieties. According to Kitschelt (1995: 48), 'The parties of the extreme right that harness success with right authoritarian or populist anti-statist messages appear only

1

in the most advanced post-industrial democracies.' Weinberg (1997: 279) concludes that, 'The sort of right-wing extremism presently manifesting itself in the advanced industrial democracies of Western Europe is a political force whose discourses are addressed to the present day concerns of many citizens.' Ignazi (1997a: 54), too, sees contemporary extreme right parties not as old, disguised, neo-fascist movements but rather as 'a response to the new post-industrial era and to the new post-material values it has created', while Merkl (1997: 18) refers to 'a largely new and disturbing phenomenon'.

The extreme right today is a complex and unevenly planted phenomenon, and the purpose of this book is to portray, examine and assess the different manifestations of this political family, from country to country, in order to understand it better, and the circumstances in which it falls or flourishes. Thus, following this introductory chapter, the first three-quarters of the book focuses on Western Europe, for the most part European Union (EU) member states. A brief panorama of these countries reveals the uneven electoral performance of the extreme right in major national-level elections. In certain cases, the extreme right has performed impressively and emerged as a significant player in national politics. In France, Austria, Italy, Belgium (Flanders) and parts of Scandinavia, the respective parties examined below have all enjoyed considerable success: 10 to 15 per cent of the vote for the *Front National* (FN) between 1984 and 1998; from 9.7 per cent (1986) progressing to 28 per cent (1996) for the *Freiheitliche Partei Österreichs* (FPÖ) or Austrian Freedom Party – which won 27 per cent in the 1999 general election, leap-frogging into second place; returns of 13.5 per cent (1994) *and* seats in the Italian government – and 15.7 per cent for the *Alleanza Nazionale* (AN) (1996) (formerly the *Movimento Italiano Sociale*, MSI – see Gallagher, Chapter 4); and 15.5 per cent in Flanders (1999) for the *Vlaams Blok* (VB), including, as Swyngedouw relates in Chapter 6, 28.5 per cent (1994) in the key city of Antwerp. In Scandinavia, too, the extreme right – often operating under the label of Progress Party – has experienced appreciable, albeit mixed, success: with 15.3 per cent of the vote (1997) for the Norwegian Progress Party, 15.9 per cent for the Danish Progress Party (1973) and 7.4 per cent (1997) for the Danish People's Party (DPP); and, less spectacularly and more fleetingly, 6.7 per cent (1991) for Sweden's New Democracy. All these parties and their performances are examined in this book. Also assessed are instances where the West European extreme right has performed less successfully, indeed quite disastrously, notably the British National Party (BNP) in the United Kingdom (UK) and the Centre Party (CP) and the Centre Democrats (CD) in the Netherlands. As Backer (Chapter 5) explains, the German extreme right's electoral fortunes fall somewhere between relative success and abject failure, with intermittent success at regional (*Länder*) and Euro-election level, but unfulfilled promise overall. Nevertheless, the reunification of Germany in 1989–90, the subsequent onset of socio-economic problems, the changed context of a new (1998) Social Democrat government after a long period of conservative Christian Democrat rule, the *potential* for coalition within the fragmented extreme right family and the struggle to come to terms with questions of national reunification, citizenship, identity, and refugee and asylum policy all feed into a fluid and possibly unstable situation from which parties such as the *Republikaner* (REP) and the *Deutsche Volksunion* (DVU) might draw sustenance.

The presence of the extreme right is not, of course, confined to Western/ Northern/Europe, and the later chapters of the book turn to post-communist Eastern and Central Europe, and the United States, in order to provide a fuller picture of extreme right forms and nature. The demise of Soviet-style communism has produced an unstable and vacuous context in which extremist alternatives could emerge. As Merkl (1997: 6) explains, 'ultra-nationalist feelings and movements are back with a vengeance, like genies from the bottles in which they were so long confined'. Szayna (1997: 111–13) assesses the growth of ultra-nationalist, populist and demagogic individuals and organizations in post-communist Europe over recent years, interpreting them as a potential threat to nascent liberal democratic forms. Warning against simply using Western terminology when discussing post-communist Central Europe, Szayna nonetheless depicts the extreme right there as 'political movements characterised by suspect allegiance or downright rejection of pluralism and democratic institutions, combined with a proclivity towards authoritarian modes of rule'.

Slobodan Milošević's Serbian extremism, as discussed by Markotich (Chapter 12), is perhaps a good example of this state of affairs. Arguably, though, it is a case apart, with ethnic cleansing commonplace and the head of state recently indicted for war-crimes. Certainly, the undisputedly *extreme* experiences of former and current Yugoslavia make the phenomenon and situation less easily comparable with other movements and countries discussed below. Nevertheless, as in other parts of Central and Eastern Europe, intolerance, extreme nationalism and ethnocentric assertiveness are conspicuous legacies in post-communist Europe and bear comparison with developments elsewhere. What also emerges from the contributions on Russia (Cox and Shearman, Chapter 10), Romania (Shafir, Chapter 11) and Serbia is the evident scope here for constructing so-called red–brown unholy alliances or 'fixes' which combine communist, post-communist, pre-communist and *ad hoc* themes and forces. Cox and Shearman and Shafir furthermore argue that 'national communism' has, in part, prepared the ground for some of the recently displayed sentiments, since it too exhibited traits such as anti-semitism, xenophobia, intolerance, authoritarianism, conspiracy theory and anti-individualism. Overall, then, this makes for a complex alchemy and we can, from the outset, agree with Cox and Shearman (Chapter 10) that 'finding an adequate term to define Russian nationalist extremism is ... not an easy task'.

At the same time, the onset of post-communism will, most likely, have consequences for what Cox and Durham (Chapter 13) define as a mixture of radical, racist and extremist rightism in the United States, all traditionally rooted in a militantly anti-communist world-view. As Zeskind (1999: 23) points out, the United States' national identity has been defined in the twentieth century as anti-communism. With the end of the Cold War, the extreme – and the not so extreme – right in the United States has set about re-imagining America: 'At the close of the century, white supremacists have joined angry middle class Americans in constructing this new nationalism.' Zeskind, in fact, sees the emergence of a backlash movement against the new world order (paradoxically US-dominated), a movement that increasingly identifies 'race' with nation (see also Perry, 1998). Cox and Shearman examine the various elements of this backlash, as well as their immediate predecessors. Indeed, the overall picture in the United States suggests a very cluttered far right, as the various components – the Patriot movement, the Ku Klux Klan, Christian Identity, Posse Comitatus, neo-Nazis, the National Alliance and others – jostle with each other for influence, and sometimes cross over into more mainstream politics.

The extreme right: definitional problems

At this point, it will be useful to explore some problems of definition. In an earlier volume (Hainsworth, 1992a), we pointed to the difficulty of defining the nature of the extreme right. Principally, it was argued that essentialist categorizations of the extreme right were fraught with problems. Thus, it is not easy to provide neat, self-contained and irrefutable models of extreme rightism which might successfully accommodate or disqualify each concrete example or candidate deemed to belong to this political family. As Blinkhorn (1990: 1–2) explains, 'the definitions, typologies and taxonomies beloved of social scientists tend to fit uncomfortably the intractable realities which are the raw material of the historian. ... Lines stubbornly refuse to be drawn ... exceptions disprove more rules than they prove.' Moreover, we can agree with Billig (1989: 146) that the term 'extreme right' is a troublesome tool of political analysis. Linz sums up the definitional problem in his perceptive analysis of pre-First World War proto- or pre-fascist movements. Confessing to 'taxonomical uneasiness' in engaging in comparative analysis, Linz (1980: 172–4) points to the fuzziness of boundaries between the above movements and traditional conservative forces. However, and again as previously argued (Hainsworth, 1992a: 3–7), the extreme right should not be seen necessarily as 'a uniform type bearing essentially homogeneous traits' (the quotation is borrowed from Payne's writings on *fascism* – see Payne, 1980: 21). Rather, it can be portrayed as a political family whose constituent parts exhibit certain things in common, but that also may be divided into subtypes. Indeed, such a perspective is highly appropriate for asse various movements covered in this volume, which range from the a not so extremist Scandinavian Progress parties to the much more ex movements in, for instance, the United States, the United Kingdc post-communist Central and Eastern Europe. Thus, while mindful of the differences between parties classified by us as being located on the extreme right, we are nonetheless conscious of the need to make sense of what Betz (1998: 6) defines as 'one of the most significant political developments of the past few years'.

In this respect, Ignazi (1997b: 300–3) distinguishes between *old*, traditional extreme-right parties and *new*, post-industrial extreme right parties, in order to come to terms with the ideological variety of different extreme right forms in Western Europe. Ignazi sees members of the extreme right as parties which are located at the far right of the political spectrum, exhibiting 'an ideal-ideological linkage with fascism' and expressing 'a set of beliefs that undermines the fundamentals of a polity'. Thus, this is taken to include old neo-fascist-type parties, such as the Italian MSI/AN, the BNP in Britain and the German DVU. But Ignazi's second category includes anti-system type parties, that – while keeping their distance from fascism – 'express anti-democratic values in their political discourse'. This subtype is seen to include the French FN, the Austrian FPÖ, the Belgium VB, the German REP and the Netherlands' *Centrumdemocraten* or Centre Democrats (CD). Examination of spatial, ideological and attitudinal criteria are utilized by Ignazi to situate extreme right forces. Griffin, too, interprets 'the modern radical right' as being composed of a neo-fascist and a 'pseudo-liberal' wing (Griffin, 1998: 292; see also 1993, 1995; Mudde, 1997).

As Linz (1980) suggests, the contemporary extreme right also overlaps with and shares, to some extent, common values with the mainstream right. Indeed, in an oft-remarked-upon statement, the French veteran Gaullist politician Charles Pasqua (see Hainsworth, 1992b: 53) appealed to FN voters, declaring that the mainstream right wing and the extreme right FN both basically shared the same values. However, despite this viewpoint (articulated, significantly and calculatingly, in mid-election circumstances), the extreme right does belong to a different political family and is distinguishable enough from the traditional right wing. Ignazi (1997b: 301) notes a certain overlap between right and extreme right on issues such as law and order, immigration and moral traditionalism, but 'these issues are dealt with in a completely different way', with radicalization, xenophobia and racism, particularly, characterizing extreme right discourse. As Westle and Niedermayer (1990:28) suggest, in discussing the German *Republikaner* (Republican Party), it represents 'extreme right topics in a harder style', than established right-wing parties.

That style, in the late twentieth century, has often been summed up as populist, neo-populist or national-populist. For instance, in an important recent study of what Betz and Immerfall (1998) refer to as 'the new politics of the right', Betz (1998: 6) points to the 'rise and dramatic gains of radical right-wing populist parties and movements' in contemporary times. Immerfall (1998: 249–50), too, reaffirms the term 'neo-populism' as the most appropriate label to describe the kind of parties referred to in my introductory comments (above). Indeed, neo-populism is an important feature of the style and discourse of some of the extreme right parties covered in this book *and* by Betz and Immerfall. However, the same authors reject the label 'extreme right', seeing this latter term as symbolizing a fundamental rejection of democracy and an acceptance of violence. Thus, according to Betz (1998: 3),

> the notion of right-wing extremism – or worse, neo-fascism – is hardly apt to capture the nature of the contemporary right in established Western democracies. Instead, what we propose is that what unites these parties and movements is programmatic radicalism and populist appeal.

Betz qualifies this stance by asserting that the parties and movements under discussion 'have been rather careful to stress their commitment to representative democracy and the constitutional order'.

While I can accept much of Betz and Immerfall's commentary on the centrality of neo-populism to the make-up of the phenomena under discussion, I nevertheless retain the label 'extreme right' as the appropriate generic term for the political family analysed in this book. Mudde (1997) usefully examines the topic using an ideological approach and contends that 'extreme right' is the broadly acceptable term used to depict a distinct enough group of parties embracing an ideology that draws together a common core of features. This is not to succumb to an essentialist interpretation of the extreme right, but rather to recognize that certain themes (and, indeed, styles) characterize and help to identify extreme right-wing parties. They help us to make sense of the extreme right and to understand it, without trying to fit all candidates for inclusion, into reductionist straitjackets. Thus, for instance, the Scandinavian Progress parties – borderline cases for inclusion, according to Ignazi (1997b: 302) – sit slightly uncomfortably within our extreme right family parameters but, as Andersen and Bjørklund argue (in Chapter 9): 'Although [they] may deviate from ideal-type extreme right parties elsewhere in Western Europe, they nevertheless seem to feed from the same sources; in particular, immigration and the deterioration of working-class organizations.' Kitschelt (1995: 158) suggests usefully that historical, cultural and political factors limit or moderate the propensity for extreme rightism in Scandinavia, but the Progress parties (and we might include here the Danish People's Party – see again Chapter 9) belong to the same broad family, even if 'they constitute a diluted version compared to their counterparts on the European continent'. Moreover, as

Andersen and Bjørklund again illustrate, these parties are certainly extreme within their own party systems and political cultures.

Minkenberg (1997: 84–5) makes a not dissimilar argument, albeit largely discussing what he conceptualizes as the new right radical parties in France and Germany: 'They are "extreme" not in terms of being against or outside the existing constitutional order but in terms of being extreme within that order.' In part, I can concur with this analysis: it captures certain character-istics of the extreme right. However, arguably it exaggerates the systemic compliance of new right radical or extreme right parties. For, as Minken-berg (1997: 67–8) himself contends – drawing upon Sartori's discussion of anti-system parties – such a party 'abides by a belief system that does not share the values of the political order within which it operates'. Thus espousal of narrow, ethnically based, exclusionary representations of the nation, combined with authoritarian political perspectives, renders such parties as extremist, intolerant and suspect participants in the realm of constitutional politics. This dichotomy between democratic pretensions and anti-democratic values is summed up well in Lucardie's (1998: 122) assess-ment of the Netherlands' Centre Democrats: 'The CD seems to accept the institutions of liberal democracy, though often grudgingly, but rejects the dominant liberal value system with respect to ethnic minorities and cultural pluralism. Its critique of multicultural society ... has ethnocentric and occasionally racist connotations.' In short, the stated respect of extreme right parties for the rules of the game should not simply be taken at face value. Furthermore, analysis of the extreme right needs to bear in mind the relationship between this political family and violence. As Michel Wie-viorka (*Libération*, 12 May 1995) explains, the discourse of the extreme right promotes intolerance and scapegoats certain groups. Thus, attacks on ethnic minority persons may not be directly attributed to extreme right elements (although, alternatively, they might be), but neither can this political family be totally dissociated from aggressive acts. Quite clearly, and as most critical observers do indeed recognize, the parties and move-ments under discussion here are not like the others within the party system. Karvonen (1997: 91–2), in her attitudinal survey using data from the European Values Study, even takes the argument on extreme rightism a little bit further: 'Although careful not to be associated with outright fascism or with violent methods, these parties display several similarities with the extreme right-wing parties of the inter-war years.' (For further discussion of the relationship between fascism and the extreme right, see Eatwell, 1995; Ignazi, 1997a: 47–9; 1997b: 301–03; Wilkinson, 1981).

Many of the key parties and movements under discussion here have, therefore, questionable credentials as participants in the liberal democratic process. Three examples from Italy, France and Austria illustrate our argument. First, as Gallagher explains (in Chapter 4), the old neo-fascistic Italian MSI may have attempted to reinvent itself, with a name-change to lubricate this process, but in-depth study of party conference delegates showed the rank and file to be still attached to the fascist era. As Ignazi (1997a: 54) also notes, 'even the recent adoption of the electoral label of *Alleanza Nazionale* (National Alliance) has not implied a radical ideological transformation'. Success and political office may have made the party 'more cautious', but 'no serious debate on the acceptance of the fundamentals of liberal democracy has started yet'. Second, in France, Le Pen's constitutionalism stretches to him wanting actually to abandon the constitution of the French Fifth Republic and replace it with a new Sixth Republic, with social exclusion or a 'national preference' (see Chapter 2) written into it, to ensure a policy and practice of 'France for the French'. Moreover, it is worth recalling that Le Pen's *de facto* espousal of apartheid-style solutions and his periodic anti-semitic and extremist outbursts are legendary. Third, as Morrow (Chapter 3) clearly shows, FPÖ leader Jörg Haider's neo-populism must be seen alongside his controversial and well-publicized eulogy to unreconstructed Nazis. Thus, nominal commitment to democracy and constitutionalism should not simply be taken as evidence of its actual realization. As Ignazi (1997a: 51) again explains, the anti-party, anti-establishment, anti-pluralistic values of the extreme right serve overall to undermine, not to strengthen, the liberal democratic representative system.

To summarize: the prevalence of extreme right political forces has been a feature of recent decades. There are problems in conceptualizing and defining the extreme right. Indeed, as we have seen, the label 'extreme right' is not acceptable to all observers. Perhaps needless to add, it is similarly not accepted by parties and movements generally attributed to the extreme right political family. As Swyngedouw (1998: 72) comments about the Belgian, or rather the Flemish, separatist extreme right: 'Whereas the VB is best defined as a culturally racist, separatist, and authoritarian party of the ultra right, for its supporters it represents at the most a populist, ethnocentric protest party.' Radical right or neo-populist right or (neo-) fascist are the preferred terms of some commentators. Eatwell (1998: 3) suggests that there is a tendency for academics in Europe to use the term 'extreme right', whereas in the United States, 'radical right' is more commonly used. The same author (and Backer, Chapter 5) points also to the German practice, which distinguishes between the extreme and radical rights: 'Put simply, while the latter shares the holistic nationalism and usually the racism of the extreme right, it is not totally hostile to liberal democracy, though it may support radical changes, such as plebiscitary legitimization or a strong president.' Eatwell warns too against usage of terms like 'neo-fascist' and 'populist', which do not necessarily locate extreme right parties *on the right*. Mudde (1995: 205) contends that the term 'right-wing extremism' has 'been in vogue as the collective term' since the mid-1970s – 'it was originally used alongside right-wing radicalism and later replaced it'.

Other interpretations put emphasis on subtypes of extreme right forms, in recognition of the complexity of the phenomena in question, while some authors portray the extreme right as a post-materialist reaction to New Left, libertarian and anti-authoritarian tendencies. According to Meijerink *et al.* (1998: 166): 'What exactly constitutes right-wing extremism is rather difficult to ascertain. An unambiguous description of the term is lacking and there is no consensus within the field.' A leading theoretician in this debate, Griffin (1998: 293), provides some useful and sobering guidelines here: 'it must be remembered that there are no rights and wrongs when such contrasting models are put forward, no question of definitive vindication or refutation. What is at stake is the relative heuristic value of different ideal types.'

The extreme right: parties, policies and perspectives

I have highlighted the pitfalls of hard-and-fast essentialist definitions. However, the parties, movements and ideas to be discussed have certain characteristics, commonalities and policy perspectives that contribute to (or undermine) their appeal, and an analysis of which enables us to identify and understand the politics of the contemporary extreme right. Recent research by Mudde (1997) examines 26 different definitions of the extreme right and specifies some 58 different features that various analysts have attributed to it. While there is considerable scope for variation here, a sift and synthesis of the various contributions reveal that certain elements emerge as more central than others to the collective analysis of the extreme right: nationalism, xenophobia, racism, anti-democracy, and support for a strong state. Welfare chauvinism and a strong emphasis upon law and order or security and upon ethnic identification and exclusion are part and parcel of the extreme right's ideological personality.

In many respects, the extreme right movements can be seen as anti-party parties. They benefit from popular disillusionment with mainstream parties. Crises of representation, anti-elitism, corruption, the electorate's disaffection with established political parties and their policies: these are the vehicles of extreme right movements. Thus in Austria, in the 1990s, the FPÖ has profited from assuming the oppositional lead role against the post-war, long-standing duopoly of the major left and right parties (see Chapter 3), while in Italy (Chapter 4), the recent AN/MSI success followed the collapse of the previously hegemonic Christian Democrats, amid widespread corruption and overhaul of the party system. Also, in France (Chapter 2), the FN has prospered by playing a populist outsider role against 'the gang of four' (or three) and the latter parties' collective inability to resolve key socio-economic problems. In much the same way, in Scandinavia (Chapter 9), the Progress parties and the Danish People's Party emerged as protest parties, initially focusing around taxation and anti-state grievances, but increasingly – as with the Belgian *Vlaams Blok* (Chapter 6) and the German extreme right (Chapter 4) – adopting immigration control as a central vote-winning theme.

Undoubtedly, immigration has become a very favoured element of the West European extreme right's discourse. In fact, it can be seen as having displaced anti-communism – a receding concern in the context of post-communism – as an identifying theme of the extreme right. Traditionally, anti-communism has been a central feature of the extreme right's make-up, serving as a bridgehead to post-war, Cold War rehabilitation and to links with mainstream right parties. Cox and Durhan (Chapter 13) illustrate the importance of anti-communism (and anti-semitism) to the US extreme right's world-view and conspiracy theory of politics. Also, as Eatwell (1989: 71) contends, the extreme right has articulated 'a highly critical view of the left, especially its internationalist and class-based aspects. Communism in particular is attacked, both in its domestic and internationalist form.' However, as Griffin (1998: 292) and Prowe (1998 [1994]) explain, multi-culturalism and the threat of immigration, rather than class struggle, have assumed increasing saliency for the radical or extreme right. Anti-semitism too, while still an important (and growing, in post-communist Eastern Europe) aspect of the extreme right's agenda (notably in the form of Holocaust revisionism), has to be seen alongside the increased emphasis upon immigration. Some authors see anti-semitism as intrinsic to the extreme right and occupying a special place in extreme right discourse (Ebata, 1997: 16–17). Anti-semitism feeds upon extreme right conspiracy theory, with the Jews traditionally portrayed as 'cosmopolitan' and 'root-less' forces, seeking and plotting to dominate the world. Arguably, though, immigrants, foreigners and, in the United States, blacks and other ethnic groups have become more prominent scapegoats. According to Harris (1990: 69), 'If anti-semitism is not the main theme of contemporary extreme-right propaganda, it is primarily because the immigrant has emerged as a more convenient target, and the immigration issue produces a more substantial opportunity for mobilisation.'

The extreme right's opposition to immigration and multiculturalism is, of course, inspired by ethnocentric, xenophobic, exclusionary and often out-right racist representations of the nation. Again, although it is principally a culturally differentialist (Tagüieff, 1986), rather than a biological, racism that informs the discourse, it is this sentiment which underlines the welfare chauvinism of the extreme right. In practice, this means propagating the idea of reserving or prioritizing state-provided goods and benefits (such as jobs, housing and social payments) for nationals, on the basis of a distinctly restrictive citizenship, rather than to the population at large, on the basis of equity. In fact, the extreme right – in Europe and the United States – portrays immigrants, asylum seekers and refugees often as privileged individuals, jumping the queues ahead of the nation's citizens and benefiting disproportionately from affirmative action programmes. In the United States (see Chapter 13) and the United Kingdom (see Chapter 8), therefore, the extreme right campaigns, pointedly and provocatively, for 'rights for whites'. That this rallying cry might strike a receptive chord can be seen from the following view from an ex-member of the British extreme right (Ray Hill, in Hill and Bell, 1988: 41):

> We were being cheated of work, good housing, a decent education for our kids, things we believed were our birthright, while thousands of interlopers seemed to have little trouble in grabbing work, houses and every state benefit on offer, they got this with help and encouragement from politicians of every political hue.

Moreover, through immigration politics and xenophobia, the extreme right scapegoats 'the Other' and contributes to racism and intolerance within society. Immigrants and foreigners, especially from the developing world, are equated with all the alleged or real problems of society: economic decline, cultural dilution, crime and disorder, falling standards in health and education, and so on. The lexicographical approach of the extreme right also involves castigating immigrants as 'invaders' and 'colonizers', 'occupying' Western countries – an interesting manipulation of the discourses of colonization and foreign domination (Hainsworth, 1992a: 7–9). Indeed, the prominence of immigration as a campaign theme for the broad extreme right owes something to FN president Jean-Marie Le Pen's post-1983 success in France in winning support around this issue. Other parties followed suit, and Glyn Ford, the rapporteur/chair of the European Parliament's committees (European Parliament, 1985, 1990) on fascism, racism and xenophobia referred to a 'ripple effect' (see Harris, 1990: ix) in this respect, as other parties jumped on the bandwagon. Without doubt, immigration politics and welfare chauvinism have been important vote-winners for the extreme right, not least among the dispossessed, the young and the male working classes, the lower middle classes and among those living in under-resourced urban and suburban built-up/run-down areas. However, it would be incorrect to see the extreme right as a single-issue movement or to draw simple correlations between levels of extreme right support and immigrant presence. The reality is more complex, with various subjective and objective variables coming into play.

The immigration discourse of the extreme right appeals certainly to a disaffected and alienated clientele. Various studies reveal the extreme right voter to be more of a pessimist than an optimist (see, for instance, Orfali, 1990). Extreme right parties, then, tap into popular grievances and resentments, and often help to manufacture these. Furthermore, some observers point to processes of marginalization (socio-economic or cultural) as the context behind extreme right and neo-populist successes. While subjective and/or objective social deprivation and a relative sense of pessimism are undoubtedly some of the key sentiments that inform a vote for these political parties, Immerfall and other commentators (see, for instance, Perrineau, 1997) rightly warn against interpreting the choice as solely and simply a protest phenomenon – an abandonment of traditional voting patterns 'just to send a message of protest against inefficiency, incompetence, and incumbents in general' (Immerfall, 1998: 258). Eatwell (1998: 5), too, rejects 'the dominant protest vote thesis': 'Whilst such voting is undoubtedly a factor, there is the more important element of rational choice, the desire to achieve change along the lines promised by insurgent right programmes.' Thus, although the anti-party and anti-elitist characteristic *is* a strong feature of extreme right voting, it is not the full picture: to some extent, an extreme right vote is also an option *for* – for nation, for identity, for leadership and for a policy or perspective – as much as *against*. Eatwell (1998: 27), drawing upon the work of Belgian authors (Billiet, de Witte and Swyngedouw), rejects the simple equation of extreme right voting with a protest vote, and sees it more as a question of rational choice:

> The VB vote emerges as something rational in the sense that supporters voted for the party that was closest to their policy preferences. They may have been protesting against existing elites, or the system, but there was an essential programmatic affinity.

Furthermore, protest votes tend often to be transient and thus associated with 'flash parties', whereas some of the more successful forces discussed in this book (and elsewhere) have had an impressive enough record in voter retention.

Nation, national identity and ethnocentrism are central to the extreme right's value system. The nation is ascribed a purity, a rootedness and a heroic personality. Hence, multinational, transnational or global forms are seen as alien and dangerous anti-national threats to the identity and cultural integrity of the nation. Third World immigration, Islam, communism, multiculturalism and globalization trends are particularly in question here. Although committed to the market and capitalism – indeed, Kitschelt (1995) defines this as a key element of the contemporary radical right – extreme right parties, such as the FN, are uncomfortable with out-and-out free trade, if this can be seen to undermine the nation (see Chapter 2). Thus, via national-populism, an economic protectionist and would-be patriotic discourse is increasingly adopted against the alleged (or real) ravages of globalization. Catchy slogans – 'Germany for the Germans', 'France for the French' – are utilized against immigration and globalization, as extreme right parties identify with 'the little man' and, at the same time, seek to accommodate their 'popular' electorate. National-populist or neo-populist appeals also help to underwrite the extreme right's tribune function, as the respective parties seek to take advantage of the decline of traditional support and solidarity structures, such as trade unions, churches, community and extended family (see, for instance, Swyngedouw's revealing case study of Antwerp, Chapter 6). Nation and nationalism are, therefore, projected as the affective bind that can provide meaning and identity to the individual in a rapidly changing world. As I have argued elsewhere (Hainsworth, 1992a: 10),

> Although nationalism is a factor common to many contemporary political strands, it is the style of nationalist assertion – usually aggressive, exclusive, chauvinistic and historically selective – closely allied to anti-immigrant, anti-communist politics, which helps to identify the nature of the extreme right. Contemporary extreme right movements offer their audience a messianic, crusading recipe of national redress and redemption often based upon simple slogans calculated to appeal populistically to the discontented and the disillusioned.

Unsurprisingly, then, unemployment and insecurity (in a broad sense) have been particular vote-winning themes for extreme right parties. Again these issues are linked by the extreme right to immigration and identity matters. Moreover, via 'national preference' and welfare chauvinist politics, tough law-and-order stances and promises of more extensive direct democracy (referendums by popular initiative), extreme right parties maximize their appeal. Thus, as the contributions in this book illustrate, votes for the extreme right are taken from the right *and* the left, the young and the old, first-time voters and customary abstentionists, white-collar and blue-collar workers, the unemployed and the urban and suburban discontented.

European integration provides a further identifying issue for the extreme right and its electorate. As mainstream left and right parties subscribe consensually to fuller integration, the extreme right – again wearing its national-populist hat – serves as an oppositional voice of protest against the undermining of national sovereignty and against Euro-elites. The European arena also provides scope – not always exploited or maximized (European Parliament, 1985, 1990; Fieschi *et al.*, 1996; Hainsworth, 1992a: 23–4) – for links with other like-minded parties, for winning prestigious seats at the European Parliament and for Europeanizing the agenda on issues such as immigration, culture, nation and identity. Significantly, at the European level (European Union, Council of Europe, political parties, anti-racist bodies, trade unions, and so on) – as well as the local, regional and national layers – the extreme right has encountered much opposition and monitoring. At the same time, though, official EU and national policies on immigration, asylum seekers and freedom of movement have been criticized by civil liberties, human rights and ethnic minority organizations for their restrictive nature and *de facto* criminalization of immigrants and refugees (Hainsworth, 1992a: 19).

Conclusion

Extreme right ideas, movements and parties are a significant feature of postwar and millennium politics. In national electoral terms, they have made an uneven but appreciable impact, stretching from the margins to the mainstream of power. At local, regional and European levels, extreme right parties have been able to exploit 'secondary' elections and win seats and influence. A certain legitimacy has been conferred upon them where mainstream politics has made alliances and reached accommodations with extreme right forces in order to retain or capture power – and there are many examples of this in the chapters that follow. At the same time, the success of extreme right parties cannot just be measured in electoral terms for, in a variety of situations, they have influenced the agendas, policies and discourses of major political parties and governments. Again, especially where the extreme right has been relatively successful, the mainstream parties have not always known how to respond consistently, effectively and ethically. Moreover, too much attention on the extreme right has allowed it to occupy centre stage, help define the issues for public debate and even to sow division among its opponents.

As we have argued, defining and conceptualizing the extreme right are problematical. Nevertheless, the issues and themes upon which the extreme right has campaigned are identifiable enough: immigration, nation, security, unemployment, culture, anti-communism, globalization, Europe, corruption, moral questions, identity, and so on. On these issues, the mainstream and establishment forces are deemed to have failed 'the people', and the extreme right often purports populistically to offer 'new' and allegedly straightforward alternative politics. As indicated above, and in this book as a whole, these parties have been able to exploit and channel popular discontent and grievances against established parties and politics and against change, insecurity and anomie. Leadership and image are obviously important here, and the most successful and prominent extreme right parties have repackaged their message, built up their organization *and* have been led by individuals (Fini, Haider, Le Pen) who were able to reach a sympathetic audience with their oratorical and media skills. The undisguised intention of extreme right politicians and parties is to restructure the political and party system and to move it more in the direction of their own ideas. However, despite the extreme right's capacity for reinvention and re-imagining and an obvious willingness to play the electoral system, there are well-founded doubts about their commitment to the norms and values of a liberal democratic and pluralist society. In societies where these values are recently and weakly implanted, liberal democratic pretensions are even more problematical, not least when – amid rapid change and systemic reconstruction – stability and order are valued as much as, if not more than, democracy.

References

Betz, H.-G. (1998) 'Introduction', in Betz, H.-G. and Immerfall, S. (eds) *The New Politics of the Right: Neo-populist Parties and Movements in Established Democracies*. Basingstoke: Macmillan, 1–10.

Betz, H.-G. and Immerfall, S. (eds) (1998) *The New Politics of the Right: Neo-Populist Parties and Movements in Established Democracies*. Basingstoke: Macmillan.

Billig, M. (1989) 'The Extreme Right: Continuities in Anti-semitic Conspiracy Theory in Post-war Europe', in Eatwell, R. and O'Sullivan, N. (eds) *The Nature of the Right*. London: Pinter, 146–66.

Blinkhorn, M. (1990) 'Introduction: Allies, Rivals or Antagonists? Fascists and Conservatives in Modern Europe', in Blinkhorn, M. (ed.) *Fascists and Conservatives*. London: Unwin Hyman, 1–13.

Eatwell, R. (1989) 'The Nature of the Right, 2: The Right as a Variety of Styles of Thought', in Eatwell, R. and O'Sullivan, N. (eds) *The Nature of the Right*. London: Pinter, 62–76.

Eatwell, R. (1998) 'The Dynamics of Right-Wing Electoral Breakthrough', *Patterns of Prejudice* 32(3) (July), 3–31.

Eatwell, R. (1995) *Fascism: A History*. London: Chatto and Windus.

Ebata, M. (1997) 'Right-Wing Extremism: In Search of a Definition', in Braun, A. and Scheinberg, S. (eds) *The Extreme Right: Freedom and Security at Risk*. Boulder, CO: Westview, 12–35.

European Parliament (1985) *Report on the Findings of the Inquiry* (Evrigenis Report). Committee of Inquiry into the Rise of Fascism and Racism in Europe, European Parliament, December, Luxembourg.

European Parliament (1990) *Report Drawn Up on Behalf of the Committee of Inquiry into Racism and Fascism* (Ford Report). European Parliament, Session Documents, 23 July, Document A3-195/90.

Fieschi, C., Shields, J. and Woods, R. (1996) 'Extreme Right-Wing Parties and the European Union: France, Germany and Italy', in Gaffney, J. (ed.) *Political Parties and the European Union*. London: Routledge, 235–53.

Griffin, R. (1993) *The Nature of Fascism*. New York: St Martin's Press.

Griffin, R. (1995) *Fascism*. Oxford: Oxford University Press.

Griffin, R. (ed.) (1998) *International Fascism: Theories, Causes and New Consensus*. London: Arnold.

Hainsworth, P. (1992a) 'Introduction. The Cutting Edge: The Extreme Right in Post-war Europe and the USA', in Hainsworth, P. (ed.) *The Extreme Right in Post-war Europe and the USA*. London: Pinter, 1–28.

Hainsworth, P. (1992b) 'The Extreme Right in Post-war France: The Emergence and Success of the *Front National*', in Hainsworth, P. (ed.) *The Extreme Right in Post-War Europe and the USA*. London: Pinter, 29–60.

Harris, G. (1990) *The Dark Side of Europe: The Extreme Right Today*. Edinburgh: Edinburgh University Press.

Hill, R. and Bell, A. (1988) *The Other Side of Terror: Inside Europe's Neo-Nazi Network*. London: Grafton.

Ignazi, P. (1997a) 'The Extreme Right in Europe: A Survey', in Merkl, P. H. and Weinberg, L. (eds) *The Revival of Right Wing Extremism in the 90s*. London: Frank Cass, 47–64.

Ignazi, P. (1997b) 'New Challenges: Post-materialism and the Extreme Right', in Rhodes, M. *et al.* (eds) *Developments in West European Politics*. Basingstoke: Macmillan, 300–19.

Immerfall, S. (1998) 'Conclusion: The Neo-populist Agenda', in Betz, H.-G. and Immerfall, S. (eds) *The New Politics of the Right: Neo-populist Parties and Movements in Established Democracies*. Basingstoke: Macmillan, 249–61.

Karvonen, L. (1997) 'The New Extreme Right-Wingers in Western Europe: Attitudes, World Views and Social Characteristics', in Merkl, P. H. and Weinberg, L. (eds) *The Revival of Right Wing Extremism in the 90s*. London: Frank Cass, 91–110.

Kitschelt, H. (1995) *The Radical Right in Western Europe: A Comparative Analysis* (in collaboration with Anthony J. McGann). Ann Arbor: University of Michigan Press.

Linz, J. J. (1980) 'Political Space and Fascism as a Late-Comer', in Larsen S. *et al.* (eds) *Who Were the Fascists? Social Roots of European Fascism*. Bergen: Universitetsforlaget, 153–89.

Lucardie, P. (1998) 'The Netherlands: The Extremist Center Parties', in Betz, H.-G. and Immerfall, S. (eds) *The New Politics of the Right: Neo-populist Parties and Movements in Established Democracies*. Basingstoke: Macmillan, 111–24.

Meijerink, F., Mudde, C. and Van Holsteyn, J. (1998) 'Research Note', *Acta Politica* 33 (Summer), 165–78.

Merkl, P. H. (1997) 'Introduction', in Merkl, P. H. and Weinberg, L. (eds) *The Revival of Right Wing Extremism in the 90s*. London: Frank Cass, 1–16.

Minkenberg, M. (1997) 'The New Right in France and Germany: *Nouvelle Droite, Neue Rechte*, and the New Right Radical Parties', in Merkl, P. H. and Weinberg, L. (eds) *The Revival of Right Wing Extremism in the 90s*. London: Frank Cass, 65–90.

Mudde, C. (1995) 'Right-wing extremism analyzed. A comparative analysis of the ideologies of three alleged right-wing extremist parties (NPD, NDP, CP'86)', *European Journal of Political Research* 27, 203–24.

Mudde, C. (1996) 'The War of Words Defining the Extreme Right Party Family', *West European Politics* 19(2) (April), 225–48.

Mudde, C. (1997) 'The Extreme Right Party Family: An Ideological Approach', PhD thesis, Department of Politics, Leiden University.

Orfali, B. (1990) *L'Adhésion au Front National: de la minorité active au mouvement social*. Paris: Kimé.

Payne, S. (1980) 'The Concept of Fascism', in Larsen, S. *et al.* (eds) *Who Were the Fascists? Social Roots of European Fascism*. Bergen: Universitetsforlaget, 14–25.

Perrineau, P. (1997) *Le Symptôme Le Pen: radiographie des électeurs du Front National*. Paris: Fayard.

Perry, B. J. (1998) 'Defenders of the Faith: Hate Groups and Ideologies of Power in the United States', *Patterns of Prejudice* 32(3) (July), 32–54.

Prowe, D. (1998, original article 1994) 'Fascism, Neo-fascism, New Radical Right?', in Griffin, R. (ed.) *International Fascism: Theories, Causes and New Consensus.* London: Arnold, 305–24.

Swyngedouw, M. (1998) 'The Extreme Right in Belgium', in Betz, H.-G. and Immerfall, S. (eds) *The New Politics of the Right: Neo-populist Parties and Movements in Established Democracies.* Basingstoke: Macmillan, 59–75.

Szayna, T. S. (1997) 'The Extreme-Right Political Movements in Post-communist Central Europe', in Merkl, P. H. and Weinberg, L. (eds) *The Revival of Right Wing Extremism in the 90s.* London: Frank Cass, 111–48.

Tagüieff, P.-A. (1986) 'L'identité nationale saisie par les logiques de racisation: aspects, figures et problèmes du racisme différentialiste', *Mots* 12 (March), 91–128.

Weinberg, L. (1997) 'Conclusions', in Merkl, P. H. and Weinberg, L. (eds) *The Revival of Right Wing Extremism in the 90s.* London: Frank Cass, 271–81.

Westle, B. and Niedermayer, O. (1990) 'Contemporary Right-Wing Extremism in West Germany: The "Republicans" and Their Electorate', paper presented at a workshop on 'The Extreme Right in Europe' at the European Consortium for Political Research Joint Sessions, Bochum, April.

Wilkinson, P. (1981) *The New Fascists.* London: Grant McIntyre.

Zeskind, L. (1999) 'From compounds to Congress', *Searchlight* No. 287 (May).

CHAPTER TWO

The Front National: *from ascendancy to fragmentation on the French extreme right*

Paul Hainsworth

Introduction

For at least fifteen years, the French extreme right has been dominated by a successful and durable *Front National* (FN). Born in October 1972, as an electoral initiative of the revolutionary-nationalist *Ordre Nouveau*, the party experienced a decade of marginalization and fragmentation. Then, in local and European elections, in 1983 and 1984 respectively, the movement burst spectacularly on to the political scene. Led since 1972 by Jean-Marie Le Pen, the FN secured 11 per cent of the poll and 10 Members of the European Parliament (MEPs) in the Euro-elections. Subsequently, the party won between 10 and 15 per cent of the vote in major elections (presidential, parliamentary, regional and European) and emerged as a significant force in contemporary French politics. Uncharacteristically for the French extreme right, the FN – under Le Pen's charismatic and controversial leadership – managed to rally together disparate ideological tendencies and factions. The initial and early FN represented a number of different components: French Algeria die-hards; revolutionary nationalists; wartime Vichyites; Holocaust revisionists; neo-fascists; neo-Nazis; monarchists; Catholic fundamentalists; former members of extreme right *groupuscules*; and so on.

However, as the party accumulated votes and influence, it increasingly attracted members from the mainstream political right, the (French) New Right and beyond. Bruno Mégret, one of these recruits – from the neo-Gaullist *Rassemblement Pour la République* (RPR) in 1985 – rose to the heights of delegate-general within the FN. In fact, it was Mégret who masterminded Le Pen's high-profile French presidential election campaigns in 1988 and 1995 and served as *de facto* number two in the party. In 1998–9, though, the rivalry between the two men erupted into a full-scale war for the

18

control and direction of the party apparatus. Special conferences in early 1999 confirmed the split within the FN, as Mégret founded a rival *Front National–Mouvement National* and Le Pen complained of betrayal. Paradoxically, the movement began to unravel at a time when it was seriously undermining traditional right-wing parties and making new inroads into political life.

To what extent, then, has the FN been a successful and influential voice in French politics? Who votes for it? What policies have mobilized the party and attracted voters? And how and why has the party imploded into internecine warfare at an otherwise objectively favourable time in its history?

From obscurity to success

The first decade of the FN's existence has been likened to a crossing of the wilderness for the party rank and file. The abject failure of the movement in the 1970s has been discussed elsewhere (Hainsworth, 1992: 35–40). Recruitment problems, poor electoral results (including Le Pen's 0.74 per cent in the 1974 French presidential election), splits, and rivalry on the extreme right (notably from the *Parti des Forces Nouvelles*) were some of the main difficulties encountered by the early movement. Suffice it to say here that the FN barely survived as a political entity. Then, in the early to mid-1980s, a weak and demoralized party reaped the rewards of mainstream right-wing radicalization, popular disaffection with the left in government, enhanced media access, painstaking grassroots work (in Dreux) and, not least, legitimation (see Schain, 1987) through right-wing alliance (again, in Dreux). The 1983–4 breakthroughs, of course, proved to be more than 'flash in the pan' successes. The high spots of the next few years included Le Pen's impressive 14.4 per cent (4.4 million voters) in the 1988 presidential election, followed by an even better haul next time round in 1995 (15 per cent, 4.6 million voters). In parliamentary elections, too, the FN performed well, winning 35 *députés* in the National Assembly in 1986 (when, uniquely in the Fifth Republic [1958–], the Socialist government had resorted to a proportional representation electoral system). With the reinstatement of France's usual majoritarian voting system, however, the FN had only isolated, individual successes in subsequent parliamentary elections (1988; 1989 by-election; 1997). Nevertheless, the most recent legislative election in 1997 produced the FN's best-ever result at this level (almost 15 per cent). This enabled the party to discomfort (mainly) right-wing rivals by retaining 132 candidates on the second-ballot run-offs. As explained elsewhere, the clear intention here was to punish and thwart the right-wing parties for ostracizing the FN (Hainsworth, 1998).

At national level, the leaderships of the main right-wing parties – the

RPR and the *Union pour la Démocratie Française* (UDF) – have been reluctant to make legitimizing alliances or electoral agreements with the FN. But at local and regional levels, a more *laissez-faire* attitude has often prevailed, if it was a question of being able to beat or oust the left. At regional electoral level, the FN has again performed well and won seats in the directly elected regional assemblies: 9.7 per cent of the vote and 137 seats in 1986; 13.9 per cent and 239 seats in 1992; and, more recently and most successfully, 15.2 per cent and 273 seats in 1998 (see Downs, 1998). In several regions (such as Languedoc-Roussillon and Rhône-Alpes), the FN regional councillors have provided crucial votes and alliances to elect presidents, ratify budgets and secure legislation. In return, the party has gained regional vice-presidencies and other posts, in addition to acquiring further legitimacy and influence. A consequence of regional elections and agreements has been the enabling of the FN to sink roots into French society, a process enhanced by municipal electoral success. While undoubtedly the flagship FN-controlled towns of Marignane, Orange, Toulon (all won in 1995) and Vitrolles (won by Catherine Mégret in 1997) have attracted most attention here, it should be noted that the party also has almost 2000 local councillors. Moreover, benefiting from the proportional voting system used for Euro-elections, the FN would regularly return 10 or more MEPs to Strasbourg, enabling it to link up with and inspire other, sister parties. The recent split in the party, however, threatened to have particular implications for the retention of European Parliament seats since, with a 5 per cent quota in operation, it was by no means certain that both components of the *fin de siècle* French extreme right would achieve this minimum target. The normally faithful FN voters were liable – sooner or later – to react negatively to the scission within their party. In the event, the June 1999 Euro-elections saw Le Pen's National Front winning only 5.7 per cent and 5 seats and Mégret winning 3.5 per cent and no seats.

Voters

Political commentators and pollsters have pointed to a relative *fidélisation* of the FN vote: more so than any other French political party in recent years, the FN has retained its electors, at the same time feeding off the volatility of rival parties' electorates. This is not to say that the party has *simply* retrieved its voters. Indeed, there have been some important fluctuations in the profile of the FN electorate from one election to another. Again, while there are certain biases in the sociological make-up of the FN's voters, stereotyping is not appropriate.

Studies of the initial 1984 breakthrough revealed the FN voter to be predominantly masculine and urban. Subsequent elections confirmed these characteristics, with the party establishing bastions of support in urbanized northern, eastern, south-eastern France and in Greater Paris. In 1984, first-time, younger and formerly abstentionist voters inclined disproportionately towards the FN. Three times as many right-wing, as opposed to left-wing, voters opted for the FN, with the party doing particularly well among shopkeepers, artisans, the lower middle classes, *pieds noirs* (former French settlers in Algeria) and small business people. Less practising in religion than mainstream right-wing voters, the FN voters were also more working-class (Plenel and Rollat, 1984). The latter characteristic became more marked in subsequent elections in the 1980s, especially as some right-wing defectors returned to their original 'homes', but were replaced by a more 'popular' electorate, again drawing upon first-time voters, abstentionists and disillusioned left- and right-wing voters (Jaffré, 1987). This 'popularization' was especially noteworthy in 1988, when Le Pen polled 20 per cent of working-class votes in contrast to the *combined* 16 per cent share obtained by his two right-wing rivals, Jacques Chirac (RPR) and Raymond Barre (Grünberg *et al.*, 1988; Shields, 1990).

In the 1990s, the 'popular' character of the FN electorate was again very much in evidence and it disturbed politicians on the right and the left, who had seen the FN cut into 'their' potential electorates. Thus (neo-) Gaullists looked back nostalgically to the 1960s, when General de Gaulle had mobilized a certain right-wing working-class vote, and, on the left, the French Communist Party (PCF) – in decline since the early 1980s – similarly recalled its own former monopolization of a 'popular' and protest tribune role. Between 1988 and 1995, the FN electorate underwent further proletarianization as unemployment emerged and insecurity persisted as key vote-winning issues. Feelings of insecurity were related to the socio-economic restructuring of French (and global) society and 'popular' disillusionment with the inability of mainstream political parties to respond effectively and reassuringly to the crisis. Le Pen's national-populist and demagogic tones ('France for the French', 'French first') proved to be persuasive – even though opponents accused him of offering simplistic answers to difficult questions. Following Le Pen's impressive showing in the 1995 presidential election (15 per cent of the vote, including 30 per cent of the 'popular' vote; see Perrineau, 1997: 9), one close observer of the FN was able to say, 'The FN president seems more successful among male blue-collar workers aged 18–25 who are politically undecided and who live and work in urban surroundings where the themes of immigration and crime are more relevant' (Mayer, 1998: 11) Indeed, the FN had now emerged as the first-choice party of blue-collar workers in France.

In the mid-1990s, with the FN having made clear inroads into the working-class and potential left-wing electorate, political commentators, such as Pascal Perrineau (see *Le Monde*, 3 June 1997; Perrineau, 1997) adopted the label '*gaucho-lepénisme*' to describe this phenomenon. Left-*lepénisme* is relatively more inclined to the left on socio-economic issues (such as wage rises or privatization), but receptive to FN ideas on immigration and law and order (including support for the death penalty) (see Mayer, 1998: 17). Disturbingly for the RPR–UDF bloc, a characteristic of 'left-wing' *frontistes* has been their unwillingness to vote for the right against the left on second-ballot electoral duels, thus depriving the right of seats. This situation was very much in evidence in the 1997 legislative election, when good first-ballot scores enabled FN candidates to proceed to second-ballot triangular contests (i.e. left, right and FN) in 76 constituencies, and 47 of these were won by the left (Hainsworth, 1998). Because of the majoritarian electoral system and cold-shouldering from other parties, the FN was able to win only 1 seat in 1997. Nevertheless, although the impact of the FN in the 1997 election should not be exaggerated, it was clear that the movement and its electorate had played an influential role in the left's return to power – by a narrow overall majority – forcing the right subsequently to engage in some rethinking as to the best way to deal with the FN.

The 1997 election was also notable for a more balanced FN vote profile, as the party did well again among the traditional middle classes as well as working-class voters. In the 1980s, traditional middle-class voters (small business owners, artisans, shopkeepers, etc.) had become radicalized by the reality of the left in power, and they became receptive to FN themes, especially as the (also radicalized) right-wing discourse and alliances with the extreme right legitimized the FN. Some traditional middle-class voters were alienated too by mainstream right-wing parties' acceptance of or support for neo-liberal economics and closer European integration, all of which seemed to favour big capital and globalization trends. In the 1990s, therefore, FN policies embracing economic protectionism and anti-Maastricht positions, and attacking the anti-national, globalizing effects of the new world order, were attractive to traditional middle-class voters. However, at the same time, the party felt compelled to acknowledge its 'popular' electorate and adopt policies to reflect this, even if this meant reversing previously held positions on, for instance, the minimum wage, welfarism and popular social gains of the 1980s Socialist government. Opinion polls also indicated that two out of three FN voters were sympathetic to the late-1995 wave of strikes in France, which the party had criticized and opposed. The net result, then, was to leave the FN captive to two electorates that, to some extent, had different (class) interests. The gap was bridged, however, by campaigning around issues such as immigration and the nation. As Bihr (1998: 117) suggests,

In short, the decline in the living standards of these different social classes together with their political marginalization have given rise to conditions that facilitate their rallying a reactionary nationalism that is both frightened and aggressive, basing national identity on the exclusion of non-nationals and thus on xenophobic and racist foundations [whilst] ... Their fusion into one social bloc and political force requires making a fetish of national unity as an imaginary space where they can be reconciled.

For FN voters, then, the nation – as imagined by the FN – is the construct around which alliances could be cemented. While it would be wrong to suggest that all FN voters agree with everything their party stands for, nevertheless there is considerable agreement around the key issues that motivate the party: immigration control, nation, disillusionment with France's mainstream parties, distrust of globalization and deeper European integration, and calls for tougher law-and-order or security measures. As regards FN members, Orfali's (1990) study shows this category to share the above sentiments, with pride in the nation and a concomitant concern to arrest its alleged fall into decadence and decline serving as particularly motivating factors for joining the party.

Perrineau's full-length study of the FN electorate concludes that the party has been successful in managing its sociologically different electorate. The same author presents an interesting typology of FN voters, dividing them into five types. First, there are the national-populists (21 per cent), who exhibit the following characteristics: they are younger, more left-wing and working-class (likely to have backed the 1995 strikers), less (formally) educated, xenophobic, racist, anti-European and professing to be uninterested in politics. Second, the right-wingers, or *droito-frontistes* (18 per cent), are economic liberals, interested in politics, nationalistic and xenophobic, older and more bourgeois (including Chirac voters in 1995), and hostile to Europe and the 1995 strikes. Third, the *gaucho-frontistes* (25 per cent) are younger, 'popular', less educated, non-political, more feminine, anti-European, disillusioned ex-left-wing voters, pro-strikers, pessimists, against immigration but uncomfortable with racism. Fourth, the *frontistes mous* (soft) (18 per cent) are young, masculine, better educated, interested in politics, economic liberals, the least xenophobic or anti-European, not so pessimistic and quite likely to have come from the mainstream right originally. Finally, the *apprentis-frontistes* (16 per cent) are *very* right-wing, older, richer, better educated, practising Catholic, economically liberal, against the strikes, xenophobic and against immigration, but distinctly more European than those belonging to the other categories. The first two cohorts are deemed to be the most faithful party supporters (see Perrineau, 1997: 212). Altogether, these categorizations testify to the diversity of the FN voter beyond the agreement around certain key themes. They also underline the point made by Bihr (above) that the party needs to perform a careful balancing act to keep its voters on board. The end result, though, is likely to be seen as a certain policy and presentational incoherence, as the FN appeals to its different electorates. And this dichotomy (not unique to the FN) has been seized upon by opponents keen to reveal the nature of the party and undermine its influence (see, for instance, Camus, 1997; Konopnicki, 1998; Robert, 1998).

Policies

As noted in the previous section, the vote-winning policies of the FN have been based around issues such as immigration, security and unemployment. Whereas immigration control is a key feature of the party's policy make-up, the FN should not simply be seen as a single-issue movement. Nevertheless, as Marcus (1995: 100) explains, immigration is for the FN an 'omnibus issue', a matrix through which most other issues can be contextualized: unemployment, law and order, culture, the economy, social services, education and so on. Eatwell (1998: 15) adds that while immigration 'may be central to its supporters' thinking . . . this in no way precludes it being part of a wider set of ideological views'. Ironically, in view of the party's successful mobilization around this issue, the early FN placed relatively little policy emphasis on the theme of immigration. Anti-communism was a much more prominent component in the *Front*'s discourse. In fact, the very creation of the FN can be seen as a reaction against the prevailing left-wing/Communist trends and challenges of the day: May 1968 and its aftermath, namely nascent Euro-communism and growing left-wing *rapprochement* which culminated in the 1972 PCF–Socialist Party (PS) Common Programme for Government.

In the late 1970s, immigration began to preoccupy the party more, especially with Jean-Pierre Stirbois's recruitment to and ascent within the party. At this time, the blunt FN discourse on immigration could be summed up by Stirbois's infamous line: 'Immigrants from beyond the Mediterranean: go back to your huts' (quoted in Bresson and Lionet, 1995: 399). It was Stirbois, of course, who did so well for the FN at Dreux in 1983, basing his local election campaign on immigration issues, securing the legitimizing deal with the mainstream right wing and in effect encouraging Le Pen to make more of the immigration issue. With the incorporation of New Right influences into the then-ascendant party after 1984, the immigration theme gathered more momentum and fine-tuning. Immigrants or 'invaders' from the Third World (and particularly the Maghreb) continued to be stereotypically associated with all France's real or imagined problems: high unemployment levels, crime, demographic regression, cultural dilution, educational difficulties, urban decay, AIDS and a general decline in moral and national values and status. As Marcus (1995: 76) explains, 'Le Pen has skilfully picked up and manipulated the issue of immigration, using it as a focus for the Front's appeal. The immigrant has been resurrected as the traditional scapegoat for all France's ills.'

Significantly, the concept of the 'national preference' became the centrepiece of the party's immigration control platform – and this figured centrally in the much talked-about *Immigration: 50 mesures concrètes* (Front National, 1991) and the extensive 1993 party programme, *300 mesures pour la renaissance de la France: Front National programme de gouvernement* (1993). Indeed, Bihr (1998: 87) sees the national preference as the principal axis of the 1993 programme. The essence of the concept is that French nationals should be given clear priority when it comes to allocating job opportunities (or avoiding redundancies) and public benefits (housing, social security or other grants). Other relevant criteria, such as social need, equity, acquisition of valid work and residence permits or payment of taxes and welfare contributions, would constitute, at best, secondary factors in FN eyes. Moreover, in the mid-1990s, Le Pen proposed to give legal substance to this policy concept by, if elected to high office, incorporating it formally into a new French Sixth Republic.

The party's adoption of the national preference has led to accusations of racism, social exclusion and apartheid against the FN. Bihr (1998: 89), for instance, defines national preference policy as 'state racism'. Borrowing again from the New Right, the FN has shied away from systematically espousing biologically racist ideas and argued instead that peoples and nations are culturally different and should be treated as such. Difference, though, is elevated by the FN into a pseudo-rationale for excluding certain categories or individuals or ethnic groups from full access to rights (for a fuller discussion of the issue of rights and the FN, see Hainsworth, 1999a). Tagüieff (1986), notably, has explained that although the party generally avoids crude biological references, it nonetheless articulates an indirect racist discourse on French national ethnic identity, which amounts to a cultural and differentialist neo-racism. However, despite the FN's declared policy orientation here, Le Pen and his movement are very prone to drop their guard – purposely or otherwise – and, as explained elsewhere (see, for example, Vaughan, 1987: 306), biological race references and instances of anti-semitism are not difficult to find in FN speeches. For example, Le Pen attracted much critical interest with his assertion that 'some races are more equal than others' (*L'Express*, 19–26 September 1996). Often, such utterances have led to a decline in support for the FN in the opinion poll ratings, but undoubtedly the party also wins appreciable sympathy (as well as a great deal of polarized opposition) for its stance on immigration and nation.

As Perrineau explains, propagation and popularization of the immigration and national preference policy have enabled the party to attract to its ideas a considerably bigger audience than it has been able to win over via the ballot box. Opinion polls thus revealed that, varying with time and circumstances, between a fifth and a third of respondents agreed with the FN on this specific policy issue (Perrineau, 1997). As Schain (1999: 8) also explains:

In 1984, relatively few voters aside from those who supported the National Front considered either immigration or law and order to be a strong priority. By 1988, the importance of these issues ranked with such issues as social inequality, and far higher than concerns about the environment, corruption, and the construction of Europe; only concern with unemployment ranked 'higher'.

The net effect here was to give the party some leverage over the setting of the policy agenda in France, and thus other political parties felt obliged to respond to the FN challenge. Two of the most commented-upon responses came, respectively, from the Socialist ex-premier Laurent Fabius and the Gaullist ex-Interior Minister Charles Pasqua. Fabius contended that the FN posed good questions but gave the wrong answers, while Pasqua (blatantly looking for support from FN voters) suggested that essentially, the FN 'shared the same values and preoccupations' as the right-wing parties in France, but that it articulated them in a different way (quoted in Marcus, 1995: 144). As critics of these positions pointed out, neither response was likely to harm the FN. On the contrary, each in its own way played into the hands of and validated the FN's discourse.

However, in regard to the national preference idea, Silverman makes an interesting contribution to the debate. In a well-researched book, he explains how the concept was put into practice in France in the 1930s, notably to repatriate Polish workers (Silverman, 1992: 79–80). The same author goes on to suggest that the ideological ground had been prepared for Le Pen through the unfortunate official tendency to link immigration to unemployment. Moreover, the notorious rallying equation, 'two million unemployed = two million [i.e. too many] immigrants', was not invented by the FN leader, but exploited and reproduced by him. Thus, in 1976, for instance, the (then) RPR leader and Prime Minister, Jacques Chirac, had said publicly, 'A country which has 900,000 unemployed but more than two million immigrant workers is not a country in which the problem of jobs is insoluble' (quoted in Silverman, 1992: 90–1). Silverman's research, therefore, is useful for establishing the broader well of support for ideas that have perhaps been too specifically associated with Le Pen. Discussing the role of Jean-Pierre Stirbois and the legitimation of the FN's discourse, Eatwell (1998: 15) also maintains that, 'His ability to court "respectable" support whilst stressing anti-immigrant themes was helped by the fact that the issue had already been mooted by mainstream parties.' What Le Pen and co. have done, in fact, is to take hold of certain pre-existing ideas and themes and concepts, and rework them in a national-populist manner, echoing extreme right-wing traditions in France.

The immigration theme is linked closely to the insecurity issue by the FN. The Third World, allegedly non-assimilable, immigrant is associated with rising crime rates and decadence (for a useful discussion on assimilation, integration and related themes, see Hargreaves, 1994). The party press and speeches are littered with examples of criminality committed by persons with 'non-French'-sounding names. The FN supports tougher law-and-order policies, including stronger sentences, a reformed (and more punitive) judiciary and more police and prisons. The party favours the reinstatement of the death penalty for large-scale drug pushers, terrorists and murderers. In this policy sphere, the FN calls for a strong and protective state: 'We know that the state is necessary and we want it strong and respected in its regalian functions: defence, policing, justice, diplomacy' (Le Pen, 1988). Essentially, the party aspires to be seen as the 'party of order' against its more lax and moribund rivals. According to Pierre Grosz (1999: 19), from the anti-racist monitoring organization *Reflex*, 'This image is fed by the higher than average number of police officers and military personnel belonging to the party.' Certainly, much FN effort in recent years has gone into creating 'trade union' structures within police, prison officer and military professions. Also, where the FN has had an opportunity to implement its law-and-order policies – in the municipalities controlled by the party – there has been a significant increase in the size of the local police forces. In Vitrolles, for example, *Searchlight*'s Graeme Atkinson (1999: 21) points to an increase from 40 to 150 officers since the FN captured the town hall in February 1997.

Security does not only consist of law-and-order matters. The FN takes the term to mean, more widely, how individuals feel while living in France. Thus subjective interpretations and the challenge of structural, social and economic change come into play here. Many commentators on the party's success in 'reaching' people have pointed to the breakdown of former solidarities and belongings – religion, trade union, village, *quartier*, community, party, job security and camaraderie and so on – and the FN's capacity to exploit this socio-psychological vacuum. In this context, the labelling of scapegoats and the rallying around the powerful idea of nation have been compensating factors. Nation is paramount for Le Pen: it implies roots, culture, identity, tradition and patrimony – values which, alleges the FN, it is difficult, if not impossible, to 'buy into'. Hence, the FN opposes all those transnational, globalizing or European forces which are seen as undermining the nation: communism, socialism, Islam, deeper European integration and, not least, globalization.

The centrality of anti-communism to the early FN discourse has already been remarked on. In the 1990s, however, the party had to adjust to 'the fall of the wall' and the decline of communism in France and Europe. At the same time, the globe has experienced the emergence of a so-called new world order, in which globalization and US economic, military and cultural predominance have featured largely. The benchmark 1993 FN programme reflected these developments. As argued elsewhere (Hainsworth, 1996: 197–8): 'The 1993 programme describes globalising trends (*mondialisme*) as *the* most serious threat to the French nation since they destroy nations, reduce differences, erode frontiers and dilute cultures.' The FN opposed, then, such measures as French participation in the 1990 US-led Gulf War and the NATO offensive in 1999 over Kosovo, US cultural hegemony (Hollywood, Euro-Disneyland, McDonald's) and the world trade talks (via the General Agreement on Tariffs and Trade or GATT) precisely because they were deemed to undermine French sovereignty. According to one prominent FN journalist, Jean Mabire, 'obsessed by Soviet ideological and military power, we have not realized that we were already colonized by American "cultural" power' (*National Hebdo*, 14–20 February 1991). The party now attacked unbridled free trade as detrimental to France's economic and national interests. Prompted by Bruno Mégret in particular, the party moved towards an economic protectionist position that contrasted with previous FN programmes and positions, which were more market- (and US-) friendly. Economics quite clearly took a back seat to politics and the nation, in FN reckoning. Indeed, writing in the FN cultural magazine that he founded (*Identité*, Autumn 1993: 5–12), Mégret described free trade as a catastrophe for France, and he called for the liberation of politics from economics and 'the sacrosanct law of international free trade'.

The FN's reworking of its economic policy orientations was accompanied by a reversing of its stance on certain socio-economic questions. Already I have alluded to the change of attitude on items such as the minimum wage, as the party responded to the concerns and preferences of its increasingly 'popular' electorate. This cohort of supporters were favourably disposed to the social gains of the 1980s left-wing government, including the 39-hour week and the fifth week of paid holidays. They also wanted to retain a stake in the welfare state and social security system. Nor were they in tune with the party – as demonstrated in Perrineau's typology (above) – on the question of industrial/public-sector strikes. Consequently, in all these matters, the FN modified its positions in order to correlate more with its status as France's leading workers' party at the polls. In addition, the FN – again 'led' by Mégret – began to dabble more in trade unionism of sorts and could even be seen at the factory gates. At the same time, the self-ascribed status as a party of the right was altered. Hitherto, the FN had posed as 'the popular and social right'. Its accusation against the RPR and UDF was that they were not right-wing enough in practice. From the mid-1990s, though, the FN adopted a 'neither right nor left' stance (see Maréchal, 1996). Critics were quick to point out that this was the old slogan of pre-war and early twentieth-century fascist movements (see Sternhell, 1986). For the FN, at this time, the slogan served to underline the movement's essentially national message. But it was also useful for conjugating a sociologically diverse electorate and for coming to terms with the FN's political ostracism. However, before long, the FN had more pressing things to concentrate on as, from a position of relative strength and consolidation, the party began to unravel.

Conclusion: schism

The 1980s and 1990s had seen several prominent resignations from the FN, usually in protest against extremist, anti-semitic or other remarks by Le Pen or his Gulf War stance (Hainsworth, 1996). However, there was nothing tantamount to a leadership challenge. In fact, as various analysts noted (Birenbaum, 1992; Camus, 1997), Le Pen kept a tight, authoritarian rein on the party, packed the upper echelons with his supporters and generally tried to balance or play off potential rivals within the party. While different tendencies certainly existed inside the party (see Camus, 1992), they never really threatened to seriously divide the movement – as long as electoral success continued unchecked. Increasingly, though, in the 1990s, Bruno Mégret strengthened his base inside the party apparatus and eventually mounted a challenge to Le Pen.

Gradually, Mégret's policy/ideology and organizational input were intensified. Having managed Le Pen's (relatively) successful presidential election campaigns in 1988 (and again in 1995), he had a leading role in formulating the party's extensive programme in 1993 and also had put his name to the FN's '50 Proposals' on immigration (1991). Within the party apparatus, he spent several years building up his support, at departmental secretary and central committee levels. Also, he was seen very much as the ideas man of the party, promoting various cultural and ideological initiatives. At local/regional grassroots level, too, he had 'worked the terrain' in the FN bastion of Bouches-du-Rhône (encompassing Marseille, Vitrolles)/Provence-Alpes – Côte d'Azur, eventually winning, with his wife's candidature, Vitrolles for the party in early 1997. The prospect of him winning a parliamentary seat in June 1997 was widely speculated to have deterred Le Pen from contesting the legislative elections – allegedly for fear of losing ground in the party if his number two, but not he himself, was elected. Conscious of the emerging threat, Le Pen had secured the election of Bruno Gollnisch (FN leader in the Rhône-Alpes region) to the post of secretary-general, in a thinly veiled attempt to contain Mégret's influence within the movement. Matters came to a head in late 1998 to early 1999, when Le Pen tried further to minimize the influence of *mégretists* within the FN. Le Pen was barred legally (albeit temporarily) from standing for election (for striking a rival candidate in a previous electoral contest). Now, instead of backing his number two's claim to head the party's list for the June 1999 Euro-elections, Le Pen advocated that his wife, Jany, should occupy this position. Also, he planned to reduce the number of Mégret's supporters on that list. Internal party meetings were noteworthy for friction and diatribes between the two sides, and in one stormy session two of Mégret's close supporters were ejected, with Le Pen's approval. Most commentators on the FN had expected a war of succession to *follow* Le Pen's death or retirement, but Mégret now opted to challenge for the leadership and direction of the movement. A special congress, called for and attended by Mégret and his supporters, was held at the flagship town of Marignane in January 1999. This formally consummated the split, as Mégret was elected president of the new, rival *Front National–Mouvement National*.

Personal rivalry certainly played a part in the fragmenting of the FN, but arguably more crucial were the differing perceptions on presentation and tactics. Mégret clearly felt that Le Pen's leadership (and extremist utterances) had pushed the party towards political isolation and made it difficult for the FN to break out of the 15 per cent electoral 'ghetto' (Longuet, 1999). Mégret favoured at least some form of tactical, mutually advantageous arrangement with the mainstream right to help the FN win more votes and translate these into tangible gains (i.e. seats). It was not lost on the *mégretists* that smaller, less popular forces in French politics (such as the PCF and the Greens) were able to win seats by virtue of being able to form alliances, notably in the context of a 'pluralist left'. Mégret, no doubt, was also impressed by the success of Gianfranco Fini in Italy, where alliance-making had enabled the re-imagined *Alleanza Nazionale/Movimento Sociale Italiano* to enter the government coalition in 1994 (see Chapter 4). Le Pen, however, was less keen on the concept of a 'pluralist right', whose formation might serve to dilute his national-populist and tribune appeal. In the 1997 legislative election, Le Pen had even seemed to favour a left-wing, as opposed to a right-wing, victory. Mégret, a former RPR politician and much less populist than Le Pen, was more convinced of the need to repackage the French extreme right. Nevertheless, the internal dispute in the FN could not simply be portrayed as one between moderates and extremists. Mégret's New Right sympathies and his close identification with FN immigration policy militated against him being portrayed as a moderate.

The divisions in the movement certainly ran deep and affected all levels of the internal organization of the FN, even splitting Le Pen's close family. Initial calculations, in early 1999, showed that the *mégretists* had attracted 58 (out of 95) departmental secretaries, 14 (out of 44) political bureau members, 51 (out of 120) members of the central committee, 139 (out of 273) regional councillors, 3 (out of 11) MEPs, 2 (out of 4) mayors, half the departmental secretaries of the *Front National de Jeunesse* (FNJ), and the majority of the leadership of the party's internal security service and also the FN's university apparatus, *Renouveau Étudiant*. Arguments over who had the right to the FN's name, logo and funds were taken to the Paris law courts. In a party that had aspired only recently to win 20 per cent of the vote and take advantage of the divisions on the mainstream right (see, for a discussion of these, Hainsworth, 1999b), the in-fighting left both rumps of the party now hoping anxiously to come out on top *and* to cross the 5 per cent quota hurdle needed to win seats in the European Parliament. As Schain (1999: 1) explained, 'the two National Fronts are engaged in a short-term struggle for domination and a long-term struggle for survival'.

In conclusion, therefore, since 1972 and especially since 1983, the FN had come a long way in French politics. Hitherto, a feature of the French extreme right had been its fragmentation and disunity. Le Pen's charismatic and forceful leadership had helped to reverse this image (Anderson, 1974; Chebel d'Appolonia, 1988). Indeed, the success of the party in the 1980s and 1990s owed much to this factor. The Le Pen–Mégret split now threatened to return the French extreme right to the more familiar patterns of the past.

References

Anderson, M. (1974) *Conservative Politics in France*. London: Allen & Unwin.

Atkinson, G. (1999) 'FN Split', *Searchlight* (London), No. 286 (April).

Bihr, A. (1998) *Le Spectre de l'extrême droite: les Français dans le miroir du Front National*. Strasbourg: Atelier.

Birenbaum, G. (1992) *Le Front National en politique*. Paris: Balland.

Bresson, G. and Lionet, C. (1995) *Le Pen: biographie*. Paris: Seuil.

Camus, J.-Y. (1992) 'Political Cultures within the *Front National*: The Emergence of a Counter-ideology on the French Far-Right', *Patterns of Prejudice* 26 (1–2), 5–16.

Camus, J.-Y. (1997) *Le Front National: histoire et analyses*. Paris: Éditions Laurens.

Chebel d'Appolonia, A. (1988) *L'Extrême-droite en France: de Maurras à Le Pen*. Brussels: Éditions Complexe.

Downs, W. D. (1998) 'The Front National as Kingmaker ... Again: France's Regional Elections of 15 March 1998', *Regional and Federal Studies* 8(3) (Autumn), 125–33.

Eatwell, R. (1998) 'The Dynamics of Right-Wing Electoral Breakthrough', *Patterns of Prejudice* 32(3) (July), 3–31.

Front National (1991) *Immigration: 50 Mesures Concrètes*. Marseille: Front National (pamphlet).

Front National (1993) *300 mesures pour la renaissance de la France: Front National programme de gouvernement*. Paris: Éditions Nationales.

Grosz, P. (1999) 'Front National politics', *Searchlight* (London) No. 286 (April), 21.

Grünberg, G. *et al.* (1988) 'Trois candidats, trois droites, trois électorats, l'élection présidentielle', *Le Monde: Dossiers et Documents* (May).

Hainsworth, P. (1992) 'The Extreme Right in Post-war France: The Emergence and Success of the *Front National*', in Hainsworth, P. (ed.) *The Extreme Right in Europe and the USA*. London: Pinter, 29–60.

Hainsworth, P. (1996) 'The *Front National* and the New World Order', in Chafer, T. and Jenkins, B. (eds) *France: From the Cold War to the New World Order*. Basingstoke: Macmillan, 193–203.

Hainsworth, P. (1998) 'The Return of the Left: The 1997 French Parliamentary Election' *Parliamentary Affairs* 51(1) (January), 71–83.

Hainsworth, P. (1999a, forthcoming) 'From Joan of Arc to Bardot: Immigration, Nationalism, Rights and the French National Front', in Hancock, L. and O'Brien, C. (eds) *Re-writing Rights in Europe*. Aldershot: Dartmouth.

Hainsworth, P. (1999b) 'The Right: Divisions and Cleavages in *fin de siècle* France', *West European Politics* 22(4), October, 38–56.

Hargreaves, A. (1994) *Immigration, 'Race' and Ethnicity in Contemporary France*. London: Routledge.

Jaffré, J. (1987) 'Trois postulats sur l'électorate d'extrême droite: ne pas se tromper sur M. Le Pen', *Le Monde*, 26 May.

Konopnicki, G. (1998) *Manuel de survie au Front*. Paris: Mille et Une Nuits.

Le Pen, J.-M. (1988) *Passeport pour la victoire*. Programme for 1988 presidential election. Paris: Front National.

Longuet, P. (1999) 'Crise au Front National: chronique d'un divorce annoncé', *French Politics and Society* 17(1) (Winter), 17–36.

Marcus, J. (1995) *The National Front and French Politics*. London: Macmillan.

Maréchal, S. (1996) *Ni droite ni gauche ... français!* Charenton-le-Pont: Alizés.

Mayer, N. (1998) 'The *Front National* Vote in the Plural', *Patterns of Prejudice* 32(1) (January), 3–24.

Orfali, B. (1990) *L'Adhésion au Front National: de la minorité active au mouvement social*. Paris: Kimé.

Perrineau, P. (1997) *Le Symptôme Le Pen: radiographie des électeurs du Front National*. Paris: Fayard.

Plenel, E. and Rollat, A. (1984) *L'Effet Le Pen*. Paris: La Découverte/Le Monde.

Robert, M. (1998) *Petit manuel anti-FN*. Lyon: Golias.

Schain, M. (1987) 'The National Front in France and the Construction of Political Legitimacy', *West European Politics* 10(2), 229–52.

Schain, M. (1999) 'The National Front and the French Party System', *French Politics and Society* 17(1) (Winter), 1–16.

Shields, J. (1990) 'A New Chapter in the History of the French Extreme Right: The National Front', in Cole, A. (ed.) *French Political Parties in Transition*. Aldershot: Dartmouth, 185–212.

Silverman, M. (1992) *Deconstructing the Nation: Immigration, Racism and Citizenship in Modern France*. London: Routledge.

Sternhell, Z. (1986) *Neither Right nor Left*. Berkeley: University of California Press.

Tagüieff, P.-A. (1986) 'L'identité nationale saisie par les logiques de racisation: aspects, figures et problèmes du racisme différentialiste', *Mots* 12 (March), 91–128.

Vaughan, M. (1987) 'The Wrong Right in France', in Kolinsky, E. (ed.) *Opposition in Western Europe*. London: Croom Helm, 289–317.

CHAPTER THREE

Jörg Haider and the new FPÖ: beyond the democratic pale?

Duncan Morrow

The rise of a new form of authoritarian right-wing populism in the 1980s and 1990s is a phenomenon of more than one country in Europe. Nowhere has this re-emergence been more rapid or more successful, however, than in Austria, where a new political star, Jörg Haider, has led his party to a series of spectacular electoral successes. In the ten years before 1996, Jörg Haider led the *Freiheitliche Partei Österreichs* (FPÖ, loosely translated as Freedom Party of Austria) or *Freiheitlichen* from being a party with less than 5 per cent support to within 2 per cent of becoming the largest single party in the state. Complacency about Haider in the 1980s gave way in the 1990s to a degree of panic among many of Haider's opponents in Austria, highlighting widespread concerns about Haider's underlying commitment to the principles of liberal democracy. No single figure, certainly from the opposition, has dominated the post-war Austrian political scene to the same extent. No one since 1945 has given rise to such fundamental fears about the security of Austrian democracy among their opponents.

Part of the reason for the panic lies, of course, in Austria's recent past. Perhaps more than anywhere else, nationalism and right-wing politics carry the burdens of history. While historical Nazism was certainly related to forms of right-wing authoritarianism elsewhere in Europe, its particular horror depended on specifically Germanic features (Bracher, 1971: 70). The sheer weight and potential damage of this legacy drove most Austrian post-war politicians to a fairly systematic policy of official repression and denial, as they sought to build a secure democratic foundation for the post-war Second Republic. An integral part of that policy was the attempt to bind former Nazis into a new democracy. Since its foundation in 1955, the FPÖ has always served as a political vehicle for integrating former Nazis. Technically, this was meant to allow those with unsavoury past connections to enter into mainstream post-war politics, avoiding the creation of a permanent and large anti-democratic opposition.

After 1945, stability was the primary political goal of all Austrian political parties. The need for Austria to prove the economic effectiveness of democracy and to avoid any return to pre-war antagonisms led to the development of social partnership, a uniquely complex accommodation between the forces of capital and labour, made possible by a political culture dominated by deals between political party elites. In the 1980s, the stability from decades of political calm and economic growth began to be challenged. Increasing frustration with the corruption of the Austrian political system and growing economic difficulties were compounded by the geopolitical earthquake of 1989–90 when the Iron Curtain, which had separated Austria from its neighbours to the north and east, collapsed.

The potential for a rapid rise in the number of migrants from Eastern Europe in Austria rose exponentially. Widespread doubts about the capacity of the Austrian political elite to manage the turbulence also surfaced. Economic and political insecurity, which had been effectively abolished in Austria between 1955 and 1985, returned to centre stage. In the light of such turbulence, Jörg Haider's populist protests against the established political order struck an ever-deeper chord across a wide spectrum of Austrian society.

Haider's domination of the FPÖ over the past decade has been accompanied by a sharp rightward turn in the party's rhetoric and activity. Haider's anti-foreigner campaigns, FPÖ flirtations with former Nazis and anti-democratic right-wing groups, active anti-Slovene policies in Carinthia and the focus on leadership rather than on participation in politics have all revived historic suspicions. He has also appeared to regularly reinterpret orthodox post-war Austrian history by focusing on the failings of the Second Republic while apparently diluting the consensus on Nazi crime and happily sharing platforms with the remnants of the Hitlerite Waffen SS.

The task of drawing distinctions between the past and the recent right wing in Austria is not made easier by the deliberate blurring of the lines between the past and the present by Haider himself. The FPÖ presents itself to some audiences as a movement of the 1990s, a decisive break with anti-democratic authoritarianism, let alone National Socialism, yet also appears to signal a desire to keep faith with a cultural and historical tradition which sees little to be ashamed of in Austria's National Socialist past. Indeed, FPÖ politicians continue to use phrases which have specific meanings from that past, thereby further alarming their opponents.

This chapter is concerned with a number of interlinked questions: What is the right-wing tradition in Austria? How do contemporary authoritarian politics in Austria relate to historical ancestors? What is the ideological core of the FPÖ? How and why did Haider establish his domination over the party? To what extent is the modern FPÖ a democratic party? Who does the FPÖ appeal to with its political programme, and why? How robust is democratic culture in modern Austria?

The pan-German tradition in Austria pre-1945

In previous centuries, the name 'Austria' signified not a national state but the extent of Habsburg power, the territories of the 'House of Austria'. Between 1867 and 1918, the term 'Austria' began to be used to describe the non-Hungarian part of the Habsburg lands. Politics in these territories was characterized by increasingly bitter divisions between German and, especially, Czech nationalists. While modern Austria lacks any sizeable indigenous ethnic minorities, the world-view of the Austrian right wing is still filled with assertions of the integrity of the *Volk* and paranoias about foreigners, with roots in the multicultural Habsburg legacy. The sense that the Germans of the empire were a frontier people, under permanent threat from lesser and dangerous enemies and requiring solidarity with all German-speakers, has left a long-lasting imprint.

German–Austrian politics divided into three separate streams: social democracy, Christian socialism and pan-German nationalism, all of which had authoritarian tendencies. In response to the general parliamentary chaos, the Habsburgs resorted to administration by decree. Parties became largely oppositional and no tradition of democratic bargaining and negotiation was established (Macartney, 1978). Instead, parties were substitute focuses of primary loyalty, fostering the growth of complex subcultures. In the classic analysis of the Austrian historian Adam Wandruszka, parties became competing and self-perpetuating *Lager* (camps), whole self-sufficient groups, rather than more restricted 'parties' in the Anglo-Saxon sense (Wandruszka, 1954). Loyalty to the *Lager* became a matter of personal identity. The protective, social and sometimes military function of the parties fostered a top-down dependence culture, incorporating 'guided movements', rather than a wide and participative democratic pluralism. The German-national or third *Lager* gathered all of those who opposed socialism and sought immediate integration into a Greater Germany.

There was never an Austrian nationalism under the Habsburgs. Imperial loyalty was one thing, but the ideology of nationalism divided the empire into its linguistic subgroups. Following Austria's exclusion from Bismarck's German Empire in 1871, many pan-Germans became alarmed by the growth of Slavic nationalism in areas such as Bohemia and Slovene Carniola. The pan-Germans were often militantly anti-clerical and anti-Habsburg. For the Austrian middle class after 1871, Germany was associated with progress and economic success, and many despised the supposed backwardness of Catholic Austria. Anti-clerical liberalism, with its emphasis on individualism and economic markets, was always closely associated with nationalism in Austria.

Virulent anti-semitism was directed against Vienna's growing Jewish middle class and the influx of poor Jews from Galicia. Bourgeois supporters of this doctrine were particularly prevalent among academics and students in the universities, the most profound interface with Jewish intellectuals. The German-nationals developed strong cultural and social ties, in clubs or *Verbindungen*, which emphasized discipline, strict gender divisions and manly Germanic activities such as gymnastics or *Jahnisches Turnen* with its emphasis on duelling for young men. Proletarian German nationalism was successful among workers in Bohemia, where the growth of a Czech industrial class changed German areas into mixed areas and mixed areas into Czech ones. These diverse strands – anti-clericalism, anti-democracy, anti-semitism, working-class economic competition, middle-class resentment and authoritarian militarism – were gathered together by Hitler in the 1930s.

Habsburg defeat in 1918 left the German-speakers of the empire demoralized, defeated and divided. The German-speaking parties agreed a new republican constitution for 'German-Austria' and called for *Anschluss*, or union, with Germany. To be nationalist in German-Austria in 1918 meant to be anti-Austrian and pro-German. Few in Austria were loyal to a separate Austrian nation, but their visions of Germany were also hopelessly divergent. The Social Democrats saw in Germany the progressive hope for proletarian progress while the Christian Socials often hankered for the previous dominance of the Catholic Habsburgs. German-nationalists, bitter in defeat, saw unification with Germany as a matter of uniting the *Volk* in one common and powerful state. Through the Treaty of St Germain of 1920, however, the allies forbade all talk of *Anschluss* with Germany. The result was a bitter and unstable Austrian Republic.

Between 1920 and 1938, Austria successively experienced economic collapse, hyper-inflation, crippling international debt repayments, and mass unemployment. The political situation was hardly less grave. Post-war unity gave way to interminable crises. After 1920, the Christian Social Party held power, though mostly only in coalition with bourgeois and rural pan-German parties. The Social Democrats were accused of bolshevism and fomenting class hatred. The weak federal army quickly became politicized, while numerous well-armed and (at best) conditionally loyal private armies sprang up on both right and left. All of the parties appeared willing to resort to violence in any self-declared emergency. None of the main Austrian parties had a complete commitment to parliamentary democracy.

The retreat into civil violence was almost inevitable. Fascism in Italy attracted many admirers in Austria, especially in the paramilitary *Heimwehr*. The demand for order, for a strong man to provide stability in the midst of chaos, grew as the economic and political crisis expanded. The weakness of political loyalty to 'Austria' left Austrian politics deeply vulnerable to developments in Germany. In this context, Hitler's anti-semitic, anti-Slavic, anti-Bolshevik and anti-Versailles politics struck deep chords. Many of the roots of national socialist ideology sprang from Austrian conditions and history (Pauley, 1981). When the Austrian parliament was paralysed in a procedural wrangle in 1933, the Catholic Chancellor, Engelbert Dollfuss, took the chance to abolish parliamentary rule. This act of authoritarian dictatorship from the right provoked a spontaneous uprising of left-wing Social Democrats in February 1934. The defeat of the left in the civil war resulted in a new Austrian dictatorship. In July 1934, when the Nazis came close to succeeding in an attempted *putsch*, Dollfuss himself was murdered. The Christian Social dictatorship found itself under constant pressure. Without strong domestic or international support, it was unable to resist German demands. Driven to assert Austrian independence by calling a national referendum, the dictatorship was swept from power in March 1938 by Hitler's invading armies.

The great hour of pan-Germanism was an apparent popular success. Hitler's armies were greeted by enormous crowds. Hitler himself addressed a mammoth demonstration in Vienna's Heldenplatz. When an, albeit flawed, referendum was held after the invasion, it returned a 99 per cent vote in favour of the *Anschluss*. Recommendations by the Cardinal of Vienna and the leading Social Democrat Karl Renner for a pro-German vote compounded the sense in foreign capitals that most Austrians were relieved rather than horrified by events (Luza, 1975). The Western allies raised no objections and Austria was integrated into the Reich.

Membership of the Nazi Party in post-*Anschluss* Austria was above the German average; conscription of soldiers to the *Wehrmacht* and participation in the SS and Waffen SS took place without difficulty. Resistance on the territory of Austria was comparable with resistance throughout the Reich. The evidence of widespread anti-semitism in Vienna in 1938, the huge popularity of confiscation of Jewish property, the attacks on Slovenes in Carinthia and the toleration of the concentration camp at Mauthausen all point to a record of collaboration. The activities of Austrian-led or -dominated units of the German armed forces in the Balkans, Italy and elsewhere were as vicious as any.

There is some suggestion that Austrians, particularly in Vienna, were antagonized by the predominance of *Altreich* or non-Austrian Germans in the bureaucracy and party apparatus. There is some evidence, also, that under central Berlin control, a certain regional oppositionalism set in (Kienzl, 1992). However, there is little proof that this could have provided a sufficient basis for the establishment of national independence in the absence of total German defeat in 1945. All in all, Austrians acted little differently from Germans under the Nazi regime (Botz, 1986).

Re-establishing Austria after Hitler

The collapse of the Nazi regime in 1945 destroyed pan-Germanism as practical politics. Allied occupation left no alternative to the pro-Austrian independence politics of the People's Party (ÖVP)–Socialist (SPÖ) coalition. There was nothing to be gained from anti-Western German nationalism. If German nationalism was out, liberal democracy was in. Despite the fact that, until 1945, Austria had failed to develop any liberal democratic political culture, the choices were now stark. Evidence of the Holocaust added to the humiliation of military defeat, and all public associations with the Nazi system had to be avoided. The virtually immediate onset of the Cold War further reduced the range of realistic political choices in Austria. Western democracy was no longer the unwanted imposition of 1918 and of the 1930s, but the only thinkable bulwark against Stalinism. Austria's inclusion in the Marshall Plan was arguably the single most critical factor in determining Austria's post-war fate. In 1945, liberal democracy was, beyond all doubt, the *sine qua non* of Austrian survival outside communist domination.

The post-war Austrian coalition faced a serious practical problem of reintegrating 536,000 former Nazi Party members, of whom about one-third were regarded as party functionaries (Stiefel, 1981: 99). Former Nazis were now supplemented by large numbers of traditionally German-nationalist refugees from the Sudetenland and elsewhere. The sheer scale of the difficulty meant that Austrian governments were faced with contradictory problems. Despite the foreign-policy necessity of presenting Austria as an anti-Nazi state, no government could afford to leave such an enormous latent protest group outside the political system for ever. The permanent exclusion of such a large group promised a return to the partisan confrontations of the First Republic. Conveniently for the Austrian coalition, Western opinion after 1946 was more concerned with anti-communism than with hunting Nazis. The pragmatic outcome in 1948 was a fairly open attempt to draw former Nazis into the new democratic political system, a *de facto* recognition of the political necessity of soft-pedalling on Austria's war record.

Ideological legacies and the memories of participants in the Nazi experiment were much more difficult to eradicate. A distinction, therefore, still needs to be drawn between the eradication of the remaining traditions – social romanticism, the worship of the strong state and the fundamental defensive hostility of German Austrians to their Slav neighbours – and the pragmatic necessity of keeping them underground. In public, legal arguments about Austria being Hitler's first victim in 1938 became standard political myth. Provided former Nazi Party members accepted the new Austrian (not German) democratic system, as the vast bulk, although not all, felt obliged to do, they were to be integrated into post-war politics. The

JÖRG HAIDER AND THE NEW FPÖ

crucial advantage of this strategy was the creation of a more promising basis for real domestic political stability, in sharp contrast to the inter-war disaster. The disadvantage was that although far right politics were driven from the official public arena, the culture and ideological challenge of Austria's collapse into totalitarianism and the responsibilities which arose from it were left dangerously unresolved.

Defining the extreme right in post-war Austria

Nazism itself remains the ultimate measuring-stick for what is meant by the extreme right, not only in Austria. Although, as Bracher (1971) points out, Nazism had a specifically German heritage, the systemic complexity of Nazism added new dimensions to the fascisms of Southern Europe and other pre-war dictatorships for right-wing groups outside Germany. In Austria, the particularly long shadow of this history means that all subsequent right-wing political movements are inevitably judged according to their relationship to Nazi ideology and ideals.

Nonetheless, Nazism itself was not a simple legacy. The personality cult around Hitler himself was so crucial to the actual nature of the German dictatorship that right-wing extremism after Hitler must inevitably be a new phenomenon. In the post-war world, the contents of Nazism and fascism have therefore been drawn upon in different combinations. So much is clear from a study by Cas Mudde (1995) of the work of 26 political researchers into post-war right-wing extremism. He demonstrates that there is now no single definition of what constitutes 'extreme' or 'far-right' politics. Instead, a number of indices have been use in different studies. H.-G. Betz (1993), for example, uses xenophobia and the strong state as his key indicators of an extreme right, Doll (1990) emphasizes the elements of nationalism and anti-democracy, while Hainsworth (1992) relies largely on racism and xenophobia.

Clearly, Nazism had all these. Bracher identified four basic strands in Germanic reactionary thought, all of which were brought together by Hitler in the 1930s: imperialistic nationalism; a conservative–authoritarian glorification of the state; a nationalistic–statist aberration of socialism which sought to combine social romanticism and state socialism; and a *völkisch* community ideology based on race, which began as simple xenophobia and turned into radical anti-semitism (Bracher, 1971: 23). All the strands had deep ideological and sociological roots in Austria. The pan-Germans of the 1930s despised the weakness and divisions of democratic politics and looked to the virtues of military discipline and communal purity embodied in the programme of a single leader, the Führer. Hitler's contribution was to bring the different strands into a single political programme crowned by rabid anti-semitism, a programme which turned German and Austrian national resentments into broadly based popular authoritarian politics.

These preliminary comments raise some further questions. How far do contemporary parties emphasize the supposed superiority of the German race and culture, including a strong tendency to anti-semitism and anti-Slav sentiment? To what extent is political vision directed towards the establishment of a strong centralized state focused around an individual leader and the utopian dream of a complete culture in which all social conflicts are subsumed in common devotion to that leader? Do Austrian (extreme) right-wing movements seek to protect the democratic mechanisms of conflict resolution or do they despise them as weakness and decadence?

Austria's own past history constitutes a crucial measuring-stick for Austria's present right wing. Loyalty to that past raises questions in Austria's democratic political culture. This particular meaning lies behind the oft-repeated phrase 'coming to terms with the past' in Austria. A clear breach from this past is, however, very difficult to achieve. Having broken from the practices of the Third Reich in 1945, the ruling SPÖ and ÖVP elites who dominated the Second Republic did not dwell any longer than necessary on its more complex and chronic aspects. In the absence of systematic public education, however, the legacy of memory retained a latent political potency.

Mudde (1995) contends that, by the early 1980s, the explicitly neo-Nazi Austrian National Democratic Party (NDP) represented an almost paradigmatic model of the modern extreme right in Europe, espousing xenophobia, nationalism, racism, anti-democracy and a strong, personal leadership demanding unconditional loyalty in a strong state. While the NDP, of which more later, was not by any means the largest political grouping occupying the extreme right wing of the Austrian polity, the tradition which it encapsulated had wider reach through the informal channels of the established pan-German third *Lager*. Across this entire spectrum, there was no complete rupture with the past. Even among the more democratic wing, there was a clear reluctance to criticize the Nazi period outright.

However, if we are to find coherent definitions of the extreme, the different degrees of attachment and the direction in which the political leadership within the third *Lager* were committed to moving are obviously of crucial significance. Extremism, defined from the perspective of democracy, always entails a fundamental challenge to democracy. For democracies, the defining criterion of the 'extreme' right, as opposed perhaps to 'far' right, is the extent to which they challenge liberal democracy itself, putting themselves beyond the pale of political inclusion by democratic parties. Accurate analysis of a party's commitment to democratic procedures is thus crucial when assessing its capacity to be integrated into the democratic system. Most of the third *Lager* in post-war Austria has never openly crossed this line. Nevertheless, a political movement which appears to be driven by authoritarianism, xenophobia, a cult of personality and an indistinct relationship to the authoritarian past gives rise to enormous suspicion. These are precisely the accusations levelled at Jörg Haider's rapidly advancing FPÖ.

Towards liberalism? The FPÖ and the integration of the third *Lager* into post-war Austria

The Second Republic was founded on a reversal of the myth of the First Republic. Independence, not *Anschluss*, meant survival. Austria was a victim of Hitler's aggression, not a participant in Nazism (Knight, 1988). An official handbook in 1946 described Austria as 'the first victim, abandoned by the world' (Rot–Weiß–Rot Handbuch, 1946). International interests during the Cold War, with the notable exception of Konrad Adenauer, conspired with domestic interests to establish this view as orthodoxy.

In 1945, the leaderships of the Socialists (SPÖ) and Christian Democrats (ÖVP) unambiguously agreed on the need for parliamentarianism and struck a crucial deal to establish basic stability in the system. Co-operation between the traditional rural and business support of the Catholic ÖVP and the urban supporters of the SPÖ enabled the emergence of a stable, definitively Austrian, centre. The political and social mechanisms for national co-operation established between the party elites in 1945 have survived for more than fifty years, even when the coalition has been out of operation. At their core lay two principles: social partnership, through which the elites of business, politics and the trade unions struck universal agreements on pay and, in the early years, basic prices; and *Proporz*, or proportionality in the allocation of jobs in the huge public sector between the followers of the two *lagers*.

In 1948, representatives of the politically disenfranchised *Ehemaligen* (former Nazi functionaries or members) made common cause with two economic liberal critics of the SPÖ–ÖVP coalition. They gathered support from industrialists who objected to the nationalization policies of the government and from anti-centralist intellectuals in Salzburg. Later that year, anti-Nazi restrictions were loosened, distinguishing between a narrow range of more serious Nazi officials, who would continue to face restrictions, and the mass of 'less tainted' members, who were granted full citizens' rights. The new League of Independents (VdU) became the first rallying point for most of the previously disenfranchised. These decisions effectively ended serious attempts by the Austrian state to pursue collaborators. For as long as the coalition parties were pre-eminent in Austrian politics, there was no immediate association between the Austrian state and National Socialism. Significantly, even the new populist right wing which has emerged since 1986 has actively sought to detach its expression of authoritarian thought from direct association with Nazism (Scharsach, 1992: 19–20).

The VdU was largely a gathering of the discontented around particular local figures and it never developed a coherent programme or ideology. The unifying policy in the party was the lifting of all remaining restrictions on the activities of former Nazis. Nevertheless, it enjoyed electoral success in the 1949 parliamentary elections, polling 490,000 votes or 11.7 per cent (Perchinig, 1983), and the VdU electorate was clearly a decisive factor in the 1951 presidential election. Most importantly, the result confirmed that post-war Austria remained a three, or at least a two and a half, party system. The VdU always risked losing voters to the dominant coalition parties, both of which controlled great opportunities for patronage through the burgeoning *Proporz* system. By 1953, the VdU was adopting more overtly German-national tones in the election, while the 1954 *Bad Ausseer* programme seemed to define the party in unmistakably German-national colours. The absence of systematic social or economic policy signalled the end of the attempt by liberals to create from the VdU a serious liberal third force in Austrian politics (Riedlsperger, 1978).

The successful negotiation of the State Treaty in 1955 led to the final collapse of the VdU. The signing of the document was probably the finest hour of Second Republic diplomacy, securing international agreement for the departure of foreign troops from Austrian soil. The deletion from the final text of the State Treaty of any reference to war guilt, and the fact that Austria signed a 'State Treaty' and not a 'Peace Treaty', gave international substance to Austria's 'first victim' status. It also accounts for the lack of any serious compensation law for Jewish or other persecuted citizens until the 1990s. Separate Austrian identity was reinforced by the declaration of permanent neutrality, which opened up a new foreign policy profile. In international politics, Austria was thereafter associated with Switzerland and Sweden, but seldom with Germany. Only occasionally, such as when the Soviet Union objected to Austrian membership of the European Community, was the matter of *Anschluss* raised. Even then, the fear of *Anschluss* was largely camouflage for Cold War concerns.

After the withdrawal of the allies from Austrian soil, a wide variety of groups from the German-national *Lager* re-emerged, 'encompassing a broad political spectrum from barely concealed neo-Nazism to more moderate German nationalism' (Bailer and Neugebauer, 1994: 98). No analysis of the form of right-wing politics in Austria can be detached from an appreciation of this variegated milieu from which various parties stem. The continuation of a *Lager* was crucial, ensuring that contact would be maintained among the huge variety of groups, ranging from sports clubs to military veterans' groups and university organizations, that constituted the culture of the third *Lager*.

The most successful branch of the German-national *Lager* was its student wing, the RFS (*Ring Freiheitlicher Studenten*). In 1953, German-national students won 33.4 per cent support in elections to the Austrian Students' Union (ÖH). The RFS was to be the breeding-ground for many of the leading figures on the Austrian extreme right during subsequent decades, and not only in the FPÖ. The students cultivated the strong traditions of Germanic sport through a number of right-wing fraternities (*Verbindungen*) and had close connections with the controversial *Freiheidicher Akademikerverhand* (Gartner, 1990: 2). The membership of the RFS included committed democrats and liberals, like Friedhelm Frischenschlager and Heide Schmidt, traditional third *Lager* figures – such as Jörg Haider – and also overtly anti-democratic figures, such as Norbert Burger. While leader of the RFS in 1960, Burger was actively involved in the first serious post-war anti-democratic right-wing activity, the bombing campaigns by German-nationalists in South Tyrol. In 1965, clashes between RFS students supporting the anti-semitic Professor Taras Borodajkewicz and anti-fascist demonstrators led to the death of one of the anti-fascists. Although Burger and other RFS right-wingers subsequently abandoned the FPÖ and formed the NDP on an explicitly authoritarian, German, anti-democratic platform, the connections within the *Lager* were ongoing. The NDP fostered a distinctly neo-Nazi subculture, campaigning as overt opponents of the post-war settlement and of all non-German influences which weakened the collective power of the *Volk*. Openly admiring Hitler and proudly anti-foreigner and anti-democracy, the NDP's modernized Nazism qualifies as extreme right wing on all criteria. In the 1980s, the party was banned under Austrian anti-Nazi legislation.

Electorally, however, the FPÖ was the only successful party of the right. In 1956, dissatisfaction with the disorganization of the VdU had led to the formation of the FPÖ, under the leadership of former SS officer Anton Reinthaller. It quickly became by far the largest political party for those in the third *Lager*. The FPÖ leadership effectively adopted the VdU's *Bad Ausseer* programme as the initial party platform, including the clear accent on German-national priorities. Seeking both to maintain its base in the third *Lager* and to extend it to a post-war constituency, the FPÖ tried to function both as the keeper of the pan-German flame and as an anti-corporatist party of protest in parliament. However, the dynamism of the Austrian economy from the 1950s until the 1970s, the successful establishment of an independent foreign policy profile for Austria during the Cold War, the security against all foreign paranoias provided by the Iron Curtain, and the historic *rapprochement* of Social Democracy and Roman Catholicism all restricted the party's appeal. The FPÖ's electoral standing stabilized at around 5 per cent of the vote by the 1960s.

By 1966, it was clear that the larger parties were interested in the FPÖ only in as far as it was useful in winning advantage over their main opponents (Bailer and Neugebauer, 1994). Under ex-SS officer Friedrich Peter, the FPÖ leadership sought to use its remaining leverage to move from the shadows of permanent opposition and into the political mainstream. This it did by making a bid for the unoccupied ground of corporatist

Austrian politics: economic liberalism. The failure of the NDP to make any electoral inroads seemed to encourage the trend away from German-nationalism. The shift in emphasis paid dividends in 1970, when the FPÖ agreed to tolerate an SPÖ minority government under the leadership of Bruno Kreisky, in return for a more favourable electoral system. The rehabilitation of the FPÖ by Kreisky was all the more surprising given Kreisky's Jewish origins. It was justified by SPÖ figures as a recognition of changes in the FPÖ and as underpinning the liberal trend. Leading intellectuals in the FPÖ, particularly those gathered in the so-called Attersee Circle, sought to secure and substantiate the image. When the FPÖ was admitted to the Liberal International in 1979 (Frischenschlager, 1980), many believed that the party had decisively shed its past Nazi associations. The surprisingly good performance by Norbert Burger (NDP) in the presidential election of March 1980, polling 3.2 per cent, did not dent this impression. To most observers, it seemed sufficiently small to warrant only minor anxiety. If anything, violent splinter right-wing groups emerging from extreme German-national circles underlined the different status of the FPÖ. The liberal faction within the FPÖ seemed to be approaching final victory when the intellectual Norbert Steger, a hate figure for the party's right wing, narrowly won the contest for national party leadership. His advance was crowned in 1983 when the FPÖ entered a coalition government with the SPÖ under Fred Sinowatz.

Problems of the Second Republic in the 1980s

Austria by the 1980s was a sharply different place from the Austria of 1918, 1933, 1938 or 1945. In contrast to inter-war experience, Austria had seen continuous economic growth for forty years. Since the mid-1960s, the welfare state had been expanded along Scandinavian lines, creating one of the largest public sectors in Europe. Meanwhile, neutrality in the Cold War allowed Austria to develop an active and distinctive foreign policy. The Social Democratic–Christian Democratic axis had apparently resulted in one of Europe's most stable political systems, the two parties polling over 90 per cent of votes cast in general elections.

Nevertheless, political tranquillity hid important problems. Not least, Austrian politics was an elite preserve. Since the Habsburgs, Austrian politics has been characterized by disciplined top-down leadership: so-called 'guided' rather than 'participative' parties, replicated on the political left as well as the right. The *Lager* tradition, translated into economic corporatism of the post-war years, generated a dangerous gulf between these elites and the populace, once the system started to falter. By 1980, social partnership had led to an unprecedented and probably unique degree of both formal and informal interpenetration of the economic and political elites. While elite co-operation could be held to have changed Austria from a violently divided society into a model consociational state (Lijphart, 1975), progress towards participative democracy remained restricted. For as long as there was continuing and general economic growth, combined with a generous welfare system, the result was widely envied social peace. By the mid-1980s, however, economic and political processes were rapidly undermining this stability.

Forty years of welfare state prosperity produced a generation increasingly adapting to Anglo-American consumerism and individual choice. Growing secularism and the ending of open hostility between Austrian Socialism and Roman Catholicism after the war made the barriers between the *lagers* at the heart of Austrian politics more permeable and their institutional coherence less complete. The party-owned press, previously dominant in Austria, was struggling to keep pace with a rapidly changing media environment (Hanisch, 1994). All these factors were increasing the potential of a dealignment from traditional loyalties, and encouraged mobility among voters. Bruno Kreisky harvested this floating vote for the SPÖ in the 1970s. The first indication that the voters might rebel came with the shock defeat of the entire Austrian political establishment in a referendum on nuclear energy in 1978.

By 1986, the tendencies against market intervention by the state in all the leading world economies were impinging on Austria. European growth was no longer creating jobs. The economic downturn of the mid-1980s slowed Austria's growth, causing increasing, if still low, unemployment. Technological development favoured small workplaces and flexible labour markets. Traditional heavy industry was shedding jobs. Even more dramatically, farming trends favoured large producers, leading to a sharp reduction in the numbers engaged in agriculture. All these changes reduced the capacity of social partnership deal-making to deliver stability to the core electorates of the SPÖ and ÖVP. Changing social and economic circumstances were compounded in the years following Kreisky's departure in 1983 by a succession of corruption scandals involving key figures in the SPÖ elite. Kreisky's successor, Sinowatz, lacked the public relations talents of his predecessor and was himself caught in the web of corruption (Sully, 1990: 136–54). The ÖVP was still unable to break the SPÖ's grip on power, and by 1986 was suffering from seventeen years of opposition at federal level. Steger's FPÖ, allied to the Socialists in government, was widely accused of abandoning its critical edge, and seemed impotent in the face of corruption and unable to change either the atmosphere or the direction of government policy (Bailer and Neugebauer, 1994: 366).

Identifiable constituencies for a party of populist protest were emerging. On the left, the SPÖ faced criticism from ecologists and discontented student groups. On the right, discontent within the German-national right wing of the FPÖ was palpable. By 1986, two further groups of discontented voters were also apparent: paradoxically, both the new rich or yuppie constituency, who resented the straitjacket of corporatist bureaucracy, and the less skilled, who were threatened by rising economic instability, were showing signs of disaffection.

The re-emergence of right-wing populism

Liberal dominance of the FPÖ was short-lived. Two specific events allowed the re-emergence of the right wing into national prominence. First, the national–liberal split in the FPÖ surfaced over the 'Reder affair'. In 1985, the high-profile, liberal Defence Minister, Friedhelm Frischenschlager, sought to mend party fences by organizing an official welcome for a convicted war criminal, Walter Reder, on his release from prison in Italy. Attacked by all other parties, Frischenschlager apologized publicly to an Israeli newspaper for his action. Initially supported by the FPÖ right wing for welcoming Reder, most vocally by Jörg Haider, the leader of the party in Carinthia, Frischenschlager was now accused of betrayal. The particular implication of an Israeli newspaper was not lost on his audience. The Reder affair focused the discontent at the grassroots in the FPÖ and galvanized the right into action against the liberal leadership. Articulating this disillusion, Jörg Haider launched increasingly bitter attacks on the federal leadership from his home province of Carinthia, where he was engaged in a campaign to reduce the amount of Slovene taught to Carinthian German-speakers. The Reder affair publicly demonstrated the lack of consensus over Austria's wartime experience, for the first time for many years.

This development was reinforced by the second crucial event: the presidential election campaign of 1986. The candidacy for the ÖVP of former UN Secretary-General Kurt Waldheim became a matter of international controversy when he was exposed as having lied, both orally and in print, about his war record. The matter was taken up by the World Jewish Congress (WJC) in New York, which suggested that Waldheim might have been involved in war crimes. Almost instantly, and very publicly, the veil was lifted from Austria's wartime past (Mitten, 1992). The very different perceptions of the meaning of Waldheim's banal lying, for many Austrians and for those outside, were laid bare. The compromises at the heart of the great silence of Austrian politics since 1945 were ripped apart. A public row between the WJC and the ÖVP leadership developed into a debate about Austria's war record and the right of outsiders (Jews) to comment. The official 'first victim of Hitler' dogma conflicted sharply with the claim that Waldheim's *Wehrmacht* service in the Balkans was that of someone 'who had only done their duty'. The fact that the campaign was led by the right-wing Christian Democratic ÖVP merely smoothed the way for more explicitly nationalist figures. A vote for Waldheim was turned by the ÖVP into a matter of patriotic duty. The boundary between the defence of Waldheim and the opportunity to restate authoritarian sentiment became very thin. Implicit anti-semitism appeared everywhere in the Austrian media (Wodak, 1991: 80).

These events allowed Jörg Haider to emerge as the undisputed spokesman for the right-wing FPÖ grassroots. With Haider leading the charge, the intense but disorganized frustration with the party leadership had now acquired political potency, stunningly demonstrated by the unanticipated internal putsch at the 1986 FPÖ Congress in Innsbruck. Planned in advance by Haider and a well-established clique of right-wingers, Steger's downfall was executed with breathtaking efficiency. Although the majority of the party elite supported Steger, Haider's grassroots support carried him to a clear victory in a leadership poll, amid scenes of right-wing jubilation, with frighteningly neo-Nazi overtones.

The SPÖ, now under the moderate leadership of the pragmatic former banker Franz Vranitzky, immediately terminated the coalition with the FPÖ. Shocked by the scenes of right-wing mayhem in Innsbruck, Vranitzky was now embarked on the policy which he was to follow consistently for the next ten years: the policy of *Ausgrenzung*, meaning 'exclusion' or 'putting beyond the pale'. In Vranitzky's eyes, Haider represented a serious threat to the democratic consensus in Austria and was both damaging to Austria internationally and morally repugnant. The personal struggle between Vranitzky and Haider was to dominate Austrian politics for the next decade. Vranitzky, Federal Chancellor throughout the period, seemed to symbolize the Social Democrats after fifty years of the Second Republic: solid, reliable and prosperous, the very personification of the new political establishment. It was left to Haider to articulate the grievances and to adopt the revolutionary and oppositional mantle which had once been the SPÖ's own.

Haider's potential as a vehicle for popular protest was sensationally underlined when the FPÖ doubled its vote to 9.7 per cent in the 1986 parliamentary elections (Luther, 1987: 394–5). Haider's electoral success contrasted even more sharply with the poll ratings of the FPÖ under Steger in government. The confrontation between the erstwhile coalition partners benefited both Vranitzky and Haider at first. Haider's internal revolution and Vranitzky's absolute abhorrence of it established the FPÖ as *the* party of opposition. A bitterly disappointed ÖVP failed to overtake the SPÖ as the largest party and was forced to enter a consociational coalition as the junior partner. Across a whole range of issues and groups, Haider could now monopolize popular discontent with the growing list of shortcomings of the Second Republic. Haider's lack of support among the previous elite in the FPÖ actually ensured his personal domination over the new party apparatus. Analysis of the FPÖ electorate in 1986 established that Haider's personality was the greatest single factor in the party's appeal. Voters apparently identified Haider's FPÖ as a breath of fresh air in Austria's frozen political landscape (Plasser and Ulram, 1992: 154).

Haider and the politics of right-wing populism

The manner of Haider's triumphs instantly made the FPÖ by far the most important focus of concern as regards the re-emergence of an extreme right in Austria. Haider's goal, however, was to transform the FPÖ from a small oppositional group into a significant party of potential government. This clearly entailed the building of a new political coalition far beyond his base among the traditional far right of the FPÖ. The rising tide of political and economic resentment presented Haider with the ideal opportunity. Haider's adoption of populist anti-establishment slogans attracted a wide popular audience. Using his status as an 'outsider' from the old governing elites, he presented himself as an uncorrupted crusader, speaking truth to corrupt power, just as the opportunities for such explicitly oppositional politics in Austria were multiplying. His extremely image-conscious presentation appealed to a consumerist generation raised on novelty and excitement. By monopolizing opposition, he was also presented with an embarrassment of rich targets to attack, including corporatist corruption, the nepotism and bureaucracy of the 'system parties', an over-bloated welfare state and the domination of the economy by vested interests. The problem for the SPÖ and ÖVP, parties of government for forty years, was the scope for opposition which the problems of the 1980s exposed, multiplied by their own apparent incapacity to confront them.

The crucial objection to Haider, and the justification for his exclusion from power, was his association with the anti-democratic Germanic right wing of the third *Lager*. As already suggested, Jörg Haider was and is a child of that *Lager*. A leading light of the German-national youth movement and one-time chairman of the RFS, he had been snubbed by Steger in the distribution of political favours in 1983. Haider returned to Carinthia to become leader of the historically right-wing, local FPÖ, where he reinforced the party's traditional anti-Slovene image and carved out a role as the leading internal opponent of the Vienna party leadership. Haider's high profile in the Reder affair ensured his support among the German-national footsoldiers in the FPÖ and beyond, but it also consolidated his status as an authoritarian anti-democrat among his many critics. He has always been careful to signal his fundamental loyalty to these roots. A regular attender at veterans' gatherings, Haider told one meeting for Waffen SS war veterans in 1985: 'I feel it incumbent on me to thank you for your active service. I am not alone, indeed, many young people think like me when I say that your sacrifice was not and should not be in vain' (in Galanda, 1987: 41).

For many democrats, Haider's reliance on the right-wing core of his movement invalidates his articulation of widely held complaints about the corporatist system. His stand against corruption and 'party' domination certainly struck a chord among broad swathes of the electorate. In building from the FPÖ core, however, Haider relied on a very specific right-wing infrastructure of political, academic, economic and cultural support. In combining that old core with the new causes, Haider's promise of necessary change appeared to many as more of a threat than a promise. The consistent difficulty for opponents of Haider, though, has been how to assess the degree of seriousness which should be attached to his authoritarian associations, while he continues to harvest votes on the back of popular protest.

Most of the former liberal leadership did not leave the FPÖ immediately. Economic liberals identified with much of the thrust of his anti-corporatist critique. At the same time, an already worried Liberal International (LI) sent a commission of inquiry to Austria in 1986 to investigate FPÖ developments, and this resulted in a very critical report. In interviews with liberal journals, Haider was careful to put clear distance between himself and any crass admiration for National Socialism (*Profil*, 18 February 1985). Yet Haider's inner circle was dominated by those from the German-national right who had supported his party *putsch*. His electoral success was paralleled by ruthless personal leadership of the party. The nature of the 1986 *putsch* meant that Haider could rely on overwhelming support among the grassroots of the FPÖ. Party advancement became increasingly reliant on loyalty to Haider himself. Electoral success reinforced this process beyond doubt. Increasingly, FPÖ representatives were dependent on Haider rather than the other way around. Internal discipline was rigidly enforced and, one by one, all rivals were driven to the margins.

The liberal presentation of the party programme thus looked like a veneer which hid an authoritarian core. There was repeated evidence of Haider's open flirtation with the anti-democratic right within the *Lager*. In 1987, Haider held a secret meeting with the leading lights of the German-national *Lager*, including Norbert Burger of the NDP and Otto Scrinzi, a leading extreme right thinker and self-declared fascist. The widely circulated extreme right German-national press, which presents a daily diet of revisionist pro-Nazi history, anti-semitism and xenophobia throughout Germany and Austria, constantly praised his anti-liberal stance (Scharsach, 1992; 1995). The willingness of many FPÖ figures to write for and to this press, and the highly permeable boundary between the press and publishing houses close to the FPÖ (notably *Aula*) and other extreme right-wing publications in Germany and Austria, ensured a constant flow of information and consultation across the full range, both democratic and anti-democratic, of the German-national *Lager*. In an interview with Austrian television in 1988, Haider described the concept of an Austrian nation as an 'ideological deformity', apparently conforming to the traditional view of Austria as integral to the Greater German nation (Scharsach, 1992:

90–3). Significantly, the Attersee Circle, the liberal think-tank which had influenced Steger, distanced itself from the FPÖ, while the distinctly racist outpourings of the Lorenzener Circle became increasingly influential (Fischer and Gstettner, 1990: 16–33).

Haider survived the defection of the liberals from the FPÖ because of his capacity to draw new supporters into the party, underpinned by his spectacular electoral successes. Haider's oppositional crusades simultaneously won new votes among the yuppie *nouveaux riches* and the disillusioned. Austria's largest mass-circulation newspaper, the *Neue Kronen Zeitung*, adopted Haider as the voice of the 'small man' against the party machines. The Haider bandwagon rolled the resentments of numerous groups into a 'coalition of the outsiders', with himself as popular tribune or 'renewer' (Mölzer, 1990). Assigned by the other parties to opposition, Haider eagerly and skilfully exploited his chance to articulate almost any popular resentment against any establishment decision or responsibility.

What took most observers and the Austrian political establishment by surprise was the depth and breadth of the resentments which proved open to Haider's exploitation. Early assessments that Haider's performance represented the return of the 10 per cent of the electorate who had supported the VdU or the pre-war *bourgeois* German-nationals (Pelinka, 1988) were quickly dashed as Haider moved from electoral victory to electoral victory. There were spectacular performances for the FPÖ in provincial elections throughout Austria in 1988 and 1989. Most of the initial gains were made at the expense of the ÖVP, a trend confirmed in the 1990 federal election, when the FPÖ broke through the 15 per cent barrier for the first time, while the ÖVP lost 8 per cent. Whereas in 1983 the FPÖ under Steger polled less than an eighth of the ÖVP vote, by 1994 the FPÖ under Haider had almost equalled the ÖVP total.

In 1989, the FPÖ overturned the long-standing Socialist domination of Carinthia and became the second largest party in the province. The result led to the first real crisis for Vranitzky's policy of exclusion. Anti-Socialist and right-wing Catholic elements in the third-placed ÖVP strongly favoured an anti-Socialist coalition. Devastated by Haider's capacity to monopolize discontent, they argued that keeping Haider out of the political system only created more opportunities for him to exploit government failings. Furthermore, the Carinthian ÖVP shared Haider's loathing of the dominant SPÖ. In an open breach with ÖVP policy at federal level, the Carinthian ÖVP entered a coalition agreement with the FPÖ, making Haider *Landeshauptmann* (governor) of Carinthia.

From the outset, Haider courted controversy. In 1990, he publicly refused to award honours to former partisans for their service in opposing the Nazis, choosing instead to praise Carinthian German resistance to Slovene encroachment in 1920 (Haider, 1993: 221). During the same year, he again attended the German war veterans' meeting at Ulrichsberg and praised the loyalty and service of the veterans (Bailer and Neugebauer, 1994: 424; Scharsach, 1992: 160–9). Ultimately, Haider's refusal to endorse the anti-Nazi fundamentals of the Second Republic brought the ÖVP–FPÖ experiment to a premature end in June 1991. In the heat of a debate on the economy, one particularly revisionist remark – 'In the Third Reich they had a proper employment policy, which your government in Vienna can't even manage' (*Protokoll der Kärntner Landtag*, 13 June 1991) – proved too much for the Carinthian ÖVP.

Events in Carinthia seemed to confirm that democratic parties had no choice but to treat Haider as a danger to the system, and the ÖVP leadership at federal level underlined their support for Vranitzky's *Ausgrenzung* strategy. In doing so, however, the scope for alternative coalition-building in Austrian politics disappeared altogether. By consigning Haider's growing band of voters to the political wilderness, the main parties allowed him to monopolize all oppositional causes, with the obvious danger that a large and angry anti-democratic opposition, so feared by the coalition of 1948, could now emerge. With both parties in electoral decline, the SPÖ–ÖVP coalition seemed locked in power by a straitjacket rather than by any significant common bond. In the face of the FPÖ's continuing electoral advances, the 'old parties' often looked tired and without ideas, committed only to remaining in power.

Successful politicians are touched by both skill and luck. Just as the momentum was running out of Haider's first anti-corruption campaigns and the novelty began to flag, world political events transformed the domestic political agenda. The fall of the Berlin Wall in 1989 and the collapse of Yugoslavia in 1991 substantially increased the flows of migrants arriving in Austria, particularly in Vienna. Moreover, the collapse of the Iron Curtain exposed the huge contrast in economic expectations between Eastern and Western Europe, and Austria found itself as one of the first ports of call for potential economic refugees. The prospect of huge waves of Slavic or Romanian immigration was deeply unsettling to elements of the Austrian working class, who were already faced with rising job insecurity as a result of other changes in the world economy.

Feeding directly off and into this fear, Haider launched a series of viciously anti-immigrant campaigns. Whereas the anti-corruption campaigns of the 1980s had netted Haider new support among the upwardly mobile new middle classes and among working-class protest voters (Plasser, *et al.*, 1992: 40–1), the anti-immigrant and anti-foreigner campaigns of the early 1990s appealed increasingly to the SPÖ's core working-class electorate. Campaigning under the slogan 'Vienna for the Viennese', the FPÖ doubled its vote in the Vienna City elections to 22.5 per cent in November 1991, seriously threatening the SPÖ's overall majority in the city for the first time since 1918.

Parallel to the rise in anti-immigrant sentiment, there were also disturbing signs that a violent, extreme right wing was re-emerging. In October 1991, Jewish graves were desecrated in Vienna. Police raided neo-Nazi paramilitary training centres and discovered bombs and home-made explosives equipment (Knight, 1992: 285). Xenophobia was spawning active terrorism among small groups on the outer fringes of neo-Nazism. For instance, the explicitly neo-Nazi group VAPO, founded in the mid-1980s, regarded itself as a modern version of the old Nazi *Sturm-Abteilung* (storm-troops, SA). In 1993, the Viennese Nazi Gottfried Küssel was sentenced to ten years' imprisonment for renewal of neo-Nazi activities and was turned into a *cause célèbre* by the extreme right press. In December 1993, ten letter-bombs were sent to a variety of anti-Nazi figures in public life, including the Mayor of Vienna and leading members of the Green Party, who had strongly opposed Haider's anti-foreigner campaign (Purtscheller, 1994: 495–514). During 1994, a new and shadowy group, the Bajuvarian Liberation Army, emerged as the authors of further waves of small bomb attacks. In early 1995, four gypsies were killed in the Burgenland village of Oberwart. Later in the same year, during the 1995 election campaign, there was a further series of letter-bomb incidents. Although there was no evidence of widespread popular support for the violence, the renewal of extreme right terror was unparalleled in the Second Republic. While there was no direct connection to the FPÖ, the social risks inherent in race politics were ominously clear.

Haider's personal commitment to the anti-foreigner campaign put further strain on the remaining liberals in the FPÖ. Throughout 1992, he campaigned vigorously for his popular initiative (*Volksbegehren*) which sought to force the government to adopt draconian anti-immigrant laws. Under the title 'Austria First' (*Österreich Zuerst*), Haider called for a million signatures to the petition. The fact that 'only' 416,000 signed was widely regarded as a failure, although the total represented over 7 per cent of the Austrian electorate (Müller, 1994: 243). Furthermore, in an internal party matter, Haider sided with the right wing of his party in a dispute over the neo-Nazi racist language of his publicist-in-chief, Andreas Mölzer.

While the anti-foreigner campaigns drew on strong traditional themes in pan-German thinking, the mass movement now being built by Haider was a new phenomenon in post-war Austria. In addition, Haider's appeal went far beyond the traditional *Lager*. In making direct appeals to the voters and using the option of the popular initiative, Haider was mobilizing a new, much more mobile political force, using highly emotive issues to undermine the traditionally solid lines of Austrian political support. With the support of the *Neue Kronen Zeitung*, Haider appealed to all those who feared the new world of globalization and the individual market, articulating their authoritarian and reactionary response. An opinion poll in 1992 found that 70 per cent of *Neue Kronen Zeitung* readers were authoritarian in orientation (*Profil*, 14 December 1992). Paradoxically, Haider was the first politician fully to exploit the political dealignment, which was itself the result of the modern marketplace, in a movement of protest against its effects.

The collapse of the Soviet Union, which released Austria from the last obstacles obstructing its full membership of the European Union (EU), presented a further opportunity for political realignment. Sensing growing anxieties in the Austrian population about the implications of membership, Haider moved to monopolize anti-EU opposition and began campaigning aggressively against the loss of power of individual states. In effect, he single-handedly reversed, virtually overnight, the FPÖ position on the European Community (now Union). The FPÖ had traditionally supported EC membership as a route to closer association with Germany, which the prospect of 'ever closer union' appeared to offer. Haider's *volte-face* on European unity and the xenophobia of the *Volksbegehren* were the final straw for the remaining liberals in the FPÖ.

In February 1993, led by the party's former general secretary Heide Schmidt and other liberal parliamentarians, all the leading figures from the Steger era, and others who had joined the party since 1986, left the FPÖ and established the Liberal Forum (LF), Austria's first internally created new party since the war. On television, on the evening of her departure, Schmidt attacked Haider for 'despising human beings' (*Menschenverachter*) and pointed to his preparedness to tolerate street violence in pursuit of the *Volksbegehren* (Bailer and Neugebauer, 1994: 391–5). In July, Haider bowed to the inevitable and withdrew the FPÖ from the Liberal International, before he was pushed. Few in the liberal press or in the SPÖ questioned Vranitzky's conviction that there was no serious alternative to continuing a policy of exclusion against the FPÖ.

The pre-1986 FPÖ had been split into two distinctly different factions, with the German-national core clearly loyal to Haider. The strength of grassroots differences in the FPÖ had prevented a coherent single party profile. By 1994, this had all changed. The remaining and new membership of the FPÖ was bound to the personality and political success of Haider. Haider's capacity to change policy-tack over Europe demonstrated the scope of his internal authority. Crucially, although the liberals were the ones who now felt obliged to leave, the *volte-face* was also a ruthless recognition that the old formulas of pan-German thought were inappropriate for a populist party in Austria in the 1990s. Paradoxically, Haider increased his personal hold on the party by abandoning the most obvious path to integration with other Germans. However, German chancellor Helmut Kohl's Europe held little in common with more strident visions of Germanic power. In recognizing that the maintenance of populist opposition was more important than unreachable goals of pan-German unity, the FPÖ put a Haider-led Austria above a Europe led by Helmut Kohl. This did not necessarily represent a fundamental philosophical change – and, indeed, German-national groups were constantly being reassured that it did not –

but there was a real recognition that the *Anschluss* did not mobilize an Austrian electorate behind authoritarian right-wing politics in the 1990s.

Haider was now transformed into an Austrian superpatriot. Although the anti-foreigner campaign represented identification with traditional Germanic xenophobia, the *Freiheitlichen Thesen*, a series of position papers published in 1993, made no explicit mention of traditional phrases such as *Volksgemeinschaft* ('the community of the *volk*', a core component of Nazi racial ideology). Instead, they substituted a determination to protect more pastoral or domestic notions like *Heimat* (hearth and home), a word with enormous romantic resonance in German (Bailer and Neugebauer, 1994: 419). Haider's mass movement, although rooted in authoritarianism and a respect for the Germanic traditions and military virtues, also represented a radical and new accommodation with post-war reality.

This synthesis of the traditional with the new, in search of a popular majority, was illustrated by Haider's continuing attacks on the Second Republic itself. Indeed, the FPÖ openly campaigned for its transformation into a new, rather ominously (though numerically correctly) titled 'Third Republic'. Haider asserted, 'In reality, Austria is not a functioning democracy but an authoritarian democracy like a developing country, under the rule of licensed parties which were never founded by the people but were permitted by the Allies' (*Basta*, March 1993). This came close to asserting that the Second Republic, and perhaps liberal democracy *per se*, was an external imposition. In 1993, a number of FPÖ intellectuals, with Haider's support, proposed the replacement of the existing constitution, the abolition of the role of chancellor, the reduction of the cabinet to seven posts and the creation of a powerful presidency (FPÖ, 1994). They called for the abolition of collective bargaining, an enhanced role for the *Länder* and an increased number of plebiscites. This preference for strong personal leadership and appeals to the people against supposedly divisive parties corresponded to traditional right-wing demands, as well as enhancing Haider's political positioning as the radical renewer and a 'can-do' strong man. Significantly, the plans for a Third Republic illustrated the scope for ideas which appeared both populist and authoritarian.

Opposing Haider remained a difficult matter. His continuing success at the polls appeared to pose serious questions about the effectiveness of the *Ausgrenzung* strategy. Within the ÖVP, there were many voices arguing that the FPÖ should be brought into government and faced with responsibilities rather than left free to monopolize popular resentments. However, the renewed antics of the Carinthian FPÖ, following further local electoral success in 1994, only served to underline concern about what strong FPÖ rule might mean. Having negotiated a new deal with the local ÖVP, and securing nearly all the key government posts for itself, the FPÖ celebrated with a show of extreme public triumphalism. The manner in which the FPÖ trumpeted its outmanoeuvring of the other parties led to such uproar that the embarrassed ÖVP had to withdraw from the coalition as in 1991.

While the governing coalition was unable to devise a workable mechanism for integrating Haider into the political mainstream, his personal domination of the opposition was strengthening rapidly, a fact best illustrated by his decision to oppose Austrian membership of the EU. The risks of the strategy appeared to be confirmed when, despite opinion polls suggesting the contrary, Austria's membership of the EU was ratified by a wide margin in a referendum in June 1994. Nonetheless, given the likely medium-term adjustment costs resulting from membership, there was a clear strategic rationale to Haider's position, and the FPÖ was now the obvious recipient of protest votes (Sully, 1995a: 67–9).

By October, the electoral benefit was visible. Haider dominated the television campaign for the parliamentary elections against the jaded leaders of the coalition parties. The master of the sound-bite, Haider consistently outmanoeuvred his opponents. Presenting himself as 'the patron saint of the hard-working' against the corruption of the corporatist state and its parties, 'spongers' on the welfare system and foreigners who committed crimes and threatened social stability, Haider made this unashamedly populist pitch under the slogan 'Simply honest, simply Jörg', posing as a modern-day Robin Hood (Sully, 1995b: 221). To complement the proposals for a Third Republic, the FPÖ called for the abolition of the compulsory membership of the institutions of social partnership and the ending of permanent neutrality.

In winning more than 22 per cent of the vote, Haider made huge inroads into the SPÖ core electorate. By 1994, the FPÖ was being shunned by the university-educated middle class but was as much a working-class party as the SPÖ, with considerable support in the lower middle classes and among the rising business class (Müller and Ulram, 1995: 151). Moreover, political momentum seemed overwhelmingly to favour Haider. For the first time since 1945, the combined parliamentary strength of the ÖVP and SPÖ alone could not assure the passage of constitutional amendments. Dubbing the ruling alliance a 'coalition of losers', Haider proclaimed his intention to be 'chancellor by 1998', as leader of a *Freiheitlichen* movement whose core would be the FPÖ, but which would contain others prepared to identify with his movement for national renewal (*Frankfurter Hefte*, 1995: 627–34). The apparent abandonment of party in favour of a broader movement was a further attack on a corporatist Austria constructed on rigid party identity. But in highlighting disillusion with party bureaucracy, Haider's proposals also corresponded to traditional German-national suspicion of 'Anglo-American' parties. The lack of accountability inherent in 'movements', more specifically their vulnerability to leader domination, simultaneously confirmed to others their deep suspicions about Haider's motives.

By 1994, Haider had shaped a new phenomenon in Austrian right-wing politics. Although anti-foreigner sentiment and an authoritarian state were still the bases of FPÖ politics, Haider's contribution was to fashion these according to the circumstances of the 1990s, rather than the 1930s, and to combine them with a strongly neo-liberal approach to the economy, reminiscent of Newt Gingrich's 'Contract with America'. The post-war welfare state would be slashed, neutrality abolished and the European Union opposed. In a complete break with the FPÖ's anti-clerical tradition, Haider also moved to exploit the increasingly bitter divisions in the Austrian Catholic Church. Conservative bishops, such as the Archbishop of Vienna and the Bishop of St Pölten, indicated their disapproval of liberal tendencies in the traditionally pro-clerical ÖVP, implying an openness to the FPÖ. The outlines of Haider's new, authoritarian, right-wing coalition were already visible.

The first evidence that Haider, like other politicians, might also experience setbacks came unexpectedly in 1995. When the bad-tempered SPÖ–ÖVP coalition broke up in acrimony in October 1995, there was widespread expectation that the FPÖ would be the main beneficiary. For the first time since 1986, the ÖVP signalled a willingness to end the *Ausgrenzung* policy, entering the election refusing to name a definite coalition partner. But in spite of renewed anti-foreigner, anti-corruption and anti-crime populism and a pledge to 'muck out' the republic, Haider failed to dominate the television campaign as in 1994. Instead, the possibility that Haider might enter government moved centre stage and he came under sustained attack from the liberal press (*News*, 9 November 1995). By election day, the Social Democrats had turned the implicit risk to democracy in an ÖVP–FPÖ government into the main plank of their campaign. Fear of Haider now appeared to polarize the Austrian electorate, largely to the benefit of the SPÖ. A rejuvenated Vranitzky could claim vindication in his preference for the exclusion of the FPÖ from government, although FPÖ losses were limited to less than 1 per cent.

Any remaining chance that the ÖVP might reverse the coalition consensus on *Ausgrenzung* disappeared when Austrian television relayed a German video of Haider's speech to Waffen SS veterans at Krumpendorf, Carinthia, in September. Attacking those who objected to his presence, Haider blamed their opposition on 'irritation that there are still decent people of character in this world, who have stood up for their beliefs in a hostile environment and who have remained loyal to their convictions up to this day'. Furthermore, he praised the 'achievements' of the Waffen SS as entirely respectable:

> With my friends, I will always speak up for extending respect to this older generation: extending respect for their way through life, respect for all they put up with and, above all, respect for the things they protected for us. These are matters of crucial importance (*Profil*, 8 January 1996).

The absence of an unambiguously democratic right-wing partner created intense frustration for the ÖVP, which was anxious to break out of its eternal junior role in the coalition with the SPÖ. Not only had worries about Haider possibly cost the ÖVP the election, but the Krumpendorf video seemed to rule him out as a serious government partner. Democratic conservatives, such as the Vienna correspondent of the *Neue Zürcher Zeitung*, lamented that,

> Jörg Haider's praise for the old comrades of the Waffen SS ... doesn't only reflect his distorted view of history, but disqualifies the Haider-led *Freiheitlichen* movement as a political coalition partner, although the Nazi rubbish in no way belongs to the core of the FPÖ reform programme or to Haider's critique of the corruption of government parties, state and corporate economy (*Neue Zürcher Zeitung*, 30 May 1996).

While consigning 22 per cent of the electorate to permanent opposition creates serious problems in all democracies, the immediate choices for the ÖVP were to subordinate itself to the SPÖ or to be accused of flirting with fascism. Nevertheless, immediately following the furore, the ÖVP and FPÖ made an unofficial deal whereby the ÖVP retained the leading role in the government of the province of Styria and the FPÖ retained one of the deputy speaker posts in the federal parliament, despite considerable concern that the FPÖ candidate, Wilhelm Brauneder, had strong German-national sympathies and a clearly revisionist approach to Nazi history (*Profil*, 22 January 1996).

For as long as fears about Haider taking power were uppermost, the SPÖ made important political capital among the middle classes and the university educated, as the primary defender of liberal democracy. Nonetheless, the reduction of the SPÖ to an anti-Haider party had serious implications for its working-class core vote. When, as a result of coalition negotiations, the SPÖ agreed to sharp budget cuts to meet the Maastricht criteria, there was widespread public disquiet. Haider's strongly anti-EU stance had already gained the FPÖ new voters among farmers in western Austria (*Der Standard*, 16 December 1995). In elections to the European Parliament in October 1996, anger about budget cuts and anti-EU sentiment combined, as the working-class core voters of the SPÖ deserted their traditional party in droves. The FPÖ took 28 per cent of the total vote, less than 2 per cent below that of each of the other two parties. Furthermore, among the working class and the unemployed, the FPÖ actually outpolled the SPÖ, which lost its overall majority in Vienna for the first time since 1918 (*Der Standard*, 16 October 1996).

The resignation of Vranitzky and his replacement by Klima, largely as a result of these results, cannot therefore be disentangled from Haider's rise to prominence. While Vranitzky had successfully kept the SPÖ in power through the turbulence of the 1980s and 1990s, he had been unable to marginalize Haider. His successor, Victor Klima, represented a return to the working-class roots of the SPÖ and a more pragmatic approach to the political landscape. The national election of 1995 left the SPÖ as the clear opponent to Haider. The immediate risk was to the People's Party, whose traditional base was eroding at an even more spectacular rate than that of the Social Democrats. Furthermore, having been elected at the nadir of SPÖ fortunes and following a series of elections, Klima had certain advantages enabling him to take attention off the obsession with Haider. A marked slowdown in the pace of change from outside robbed Haider of new big issues, while Klima himself now enjoyed the novelty which had once been Haider's.

Nonetheless, the provincial elections of March 1999 – the first significant electoral test for the FPÖ since the 1996 European elections – illustrated that the political landscape of Austria has been radically reshaped by Haider. Whereas the FPÖ did not advance in Salzburg, where the SPÖ had established its own clear agenda, it emerged as the largest single grouping in Carinthia, polling a post-war record share of the vote (43 per cent). Jörg Haider returned in triumph to reclaim the provincial leadership which he had lost so controversially eight years earlier. Even more significantly, in a year of European and federal elections, the threat to the post-war consensus from the extremist right remained powerful. That the FPÖ share of the vote declined slightly (to 23.2 per cent, 5 MEP seats) in the June 1999 Euro-elections is unlikely to hurt the party. It will continue its campaigning at the national level.

Conclusions

The Austrian right inherited a poisonous legacy from 1945, scarred indelibly by Nazism. However, the requirements of state-building in Austria meant that Nazism could not be confronted directly in 1945, and it was addressed only obliquely until 1986. The cost of this postponement was the absence of a clean break with the discredited politics of the past. By adopting a 'let sleeping dogs lie' policy, Austria's post-war leadership relied largely on the passage of time and economic success under democracy to erode Austria's undemocratic traditions.

The explicitly neo-Nazi far right was not electorally successful after 1945 and the liberal position of the FPÖ seemed to secure the Austrian political system on its right flank. An unproven or unreliable democratic political culture in 1945 seemed to have flowered miraculously into a flourishing social democracy by the 1970s. However, the political success of the FPÖ under Jörg Haider, based on a platform of populist authoritarianism, has raised some serious questions about the long-term stability of the post-war consensus. Until the mid-1980s, the post-war settlement had delivered virtually uninterrupted socio-economic security. When it faltered, grievances about elite domination and the adjustment problems posed to the Austrian political and economic system by global economic forces coalesced with previously dormant resentments about the continuing legacy of the war to create a new political discontent.

In the Second Republic, political peace was bought for fifty years through deal-making among the political and economic elites. The electoral system and a tradition of political patronage gave a huge advantage to party insiders. Haider, although an FPÖ party insider all his life, campaigned as an outsider by capitalizing on his rejection by the governing parties and exploiting his associations with the right-wing grassroots of the FPÖ. Freed of the constraints of supporting corporatist patronage, he could articulate anger at a fairly full range of problems – nepotism, financial corruption, economic rigidity, bureaucracy and a culture of compromise – which had emerged through the years of prosperity. On one level, Haider represents the first sustained opposition in Austrian politics since World War II. The inability of SPÖ–ÖVP governments seriously to reform their own vested interests left potential problems for the Austrian system which have been ruthlessly exposed by Haider. His willingness to highlight multiple resentments without any reference to context or to their relative size as problems and his domination of the crucial medium of television have made him a potent and dangerous politician. Furthermore, as technological change gathers pace, the number of potential losers from a reformed social system grows, and voters may someday be willing to vote for the combination of renewal and security which an authoritarian populist like Haider embodies. The politics of exclusion, designed to protect Austria from any association with the Nazi past, do not seem to have stopped Haider's progress and threaten to become untenable if the FPÖ polls more than 30 per cent in a future election.

Haider's willingness to exploit the petty weaknesses of the Second Republic has been paralleled by a consistent unwillingness to acknowledge the much more serious problems of his approach to the Nazi past. He has been the first senior politician in post-war Austria to glorify in and profit from the undermining of the official history of the Second Republic. Since before his election as party leader, Haider has made his defence of World War II Nazi veterans a pattern. In praising the activities of the Waffen SS and in dismissing his critics, Haider has undermined his claim to be accepted as a democrat. By 1995, the Austrian courts were dismissing slander actions by Haider against those who called him the 'godfather of the extreme right', and a leading journalist labelled him 'a completely normal Nazi boy' (*Der Standard*, 22 December 1995). As the editor of *Profil* commented, the most persuasive argument against the FPÖ leader, who is probably not a National Socialist in the sense meant by criminal law, was and is that no one who has ever held a seat in the Second Republic has attempted so unashamedly to portray the Nazi period as harmless (*Profil*, 23 December 1995).

Jörg Haider is not a Nazi in any traditional sense. Ideologically, his party does not stand for an equivalent of the *Nationalsozialistische deutsche Arbeiter Partei* (Nazi Party, NSDAP). The FPÖ has never developed any of the paramilitary trappings of the SA or other such groups. Any links between the FPÖ and the openly anti-democratic right are implicit and informal. Furthermore, the FPÖ under Haider has adopted a radically neo-liberal economic policy, demanding full-scale privatization and the private tendering of public services. But if Jörg Haider is not a Nazi, there are legitimate doubts about his long-term commitment to anything other than the shell of democracy. The FPÖ remains integral to the historic German-national *Lager* in Austria, which includes many with a fanatical devotion to the Third Reich. There are clear continuities with its traditional emphases as identified by Bracher (1971). The contemporary FPÖ has adopted a conservative–authoritarian approach to both party and states, as well as a *völkisch* commitment to an organic Germanic *Heimat*. Very publicly, Haider has attacked multicultural or cosmopolitan developments, proposing to dismantle the welfare state to the benefit of the small, hard-working man against the designs of parasitical 'spongers' and big capital. Haider's plans for a Third Republic indicate his deep preference for a strong-man presidential system over a parliamentary democracy. The FPÖ is a strongly authoritarian party devoted to Haider's leadership. As Luther (1999: 141) also explains, 'the loyalty of the FPÖ party elite is oriented less to the party as such than to Haider himself, to whom most directly owe their positions'. During the 1994 referendum campaign, the 1995 election campaign and the 1996 EU elections, the FPÖ was *de facto* synonymous with Haider. Moreover, events in Carinthia in 1994 suggest that the FPÖ is not so much against patronage in principle as resentful of the current elite. The structure of the Haider party is so authoritarian as to suggest that FPÖ patronage would be a considerably more narrowly authoritarian phenomenon than patronage by the other parties.

Nevertheless, the FPÖ under Haider has usually taken care to position itself as the far right of the democratic political spectrum, rather than the extreme anti-democratic right. Haider's embrace of Austrian independence represents a compromise with post-war realities. Pan-Germanism, at least in its crude form, has no contemporary resonance. The FPÖ's politics are tailored for a small state, in which xenophobia is characterized by a hostility to invading outsiders, rather than for those of an imperialist, externally aggressive power. The contemporary FPÖ does not represent a military threat to Austria's neighbours. Although Haider calls for a more authoritarian social regime, there is no political campaign for a return to pre-war-style one-party rule. Also, Haider has clearly distanced himself from right-wing terrorism. For as long as democracy is secure in the large countries of Europe, Haider's support of the electoral system itself is unlikely to change.

The problems for any assessment of the FPÖ lie in the unspoken, the informal and the murky relationships of the language and culture of the third *Lager*. In the sense of Mudde's classification of extreme right-wing groups, the FPÖ clearly displays three of the five characteristics in full: xenophobia, nationalism and a strong, centralized leadership with a demand for a strong state. It is also difficult to assess where xenophobia becomes racism. The language of 'immigration' and overt and covert anti-semitism within the third *Lager* suggest an intimate connection between the two. The most difficult criterion to judge is the FPÖ's commitment to democracy. As we have seen, anti-democracy in the FPÖ is a 'whiff' or a 'rumour' which must remain unproven.

Haider's FPÖ thus represents a refiguring of the authoritarian tradition associated with the third *Lager*, a slick and modern movement of the far right. Its dependence on the capacity of its leader to make direct appeals to the electorate on the back of reactionary populist causes such as anti-foreigner sentiment, fear of crime and anti-elite resentment has made it highly effective in an age of presidential politics. Haider has transformed the FPÖ from a relatively insignificant party based on nostalgia to a serious and ambiguous authoritarian movement fashioned on populist causes.

The ambiguous nature of the FPÖ's commitment to liberal democracy is nevertheless strong enough to present both the ÖVP and SPÖ with a critical dilemma. The charge of anti-democratic intentions will remain unproven unless and until Haider enters government. The policy of *Ausgrenzung* associated with Franz Vranitzky stemmed largely from his determination to protect the Second Republic from any associations with the fascist past. Haider's antics at Waffen SS gatherings became the measuring-stick of his political unacceptability. Problematically, however, Haider has continued to make serious inroads into the electorate of both large parties, monopolizing the anxieties of large swathes of Austrian society, particularly the working class. After the 1996 European and 1999 Carinthian regional elections, many argued that *Ausgrenzung* itself was giving Haider's demagogic tendencies the free reign they needed and failing to provide the challenge of governmental responsibility.

The resignation of Vranitzky as SPÖ leader and chancellor in February 1997 and his replacement by Viktor Klima promised a new era. Deeply rooted in the traditions of the SPÖ, Klima was widely held to herald a new pragmatism in dealing with the FPÖ, less hostile to co-operation and geared towards reintegration. Including Haider in power, however, unavoidably implies weighing up a balance of risks, and making a decision of a kind that has not been necessary in Austrian government since 1945.

References

Bailer, B. and Neugebauer, W. (1994) 'Die FPÖ: Vom Liberalismus zum Rechtsextremismus', in *Handbuch des Österreichischen Rechtsextremismus*. Vienna: Dokumentationsarchiv des österreichischen Widerstandes.

Betz, H.-G. (1993) 'The Two Faces of Radical Right-Wing Populism in Western Europe', *Review of Politics* 55(4), 663–86.

Botz, Gerhard (1986) 'Eine deutsche Geschichte 1938 bis 1945?' *Zeitgeschichte*, 23, 19–38.

Bracher, K. D. (1971) *The German Dictatorship*. London: Penguin.

Doll, H. (1990) 'Aktuelle Situation der Rechtsextremismus in der Bundesrepublik Deutschland', in *Rechtsextremismus in der Bundesrepublik Deutschland*. Bonn: Bundesministerium für Inneres.

Fischer, G. and Gstettner, P. (1990) *Am kärntner Wesen könnte diese Republik genesen*. Klagenfurt/Celovec: Drava.

FPÖ (1994) *Weil das Land sich ändern muß! Auf dem Weg in die Dritte Republik*. Vienna: Freiheitliches Bildungswerk.

Frischenschlager, F. (1980) 'Wie Liberal ist die FPÖ?' *Österreichisches Jahrbuch für Politik*, pp. 135–81.

Galanda, B. (1987) *Ein Teutsches Land*. Vienna: Löcker.

Gartner, R. (1990) 'The Extreme Right in Austria: Its Connection to the FPÖ', paper delivered to the European Consortium of Political Research (ECPR), Bochum.

Haider, J. (1993) *Die Freiheit, die ich meine*. Frankfurt am Main/Berlin: Springer-Verlag.

Hainsworth, P. (ed.) (1992) *The Extreme Right in Europe and the USA*. London: Pinter.

Hanisch, Ernst (1994) *Der lange Schatten des Staates*. Vienna: Überreuther.

Kienzl, H. (1992) 'Identität oder Zusammengehörigkeitsgefühl', *Österreichische Zeitschrift für Politikwissenschaft* 2(2), 221–4.

Knight, Robert (1988) *Ich bin dafür, die Sache an die Länge zu ziehen*. Frankfurt am Main: Athenäum.

Knight, Robert (1992) 'Haider, the Freedom Party and the Extreme Right in Austria', *Parliamentary Affairs* 45(3), 285–99.

Lijphart, A. (1975) *Democracy in Plural Societies*. New Haven and London: Yale University Press.

Luther, K. R. (1987) 'Austria's Future and Waldheim's Past', *West European Politics* 10(3), 376–99.

Luther, K. R. (1999) 'Austria: From Moderate to Polarised Pluralism?', in Broughton, D. and Donovan, M. (eds) *Changing Party Systems in Western Europe*. London: Pinter, 118–42.

Luza, R. (1975) *Austro-German Relations in the Anschluss Era*. Princeton, NJ: Princeton University Press.

Macartney, C. A. (1978) *The House of Austria: The Habsburg Empire 1790–1918*. Edinburgh: Edinburgh University Press.

Mitten, R. (1992) *The Politics of Anti-semitic Prejudice*. Boulder: Westview Press.

Mölzer, A. (1990) *Jörg, der Eisbrecher*. Klagenfurt/Vienna: Suxxes.

Mudde, C. (1995) 'Right-Wing Extremism Analysed', *European Journal of Political Research* 27, 203–24.

Müller, W. C. (1994) 'Austria', *European Journal of Political Research* 26, 241–46.

Müller, W. C. and Ulram, P. A. (1995) 'The Structure of Austrian Parties', *Party Politics* 1(1), 146–60.

Pauley, B. F. (1981) *Hitler and the Forgotten Nazis: A History of Austrian National Socialism*. London: Macmillan.

Pelinka, A. (1988) 'Alte Rechte, neue Rechte in Österreich', *Frankfurter Hefte/Neue Gesellschaft* 36, 103–9.

Perchinig, B. (1983) 'National oder liberal, die Freiheitliche Partei Österreichs', in Gerlich, P. and Müller, W. (eds) *Zwischen Koalition und Konkurrenz: Österreichs Parteien seit 1945*. Vienna: Braumüller.

Plasser, F. and Ulram, P. A. (1992) 'Überdehnung, Erosion, und rechtspopulistische Reaktion', *Österreichische Zeitschrift für Politikwissenschaft* 21(2), 150–76.

Plasser, Fritz, Ulram, P. A. and Grausgruber, A. (1992) 'The Decline of *Lager* Mentality and New Model of Electoral Competition in Austria', *West European Politics* 15(1), 16–46.

Purtscheller, W. (1994) '10 Briefe für 10 Jahre: Von der VAPO zum Briefbomben-terror', in *Handbuch des Österreichischen Rechtsextremismus*. Vienna: Dokumentationsarchiv des Österreichischen Widerstandes.

Riedlsperger, M. E. (1978) *The Lingering Shadow of Nazism: The Austrian Independence Party Movement since 1945*. New York: Columbia.

Rot–Weiß–Rot Handbuch (1946) Vienna: Bundeskanzleramt.

Scharsach, H.-H. (1992) *Haiders Kampf*. Vienna: Orac.

Scharsach, H.-H. (1995) *Haiders Clan*. Vienna: Orac.

Stiefel, D. (1981) *Entnazifizierung in Österreich*. Vienna: Löcker.

Sully, M. (1990) *A Contemporary History of Austria*. London: Routledge.

Sully, M. (1995a) 'The Austrian Referendum 1994', *Electoral Studies* 14(1), 67–9.

Sully, M. (1995b) 'The Austrian Parliamentary Elections 1994', *Electoral Studies* 14(3), 219–22.

Wandruszka, A. (1954) 'Österreichs politische Struktur', in Benedikt, H. (ed.) *Geschichte der Republik Österreich*. Vienna: Verlag für Geschichte und Politik.

Wodak, Ruth (1991) 'Anti-semitic discourse in post-war Austria', *Discourse and Society*, 2(1), 65–83.

Newspapers, magazines, journals

Basta
Frankfurter Hefte/Neue Gesellschaft
Neue Kronen Zeitung
Neue Zürcher Zeitung
News
Profil
Protokoll der kärtner Landtag
Der Standard

CHAPTER FOUR

Exit from the ghetto: the Italian far right in the 1990s

Tom Gallagher

On the weekend of 27–29 January 1995, at a special congress held at the resort of Fiuggi, south of Rome, the Italian Social Movement (MSI) formally dissolved itself. It was only the latest familiar landmark in Italian politics to disappear under the tidal wave of change that had transformed the political landscape during the early 1990s. In 1994, voters, angry at the scale of the corruption which the Christian Democrats and their chief governing ally, the Italian Socialist Party (PSI), had presided over from the 1980s, consigned these once mighty parties to electoral oblivion. Already in 1991, the Italian Communist Party (PCI), which had vied with the Christian Democratic Party (DC) for influence and power in the post-war Italian republic, had dissolved itself, largely abandoning Marxism and changing its name to the Party of the Democratic Left (PDS). The MSI, which had always claimed to be the only genuine opposition to the *partitocrazia* (party-controlled Italian democracy), decided, in turn, to adjust to changing times, but very much on its own terms.

The collapse of the post-war party system in Italy occurred for a variety of reasons. Certainly, the ending of the Cold War and the decline of the international tensions which had made Italy a front-line state in the ideological battle between East and West was an important catalyst in prompting voters to be more critical of the performance of the parties which they had hitherto supported. The pace of social change witnessed in Italy during the boom years of the 1980s weakened the traditional values on which the parties of right and left had rested and created interest groups with expectations and values that could not easily be accommodated by a complacent ruling establishment (see Ginsborg, 1990: ch. 11). Above all, the work of investigative magistrates in revealing the extent to which hundreds of politicians had been diverting state funds for their own political or personal uses created an angry public mood which the DC and its allies in government were unable to placate (see Gilbert, 1995: ch. 8).

By virtue of being Europe's oldest party of the extreme right, the *Movimento Sociale Italiano* (MSI) had been rigorously excluded from government in the past, and therefore was not caught up in the tide of sleaze which had engulfed its much stronger rivals. In the election of 27–28 March 1994, which was supposed to inaugurate a pure and undefiled Second Republic, the MSI had received its reward from voters disorientated by the pace of political change and fearful of chaos and instability: one in seven Italians, or more than 5 million voters, backed the MSI (running under the title of *Alleanza Nazionale*: National Alliance), giving it 13.5 per cent of the vote. One month later, the MSI became the first neo-fascist party to enter government in post-war Europe when it acquired five cabinet posts in the government of media tycoon-turned-politician Silvio Berlusconi.

The MSI had benefited from the anti-party mood prevalent across much of Europe but which, in Italy, had led to the destruction of an entire party political system, given the way that the ruling parties had systematically abused the electoral trust invested in them. Even more remarkable, in some ways, than the surge in support for the MSI was the popular endorsement given to its electoral ally, *Forza Italia* (FI), a populist right-wing force set up in a matter of weeks over the winter of 1993–4 by television mogul Silvio Berlusconi (see McCarthy, 1995a). The alliance between neo-fascists, who had acquired valuable lessons in political survival by operating in the political wilderness, and a businessman who had earned his fortune by being able to anticipate shifting popular tastes, set the country apart from the rest of Western Europe and seemed to be propelling Italy into an uncertain political future.

One year or even six months before the March 1994 election, few, even in the MSI, would have anticipated that they were on the verge of such astounding success. The party had not played an active role in subverting the old regime. Protest politics had been associated instead with the separatist *Lega Nord* (Northern League) and the anti-mafia *La Rete* (The Net) movement. Moreover, the 1991 referendum on electoral reform, which had produced a near-unanimous demand for changing the voting system, had been the initiative of constitutional reformers (Donovan, 1995: 48).

The MSI had largely sat through the gathering political crisis, which first ignited in the April 1992 national election when the *pentapartito* (the parties making up the governing alliance) received only 48.8 per cent of the votes. It was conspicuous by its absence from public protests and it was unable to make common cause with new forces demanding root-and-branch reform of a corrupt political system. Indeed, the MSI was troubled by its own uncertain prospects until some time after the 1992 election. If the wishes, overwhelmingly expressed by voters in referendums in 1991 and in 1993, for replacing proportional representation with a simple majority system had been heeded by the framers of a new election law in 1993, it looked at the time as if the MSI would have been eliminated from parliament. In the preceding years, it had registered some its lowest-ever electoral scores. It had to watch helplessly as the electorate became radicalized but not in ways amenable to the MSI: the rise of the separatist *Lega Nord* was especially painful because it challenged the unitary character of Italy. The ability of the *Lega* in 1990–1 to make enormous capital out of immigration, which had been a standard extreme right cause elsewhere in Europe, also highlighted the weakness of Italian neo-fascism.

At the start of the 1990s, as the tarnished DC-led regime was facing mounting pressure, the MSI was engaged in a fiercely introspective dispute about the future direction of the movement. Should it accommodate itself to a system based on liberal democracy or instead act as a radical alternative for those sections of society which felt excluded or let down by the system? The debate between radical populists unafraid of embracing the fascist heritage, and moderates prepared to be part of the respectable right, had shaken the MSI since the late 1940s and led to periodic splits and defections.

In 1990–1, as the Italian left was retreating from espousing ideology, the MSI found itself briefly led by Pino Rauti, a radical figure who wanted to build alliances with groups left behind as Italy had swung in an increasingly pro-American and consumerist direction, his biggest target being those workers disillusioned by the increasingly pragmatic character of Italian communism (Sidoti, 1992: 158–9). However, Rauti's dream of the MSI acquiring influence in civil society by placing itself at the head of a rainbow coalition of environmentalists, ex-communists, animal lovers, people with disabilities, pensioners and others whose needs were not catered for by conventional forces, never stood a chance of getting off the ground. It was proof of the rut which the MSI found itself in that the leadership was captured, albeit briefly, by a figure with such an unusual agenda. The party's disastrous results (4 per cent of the vote) in the 1990 local elections showed that it was in danger of losing its traditional supporters in the southern middle classes. But although Rauti's attempt to redefine the movement may have been ill-conceived, it was clear that the MSI could not escape from political isolation by standing still. Rapid economic growth in the 1970s and in the 1980s had undermined the traditional values of family and religion which the MSI had always defended. Accelerating European integration was making the defence of national values increasingly difficult. Above all, anti-communism was diminishing in importance as the Cold War drew to a close and Italy's Communists sought to adjust to new political realities.

The MSI's introspective character appeared to be confirmed by a survey into the political outlook of delegates carried out at the party's seventeenth congress in 1990. Only 13 per cent of delegates were prepared to define themselves as 'democrats' (Ignazi, 1994: 88–9). For 88 per cent of them, fascism was the key historical reference; 92 per cent were unable to countenance the view that all men were equal; 25 per cent expressed openly anti-semitic views; and the formative influences on their beliefs were all from the fascist era: Mussolini, Julius Evola, Giovanni Gentile, the Romanian fascist leader Codreanu, and the Spaniard José António Primo de Rivera being repeatedly invoked by delegates (Ignazi, 1994: 87). The MSI seemed destined to be a memorialist movement paying homage to a distinctive epoch in Italian history but unable or unwilling to adapt to changes which had rendered fascism, and the ideas associated with it, increasingly marginal to the existence of many Italians. After the traumatic interlude under Rauti, it was led by the tenacious and much younger Gianfranco Fini, who revived the long-term strategy of integrating the MSI into the political system without abandoning the party's original identity. The MSI's experience in the period from 1950 to 1990 suggested, however, that such a project was likely to produce internal tension and few electoral rewards.

The years of endurance, 1946–90

Fascism had sunk sufficiently deep roots in Italian society for there to be a successor movement ready to promote the nationalist and corporatist values of the Mussolini era, even in the hostile environment of a fledgling Italian democracy. The virtual civil war that had been waged in 1944–5 between left-wing Partisan forces and the Italian Social Republic, the Nazi-backed state formed by Mussolini and based at Salò in northern Italy, made it difficult, though, to revive the former ruling *Partito Fascisti Italiano* (PFI). Fascists therefore took refuge in the monarchist party or in the *Uomo Qualunque* (Everyman Party, UQ). The UQ was a populist movement which performed well in the South during the late 1940s by expressing and representing early disenchantment with the conduct of the national parties and, more significantly, by questioning the view that anti-fascism enjoyed unmistakable moral superiority over the extremist and right-wing ideology it had come into being to oppose (Allum, 1973: 278–82). The UQ proved to be a transitory electoral phenomenon, but its strong showing in parts of the South was bound to be encouraging to fascists intent on remaining active in politics on their own terms.

The *Movimento Italiano Sociale* itself was founded on 26 December 1946. It drew its inspiration from the late flourishing of radical fascism at Salò, where anti-bourgeois and anti-capitalist rhetoric had been conspicuous. Giorgio Almirante, one of its architects who would go on to be the MSI's longest-serving leader between 1969 and 1987, had been, in 1944–5, cabinet chief in the ministry of popular culture, whose activity was almost wholly concerned with emitting propaganda (Cheles, 1991: 43–4). The radical and quasi-socialist values supposedly exemplified by the ephemeral republic at Salò would always be invoked as the heritage which the MSI was seeking to uphold.

Initially, the MSI displayed implacable hostility to the institutions and values of Italian democracy. It was firmly anti-republican and would ally itself with monarchist groups intent on overturning the verdict of the 1946 referendum, by which a majority of Italians had opted for a republican form of government. It expressed opposition to the peace treaty imposed on Italy by the Allies and also to the presence of foreign troops on Italian soil. Its defiant nationalism extended to a commitment to recover territory lost by Italy after 1945, especially to Yugoslavia, the fate of the city of Trieste (eventually restored to Italian control in 1954) being a burning issue for the MSI. Finally, the movement made no bones about characterizing Italian democracy as counterfeit and as unable to express the true wishes of the Italian people.

By the early 1950s, the MSI's approach to the political system was starting to be modified as it became clear that hard-line opposition to democracy might prevent its enjoying a legal existence. The 1948 constitution outlawed any efforts to restore Mussolini's ruling party, but the 1948 general election showed that, under the pure electoral system of PR acquired by Italy, the MSI could enjoy modest success in conventional politics. In the elections, the MSI returned 6 parliamentarians on 1.9 per cent of the national vote; all were from the South. There was residual appreciation in a number of southern cities for the public works projects of the fascist era (Tarchi, 1995: 33). Anti-fascism and the Partisan struggle had largely been northern phenomena, while monarchist sentiment and the strength of patron–client relations had made the South stony ground for reformist parties, and thus a region where the MSI faced significantly less opposition to its presence than in northern Italy.

The MSI also found itself the beneficiary of the fact that the Italian state machine was not subject to a wholesale purge of officials deemed to have collaborated with fascist tyranny, as had taken place in Germany after 1945. Officials with firmly authoritarian values who had pursued their careers by serving the fascist state were now in a position to protect the MSI and offer it political assistance; this was particularly true of officials found in branches of Italian government dealing with law and order (Ruzza and Schmidtke, 1995: 149). The normally brief time span of Italian governments, despite the electoral strength of Christian Democracy, gave important freedom of action to unreconstructed sections of the bureaucracy. The surface instability of Italian political life, resulting from the failure of the DC to translate its electoral vitality into governmental effectiveness, also benefited the MSI: it lost no opportunity to contrast the occasional chaos and perennial indecision of Italian democracy with the authority and continuity that it felt were positive hallmarks of Italian fascism.

The onset of the Cold War relieved pressure on the MSI as its activists were emerging from clandestinity. Henceforth, it was the Italian communists who were seen as the chief threats to democracy, something the hard-fought 1948 election graphically revealed. Pragmatists within the MSI, who believed there was a chance of merging their neo-fascist ideas within a broad anti-communist front, derived encouragement from this (Ignazi, 1994: 27). But the DC preferred to view itself as an indispensable pivot between two illegitimate extremes on the right and left of politics. In the 1950s, the MSI sustained different DC governments with its parliamentary votes, including that of Antonio Segni (later president of Italy from 1962 to 1964), who privately described the *missini* (members of the MSI) as 'those who in their hearts are committed to the consolidation of our democratic institutions' (Ignazi, 1994: 27). The limits of such collaboration were shown in 1960 by the violent public reaction to the formation of a DC government, led by Fernando Tambroni, which was all too clearly dependent upon neo-fascist support.

The formation of centre-left governments, starting in the early 1960s, increased the political isolation of the MSI. The term 'right' remained one of political opprobrium in Italy and, as long as the *missini* refused to abandon an ideology that placed them outside the democratic camp, no party was prepared to seriously treat with them. The MSI's stubborn conviction that the 'nation' enjoyed a higher political value than the individual, or than any class or social group, also made the MSI an unwelcome partner. Mussolini's aggressive foreign policy, which had resulted ultimately in military defeat and occupation, had inoculated most Italians against forthright displays of nationalism; the political class could see no advantage in reviving pugnacious nationalism when far greater rewards seemed to await Italy by promoting the economic and eventual political union of Western Europe.

The era of left-wing radicalism at the end of the 1960s perhaps had a greater impact in Italy than in any other European country, and kindled hopes within the MSI that its hour might come if Italian democracy broke down. The upsurge of worker and student militancy in 1969 coincided with the appointment of Giorgio Almirante as MSI leader. While the legal far right stepped up its attacks on the centre-left alliance in government, subversive groups attacked state institutions. Thus, 95 per cent of political violence occurring between 1969 and 1973 has been attributed to the extraparliamentary right (Ignazi, 1994: 48). Ultra-rightists were promoting a 'strategy of tension' to produce a conservative backlash and goad the military into closing down civilian political institutions. Only perhaps a violent fracture of the country along communist/anti-communist lines would have been able to narrow decisively the gulf between the MSI and other non-communist forces. In 1972, this strategy seemed to be getting somewhere when, with 8.7 per cent of the vote, the MSI received its best-ever result. These votes were at the expense of the DC, and the decline of the centre appeared to suggest that the country was becoming polarized in the face of mounting political disturbances. Almirante now dreamt of bringing together the conservative middle classes of the North ('the silent majority') with the disaffected social groups in the South that had acted as the MSI's electoral reservoir. He was 'a clever exponent of a politics of double language', who often sounded moderate but around whom extremists gathered (Tarchi, 1995: 86). As late as 1990, a survey of delegates at the 1990 MSI conference found that 32 per cent believed armed struggle to be an acceptable way of securing political change (Ignazi, 1994: 88). In 1970–1, Almirante had given discreet backing to the violent revolt in the southern city of Reggio Calabria against the state's decision not to grant the city regional-capital status. Almirante even talked of the MSI as 'a proletarian party with a southern base ... [and as] a movement above all of the marginalized' (Sidoti, 1992: 155).

However, its strategy of acting as a party of protest, seeking to harness anti-communist sentiments in the North, failed to bring the MSI in from the cold. Italian democracy proved strong enough to resist challenges from both the radical left and the radical right. Furthermore, despite the existence of coup-minded generals, the armed forces remained loyal to liberal democracy. Poor MSI election results in the late 1970s led to some desire for respectability, with a large number of the more moderate deputies breaking away from the party, alarmed at some features of Almirante's leadership (Gilbert, 1995: 155). When Almirante eventually retired in 1987, the MSI was in a fractious and disunited state. The strategy of 'insertion' within the political system, while flirting with extremist political violence, had yielded few long-term rewards. Nevertheless, Gianfranco Fini, Almirante's protégé and his designated successor, revived the project of 'insertion' without abandoning neo-fascism. There then followed the odd interlude in 1990–1 when, under Pino Rauti, the revolutionary rather than the conservative character of fascism was emphasized. Racism, less conspicuous in Italian neo-fascism than in the French or German variants, was played down in favour of the environment and a host of New Age concerns (Tarchi, 1995: 153, 156).

Escape from the ghetto

If any party seemed destined to disappear completely from the Italian political scene in the early 1990s, it was the MSI. But in Fini (restored as leader in 1991) it found a capable helmsman who had grown in stature since being appointed head of the MSI youth in 1977, aged 25. Fini became a polished performer on television, which was increasingly the medium from which Italians acquired their information on political events, as well as their impressions of the leaders contending for power. Fini's eloquence and his ability never to 'lose his cool' appealed to voters increasingly disorientated by the crisis of the party system after 1992 and fearful of the effects it would have on their economic security. The stock of a former untouchable force like the MSI slowly rose, as the spectacular nature of the corruption, which nearly all of the major parties had engaged in to some degree or other, burst into the open during 1992–3. The 'neo-fascist' image of the MSI was ceasing to be a handicap as memories of the 1922–45 era were increasingly confined to a shrinking number of Italians, while the Communists, the main purveyors of anti-fascism, were preoccupied with defining their own role in post-Cold War politics.

Discreet overtures had already been made to the MSI in the 1980s by the ambitious Socialist leader Bettino Craxi, who believed that the PSI's chances of supplanting the DC at the heart of the political system could be enhanced by encouraging the MSI to steal DC votes (see Gilbert, 1995: ch. 7). Far more crucial in transforming the image of the MSI was President Francesco Cossiga, who, in the early 1990s, as his seven-year mandate drew to a close, turned on the DC, his own party, accusing it and the *partitocrazia* of a wide range of political sins (Tarchi, 1995: 203). Cossiga, in his attacks on the government parties' conduct in office, borrowed much of his populist rhetoric from the MSI and articulated many popular frustrations, thereby legitimizing the MSI's own critique of the post-war order (see Gallagher, 1992).

The most violent onslaught on the party establishment in Rome came from the *Lega Nord*, which was committed to detaching northern Italy from the control of the centre and making it virtually self-governing (*La Repubblica*, 24 November 1993). The Lega's growing support in the early 1990s prevented the MSI making converts among lower-middle-class and small-town north Italians, alienated by the effects of rule from Rome. But the violence of the Lega's rhetoric made the MSI look moderate and respectable in comparison; the *Lega*'s demagogic leader, Umberto Bossi, revived a rabble-rousing style of politics not seen in Italy for fifty years and which enabled the MSI to be viewed in a less condemnatory way. Moreover, although the *Lega* was instrumental in destabilizing the political system by depriving the ruling parties of legitimacy across much of the North and of the votes to form workable governments, it had no project for filling the political vacuum except a rhetorical cry of 'the North alone'. Nor did any of the other forces in the centre of Italian politics which had undermined the political establishment (Mario Segni's DC dissidents, President Cossiga, the anti-mafia movement) have any coherent plans for uniting aggrieved or reform-minded Italians in a newly launched Second Republic.

The MSI's opportunity to project itself as a genuine political alternative came in 1993 as the DC and the PSI, the parties that had made and unmade governments in the previous three decades, broke up. Their leaders were indicted on corruption charges, their membership slumped, splits occurred, funds dried up, and voters deserted them in millions. The reformed left seemed destined to triumph in the general election that was widely held to be necessary in order to clear the political air and remove parliamentary deputies, one in six of whom were the subject of criminal investigations. Municipal elections held in November–December 1993 were regarded as a trial run that would decide the country's political future. Fini stood for the post of mayor of Rome, while in Naples the party's candidate for that office was Alessandra Mussolini, granddaughter of the Duce. The MSI emphasized the fact that it was the only party not caught up in the *mani pulite* (clean hands) investigation (by reforming magistrates) which had helped bring down the old parties. Having been offered respectability by President Cossiga, the MSI won the open endorsement of Silvio Berlusconi, Italy's most dynamic entrepreneur, a man who enjoyed great political influence owing to the control he exercised over the Italian media. On 23 November 1993, Berlusconi declared that, 'if I were in Rome, I would certainly vote for Fini' (*La Repubblica*, 24 November 1993). The owner of the AC Milan football club, with its long history, and of three national television channels was expressing the view that Fini was a political actor no different from, and perhaps a great deal better than, the others. Neither Fini nor Mussolini won their respective battles, but they got into the second round, Fini only narrowly losing, on 47 per cent of the vote, and Mussolini acquiring 43 per cent. Clearly, huge numbers of DC and PSI voters had been more impressed by the credentials of the MSI than by those of the left parties. Anti-communism was still an important enough variable in Italian politics, even though the PDS claimed to have dropped the ideology and rhetoric of communism. The MSI was also able to trade upon issues relating to economic insecurity, high taxes and the mounting tide of illegal immigration to Italy. With the political centre having imploded, inhibitions about backing a party which made no bones about being on the right, albeit the modern right, were far less than many observers had expected.

In mid-January 1994, President Scalfaro dissolved parliament, and national elections were announced for 27–28 March 1994. Beforehand, Fini decided to press home his advantage by taking steps to convince voters orphaned by the demise of the mainstream parties that yesterday's neo-fascists had become today's post-fascists. In December 1993, he had won backing from the MSI central committee for the formation of the *Alleanza Nazionale* (AN), which would act as a new moderate shell around the old ideological party. Thereafter, events moved quickly. On 22 January 1994, an MSI congress – attended by 800 delegates – adopted the AN symbols and joint title for the forthcoming election. The revamped movement was presented as 'a common home of all the right', and the five key speeches made at its launch were by moderates who had no roots in the MSI's anti-system culture (Bull and Newell, 1995: 78).

Italian neo-fascism would be fighting the March elections under the AN banner, as Fini proclaimed that he was transforming his party into a modern conservative movement along Gaullist lines. From the outset, questions were asked about the genuineness of the transformation, given the way it was suddenly engineered from the top without the grassroots having any chance to debate the efficacy of the new departure. It was noted that a close ally of Fini, Ignazio La Ruzza, running in Milan, nominated (in a newspaper interview) Mussolini as the historical figure he most admired and that his AN running-mate, Roberto Predolin, singled out the even more extreme figure of the Romanian fascist Corneliu Codreanu as his historical hero (*Corriere della Sera*, 19 March 1994). But the AN's respectability was underscored by the willingness of Berlusconi to give it a key role in the electoral alliance of the right which he put together after announcing, in January 1994, that he was launching himself into politics.

Berlusconi used the media and advertising wings of his commercial empire to launch *Forza Italia* (Go for It, Italy), which created supporters' clubs loosely modelled on those of his top soccer club, AC Milan. *Forza Italia* (FI) was presented as a new, modern force untarnished by party politics. It was, in fact, a mixture of old and new, a movement harnessing the technical and cultural changes that had brought many American values into Italian society, and one also designed to block rapid change that might endanger vested interests, not least Berlusconi's Fininvest empire, which had prospered through adept use of the politics of patronage. Defence of his private interests had been the chief factor that had pushed Berlusconi into the political arena, according to his opponents (McCarthy, 1995b: 163). Undoubtedly he feared that a left-wing government might deprive him of the monopoly control which he exercised over national commercial television, and investigate the origins of his copious wealth. Berlusconi's emergence was the factor that enabled the MSI to break out of the ghetto in which it had been stuck for nearly fifty years. He legitimized some of the core concerns of the party. Anti-communism became the chief rallying cry of *Forza Italia* in order to prevent centrist voters switching to the left. Berlusconi's media outlets were used to present a novel message in Italy: that identifying with the political right was respectable and that it was from this part of the spectrum that solutions to Italy's fundamental problems in political and economic life were most likely to emerge.

In southern and central Italy, FI and Fini's party were able to agree to run on a common platform, the Pole of Good Government, which produced a common slate of FI and AN candidates. Berlusconi struck a similar deal with the *Lega Nord* in the rest of the country, but Bossi insisted that the AN be excluded, with the result that Fini's party ran on its own in the North. *Forza Italia* aimed to be the first party in Italian politics that represented the conservative instincts and pro-business outlook of the Italian bourgeoisie. The partnership between Berlusconi and Fini worked smoothly (in contrast to the difficulties both men encountered with Bossi, who had entered the alliance with the greatest reluctance, fearing that to remain in isolation risked the electoral fall of his movement). There was plenty in the AN programme that FI could endorse. The programme attacked *partitocrazia* and advocated a mixed parliament stressing corporatism, in which one of the houses would consist of representatives of the social partners. It reaffirmed Catholic values and embodied a pro-family outlook. Regionalism was dismissed as a negative 'tribal dynamic'. The Maastricht Treaty was rejected as 'a treaty between bankers', and fears were expressed about German hegemony in Europe (Sznajder, 1995: 90–1). There were also great contrasts between the programmes of the AN and FI, and these did not diminish with the passage of time. The AN defended big government, and its manifesto stressed social protection, the special concerns of the South, and the need to protect citizens dependent upon the state. By contrast, FI emphasized a Reagan–Thatcher formula of tax cuts, sweeping privatization and a drastic reduction in other ways of the state's role. However, these discrepancies were masked by an all-out assault on the left's fitness to rule. The AN was given unprecedented access to television, where Fini proved to be the most effective performer.

The results showed that the AN had increased its national percentage of the vote considerably from 5.4 (1992) to 13.5 per cent and had become the third party in Italy in terms of votes and seats. It tripled its vote in the central and southern regions, going from 6.9 and 7.2 per cent to 19.4 and 21.8 per cent respectively (Bull and Newell, 1995: 89). In Lazio, the area which included Rome, the AN emerged as the largest party, with 21.2 per cent of the vote. But it also doubled its vote in the North, jumping from 3.8 to 7.5 per cent, almost doubling its vote in Tuscany (9.5 per cent) and registering a big increase in Emilia-Romagna, another left stronghold. In 1994, the results showed that the Pole of Good Government had not been penalized in areas where AN candidates figured prominently on its lists, whereas the rival centre-left electoral alliance did suffer greater voter rejection where members of the hard left rump of the PCI, Communist Refoundation, were included (Tarchi, 1995: 218). So, fascism had become a lesser negative symbol than communism in the minds of many floating Italian voters. Around 20 per cent of new AN voters came from the DC and the PSI, a lower percentage than that going to FI. But the biggest influx of new blood came from first-time voters and those generally under the age of 25; even in the North, the AN was the most popular choice for this age group (Ruzza and Schmidtke, 1995: 155). The AN's popularity among an age group influenced by American popular culture, and with barely the dimmest memory of fascism, was shown by the Senate election results, in which the AN did less well than in those for the Chamber of Deputies (the minimum age for voting in the Senate elections is 25).

The March 1994 election gave the Freedom Alliance a convincing victory over its centre-left rivals and, in May 1994, a government was sworn in under Berlusconi which included five AN members in a coalition with FI and *Lega Nord*. The entry of perceived neo-fascists into the government of a major West European country caused unease elsewhere. Officials from

Germany, Spain, Greece and Portugal were concerned that working with neo-fascists in the European Union's Council of Ministers would make neo-fascism appear more respectable in their own countries. On 29 May, the Danish and Belgian telecommunications ministers refused to shake hands with their AN counterpart. But Douglas Hurd, the British Foreign Secretary, stated that his government had 'no reservations' about working with the new Italian government (*Keesing's Contemporary Archives*, 1994).

Berlusconi's claim that all sections of his Freedom Alliance were committed to democracy was undermined by a locally authorized demonstration on 15 May, which allowed 200 black-shirted and Nazi-saluting skinheads to parade through the northern city of Vicenza, celebrating the AN's inclusion in government. Further doubt about the sincerity of the AN's disavowal of fascism was cast on 16 May, when it emerged that it had tabled a proposal in parliament to revoke the long-standing constitutional ban on the revival of the Fascist Party (*Guardian* editorial, 18 May 1994). This resolution had been regularly tabled since 1978, and in 1993 it had been Fini himself who had proposed it, although in 1994 he declared the initiative to have been 'a terrible mistake'.

Unease over AN participation in government was heightened by the fact that, as Italy's 53rd government was being formed, Europe was marking the 50th anniversary of the defeat of fascism. Fini caused controversy by remarking that, with the Normandy landings, Europe reconquered its liberty but lost its independence of spirit (Ignazi, 1994: 110). He preferred to define the events in Italy between Mussolini's fall in July 1943 and the final liberation of Italy in 1945 as a civil war between 'fascist patriots' and 'communist Partisans'. Since millions of Italians had, by their votes, shown they had no qualms about seeing the lineal descendants of the Fascists assume government responsibility, he argued that it was time to take this controversial period of Italian history out of politics, and he offered to bury it as an issue if his left-wing opponents also promised to refrain from deriving political capital from it (Gumbel, 1995b).

A poll published by the Italian weekly *L'Espresso* (22 April 1994), in which respondents were asked to judge who had the greatest responsibility for events in the last years of the war, gave some comfort to the AN: 20.6 per cent of respondents were prepared to blame the Partisans, another 25.5 per cent blamed both them and the Fascists, while 38.3 per cent blamed the Fascists, another 15.6 per cent not answering or offering an opinion. Respondents were also asked if they agreed with a recent statement by Fini in which he described Mussolini as undoubtedly the greatest statesman of the century. Fini's remark had probably been the chief factor which had raised foreign doubts about the genuineness of his conversion from neo-fascism, and nearly one-quarter of respondents (23.2 per cent) endorsed it, compared with 71.6 per cent who rejected it wholly or mostly. More doubt was cast upon Fini's conversion to fully democratic politics when, in an interview with *La Stampa* on 3 June 1994, he declared that 'there are periods in which liberty is not the most important value. Fascism suppressed liberty of association for the benefit of social progress.' He went on to claim that 'until 1938, a minute before the racial laws were signed (introducing Nazi-inspired restrictions on Italy's Jews), it was very difficult to judge Fascism in a negative way' (Fuentes, 1994).

Statements and actions of the AN during the Berlusconi government showed that it had not repudiated another core element of fascism: ultra-nationalism. In April 1994, concern was expressed in Europe that Italy might become actively involved in the Balkan conflict when Mirko Trem-aglia, an AN deputy, soon to be appointed head of the foreign affairs committee of the Chamber of Deputies, demanded that Rome should disown the 1975 Treaty of Osimo, which defined Italy's north-eastern frontier with Yugoslavia. He argued that since Yugoslavia had disinte-grated, Italy was not bound to honour this treaty, and he advocated that the Istrian peninsula and parts of Dalmatia, which had belonged to Mussolini's Italy, should be returned to Rome's jurisdiction (*Independent*, 23 April 1994). Tremaglia was not repudiated by his party leader, even though President Scalfaro had earlier intervened to ensure that this veteran neo-fascist, who had fought for the Salò Republic in 1944–5, would not be given the cabinet post of Minister for Italians Abroad. On the contrary, his irredentist views were found to have official favour in the AN and perhaps further afield when the Berlusconi government vetoed Slovenia's attempt to be considered for European Union (EU) membership, reviving a long-buried dispute over property rights of former Italian residents in this ex-Yugoslav republic. Speculation mounted that the AN was cultivating links with the rebel Serb regime of Radovan Karadžić in Bosnia, in the hope that Italian influence in the eastern Adriatic could be restored. Marco Tarchi, a former rising star in the MSI who has become one of Italy's leading analysts of the far right, reckoned that Fini hoped to reach an agreement with the President of Serbia to acquire former Italian territory in Istria and Dalmatia (Tarchi, 1995: 182). Because of its destabilizing role in the former Yugoslavia, Italy was refused entry to the 'Contact Group' set up in April 1994 to work towards a Bosnian cease-fire (*Keesing's Contemporary Archives*, 1994).

Fini was unabashed about the need to restore nationalism as a defining value in Italian political culture and, like Berlusconi, he saw it as an ideal neglected by other parties since 1945 and one which offered real possibilities for the right to establish its credibility in Italian political life. In his June 1994 *La Stampa* interview, Fini declared:

> I think Italy has lost its memory because it has not placed any value on the concept of 'nation' ... It was also the fault of Fascism, which sometimes confused 'the nation' with nationalism and impermissible

excesses. As a result the nation was removed along with nationalism (Fuentes, 1994).

The ambiguities contained in Fini's comments about the respective merits of fascism and democracy, not to mention his flirtation with irredentist nationalism, gave ammunition to critics convinced that his adherence to post-fascism owed more to public relations requirements than to a serious change of mind about the validity of former core political beliefs. Up to May 1994, the AN had not produced a manifesto distinct from that of the MSI. There was no attempt to alter the tight-knit authoritarian structure of the MSI that dated from Almirante's time. No new cultural references or new leaders emerged on the scene to distinguish the AN from the MSI (Ignazi, 1994: 113). Only 30 out of 107 AN deputies (and 14 out of 47 AN senators) could claim not to have an MSI background. But Fini was able to increase the respectability of the AN during the seven-month life of the Berlusconi government. So effective was the partnership the two men established that it was normal to hear predictions from mainstream commentators that Fini was capable of becoming leader of a united movement of the Italian right if Berlusconi quit politics, depriving FI of its linchpin. By contrast, the *Lega Nord* leader, Bossi, was a disruptive influence in a coalition which he would bring down at the end of 1994, because he felt it was undoing his goal of a federal Italy. Many Italians who observed the different approaches to politics of the raucous and sometimes foul-mouthed Bossi and the smooth, even-tempered Fini would have had no difficulty in branding the former a natural extremist and the latter an innate moderate. Not surprisingly, Fini's poll ratings climbed steadily between 1994 and 1996, even among Italians whose voting preferences remained centre-left.

The AN's image was strengthened by the low-key behaviour of its members in government, who came from the pragmatic wing of the party. Giuseppe Tatarella, a deputy prime minister and Minister of Posts and Telegraphs, had been a driving force behind the creation of the AN; Domenico Fisichella, the Minister of Culture, was a monarchist; the post of Environment Minister was given to Altiero Matteoli; while Adriana Poli Bortone, the Agriculture Minister, was the only woman in the government. Meanwhile, Publio Fiori, the Transport Minister, stood out on account of having previously been a leading figure in the DC faction that supported the veteran power-broker Giulio Andreotti, currently on trial for complicity with the mafia.

It is likely that the AN will obtain more recruits from the DC, especially in parts of the South, where local political chiefs may find that the politics of clientelism and corporatism are best furthered by attachment to the conservative right. In January 1994, AN clubs had been set up with the specific purpose of attracting members of former established parties. Membership was withheld from existing MSI members and, if the number eventually formed – 850 – is of any significance, it may have proved an effective means of overcoming the inhibitions that political conservatives had of linking up with neo-fascists (Endean, 1995). In 1995, one seasoned observer of the far right, Marco Tarchi, even claimed that it was the clear aim of some sections of the MSI leadership to inherit the mediating role of the DC on behalf of a number of social groups that, especially in the South, were effectively orphaned by the demise of Christian Democracy (Tarchi, 1995: 253).

By the time these words had been written, the MSI had disappeared into history. At the aforementioned conference held in Fiuggi, in January 1995, the MSI was formally wound up and replaced by the *Alleanza Nazionale*. The new party was presented as one which had abandoned corporatism and accepted democracy, one that disavowed racism and saw the Mussolini era as a unique period of history, the circumstances that produced it being unrepeatable. So the time had finally come when neo-fascism had given way to post-fascism. Fini wanted to make the term 'right-wing' not only legitimate but popular. However, it was not difficult to find delegates anxious to cling on to the fascist inheritance. Andrew Gumbel of the London *Independent on Sunday* interviewed a 20-year-old delegate, Alessandro Veronese, a law student from Bologna, who was unabashed by what he saw as the superficial nature of the change of image that Fini was bringing about: 'Of course we are not rejecting fascism. The National Alliance would be nothing without fascism and the MSI would be nothing without fascism. You cannot let go of that history' (Gumbel, 1995a). Veronese said he supported Fini because of his ability to hold contradictory views on such issues as state control of the economy: 'he says he is a liberal while remaining a corporatist. It's like Mussolini whose greatness was his ability to remain coherent even when he changed his mind' (Gumbel, 1995a).

Fini's moderate stance received a boost, however, when Pino Rauti and MSI radicals who did not repudiate the label 'fascist' left the AN. Rauti had always rejected the label 'right-wing' on account of its affinity with capitalism and conservatism, since he wanted fascism to be a revolutionary alternative. In search of respectability, Fini saw advantage in the departure of these die-hards. But the defections were small-scale, which meant that many who had been able to live with the neo-fascist appellation stayed on in the new party. One of these was Pasquale Squitieri, an AN Senator from 1994 to 1996, who believed that the anti-semitic Protocols of the Elders of Zion, far from being a fabrication, were the genuine article (*L'Espresso*, 8 April 1994). However, foreign parties, like the US Republicans, the French Gaullists and even Israel's Likud, were prepared to give Fini the benefit of the doubt by sending observers to the refounding conference in 1995 (Tarchi, 1995: 254). A sign that some of the heat had gone out of the left–right confrontation in Italy was the presence also of observers from the PDS.

Fini emerged stronger from the experience of government than did

Berlusconi. The media tycoon made elementary mistakes, not least his open attempts to muzzle the investigating magistrates when the financial affairs of his own Fininvest company came under scrutiny. He failed to solve the conflict of interest between his political ambitions and the monopoly he enjoyed over commercial television. Nor did he appear to be a natural politician: his background as a wealthy business autocrat meant that he expected compliance when persuasion might have enabled him to achieve his goals much more easily. Significantly, Fini had stayed outside government, which meant that he was much less exposed to media criticism than was Berlusconi. Those AN members in the cabinet tended to keep a low profile, unlike some of their FI colleagues, plucked from the commercial and media wings of Berlusconi's empire. Fini had acquired the trappings of a national leader by staying aloof from the controversy-strewn Berlusconi administration; by the time it had lost its majority, owing to the defection of the *Lega*, it bore more similarity to its short-lived predecessors than to the reforming administration which Berlusconi claimed he would inaugurate.

It was hard to point to any administrative improvements or policy reforms which suggested that Berlusconi had launched a 'Second Republic' from the ashes of the discredited 1946–94 party-led regime. Fini argued that the failure lay with the cumbersome rules of the Italian parliamentary democracy in which Berlusconi had to operate. During the caretaker government of the economist Lamberto Dini (a former Berlusconi backer) in 1995–6, Fini launched a campaign for constitutional reform which he claimed would finally unblock the process of government. He believes that only a directly elected political leader can acquire sufficient authority to avoid becoming a hostage of inter-party bickering. In his model of a presidential republic, voters would elect a 'head of state' or 'national mayor', who would appoint the government. Parliament would be demoted in importance and the principle of the separation of powers overturned. Polls showed that support for this proposal among voters extended far beyond those Italians who could normally be expected to vote for the AN. Critics thus took fright, believing that, under such a system, the AN would acquire complete control over the machinery of state and that independent power centres such as the judiciary would be suborned. They pointed to the zeal which AN ministers had shown in placing supporters in key jobs in the agriculture ministry and in state television and claimed that, in Fini's muscular democracy, little opportunity would exist for corruption to be rooted out by vigilant public servants (McCarthy, 1995b: 18). They got powerful ammunition when Fini's closest constitutional adviser, Domenico Fisichella, left the AN in January 1996, claiming that his leader's blueprint was 'essentially illiberal', though he subsequently returned to the fold (Gumbel, 1996).

Sensing the degree of popular support for his presidential democracy, Fini forced a vote of no confidence in the caretaker government that

President Scalfaro tried to create following Dini's resignation, and these developments resulted in new elections being called. In the spring of 1996, therefore, the AN entered Italy's third general election campaign in four years in an apparently strong position. Although Berlusconi had distanced himself from Fini's constitutional proposals, both their parties once again formed a common list of candidates in a Freedom Alliance, which this time covered the whole of Italy. Polls had shown Fini to be Italy's most popular politician in the winter of 1995–6, thereby confirming his new-found status as a respected and charismatic figure in the eyes of many Italians, not all of whom belonged to the political right (*The Economist*, 27 April 1996). The irony is that the Freedom Alliance was now a firmly right-wing force, with Berlusconi having purged his centrist deputies. Some commentators even predicted that the AN would acquire more seats and votes than the FI, but this was never a serious possibility, owing to the good placings FI obtained as the common lists were being drawn up.

Despite the abundant finance and access to the media which the Freedom Alliance had enjoyed in 1996, it had lost credibility in important respects. In particular, it no longer had the advantage it undoubtedly possessed in 1994, when, with no compromising past, it had appeared to be a potential remedy for Italy's problems. Its short period in office, however, showed that it did not really know what to do with the responsibility of government. It had also lost credibility as a force for moderate change. Instead, the left finally acquired the mantle of moderation. A grouping of the left and parts of the centre, called the Olive Tree Alliance, was formed and it agreed to a pragmatic programme that could be summed up as building social capitalism. Romano Prodi, the former progressive technocrat close to the Christian Democrats, was its prime ministerial candidate, calming fears on the financial markets about the presence of ex-communists in government. The United States, having already enjoyed good ties with governments led by ex-communists in Poland and Hungary, also declared that it was unconcerned by such an eventuality. Even the Catholic Church decided to stay out of the election and to refrain from giving advice about how to vote. So, the 1996 election was something of a turning-point which indicated the sharply reduced significance of the Cold War or religion as factors determining voting preferences. This was bad news for the nascent right, which showed itself divided over economic strategy: the AN continued to emphasize social paternalism, while FI promised a programme of swingeing tax cuts which would make it very difficult for Fini to protect his southern supporters from economic hard times.

The result of the 21 April 1996 ballot showed little change in the respective strengths of left and right compared with 1994. The combined vote for the AN and FI in the 25 per cent of seats elected by proportional representation was 36.3 per cent compared with 34.5 per cent in 1994, the AN having gone up from 13.5 to 15.7 per cent and FI having slipped slightly from 21.0 to 20.6 per cent. But the Olive Tree Alliance had a majority in both houses of parliament via the centre votes it had acquired, though it was dependent on the backing of the Marxist Communist Refoundation. Even though the AN increased its share of the poll, Fini's electoral gamble was seen to have failed; his reputation as a political tactician was dented as it became clear that he would have acquired more political capital if he had supported Berlusconi at the start of 1996, when he was prepared to make a pact with the left about redrawing the rules of the Italian political system (Scalfari, 1996). To make matters worse, Pino Rauti's Social Movement, although it obtained only 0.9 per cent of the vote and 1 seat (in Sicily), deprived the AN of victory in at least 33 seats. Fini claimed that voters had been confused by the electoral symbols used by the Social Movement, but it still meant that some of his ablest young lieutenants failed to enter parliament (*La Repubblica*, 23 April 1996).

Confined to the opposition benches, perhaps for a considerable period if the incoming government of Romano Prodi managed to remain united and to introduce an acceptable programme of structural reforms, the AN received an unexpected boost from the newly sworn-in President of the Chamber of Deputies, Luciano Violante. A former Communist, who as a magistrate had been deeply involved in the struggle against the mafia, Violante surprised deputies during his inaugural address, on 10 May 1996, by speaking well of the 'men and women of Salò' and by asking for the past to be forgotten. He received applause from the right-wing benches, as did his warning to the *Lega* that the army would be used to quell any secessionist bid on its part (*La Stampa*, 11 May 1996). Violante's speech was a carefully modulated appeal for national unity and an end to political warfare based on rival interpretations of the past. Perhaps it was a sign that the left was prepared to give the AN the benefit of the doubt when he suggested that it was now part of the 'civilized right'. A survey of delegates at the founding congress of the AN in 1995, carried out by the Cattaneo Institute, seemed to confirm that the outlook of the new party differed from that of the MSI in significant respects. With 576 delegates returning completed questionnaires, this suggested a growing acceptance of the rules and values of liberal democracy. Also, 85 per cent did not accept violence as a method for achieving political goals, only 23 per cent supported limitations on press freedom, and no more than 30 per cent favoured the death penalty. Only one-third of delegates believed that immigrants were the cause of increasing social delinquency, while two out of three delegates wished to extend to them the rights of social protection enjoyed by other citizens; however, a surprising 90 per cent supported Italian territorial claims over the former Yugoslavia. According to Piero Ignazi, these results were encouraging, but liberal values 'continue to coexist with anti-democratic instincts, ones that retain a strong appeal for new recruits. To remove this blemish, more needs to be done than simply uttering reassuring phrases' (*Corriere della Sera*, 17 April 1996).

Conclusion

The startling rise in support for the MSI/AN after decades in the political wilderness appears baffling to anyone unaware of just how volatile the behaviour of Italian voters had become in the 1990s. The voters' disdain for the main custodians of Italian democracy, the DC and the PSI, outweighed any inhibitions they might have had about supporting a party widely seen as neo-fascist and, each time, over 5 million backed the AN in the 1994 and 1996 general elections. The misrule of the clutch of parties that were permanently in government from the 1960s to the early 1990s robbed fascism of many of its negative connotations and enabled the MSI to go on the offensive, reaping rewards for claiming that it had been the only genuine opposition force during the Italian First Republic. The party also prospered as a result of persuading many voters who hitherto had been content with the politics of patronage to transfer their support to it after the DC and PSI ceased to be able to defend their interests. To accommodate a much broader constituency of support than it had known before – reactionaries and neo-fascists; conservatives deserting mainstream parties; clients of the government looking for new parties to safeguard their interests; apolitical young people – the AN has needed to promote a subtle political discourse in which it stands for political change while respectful of tradition, conservatism and modernization, national assertion and an active Italian role in the EU, and a strong economic role for the state while believing in market economics.

A prolonged period in government might have made it difficult for the AN to reconcile what are contrasting policies. This option was removed by the electoral success of the centre-left in April 1996. Barring any serious dissension in its ranks, the centre-left could expect a number of years in office, given the size of its majority and the degree of consensus it appeared able to elicit for a programme of economic and institutional reform.

Indeed, when the Prodi government collapsed in October 1998, it was the second-longest-serving government since 1945. Moreover, it was a sign of the post-Cold War times that the Olive Tree coalition remained intact as the PDS leader Massimo D'Alema formed the new government. In opposition, the character of the AN may become more clear-cut as it responds to the legislative initiatives of the centre-left governments. At the party conference in Verona in March 1998, Fini announced that he was relaunching the AN as a 'modern, open, right-wing party', now that it had retreated from its fascist past (*Keesing's Record of World Events*, March 1998). The main question still to be asked, though, is whether the AN has become a modern conservative movement on broadly Gaullist lines, and has abandoned the anti-democratic values sustaining it into the early 1990s. No categorical answer is possible, and one may be difficult to provide for many years. The large number of activists who, according to Ignazi's survey of MSI delegates in 1990, acquired their political references from the fascist era and were profoundly illiberal in their attitude to representative government have remained with the AN; in most cases, those who showed the strength of radical, anti-system values in the MSI have not forsaken the successor party. The relaunch of the MSI as a democratic movement of the right did not lead to the mass defections which afflicted the PCI when it abandoned Marxism and the title 'communist' in 1991. One-third of the PCI's membership and voters rallied behind the new Marxist party, Communist Refoundation, but Pino Rauti's efforts to preserve the founding aims of the MSI have attracted only a trickle of adherents. Perhaps many neo-fascists have modified their hostility to liberal democracy as it became clear that at last they can prosper by playing according to its rules. Gianfranco Fini's claims to have made a genuine conversion to post-fascism, while genuflecting to Mussolini's memory, have cast doubt on how complete the rethink has been.

Perhaps ambiguity in speech and gesture and a willingness to endorse parts of Mussolini's programme, such as his public works projects or his nationalism, were necessary if Fini was to keep the MSI largely united behind his new departure. Fini himself has been the key figure in transforming the image and appeal of the MSI/AN. His urbanity and pragmatism have disarmed many Italians hitherto suspicious of the MSI/AN and have turned him into a respectable leading player in politics at a time when few political heavyweights stand out, owing to the fall of the major parties. Yet he began his political career as a protégé of the unapologetic neo-fascist Giorgio Almirante at a time when the party was promoting 'a strategy of tension' to bring down Italian democracy by force. During his fifteen-year rise before becoming party leader for the first time in 1987, he was fully in tune with the strategy of acquiring political respectability while remaining true to the party's radical origins in the Fascist era. Now he describes Fascism as an exceptional historical episode that cannot be repeated and stresses his fidelity to democracy – that is, to a presidential pluralism in which more power would be invested in a chief executive than anywhere else in Western Europe.

Just as the MSI was plucked from a cul-de-sac to the fast track of Italian politics in the 1990s by events beyond its control, it is likely that the future character of the AN will be determined by events which even Fini will have a limited role in shaping: the extent to which new recruits either from the younger generation or from the old parties are able to transform the party's outlook; the amount of time the party remains in opposition; the opportunity it has to exercise municipal authority by running large cities and towns in the South; the extent to which the fiscal crisis in Italy bears down on the

South; and the extent to which illegal immigration, or instability in the eastern Adriatic, produce demands for a more assertive Italian nationalism. It may well be the fate of the AN to become a super-regional party defending the interests of the South against a central government promoting austerity and in which southern influence is a shadow of its former self. The AN may even prove to be a more successful regional party than the self-consciously northern Leagues of Umberto Bossi. But a party enmeshed in the clientelistic practices of southern politics would probably be deradicalized rapidly, and therefore be incapable of offering inspiration to Italians, who continue to be profoundly alienated by the defects of their political leaders at national level.

It is unlikely, however, that Fini would rest fully content with the AN becoming a powerful but essentially regional force. There may well be scope for the party to advance its claim to be a national force by expanding its political base in the North. The AN made striking advances in different parts of northern Italy during the 1994 and 1996 elections. The changes in political culture, displacing the old 'red' and 'white' subcultures, and the disappearance of the Marxist and confessional mass parties which reflected these political fault-lines, all have had their greatest political impact there. A shrewd political operator like Fini appears convincing to many younger north Italians who are without firm political attachments and whose political outlook is shaped by television images, a medium where Fini is unsurpassed.

It is in the North that the AN has the greatest potential for growth and where able teams of activists already exist capable of filling the vacuum left by the retreat of older parties. The success of the *Lega Nord* in rising from nowhere to becoming the largest electoral force across much of northern Italy in the early 1990s must be encouraging for Fini and his lieutenants. In many ways, the *Lega* has smoothed the AN's path to respectability. The extremism of its leader, Bossi, the emergence of a green-shirted movement, and the provocative marches staged when 'a republic of Padania' was proclaimed one weekend in September 1996 before the world's media, but with 'Padanians' mostly staying at home, have aided the AN's efforts to enter the mainstream of Italian politics.

The national parties and institutions like the Catholic Church and the armed forces deplored Bossi for flirting with insurrection, but it was the AN which took the counter-initiative in favour of Italian unity by attracting 150,000 people to a rally in Milan on 15 September 1996, more than the *Lega* could assemble at any of its independence stunts. By threatening to dismember the nation, Bossi may only succeed in giving Italian nationalism, or at least a commitment to national unity, a value which it has never enjoyed in the fifty-year history of the Italian republic, something which the AN, given its character, is likely to profit from handsomely. If the incoherence and extremism of the *Lega* alienate many former supporters from Bossi, the

AN is quite capable of picking up many of these votes by deft appeals to some of the grievances which caused them to desert the established parties at the end of the 1990s. Thus by championing the unity of the state, the AN may be acquiring the legitimacy which the MSI dreamt of obtaining in the 1950s and 1960s by promoting anti-communism as a shield behind which it could assemble with the DC and other anti-left parties.

Opposition probably gives Fini more scope to mould the AN in the direction in which he wants it to go. He may not be completely clear about what that direction is, and he may not be entirely sure what the ultimate destination is. He is not another Mussolini in the making but he has in full measure the ability of the Duce to mask uncertainty with a convincing display of public self-confidence. Yet his tactical agility in the shifting sands of post-1991 Italian politics deserted him in 1996 when he rashly forced an election in which the right lost to its rivals. If Fini's vote-winning powers desert him in the future, there is always the danger that sections of the AN will seek to give the party a sharper ideological edge, thereby emphasizing continuity with the past. This scenario became more speculated upon after the June 1999 Euro-elections, when the AN's share of the vote dropped to 10.3 per cent (from 12.5 in 1994) and the party lost 2 MEPs. Italy remains a political laboratory within which the evolution of the AN has a long way to go and may take surprising detours before a political resting-place is finally reached.

References

Allum, P. (1973) *Politics and Society in Post-war Naples*. Cambridge: Cambridge University Press.

Bull, M. J. and Newell, J. (1995) 'Italy Changes Course: The 1994 Elections and the Victory of the Right', *Parliamentary Affairs* 48(1), 72–99.

Cheles, L. (1991) ' "*Nostalgia dell'avenire*": The New Propaganda of the MSI between Tradition and Innovation', in Cheles, L., Ferguson, R. and Vaughan, M. (eds) *Neo-fascism in Europe*. Harlow: Longman, 43–65.

Corriere della Sera (1996) 'An, violenza no ma nostalgia si', 17 April.

Donovan, M. (1995) 'The Politics of Electoral Reform in Italy', *International Political Science Review* 16(1).

The Economist (1996) 'Something New in Italy', 27 April.

Endean, C. (1995) 'Italy's new smooth-talking Mr Right takes the helm', *The European*, 3–9 February.

Fuentes, J. (1994) 'Fini insiste en sus loas a Mussolini a pesar de las encendidas protestas de la oposición italiana', *El Mundo* (Madrid), 5 June.

Gallagher, T. (1992) 'Rome at Bay: The Challenge of the Northern League to the Italian State', *Government and Opposition* 27(4), 470–86.

Gilbert, M. (1995) *The Italian Revolution: The End of Politics Italian Style*. Boulder, CO:Westview Press.

Ginsborg, P. (1990) *A History of Contemporary Italy: Society and Politics 1943–88.* Harmondsworth: Penguin.

Gumbel, A. (1995a) 'Mussolini's Heirs Shake Off Their Fascist Mantle', *The Independent on Sunday* (London), 29 January.

Gumbel, A. (1995b) 'Italians Divided over Anniversary of Fascism's Fall', *The Independent* (London), 6 April.

Gumbel, A. (1996) 'Right-Wing Prolongs Italy's Political Agony', *The Independent,* 30 January.

Ignazi, P. (1994) *Postfascisti? Dal movimento sociale italiano ad Alleanza Nazionale.* Bologna: Il Mulino, 1–21.

Keesing's Contemporary Archives (1994) News Digest for May 1994, 40022.

Keesing's Record of World Events (1998) March.

L'Espresso (1994) 'Nomenklatura della destra', 8 April.

McCarthy, P. (1995a) '*Forza Italia*: The New Politics and Old Values of a Changing Italy', in Gundle, S. and Parker, S. (eds) *The New Italian Republic.* London: Routledge, 130-145.

McCarthy, P. (1995b) *The Crisis of the Italian State: From the Origins of the Cold War to the Fall of Berlusconi.* London: Macmillan.

Ruzza, C. and Schmidtke, O. (1995) 'Towards a Modern Right: *Alleanza Nazionale* and the "Italian Revolution" ', in Gundle, S. and Parker, S. (eds) *The New Italian Republic.* London: Routledge, 147–158.

Scalfari, E. (1996) 'Le speranze d'Italia', *La Repubblica,* 23 April.

Sidoti, F. (1992) 'The Extreme Right in Italy: Ideological Orphans and Counter-mobilization', in Hainsworth, P. (ed.) *The Extreme Right in Europe and the USA.* London: Pinter, 15–174.

Sznajder, M. (1995) 'Italy's Right-Wing Government: Legitimacy and Criticism', *International Affairs* 71(1), 83–102.

Tarchi, M. (1995) *Cinquant'anni di nostalgia: la destra italiana dopo il fascismo (intervista di Antonio Carioti).* Milan: Rizzoli.

CHAPTER FIVE

Right-wing extremism in unified Germany

Susann Backer

Following the collapse of Nazi Germany, the wartime Allies wanted to ensure that the extreme right would never again become a dominant political force in Germany. Accordingly, West Germany's liberal democratic constitution, the *Grundgesetz* (1949), provided for the banning of anti-democratic parties and organizations, and the German Democratic Republic (GDR) enshrined anti-fascism in its 1968 constitution long after it had claimed to have rooted out all traces of National Socialism. Right-wing extremism, indeed, at no time became a mass movement in the two states. However, sporadic electoral successes for the extreme right in reunified Germany show that affinity to right-wing extremism continues to be a force.

This chapter looks at the development of right-wing extremism in Germany since 1945, with particular emphasis on the unified state since 1990. It analyses the conditions which foster affinity to the extreme right and examines the changing nature of right-wing extremism. After a brief definition of the terms used in this chapter, I shall sketch the development of the extreme right in the old *Länder* (West Germany), then discuss the role of the *Republikaner* in the unified state. A subsequent section concentrates on the development of right-wing extremism in the new *Länder* (the former GDR), with particular emphasis on its roots in the GDR and the role played by system transformation in fostering extreme right violence. The chapter then deals with the question of asylum seekers, which has been a salient election issue for extreme right-wing parties during the early 1990s, followed in a final section by a brief analysis of the influence of the extreme right on the political climate of unified Germany.

A brief definition of right-wing extremism

The literature on right-wing extremism abounds with terms such as the 'extreme right', the 'radical right' and the 'New Right'. There is no agreed definition of political right-wing extremism (see Hainsworth, Chapter 1), and the various concepts are often confused. It would be helpful, therefore, to provide a brief definition – or at least a short description – of the terms used in this chapter.

Lipset and Raab define political extremism as the rejection, in action or thought, of democratic political pluralism. Democratic political pluralism is expressed in an 'open democratic market place for ideas, speech and consonant political action' (Lipset and Raab, 1978: 428). Germany has taken a similar approach. Paragraph 4 of the Law for the Protection of the Constitution defines political extremism as the rejection of the liberal democratic principles set down in the *Grundgesetz*. These principles include, among others, political pluralism, the accountability of government, the independence of the judiciary, free and universal democratic elections, the rule of law, and respect for human rights and civil liberties (*Verfassungsschutzbericht*, 1994: 3f.).

Right-wing extremism is a particular expression of political extremism. The extreme right usually rejects democratic political pluralism in favour of a totalitarian or authoritarian form of government. The government envisaged normally takes the shape of a unitary party or an elite which claims to represent all sectors of society and governs in the common interest of the national community. Authoritarian forms of government may permit the existence of other parties and interest groups; they have, however, no real rights of control and participation (Stöss, 1988: 35). The exercise of power in both forms of government is often arbitrary and violent; the individual is considered subordinate to the state. There is a belief in social, political and often also genetic human inequality, based on criteria such as nationality, race and social background. This belief sharply contrasts with left-wing thought, which is rooted in the idea of equality (Saalfeld, 1993: 181).

Right-wing radicalism is not a particular form of political extremism. Although it is anti-democratic in orientation (like its more extreme sister), its ideals remain within the parameters of liberal democracy, whereas the extreme right clearly moves outside the liberal democratic consensus. A radical right party may want to see the abolition of the right to political asylum in Germany (see below), but it may support free and universal democratic elections.

The New Right is a modern intellectual and metapolitical movement. Arguing that cultural power must precede political (e.g. electoral) power, it seeks to construct a modern and theoretical foundation for right-wing extremism by means of a 'cultural revolution' which aims at the revaluation of neo-conservative, liberal and left intellectual positions. Clearly breaking

Table 5.1 Elections to the 1949 *Bundestag* (seats)

Party	No. of seats	Party	No. of seats
KPD	15	WAV	12
SPD	131	DRep	5
Z	10	SSW	1
CDU/CSU	139	Indep.	3
FDP	52		

Notes:
Total seats: 402 (+7 West Berlin), 21 seats for the extreme right (WAV, DRep, SSW, Independent candidates).
KPD: *Kommunistische Partei Deutschlands*
SPD: *Sozialdemokratische Partei Deutschlands*
Z: *Zentrum*
CDU/CSU: *Christlich-Demokratische Union/Christlich-Soziale Union*
FDP: *Freie Demokratische Partei*
WAV: *Wirtschaftliche Aufbauvereinigung* (existed only in Bavaria)
DRep: *Deutsche Rechtspartei*
SSW: *Südschleswigscher Wählerverband*

Source: Staritz (1980: 88).

with the electoral tradition and jackboot nationalism of Old Right politics, the New Right is an ideological enterprise, a network of intellectual discussion circles and groups which propagate their ideas by way of literature. The New Right adheres to apparently 'normal' concepts and it is therefore able to mobilize sections of the population which the extreme right, with its more extremist inclinations, has so far found difficult to reach.

West Germany: the three waves of right-wing extremism[1]

Right-wing extremism in West Germany developed in three separate but interlinked waves. The first wave came in 1949 and lasted until the mid-1960s. The wartime Allies had banned National Socialist parties in the early years of occupied Germany, but after restrictions on party formation were made less stringent in 1947 (they were lifted altogether in 1949), a relatively large number of small nationalistic and neo-Nazi parties emerged. The most relevant parties were the *Sozialistische Reichspartei* (SRP) and the *Deutsche Reichspartei* (DRP). In the first *Bundestag* (the national parliament) in 1949, 5 per cent of seats were taken by elected members of the extreme right (Table 5.1). Between 1949 and 1952, six extreme right-wing parties gained seats in parliament at regional or national level. These were the *Wirtschaftliche Aufbauvereinigung* (WAV, 1949), the *Deutsche Rechtspartei* (DRep, 1949), the *Deutsche Gemeinschaft* (DG, 1950, 1952), the *Deutsche*

Table 5.2 Electoral support for the extreme right in the *Bundestag*, 1949–61 (%)

Party	14.8.1949	6.9.1953	15.9.1957	17.9.1961
DP	4.0	3.2	3.4	—
BHE	—	5.9	4.6	—
BP	4.2	1.7	0.5	—
DG	—	0.3	0.1	0.1
DRep	1.8	—	—	0.1
DRP	—	1.1	1.0	0.8
WAV	3.7	—	—	—

Notes:
DP: *Deutsche Partei*; BHE: *Bund der Heimatvertriebenen und Entrechteten*; BP: *Bayernpartei*.
For other parties, see Table 5.1

Source: Staritz, (1980: 131); Stöss (1983: 242–3).

Soziale Partei (DSP, 1951), the DRP (1951) and the SRP (1951). From 1952–3 onwards, however, electoral support for extreme right-wing parties waned considerably at both levels. By 1961, no party of the extreme right was represented in the *Bundestag* or any of the *Land* (state) parliaments (Table 5.2). At the national level, the total vote for the extreme right fell from over 1 million in 1949 to roughly 350,000 in 1953 and 290,000 in 1961 (Stöss, 1988: 40). Membership of right-wing extremist organizations also declined: from 78,000 in 1954 to 24,600 in 1963 (Backes and Jesse, 1993: 77).

Towards the late 1950s, a constitutional and popular consensus developed which severely curtailed the electoral prospects for extreme right-wing parties (Stöss, 1988). The banning of the SRP by the Federal Constitutional Court in October 1952 removed this party from electoral contention and deterred many voters from voting for a party of similar vintage. The introduction in 1953 of a 5 per cent qualifying electoral threshold for *Bundestag* elections was a step towards the electoral elimination of small parties such as the *Bund der Heimatvertriebenen und Entrechteten* (BHE). By 1961, the party system had developed from a multi-party variant, reminiscent of that of the Weimar Republic (with more than ten parties represented in the 1949 *Bundestag*), to a stable three party-system based on the *Christlich-Demokratische Union* (CDU), the *Sozialdemokratische Partei Deutschlands* (SPD) and the liberal *Freie Demokratische Partei* (FDP).

The economic miracle, the socio-economic integration of displaced persons (which had been the target of right-wing extremist parties), and integration with Western Europe produced a broad legitimation of the

Table 5.3 Regional and federal election results for the NPD (%)

1965 *Bundestag*	2[a]
1966 Hesse	7.9
Bavaria	7.4
Hamburg	3.9[a]
North Rhine-Westphalia	[b]
Saarland	[b]
1967 Rhineland-Palatinate	6.9
Schleswig-Holstein	5.8
Lower Saxony	7.0
Bremen	8.8
Baden-Württemberg	9.8
1969 *Bundestag*	4.3[c]

Notes:
[a]The NPD did not enter Parliament.
[b]It did not participate in these elections.
[c]In the 1972 *Bundestag* election, the NPD polled only 0.6%.

Source: Compiled from Backes and Jesse (1993: 76–83).

democratic state and also made for the rapid integration of extreme right-wing parties into the bourgeois camp. Some extremist supporters, however, withdrew from party politics and joined parapolitical organizations. Former SRP and DRP members, for instance, infiltrated the neo-Nazi *Hilfsgemeinschaft auf Gegenseitigkeit ehemaliger Angehöriger der Waffen-SS* (HIAGS), founded in 1949. Other supporters of the extreme right subscribed to the large network of extreme right journals, newspapers and book clubs which existed alongside organized right-wing extremism.

The rise of the *Nationaldemokratische Partei Deutschlands* (NPD) signalled the beginning of the second wave of the extreme right, which lasted from 1964 to the mid-1980s. Founded on 28 November 1964 as an umbrella organization of several right-wing extremist and national-conservative parties, such as the neo-Nazi *Deutscher Block* (DB) and the national conservative BHE, the NPD entered seven *Land* parliaments and won 61 seats between 1966 and 1967 (Table 5.3), and by 1969 it had gained almost complete control of the right-wing extremist camp. In the 1969 *Bundestag* election, the NPD captured 4.3 per cent of the vote, the best national result that a party of the extreme right has ever achieved in West Germany. The early successes, however, were not repeated, and the party suffered an electoral decline that has continued to the present: between 1972 and 1994 its best result in *Bundestag* elections was 0.6 per cent in 1972 and 1987. The electoral demise of the NPD was matched by declining membership: it fell from a high point of 28,000 in 1969 to 5900 in 1982 and to 4500 in 1994

Table 5.4 NPD membership trends

Year	No. of members	Year	No. of members
1965	13,700	1978	8,500
1966	25,000	1979	8,000
1967	28,000	1980	7,200
1968	27,000	1982	5,900
1969	28,000	1986	6,100
1970	21,000	1987	6,100
1971	18,300	1988	6,400
1972	14,500	1989	7,000
1973	12,000	1990	6,500
1974	11,500	1991	6,100
1975	10,800	1992	5,000
1976	9,700	1993	5,000
1977	9,000	1994	4,500

Sources: Compiled from Backes and Jesse (1993: 81); and *Verfassungsschutzbericht* (1994: 77).

(Table 5.4). By 1998, the NPD's *Bundestag* election share of the poll was down to 0.3 per cent, with a similar return (0.4 per cent) in the 1999 Euro-elections.

In more recent years, the NPD has made some changes to its programme, and has undergone structural changes. Most notably, it has adopted a militant campaign based around social issues. At the same time, it has increased its efforts to woo young extreme right voters into its rank, presenting the party as a gathering-point for all neo-Nazis. The new strategy seems to have paid off: between 1996 and 1997 the NPD increased its membership, while neo-Nazi organizations have been losing members (see Table 5.10). In Saxony, the NPD almost tripled its membership and threatens to overtake the Greens.

In 1966, the first economic crisis in West Germany led to the formation of a grand coalition between the CDU/CSU[2] and the SPD. Although the new government was formed under the leadership of the CDU/CSU, a broad section of the nationalistic and rigidly anti-communist electorate strongly disapproved of a coalition with the SPD, which they perceived to be a left-wing socialist party. Moreover, the ruling parties shared 87 per cent of the total vote between them and left the parliamentary opposition party, the FDP (9.5 per cent), without effective leverage. When the economic climate improved and after the grand coalition came to an end in 1969, electoral support for the NPD began to wane. In subsequent years, the CDU, which started a campaign of vociferous opposition to the new social-liberal government, absorbed nearly three-quarters of the NPD vote. Many NPD supporters joined one or even several of the many militant neo-Nazi action groups which sprang up during the 1970s. In fact, a discernible subculture of militant extra-parliamentary groups emerged following the electoral demise of the NPD: between 1970 and 1975, a minimum of 62 (1973) and a maximum of 91 (1975) such groups were recorded (Zimmermann and Saalfeld, 1993: 61). During the same period and even beyond, the extreme right literature network registered higher circulation figures as Gerhard Frey, owner of the publishing house *DSZ – Druckschriften und Zeitungsverlag* and editor of the *Deutsche Nationalzeitung*, expanded his readership to include members of various newly founded organizations such as the *Deutsche Volksunion* (DVU), which Frey himself established in 1971.

The third wave of West German right-wing extremism began in the mid-1980s and has lasted to the present. It is marked by the rise of the *Republikaner*, which is a radical right-wing populist protest party. The protest nature of the party places it at an advantage compared with competitors on the right of the political spectrum. The *Republikaner* was founded on 26 November 1983 in Munich by Ekkehard Voigt and Franz Handlos, two former members of Bavaria's governing CSU, and by a former producer of Bavarian television, Franz Schönhuber, in protest against the CSU's role in brokering a loan of DM 1 million to the GDR. The *Republikaner*, whose organization is strongest in south Germany (especially Bavaria and Baden-Württemberg), participated in elections from 1984 onwards, but did not make significant gains until after 1989 (see below).

The electoral rise of this party has been fostered by the process of economically fuelled modernization, undergone by Germany since the mid-1970s. Technological modernization led to economic deprivation for certain groups in society, in effect leaving them susceptible to radical right-wing populist propaganda. It has led to the polarization in the workforce between hi-tech specialists with a solid educational background and secure full-time jobs, and an unskilled and semi-skilled workforce with insecure, often part-time, jobs (Kern and Schumann, 1984). Accelerated modernization, particularly during the incumbency in government of the CDU/CSU since 1982, has produced a '*Zwei-Drittel-Gesellschaft*' (a 'two-thirds society'), in which some two-thirds of society enjoy greater affluence, better working conditions and better qualifications (Glotz, 1989). Those in bottom third, however, feel threatened by the reverse side of modernization, such as the erosion of traditional qualifications, increased competition and a 'new poverty'. These are the low-income workers, the semi-skilled and unskilled, the young, and the long-term unemployed. It is from these losers through modernization that the *Republikaner* draws the majority of its support (Roth, 1989: 10–20). According to a 1989 survey, a disproportionately large number of *Republikaner* supporters perceived themselves as belonging to the bottom third of society and were anxious about their socio-economic future (Emnid, 1989). Deprivation, however, may be as much apparent as real. It can be based upon the subjective feeling of insecurity rather than upon an objective process of economic marginalization.

A comparison of the three waves of right-wing extremism reveals several interesting characteristics and trends. First, ever since the birth of post-war West Germany, the extreme right has been structured along three separate – but interlinked – organizational strands: (a) parties, (b) militant neo-Nazi action groups, and (c) a network of literature circles. Second, at times of electoral failure for the extreme right during the first and second wave, many supporters retreated into a subcultural milieu of militant parapolitical organizations. Even the third wave has witnessed a steady growth of these groups following the banning of extreme right organizations which participated in elections (see below): they increased in number from 23 in 1989 to 71 in 1994 (Zimmermann and Saalfeld, 1993: 61; *Verfassungsschutzbericht*, 1994: 78). The militant action groups provided the political training ground for subsequent generations with extreme right views (Kolinsky, 1992: 62). The retreat into a subcultural milieu at times of electoral failure demonstrates that a right extremist mentality is not bound by organizational structures. When right extremist groups disintegrate, the potential affinity continues to exist.

Third, the experience of economic crisis and resulting phenomena of socio-economic deprivation were an important explanatory variable for extreme right gains at the ballot box in the three waves of right-wing extremism. Socio-economic insecurities, associated with the early post-war period, the economic crisis of 1966–7 and the effects of modernization, contributed to the electoral rise of extreme right parties in the 1950s, the NPD and the *Republikaner* respectively, but they are not sufficient explanatory variables. After all, the economic crisis of the mid-1970s did not halt the electoral decline of the NPD. An analysis of votes cast for the NPD and the *Republikaner* revealed that disaffection from the established parties played an important part in explaining extreme right electoral gains: a large proportion of NPD and *Republikaner* voters believed that the main parties appeared incompetent and were unable to address day-to-day problems of the person in the street (Zimmermann and Saalfeld, 1993: 66–73). Disenchantment with the main parties (*Parteienentfremdung*) was expressed in the fact that the combined share of the vote for the CDU and the SPD fell from 91.2 per cent in 1976 to 70.1 per cent in 1994. This allowed right-wing extremist parties more potential to gain votes (Irving and Paterson, 1991: 370). *Parteienentfremdung* has its source in (a) a perceived decline in ethical and moral standards as the established parties were affected by moral and financial scandals; (b) an increasing gap in representation between party composition and the social profile of the population (see Padgett, 1989: 136–9); (c) a general decline in popular party identification (Beyme, 1991: 129); and (d) changing forms of participation (Wiesendahl, 1990: 12).

The involvement of the individual in party politics decreased during the 1970s and 1980s by 4 per cent while willingness to engage in unconventional action increased by roughly 11 per cent (Jaide and Veen, 1989: 140).

Fourth, the second wave of the extreme right differs from the first wave in that it witnessed the arrival of issue and protest politics, and this in turn gave birth to right-wing populism. The right-wing extremist groups of the 1950s drew their support, in the main, from ideological supporters whose attitudes had been shaped by the National Socialist indoctrination of the Third Reich (Peukert and Bajohr, 1990: 33). The NPD, by contrast, whose party programme displayed neo-Nazi as well as national-conservative tendencies, attracted not only former Nazis but also people who voted for it in protest against changes in the economic and political climate (Nagle, 1970). Studies on electoral support for the NPD showed that it drew protest voters from all established parties, including the opposition SPD. In this sense, the NPD was a small people's party (Dudek and Jaschke, 1984).

The trend towards issue and protest politics was accelerated in the mid-1970s by socio-economic changes associated with advanced industrial society (such as greater social mobility and technological innovation). These changes led to the de-freezing of traditional electoral cleavages which had existed along class lines and attachment to value systems (Flanagan and Dalton, 1984). Voters became less inclined to vote by party preference and more inclined to vote for a party which they perceived to be able to address those issues most important to them. The shift from social group cleavages to issue-group cleavages provided for group re/dealignment and allowed the populist *Republikaner*, whose existence is explained in terms of issues, to function as a protest party. In fact, two-thirds of electoral support for the *Republikaner* may be seen as protest votes (Hundseder, 1993: 27). The rise of issue and protest politics and the arrival of right-wing populism have occurred across Western Europe. Unlike the first wave of German right-wing extremism, that of the 1980s and 1990s was no longer a unique German case; it adopted a Western European face in terms of its causes and ideology.

Last but not least, the third wave of the extreme right has seen the re-definition of German national identity. Issue and protest politics have given birth to the Green Party, which introduced a 'new politics' cleavage into German politics in the 1980s (Kvistad, 1985). The German extreme right has responded to this challenge with a conservative counter-attack, expressed via a renewed interest in German national identity. Based on the reassertion of values and virtues traditionally associated with the Germans (such as hard work and a sense of duty), it rejects all that is seen as 'un-German', ranging from new technologies to foreign immigration. The re-definition of Germany's relationship to its past and the application of that relationship to the present is part of this new historical paradigm and distinguishes the third wave from the first and second waves. Central here is the creation of a national consciousness freed from the shadow of Hitler, since the ghost of National Socialism is seen as impeding the development of a healthy German patriotism and German *völkish* identity, as shown by the so-called *Historikerstreit* (historians' debate) (see Nolte, 1986; Wehler, 1988).

The *Republikaner* in unified Germany

The *Republikaner* has made some significant electoral gains in unified Germany; these electoral successes were, however, short-lived and did not prevent adverse membership trends for the party.

Elections and membership trends

Until 1987, the *Republikaner* took part in elections only in Bavaria, where it made some relatively insignificant gains in the local elections of 1984. The party had its first big success in the 1986 elections to the Bavarian *Landtag*, where it polled 3 per cent of the total vote (the governing CSU lost 2.5 per cent). Since 1987, the *Republikaner* has competed in elections across Germany. In the *Land* elections of Bremen (1987), Schleswig-Holstein (1988) and Baden-Württemberg (1988), it polled 1.2 per cent, 0.6 per cent and 1.0 per cent of the total vote respectively. In 1989, the *Republikaner* won 7.5 per cent of the vote in the West Berlin elections and 7.1 per cent of the vote in the European Parliament elections (Tables 5.5 and 5.6). However, in 1990, electoral success waned as rapidly as it had come. In West Berlin, the *Republikaner* lost the 11 seats it had held since 1989, and in the regional elections in the new *Länder* it polled a mere 0.6 to 1.2 per cent of the vote (Table 5.7). In the first all-German *Bundestag* elections in 1990, the *Republikaner*, competing for the first time at the national level, captured 2.1 per cent of the vote (2.3 and 1.3 per cent in the old *Länder* and the new *Länder* respectively (Table 5.8). The year 1992, however, marked the high point of electoral success for the *Republikaner* when it stormed the *Landtag* of Baden-Württemberg with 10.9 per cent of the vote. It was the first time that the party had been represented in a regional parliament. And in the 1993 regional elections of Hamburg, the *Republikaner* only narrowly missed the national electoral threshold of 5 per cent. Its competitor, the DVU, gained 2.8 per cent of the vote (Table 5.5).

Success at the ballot box, though, could not be repeated during 1994, as the party's share of the vote declined to 1.9 per cent in the *Bundestag* elections. The *Republikaner* made minor gains in some of the eight *Land* elections that were held in 1994 but it lost 3.2 and 0.2 per cent respectively in the elections to the European Parliament and the *Bundestag*. In the local elections in June 1994, it gained mandates in Bavaria, Saxony, Mecklenburg-Pomerania and Saxony-Anhalt, but in many cities it could not

Table 5.5 Election results for the *Republikaner* in the old *Länder*

Land	Year	%	Year	%	Year	%
Baden-Württemberg	1992	10.9	1996	9.1	—[g]	—
Bavaria	1990	4.9	1994	3.9	1998	3.6
Berlin (West)	1989	7.5	1995	3.1	—	—
Bremen	1991	1.5[a]	1995	—[b]	—	—
Hamburg	1991	2.2	1993	4.8[c]	1997	1.8[f]
Hesse	1991	1.7	1995	2.0	1999	2.7
Lower Saxony	1990	1.5	1994	3.7	1998	2.8
North Rhine-Westphalia	1990	1.8	1995	0.8	—	—
Rhineland-Palatinate	1991	2.0	1996	3.5	—	—
Saarland	1990	3.4	1994	1.4	—	—
Schleswig-Holstein	1992	1.2[d]	1996	—[e]	—	—

Notes:
[a]DVU (*Deutsche Volksunion*) 6.18%; [b]DVU 2.5%; [c]DVU 2.8%; [d]DVU 6.3%. [e]DVU 4.3%, [f]DVU 4.9%. [g]The *Land* elections of Baden-Württemberg, Berlin, Bremen, North Rhine-Westphalia, Rhineland-Palatinate, Saarland and Schleswig-Holstein have not taken place yet at the time of writing.

Sources: Results compiled from *Zeitschrift für Parlamentsfragen*, V. 22(1) (1991), 16–20; Irving and Paterson (1991: 366); *Der Spiegel*, No. 41 (1992), 45; Zimmermann and Saalfeld (1993: 58–64); Roberts (1995: 20); *Die Welt*, (1996b); Golz (1996); press release *Bayerisches Landesamt* (15 September 1998), press release *Landesamt Hessen* (9 February 1999); *Frankfurter Allgemeine Zeitung*, 3 March 1998, 7; press release *Amt für Statistik*, Hamburg 1997.

Table 5.6 Returns for the *Republikaner* in the European Parliament elections (1989–99)

Year	%
18.6.1989	7.1
12.6.1994	3.9
13.6.1999	1.7

Sources: Results compiled from Dalton (1993: 6); Roberts (1995: 20); *Le Monde*, 15 June 1999.

even compete because of its lack of support (Table 5.9). Two years later, the *Republikaner* vote fell by 1.8 per cent in the *Land* elections of Baden-Württemberg, but the result is nonetheless significant in that for the first time in thirty years, a party of the radical right was re-elected to a *Land* parliament. In the 1997 regional election of Hamburg, its share of the vote

Table 5.7 Election results for the *Republikaner* in the new *Länder* (%)

Land	1990	1994	1998
Volkskammer	—[a]	—	—
Saxony	—	1.4	—+[b]
Brandenburg	1.2	1.1	—
Mecklenburg-Pomerania	0.9	1.2	0.5
Saxony-Anhalt	0.6	1.4	0.7
Thuringia	0.8	1.4	—

Notes:
[a]The *Republikaner* was banned from the election to the *Volkskammer*. The rival DVU scored 6.3 per cent of the total vote and the DA (*Deutsche Alternative*) 0.9 per cent
[b]The *Land* elections of Saxony, Brandenburg and Thuringia had not taken place yet at the time of writing.

Sources: Golz (1994a); *Pressebericht Statistisches Landesamt Mecklenburg-Vorpommern* (29 September 1998); *Frankfurter Allgemeine Zeitung*, 28 April 1998.

Table 5.8 Election results for the *Republikaner* in the *Bundestag* (1990–1998)

Date	%
02.12.1990	2.1
16.10.1994	1.9
27.09.1998	1.8

Notes: In the 1990 Bundestag election, the *Republikaner* competed for the first time at the national level.

Sources: as for Table 5.5, plus *Frankfurter Allgemeine Zeitung*, 29 September 1998.

more than halved, while the DVU increased its support by 2.1 per cent (Table 5.5). The drop in electoral fortunes of the *Republikaner* by 50 per cent or more was mirrored in the 1998 regional elections in two new *Länder*, Mecklenburg-Pomerania and Saxony-Anhalt (Table 5.7). In the 1998 *Bundestag* election the party stagnated at 1.8 per cent, ahead of the DVU, which polled 1.2 per cent. A similar return (1.7 per cent) was achieved by the *Republikaner* in the 1999 European elections (Table 5.6).

The *Republikaner*'s electoral results demonstrate several points. First, the party draws protest votes across the left–right dichotomy. Studies on

Table 5.9 Election results for the extreme right in local elections in the new *Länder* in the 1990s

Land	Year	Party	%	Year	Party	%
Brandenburg	1989	—	—	1993	—	—
Thuringia	1994	DSU	1.4	1990	DSU	3.3
Saxony-Anhalt	1994	Rep	0.5	1990	Rep	0.9
		DSU	—			1.7
Mecklenburg-Pomerania	1994	—	—	1990	—	—
Saxony	1994	Rep	0.1	1990	Rep	1.2

Source: Golz (1994b).

electoral support for the *Republikaner* in the 1990s show that this party gained votes from all established parties, including the opposition SPD (see Roth, 1989; Betz, 1991). Second, electoral support for the *Republikaner* is relatively low in the new *Länder*; it lacks the protest function it has assumed in the old *Länder*. In the 1998 *Bundestag* election it trailed behind the DVU in the East, despite surpassing the latter overall. The organization of the *Republikaner* is very weak in the new *Länder*, and flirtations with neo-Nazi organizations induced well-publicized divisions in the party (see below). Taken together with the fact that the party had been banned from the first democratic elections in the new *Länder* in March 1990 (the *Volkskammer* elections), these developments deterred many potential protest voters in subsequent elections. Third, the correlation between electoral gains and true affinity is far from perfect. While the *Republikaner* suffered electoral setbacks during the period 1993 to 1997, recruitment to militant neo-Nazi groups increased by slightly more than 50 per cent, from 1550 members in 1990 to 2400 in 1997 (Table 5.10). The increase in neo-Nazism has been particularly pronounced in the new *Länder* (see Backes and Jesse, 1993: 112–25). It seems that in eastern Germany, dissatisfaction was expressed in membership rather than in protest votes, given the lack of electoral tradition – at least in the early to mid-1990s – in the former communist country.

Policy platform

The 1990 party programme of the *Republikaner* targeted disillusioned voters of established parties as well as supporters of traditional right-wing extremist parties. The programme is the reflection of a careful balance between the conservative values articulated by the CDU/CSU (such as on

Table 5.10 Membership of extreme right organizations, 1990–7

Year	*Republikaner*	DVU	NPD	Neo-Nazis
1990	25,000	22,000	6,500	1,550
1991	23,000	24,000	6,100	2,300
1992	20,000	26,000	5,000	2,200
1993	23,000	26,000	5,000	2,450
1994	20,000	20,000	3,830	2,940
1995	16,000	15,000	4,000	1,980
1996	15,000	15,000	3,500	2,420
1997	15,500	15,000	4,300	2,400

Notes:
DLVH: *Deutsche Liga für Volk und Heimat*; DVU: *Deutsche Volksunion*.
Membership of the *Republikaner* party in the new *Länder*: 1990: 3000; 1992: 2800; 1993: 4500; 1994: 3500.

Sources: Figures compiled from *Verfassungsschutzberichte 1994/1998*; Zimmermann and Saalfeld (1993: 55); *Der Spiegel* (1992b: 102).

law-and-order issues) and the extreme right attitudes articulated by the DVU and the NPD (such as the aggressive polemics against foreigners and scepticism towards the North Atlantic Treaty Organization (NATO)). The *Republikaner* has also adopted certain aspects of New Right ideology, such as the neo-liberal critique of the modern welfare state. A militant evocation of nationalism combined with a populist strategy which addresses high-priority national issues and articulates grievances against the state and society (such as the rise in crime and the alleged squandering of taxpayers' money by the incumbent federal government) bridges contradictions in the party's programme (e.g. between neo-liberal and traditionalist values), resulting in the *Republikaner*'s relatively widespread appeal (Saalfeld, 1993: 177–89).

The *Republikaner* is a typical example of a new type of right-wing populist party, examples of which have emerged across Europe, such as the National Front in France and Haider's FPÖ in Austria. Like that of its counterparts in France and Austria, the propaganda of the *Republikaner* focuses primarily, though not entirely, on hostility towards foreigners. It is an underlying theme across a whole range of issues, ranging from religion to social benefits. This focus has enabled the party to act as a channel for political and economic discontent. However, it also makes the party very vulnerable to changes in the tides of popular discontent, whose ebb and flow can be influenced by different social agents. The recent asylum-seeker issue serves as a case in point. In 1992, at the high point of electoral success for the *Republikaner*, the asylum-seeker issue topped the list of public concerns in the old *Länder*, and in the new *Länder* it came second (Gibowsky, 1995: 30; Kolinsky, 1995: 15). However, when the asylum-seeker issue lost its urgency (it was relegated to second place and fourth place in the old and the new *Länder* respectively, following a change in the asylum law), electoral support for the *Republikaner* waned (Gibowsky, 1995: 30). In fact, the *Republikaner*'s electoral comeback and decline paralleled exactly the rise and fall in importance of the asylum-seeker issue (see below).

Internal division

The *Republikaner* attracts two types of members. On the one hand, it recruits traditional right-wing extremists, who often want to move the party further to the right of the political spectrum. On the other hand, it recruits many new members with no previous right-wing extremist history, who often desire to take the party on a more moderate course. This duality led in early 1990 to deep internal splits in the party, which culminated in May 1990 in the resignation of the 'moderate' party chairman, Franz Schönhuber, enforced by the more extremist members. Upon his re-election as party chairman in July 1990, Schönhuber banned his rivals and replaced almost the entire party executive. In spite of this move, some extremist members flirted with the DVU, the NPD and the neo-Nazi *Wiking Jugend*. In fact, question marks over the *Republikaner*'s liberal-democratic pretensions have led to surveillance by the Federal Office for the Protection of the Constitution since 1992.

In an attempt to give the *Republikaner* a more moderate image, Schönhuber called for the banning of certain right-wing extremist parties, such as the *Deutsche Liga für Volk und Heimat*, a splinter party of the *Republikaner* formed in January 1991. However, in view of Schönhuber's meeting with the chairman of the extreme right DVU, Gerhard Frey, in August 1994, this ban was seen by many moderate members as a gesture only. It merely added to the growing dissatisfaction with the leadership style of Schönhuber, who was also blamed for electoral losses and declining membership. Schönhuber was subsequently dismissed from his chairmanship by the party executive in October 1994, but then reinstated after his dismissal was contested in court. At the party conference in Sindelfingen (Baden-Württemberg) in December of the same year, Schönhuber, who was very unsure whether he would be re-elected as party chairman, stepped down from candidature for chairmanship, and Rudolf Schlierer (32 years his junior) was voted in. Schlierer is an intellectual in the New Right mould who wants to set the party on a new and more moderate course in order to attract voters from the national-conservative ranks of the CDU/CSU. Schönhuber stood as a DVU candidate in October 1998 and the *Republikaner* suffered other defections to Frey's party. Following the general election, the DVU looked to future collaboration with the *Republikaner*.

Table 5.11 Racially motivated violent offences, 1985–94

Year	No. of offences
1985	120
1986	189
1987	192
1988	193
1989	255
1990	309
1991	1,492
1992	2,639
1993	2,232
1994	1,489

Source: *Verfassungsschutzbericht* (1994: 81).

Right-wing extremism in the new *Länder*

Since unification, researchers of right-wing extremism have been particularly interested in the new *Länder* (Staab, 1998). There has been a steady growth in racially motivated violence since 1990 in both parts of Germany (see Table 5.11). The majority of offences were committed in the new *Länder* (Oesterreich, 1993). The Unification Treaty stipulated the allocation to the new *Länder* of 20 per cent of all asylum seekers, although in the early 1990s they took just 10 per cent of the agreed quota (Kolinsky, 1995: 14). Violence has escalated in particular since the arrival of these newcomers in 1991, with a spate of attacks against hostels for asylum seekers during 1991 and 1992 (notably in Hoyerswerda and in Rostock) sending shock waves through Germany and abroad.

In the new *Länder*, the readiness to tolerate or even participate in violence against foreigners is higher than in the old *Länder* (Willems, 1993: 110ff.). This readiness is linked to xenophobia, which is much more widespread in the new *Länder* than it is in the old (Förster *et al.*, 1993: 114ff.). In the GDR, foreigners constituted roughly 1 per cent of the population, and the state pursued an active policy of segregation. As a result, the citizen had little opportunity to develop tolerance towards foreigners. The correlation between attitude potential and violence, however, is not flawless. A recent study has revealed that in the new *Länder*, members of the older generation (over 65) of both sexes display more pronouncedly xenophobic views than do younger people, yet offenders belong almost exclusively to the younger generation, with the majority of offenders being males under the age of 25 (Willems, 1993: 110ff.). In fact, violence against foreigners in the new

Länder is linked to a right-wing extremist youth culture which had existed before the Berlin Wall came down.

Anti-fascism in the GDR

In the 1980s, a number of fringe subcultures such as skinheads, *faschos*, heavy metal enthusiasts and punks emerged in the GDR. The common denominator of these youth subcultures was dissatisfaction with the socialist GDR state, which they perceived as rigid, anachronistic and unable to cater for their interests. A survey by the *Zentralinstitut für Jugendforschung* in Leipzig revealed that in 1988, fewer teenagers and young adolescents unconditionally identified with socialism than in the 1970s, and a large proportion felt that the GDR state was out of touch with the younger generation. The majority of the disillusioned youth were blue-collar workers, and disaffection was also widespread among members of state elite organizations such as the *Freie Deutsche Jugend* (FDJ), who had been particularly dissatisfied with the official GDR youth culture (Brück, 1988: 22). The youth subculture represented a generation whose relationship to the state was different from that of their parents. Communist rhetoric may have been plausible to the first generation but it no longer attracted the second generation (Hockenos, 1993: 71).

Initially, the youth movement was a loose organization of different, and mainly apolitical, groups which were united in protest against the state. Towards the mid-1980s, however, a more distinct youth culture (e.g. skinheads and *faschos*) developed which adopted the Nazi convictions of German and Aryan superiority. Studies on the social origin of neo-Nazis in the new *Länder* revealed that they had a profile similar to that of their counterparts in the old *Länder*: the majority were male, final-year school pupils, apprentices or blue-collar workers with a low level of education (Süß, 1993).

As intimated above, the GDR had long claimed to have eliminated, through state-ordained anti-fascism, all roots and traces of National Socialism. Yet the emergence of the extreme right youth culture attested to the failure of the state to realize a clean break with Germany's Nazi past. In fact, GDR society was not purged of Nazism at all. Former members of the *Nationalsozialistische deutsche Arbeiter Partei* (NSDAP, Nazi Party) were lobbied to join the *National-Demokratische Partei Deutschlands* (NDPD), a satellite party of the ruling *Sozialistische Einheitspartei Deutschlands* (SED). The granting of equal opportunities to former NSDAP members in September 1952 meant that such people took up leading positions in the state apparatus. Because the GDR state blamed capitalism for National Socialism, anti-fascist measures primarily targeted the economic level but failed to address the psychological level, thereby preventing any attempt at *Vergangenheitsbewältigung* (coming to terms with the past). Extreme right currents were attributed to an overspill from the 'fascist' West, which was seen as the successor state of the Third Reich. The fight against fascism became synonymous with the fight against capitalism. In addition, the GDR citizen was living in conditions which promoted authoritarian and undemocratic attitudes (usually considered receptive to right-wing mobilization). State control meant subordination and conformity, authoritarianism, dogmatic anti-pluralism and a militant intolerance towards those who were different (Butterwege and Isola 1991: 16–21). Anti-democratic, antipluralistic and authoritarian value orientations therefore continued to exist, albeit latently, in the GDR state (which was, of course, anti-democratic in itself). In 1988, 10–15 per cent of youth sympathized with Nazi ideology (Schubarth and Schmidt, 1992: 12–28). In 1990, 6 per cent of youth had very strongly anti-semitic attitudes and 53.5 per cent wanted to close the books on Germany's National Socialist past (Wittenberg *et al.*, 1991: 102).

Affinity with right-wing extremism is thus seen, at least in part, as the legacy of a failed anti-fascist strategy. Further, it is seen as the heritage of '*Realsozialismus*', the result of specific authoritarian and repressive conditions. Nevertheless, this is not a sufficient explanation. Social opposition groups (e.g. the Church-based ecology and peace movement) and some youth groups (e.g. the Goths) in the GDR remained immune to right-wing extremist propaganda. Moreover, the middle generation (these aged 35 to 64) showed markedly less inclination towards right-wing extremism than the older and the younger generations (Bergmann, 1994: 270). Hardly surprisingly, this demonstrates that not every citizen who lived under the repressive conditions of the GDR state adopted the values of the extreme right. It also attests to the fact that the adoption of right-wing extremist attitudes in some people but not in others (who, after all, live under the same conditions) is promoted by the subjective interpretation of day-to-day experiences (Backer, 1995: 169). This subjective interpretation is determined partly by experiences occurring in the early, formative years of life. Representatives of the oldest cohort (older than 64) were born during the closing years of the Weimar Republic and grew up in the Third Reich, when hatred towards foreigners informed public policy. The younger cohort (younger than 25) grew up at a time when the GDR, in its struggle to keep pace with the West, was increasingly being left behind.

System transformation

There are several theories which explain affinity to right-wing extremism in the new *Länder*. One theory attributes these affinities to the ending of socialist state control (Brück, 1992: 37ff.). The collapse of the GDR system entailed the ending of repression and released a right-wing extremist potential that was lurking under the surface of the GDR. Another theory focuses on the discrediting of socialism as an ideology. The disintegration of the socialist GDR and of the Soviet Union entailed the discrediting of leftist ideology. In search of new orientations, the individual escapes into the arms of right (or even extreme right) ideology, which is seen as the victor (Kühnl, 1993: 162ff.). Disintegration caused by societal transformation opens the way for susceptibility to right-wing extremist mobilization.

Perhaps the most convincing theory is that of system transformation. The unification of the GDR with West Germany in October 1990 marked the transformation from an 'aligned' society to an individualized society and has produced 'asynchronic' developments, expressed in social, economic and political disintegration processes (Butterwege and Isola, 1991: 112). West Germany is a highly individualized *'Risikogesellschaft'*, a 'risk society' (Beck, 1986). Amid a general climate of high socio-economic insecurity and risk, and given the disintegration of security derived from previous social anchorages, the individual must increasingly shape his or her life on their own. The individual alone is now responsible for perceived or real failures in their career plan. The GDR, by contrast, was a functionally adaptive, self-regulating society characterized by a high degree of collectivism and state protection. In fact, life in the GDR was virtually the opposite of life in West Germany. It was regulated and followed secure and predictable paths.

The sudden change from a socialist state to a dynamic capitalist state has resulted in an *'Individualisierungsaufprall'*, an 'individualization shock', in the new *Länder* (Heitmeyer, 1992: 101). This shock is a product of the transformation from a life of certainties to one of uncertainties on the economic and social level. Although the government adopted a gradualist approach to transformation of the system, the process entailed an unex-pected collapse of economic and social expectations. Promises by the CDU/CSU–FDP government of change without individual sacrifices or cost (such as tax increases) gave rise to high and unrealistic expectations in both parts of Germany. Yet in the new *Länder*, mass unemployment and massive deskilling (caused by de-industrialization), the freeing of prices, and the cutting of state subsidies in a climate of economic decline all led to a deep sense of dissatisfaction. In the old *Länder*, the payment of a *Solidaritätsbeitrag* ('solidarity tax') of 7.5 per cent levied on income, plus other tax increases (for instance on petrol, tobacco and VAT) and an increase in social insurance and welfare contributions, led to dissatisfaction with the government and resentment towards eastern Germans, who were blamed for sacrifices that needed to be made. For eastern Germans, the new status as *de facto* second-class citizens fostered a growing discontent. Dis-illusionment with *'Realsozialismus'* was now substituted by disillusionment with the new system. According to a survey in 1991, 80 per cent of citizens of the former East Germany were dissatisfied with the present political system (Schubarth, 1992: 80ff). In this context, right-wing extremism in the new *Länder*, then, gains its dynamic force from the delegitimization of the new state.

The above theories have some credibility, yet they can provide only a partial explanation for extreme right sympathies. Present-day affinity to right-wing extremism in the new *Länder* is, in fact, the product of a combination of factors: system transformation; the ending of the repressive conditions of socialist state control; the failure of the left to present itself as a viable alternative; the lack of thorough democratization of society in the GDR prior to system transformation; and the failure to prepare the East German citizens psychologically for the difficulties ahead.

The Land elections of 1998 in Saxony-Anhalt

The electoral gains of the extreme right DVU in the *Land* elections of Saxony-Anhalt on 26 April 1998 seem to confirm several of the above explanations for the rise of right-wing extremism. The DVU captured 12.9 per cent of the vote, more than any other right extremist or radical party had achieved in Germany since the 1980s. With 16 seats in the *Landtag*, the party gained parliamentary representation in a new *Land* for the first time. The DVU, which had not competed in the Saxony-Anhalt elections four years earlier, made gains at the expense of the *Republikaner*, which lost 50 per cent of its vote compared to 1994 (−0.7 per cent). More significantly, however, the DVU made heavy inroads into the CDU, which lost 12.5 per cent of its vote compared to 1994 and a third of its electoral support as compared with 1990 (*Frankfurter Allgemeine Zeitung*, 28 April 1998). The electoral decline of the CDU is mirrored in other eastern German states, too, and points to a lack of profile and a weak electoral core for this party in the new *Länder*.

According to the *Forschungsgruppe Wahlen* in Mannheim, 65 per cent of electoral support for the DVU came from split-ticket voting across the left–right dichotomy. Voters in Germany cast two votes: the first (*Erststimme*) is for a constituent candidate and the second, more crucial, vote (*Zweitstimme*) is for a party. Twenty-three per cent of DVU supporters gave their first vote to the extreme-left *Partei des Demokratischen Sozialismus* (PDS), 22 per cent to the SPD and 20 per cent to the CDU. The DVU also attracted many of those who had abstained in the previous elections or who had never voted before. Every second first-time voter in Saxony-Anhalt voted for the DVU (*Die Zeit*, 29 April 1998). Thirty per cent of the DVU's electoral supporters were young, and male, either apprentices, blue-collar workers or unemployed (*Frankfurter Allgemeine Zeitung*, 28 April 1998). German neo-Nazis have a similar socio-economic profile.

What conclusions can be drawn from these observations? First, in the main, the DVU attracted protest voters, a group it had targeted during the election campaign (one of its election posters invited the electorate to vote for the party as a protest). Against the background of rising unemployment (from 17.6 per cent in 1994 to 24.7 per cent in 1998), these voters were disillusioned with the economic and political climate in Saxony-Anhalt (*Die Zeit*, 29 April 1998). Two-thirds believed that the economic situation was 'very bad'; 30 per cent did not trust the mainstream political parties to provide viable solutions; and the great majority saw themselves as victims of system transformation (*Frankfurter Allgemeine Zeitung*, 28 April 1998). It seems that in the new *Länder*, the DVU has assumed the protest function which the *Republikaner* has failed to provide.

The second conclusion follows from the first one: the majority of DVU voters are not right-wing extremists. This view is confirmed by the fact that in many areas with a strong presence of extreme right militancy, the DVU received fewer votes than its regional average. According to Wilhelm Heitmeyer, three different types of people voted for the DVU in the elections of Saxony-Anhalt: (a) neo-Nazis; (b) those in search of new political directions; and (c) protest voters (*Die Zeit*, 29 April 1998). As with the *Republikaner*, the DVU does not have a large and stable extreme or radical right electoral core to draw upon. This makes the DVU very vulnerable to ups and downs in the economic and political climate, with major implications for its future electoral successes.

Third, protest voting behaviour in Saxony-Anhalt seems to be assuming dimensions hitherto known only in the old *Länder*. In previous local and regional elections, Saxony-Anhalt had registered a relatively low level of protest support for the extreme right (see Tables 5.7 and 5.9). In 1998, however, the state witnessed a sudden and drastic increase in votes for the DVU that even surpassed electoral gains for the *Republikaner* in the 1992 Baden-Württemberg elections. Recent surveys conducted by the *Institut Infratest dimap* in Berlin revealed that certain conditions which make it difficult for the extreme right to make gains in the old *Länder* are not as prevalent in Saxony-Anhalt (or in other new *Länder*). Identification with parties and the parliamentary system, for instance, is weaker, and so are social anchorages (such as Church membership) which bind the voter psychologically to non-extremist parties. Furthermore, voters in the new *Länder* are more likely to switch parties than their counterparts in western Germany: every second voter is prepared to vote for a different party in the next regional elections. This compares to every third voter in the old *Länder* (*Der Spiegel*, 11 May 1998). The volatility of DVU voters was only too evident in the October 1998 *Bundestag* election, when the party's vote dropped to 3.2 per cent in Saxony-Anhalt.

The asylum-seeker issue

After the fall of the Berlin Wall in November 1989, West Germany received a steady influx of *Umsiedler* (East German migrants) and *Aussiedler* (ethnic German immigrants from the eastern countries). By the end of 1990, twice

Table 5.12 Asylum seekers in Germany

Year	No. 1 asylum seekers
1983	19,737
1984	35,278
1986	99,650
1987	57,379
1988	103,076
1989	121,318
1990	193,063
1991	256,112
1992	438,191
1993	423, 670

Sources: Figures compiled from *Jahresbericht der Bundesregierung* (1992: 125); *Die Welt*, 29 January 1996.

as many *Aussiedler* (375,000) and eight times as many *Umsiedler* (345,000) as in 1988 were living in Germany (Benz, 1993: 122). During the same period, there was a drastic increase in the number of asylum seekers, notably from Third World countries and Eastern Europe. In 1988, 103,076 people sought asylum in West Germany. In 1992, this figure rose to 438,191 applicants for both parts of Germany (Table 5.12). In the same year, Germany accepted 79.8 per cent of all the asylum applicants from outside the European Union (EU), four times as many as all other EU member states put together (*Die Zeit*, 11 June 1993). Hamburg alone took as many as Great Britain (*Die Zeit*, 16 July 1993).

The *Grundgesetz* grants citizens' rights to *Umsiedler* and *Aussiedler*. They have the same employment status as German natives, and they are given equal access to social assistance and welfare provision. *Aussiedler* usually speak little or no German and they are largely seen by the extreme right as foreigners. In 1989, 83 per cent of right-wing extremist supporters wanted to refuse them German citizenship (Roth, 1989: 17). They are also regarded as unwanted competitors for employment and social security entitlement by those hardest hit by *Modernisierung* and unemployment, since a disproportionately large number of *Aussiedler* are looking for employment in the bottom third of the '*Zwei-Drittel-Gesellschaft*' (Kolinsky, 1992: 88).

In the wake of these arrivals, hostility against foreigners has emerged as a salient political and electoral issue. In 1992, 51 per cent of eastern Germans and 60 per cent of western Germans favoured the return of foreigners to their country of origin, and 70 per cent of eastern Germans and 60 per cent of western Germans felt that there was a need for constitutional change in order to revise the status of immigrants (*Süddeutsche Zeitung*, 16 July 1992). A substantial part of the population also supported recourse to unconventional political action against foreigners. In April 1992, 37 per cent of the German population expressed sympathy for right-wing extremist tendencies because of the 'problem with foreigners' (*Der Spiegel*, 1992a). Significantly, the extreme right made electoral gains parallel to the emergence of the asylum issue. The long and intense national debate on the immigration issue, fuelled by right extremist rhetoric, led to an escalation of racially motivated violence and boosted recruitment to right extremist organizations. Between 1990 and 1992, the number of violent offences against foreigners rose from 309 to 2639, and recruitment to the DVU and neo-Nazi organizations rose by roughly 18 per cent and 43 per cent respectively (Tables 5.10 and 5.11).

In an attempt to deflate a potentially damaging electoral issue, the government has taken several steps since 1990 to restrict the influx of newcomers, such as facilitating expulsion and limiting the right of appeal for asylum seekers.[3] *Aussiedler*, who could previously arrive in Germany without proof of citizenship, must now prove their German origin before they are allowed to cross German borders (see Kolinsky, 1995: 13ff.). The government has also introduced several repatriation programmes for Croats and Bosnians who fled to Germany to escape civil war in the former Yugoslavia.

Most importantly, a new asylum law came into force in July 1993, which was a compromise agreement between the CDU/CSU–FDP government and the opposition SPD. It rests on three main pillars. First, the politically persecuted have a right to asylum. This right had already been granted under the old asylum law (1949; the most recent amendment was in 1992). Second, no political asylum is granted to those arriving in Germany from a safe third country ('*Drittstaatenregelung*'). This includes all EU member states and states which recognize the Geneva Convention as well as the European Convention on Human Rights. Under the *Drittstaatenregelung*, more than 145,000 asylum seekers were sent back during the first half of 1995 (*Die Welt*, 29 January 1996: 6). The third pillar deals mainly with procedural matters, such as shortening the procedure for looking at asylum applications by foreigners from persecution-free countries.

The change to the Basic Law bore fruit: by the end of 1993, the number of those seeking asylum in Germany fell for the first time since 1987 (Table 5.12), and in 1994 the figure of violent offences committed against foreigners fell below the 1991 level (Table 5.11). Before the new asylum law came into effect, press coverage of the asylum-seeker issue and statements made by some politicians fuelled popular fears and anxiety that Germany would be flooded with foreigners, thus playing into the hands of the extreme right. Although a reciprocal relationship between the number of asylum seekers and the level of violence cannot be established in the German case, the fall in asylum seekers has – at least temporarily – defused a potentially damaging election issue. Nevertheless, the new asylum law has pitfalls. First, it fails to deal with those asylum seekers whose applications have been turned down but who have escaped the net of deportation. Second, criticism has arisen over the way in which decisions either for or against the granting of political asylum are reached. Under the '*Drittstaatenregelung*', decisions are based on the origin of the application rather than on the merits for achieving political asylum, a process which is generally held to constitute a violation of the European Convention on Human Rights. Third, there have been cases where 'secure third states' have sent applicants for political asylum back to a country that did not recognize the Geneva Convention or the European Convention on Human Rights. Consequently, popular support for the new asylum law has not been forthcoming: in 1993, only 30 per cent of the population in the new *Länder* and 25 per cent of the population in the old *Länder* considered the new law to be effective (Kuechler, 1994: 58). The renewed criticism over the deficiencies of the asylum law provided a new impetus for the *Republikaner*, as the electoral gains for this party in the 1996 Baden-Württemberg elections demonstrated. During 1996 and 1997, the party also increased its membership for the first time since 1993 (Table 5.10).

Influence on the political climate

The extreme right has an influence on the political climate that is greater than one might expect from looking at election results and membership trends. First, its aggressive propaganda has contributed to a 'more anxious, less liberal political culture' (Roberts, 1992: 343). It has resulted in an escalation of racially motivated violence, and has boosted recruitment to right extremist organizations.

Second, the established parties have incorporated the key issues of the extreme right in order to blunt its cutting edge. For instance, in 1996 the FDP introduced a document on controlling immigration, in which it supported the restriction of immigration in proportion to Germany's ability to accommodate foreigners. The SPD, when it was an opposition party, agreed to the new asylum law that came into effect in 1993, thus breaking with its tradition of welcoming applications for political asylum 'unreservedly'. Three years later, on the eve of the regional elections in Baden-Württemberg in 1996, the SPD candidate (Dieter Spöri) openly advocated further restrictions to immigration. Now that the SPD is in power, it plans to introduce a reform of the citizenship law, which would grant dual citizenship (the *Doppelpass*) to foreigners resident in Germany who fulfil certain criteria. The planned reform has already played into the hands of the *Republikaner* (see below).

Third, it appears that the *Republikaner* has become a bridge between the moderate and the extreme right. Traditionally, the party has contacts with New Right circles in the CDU/CSU, such as the *Vogelsbergkreis*, the *Deutschlandforum* and the *Petersberger Kreis* (*Der Spiegel*, 1992c). Unofficially, there have been contacts with the NPD and neo-Nazi organizations. There is also evidence of membership fluctuations between the moderate right, the *Republikaner* and the extreme right (see *Der Spiegel*, 1993). Peter Recknagel, for instance, is one of several CDU/CSU members who have moved to the extreme right via the *Republikaner*. He deserted the moderate CSU to join the *Republikaner* and later joined the *Deutsche Liga für Volk und Heimat* (DLVH), which splintered from the CSU in 1991. These membership fluctuations testify to the Republikaner's bridge-building function and also provide evidence that the party facilitates the conversion of moderate right to extreme right values.

Fourth, New Right ideology has contributed to a shift in right-wing extremist argumentation. For instance, the 'genetic racism' of the extreme right, which is based on what it sees as genetic inferiority, is shifting towards a 'cultural racism', based on cultural differences. Also, traditional anti-semitism, which was linked to the presence of Jews in Germany is shifting towards an 'anti-semitism without the Jews' (Silbermann and Hüser, 1995), which is expressed in resentment towards Jews for not allowing Germans simply to forget the past. The *Historikerstreit* which is propagated by the New Right, has made a major contribution to this shift in extreme right argumentation. Last, but not least, New Right ideology has become a common denominator between the CDU/CSU, the *Republikaner* and parties even further to the right, such as the NPD. With its adherence to concepts such as 'cultural racism' and 'anti-semitism without Jews', New Right argumentation has become a useful shield for right-wing extremists, behind which they can hide without having to water down their own convictions. By the same token, 'moderate' right-wingers who resent foreigners but have reservations against the aggressive and populist polemics of the *Republikaner* have found a home in the New Right. The adherence to New Right concepts by representatives across the right spectrum poses a threat to society.

Conclusion

Despite attempts to do away with National Socialism and ideologies of similar vintage, extreme right views have persisted in both parts of post-war Germany. Right-wing extremism has been expressed in three waves, whose flow has been influenced by a combination of factors: disillusionment with the political system; socio-economic insecurities; and structural changes in society. The rise of right-wing populism has introduced a third strand to right-wing extremism (the first two are the New Right, which existed as far back as the early post-war years, and traditional right-wing extremism, as expressed, for instance, in neo-Nazism).

Right-wing populism is channelled via clearly identifiable structures (party membership and votes for the *Republikaner*), and it can thus be monitored by looking at election results and membership trends. Affinity to the New Right, by contrast, is more difficult to detect in unified Germany because it is an ideological enterprise not linked to party structures or a clearly recognizable membership.

Adherence to traditional extreme right ideology has become less identifiable in unified Germany. In the new *Länder*, the right-wing extremist youth culture is, with few exceptions, not tied to rigid organizational – and thus clearly recognizable – structures. It is part of a wider extreme right environment, which forms the basis of a right-wing extremist social movement similar to that of the left-wing scene (Bergmann, 1994: 265-76). In the old *Länder*, right-wing extremism was, until the early 1990s, much more bound by specific organizational ties, although even then it was part of a broader social movement. However, it now appears to be retreating back into this subculture, aided by the proscription of right-wing extremist organizations in the 1990s. Although proscription has led to a decline in the number of officially registered extreme right organizations (from 83 in 1992 to 78 in 1993), it has caused a shift from organized to autonomous, 'underground' right-wing wing extremism. Three trends appear to confirm this shift. First, in order to escape proscription, extreme right groups increasingly break into autonomous cells. Siegfried Borchert, the former chairman of the *Freiheitliche Deutsche Arbeiterpartei* (FAP), said, after the banning of his party, 'We no longer need party organizations nor do we need a party chairman. The FAP can be grouped into autonomous cells, without a chairman or treasurer' (*Der Spiegel*, 1995). Second, the extreme right has built up a network which is co-ordinated by modern communications technology and which enables it to organize outside the embrace of state control. Third, resurgent nationalism in Eastern Europe has presented the German extreme right with an opportunity to expand its contacts eastward, outside the reaches of German state surveillance. Contacts have been made with right-wing extremist organizations across Eastern Europe and the former Soviet Union. The *Republikaner*, for instance, has contacts with the Ukrainian Republican Party, and the DVU has extended its hands to the Russian Liberal Democratic Party (LDP) of Vladimir Zhirinovsky (Annaun, 1995: 9–12).

The accession to power in 1998 of the SPD–Green coalition government has ended sixteen years of conservative–liberal rule. As for the extreme right, it is too early to speculate about its long-term electoral prospects. As so often before, its success is linked to developments in the mainstream CDU and CSU. Two scenarios are possible. First, the CDU could drift to the centre of the political spectrum by moving away from the hard-line positions promoted by the former federal Minister of the Interior, Manfred Kanther. Significantly, the leader of the CDU in the Saarland, Peter Müller, has demanded that issues of social justice be put back on the agenda. A move to the centre would leave a vacuum on the right that could easily be filled by extreme right parties at the expense of the CDU/CSU.

Second, the CDU, free from the centripetal bind which coalition politics imposed upon it in government, could tilt further to the right. There is evidence that such a move has already been made. In the 1999 *Land* election in Hesse, the CDU campaigned against the government's plans to reform the citizenship law, in an attempt to reverse its poor performance in the 1998 *Bundestag* election. The party increased its vote by 4.2 per cent, as compared with its 1995 performance (from 39.2 per cent to 43.2 per cent). It was successful in mobilizing many of those who usually do not vote and 61 per cent of whose who switched parties (*Die Zeit*, 11 February 1993). Moreover, the government lost its absolute majority in the *Bundesrat* following the Hesse election, leaving the CDU with increased bargaining power.

A key question is: how far can the CDU drift away from centre-right positions without alienating its moderate wing? The campaign referred to above has already caused tension among moderate members of the party. A move to the right would potentially increase the CDU's chances of gaining votes from the *Republikaner*. At the least, it would act as a brake on the electoral performance of this party. This was the case in the 1999 *Land* election in Hesse, where the *Republikaner* made only minor gains, owing to the CDU's strong opposition to the reforms of the citizenship law (see Table 5.5). The CSU has already tilted further to the right of the political spectrum. According to the DVU, it did not contest the 1998 Bavarian *Land* election because 'the CSU already represents the view of the DVU' (*Frankfurter Allgemeine Zeitung*, 1 January 1998).

Another scenario is that the parties of the extreme right merge. The total aggregate vote of the NPD, DVU and the *Republikaner* in the 1998 *Bundestag* election came to 4.6 per cent, only 0.4 per cent short of the electoral threshold. The demarcation lines between the parties of the extreme right are blurred, which facilitates movement of volatile voters and members between these parties. In the *Land* election of Saxony-Anhalt, for instance, many voters switched from the *Republikaner* to the DVU (*Frankfurter Allgemeine Zeitung*, 15 January 1998). The NPD has absorbed former members of outlawed organizations such as the *Nationalistische Front* (NF) and the FAP. Some of these members now sit on the executive committee of the NPD. There is also support for a united right-wing extremist front between supporters of various extreme right groups. Some grassroots members of the *Republikaner*, for instance, have openly called for unification with the DVU, shortly after their former leader, Schönhuber, announced that he would stand as a DVU candidate in the 1998 election to the *Bundestag* (*Der Spiegel*, 1998). However, the chances that extreme right parties will unite are slim. Gerhard Frey of the DVU was turned down by the leader of the NPD, Udo Voigt, when he suggested an electoral pact between the two parties in forthcoming local and regional elections. Voigt was clearly concerned that his party would lose its new and emerging profile among young voters. Schlierer, the leader of the *Republikaner*, has openly voiced his opposition to any co-operation with the DVU. He fears that formal alliances would split the *Republikaner*, with the moderate members running to the CDU/CSU. His potential successor, Christian Käs, is also against unification with other parties of the extreme right. (The 1999 Euro-elections witnessed fragmentation and failure for the extreme right in Germany. In the same poll, the CDU/CSU triumphed convincingly against the SPD.)

It is unlikely that the extreme right will play a major role in federal politics, now that the CDU/CSU has been relegated to forming the opposition to the SPD–Greens government. However, the debate surrounding the planned reform of the citizenship law could reverse the adverse electoral trend of the *Republikaner* and ensure that the extreme right remains a relatively strong voice, at least at the regional level, in the near future. Although much depends on the ability of the CDU/CSU to absorb disillusioned and volatile voters, the extreme right will continue to be a lasting force, given the emergence of a sympathetic and sustained subculture which is not simply determined by the ebb and flow of electoral politics.

Abbreviations used in this chapter and organizations mentioned

BHE	Federation of the Homeless and Dispossessed
BP	Bavarian Party
CDU	Christian Democratic Union
CSU	Christian Social Union
DA	German Alternative
DB	German Block Party
DG	German Community
DLVH	German League
DP	German Party
DRep	German Rightist Party
DRP	German *Reichs* Party
DSP	German Social Party
DVU	German People's Union
EU	European Union
FAP	Free German Workers' Party
FDJ	Free German Youth

FDP	Free Democratic Party
GDR	German Democratic Republic (East Germany)
HIAGS	Mutual Aid Society of Former Armed SS
KPD	Communist Party of Germany
LDP	Liberal Democratic Party (of Russia)
NATO	North Atlantic Treaty Organization
NDPD	National Democratic Party of [East] Germany
NF	National Front
NO	National Offensive
NPD	National Democratic Party of [West] Germany
NSDAP	National Socialist Workers' Party
PDS	Party of Democratic Socialism
Republikaner	Republicans (Party)
SED	Socialist Unity Party
SPD	Social Democratic Party
SRP	Socialist *Reichs* Party
SSW	Electoral Union of Southern Schleswig
WAV	Economic Reconstruction Association
Wiking Jugend	Viking Youth
Zentrum	Centre Party

Notes

1. This section is based on a revised version of 'A Future for Right Extremism in Germany?' (Kolinsky, 1992).
2. The acronym CSU stands for *Christlich-Soziale Union*.
3. Several factors aid the state in its fight against right-wing extremism. Article 21(2) of the *Grundgesetz* provides for the banning by the Federal Constitutional Court of anti-democratic parties. Article 9(2) equips the Minister of the Interior with the power to ban anti-democratic groups and organizations. In 1992 and 1993 alone, at least eleven such organizations/parties were banned, including the *Deutsche Alternative* (DA), the *Nationale Offensive* (NO), the *Nationalistische Front* (NF) and the *Wiking Jugend*.

References and further reading

Annaun, W. (1995) 'Die Braune-Armee-Fraktion', *Die Zeit*, 13 January, 9–12.

Assheuer, T. and Sarkowics, H. (1992) *Rechtsradikale in Deutschland: Die alte und die neue Rechte*. Munich: Beck.

Atkinson, G. (1993) 'Germany: Nationalism, Nazism and Violence', in Björgo, T. and Witte, R. (eds) *Racist Violence in Europe*. Basingstoke: Macmillan.

Backer, S. (1995) 'New Perspectives on the Far Right in Germany', *German Politics* 4(2), 165–71.

Backes, U. and Jesse, E. (1993) *Politischer Extremismus in der Bundesrepublik Deutschland*. Bonn: Bundeszentrale für Politische Bildung.

Beck, U. (1986) *Die Risikogesellschaft*. Frankfurt am Main: Suhrkamp.

Benz, W. (1993) *Rechtsextremismus in der Bundesrepublik*. Frankfurt am Main: Fischer.

Bergmann, W. (1994) 'Antisemitism and Xenophobia in the East German *Länder*', *German Politics* 3(2), 265–76.

Betz, H. G. (1991) *Postmodern Politics in Germany: The Politics of Resentment*. London: Macmillan.

Betz, H. G. (1994) *Radical Right-Wing Populism in Western Europe*. Basingstoke: Macmillan.

Beyme, K. von (1985) *Political Parties in Western Democracies*. Aldershot: Gower.

Beyme, K. von (1991) *Das politische System der Bundesrepublik Deutschland nach der Vereinigung*. Munich: Piper.

Brück, W. (1988) *Das Skinhead-Phänomen in jugendkriminologischer Sicht*. Leipzig: Zentralinstitut für Jugendforschung.

Brück, W. (1992) 'Skinheads – Vorboten der Systemkrise', in Heinemann, K. H. and Schubarth, W. (eds) *Der antifaschistische Staat enläßt seine Kinder: Jugend und Rechtsextremismus in Ostdeutschland*. Cologne: Pappy Rossa.

Butterwege, C. and Isola, H. (eds) (1991) *Rechtsextremismus im vereinten Deutschland*. Bremen: Steintor.

Cheles, L., Ferguson, R. and Vaughan, M. (eds) (1991) *Neo-fascism in Europe*. London: Longman.

Childs, D. (1991) 'The Far Right in Germany since 1945', in Cheles, L., Ferguson, R. and Vaughan, M. (eds) *Neo-fascism in Europe*. London: Longman.

Dalton, R. J. (1993) *The New Germany Votes*. Oxford: Berg.

Delfs, S. (1993) 'Heimatvertriebene, Aussiedler, Spätaussiedler', in *Aus Politik und Zeitgeschichte*, Beilage zur Wochenzeitung 'Das Parlament' B48, 3–11.

Der Spiegel (1992a) 'Bleibt es beim Rechtsdruck? Spiegel-Umfrage über die politische Situation im Monat April', 46(18), 58–65.

Der Spiegel (1992b) 'Republikaner bekommen Zulauf von alten SED-Genossen', 46(19), 102–5.

Der Spiegel (1992c) 'Das Böse in den Genen', 46(31), 30–2.

Der Spiegel (1993) 'Rechter Schatten', 47(31), 50–2.

Der Spiegel (1995) 'Werwolf der Zukunft', 49 (10), 3.

Der Spiegel (1998) 'Die Republikaner vor dem Zerfall', 52(22), 20.

Die Republikaner (1990) *Parteiprogramm*. Bonn: Bundesgeschäftsstelle der Republikaner.

Die Welt (1996a) 'Streit um das Asylrecht neu aufgeflammt', 29 January, 6.

Die Welt (1996b) 'Republikaner wollen nicht Partei der Verlierer sein', 26 March, 4.

Die Zeit (1993a) 'Europa wird zur Festung ausgebaut', 11 June, 2.

Die Zeit (1993b) 'Die Gewalt an den Wurzeln bekämpfen', 16 July, 3.

Diwald, H. (1978) *Die Geschichte der Deutschen*. Frankfurt am Main: Propyläen.

Dudek, P. and Jaschke, H. G. (1984) *Entstehung und Entwicklung des Rechtsextremismus in der Bundesrepublik Deutschland*. Opladen: Westdeutscher Verlag.

Eldinger, L. J. (1988) *Germany*, 2nd edn. Boston: Little, Brown.

Emnid (1989) 'Die Einstellung der Bundesbürger zum Nationalsozialismus', *Der Spiegel* 43(15), 56–62.

Feist, U. and Krieger, H. (1987) 'Alte und neue Scheidelinien des politischen Verhaltens', *Aus Politik und Zeitgeschichte*, Beilage zur Wochenzeitung 'Das Parlament' B12, 33–47.

Feit, M. (1987) *Die 'Neue Rechte' in der Bundesrepublik*. Frankfurt am Main: Campus.

Flanagan, S. C. and Dalton, R. J. (1984) 'Parties under Stress: Realignment and Dealignment in Advanced Industrial Societies', *West European Politics* 7(1), 7–21.

Ford, G. (1992) *Fascist Europe: The Rise of Racism and Xenophobia*. London: Pluto.

Förster, P. F., Müller, H. and Schubarth, W. (1993) *Jugend Ost: Zwischen Hoffnung und Gewalt*. Opladen: Leske and Budrich.

Fuchs, D., Klingemann, H. D. and Schrobel, D. (1991) 'Perspektiven der politischen Kultur im vereinigten Deutschland', *Aus Politik und Zeitgeschichte*, Beilage zur Wochenzeitung 'Das Parlament', B32, 35–46.

Gibowsky, W. G. (1995) 'Election Trends in Germany: An Analysis of the Second General Election in Reunited Germany', *German Politics* 4(2), 26–53.

Glotz, P. (1989) *Die Deutsche Rechte*. Munich: Wilhelm Heyne.

Golz, G. H. (1994a) 'Der Wechsel fand nicht statt', *Deutschlandarchiv* 27(11), 1129–34.

Golz, G. H. (1994b) 'Halbzeit im Superwahljahr', *Deutschlandarchiv* 27(7), 677–9.

Golz, G. H. (1996) 'Ende der Spekulation', *Deutschlandarchiv* 29(3), 341–3.

Gress, F. and Jaschke, H. G. (1982) *Rechtsextremismus in der Bundesrepublik seit 1960: Dokumentation und Analyse von Verfassungsschutzberichten*. Munich: Pressedienst Demokratische Initiative.

Heinelt, H. (1993) 'Immigration and the Welfare State', *German Politics* 2(1), 78–96.

Heitmeyer, W. (1992) 'Die Wiederspiegelung von Modernisierungsrückständen im Rechtsextremismus', in Heinemann, K.H. and Schubarth, W. (eds) *Der antifaschistische Staat enläßt seine Kinder: Jugend und Rechtsextremismus in Ostdeutschland*. Cologne: Pappy Rossa.

Heitmeyer, W. (1993) 'Hostility and Violence towards Foreigners in Germany', in Björgo, T. and Witte, R. (eds) *Racist Violence in Europe*. Basingstoke: Macmillan.

Henning, E. (1991) *Die Republikaner im Schatten Deutschlands*. Frankfurt am Main: Suhrkamp.

Hockenos, P. (1993) *Free to Hate: The Rise of the Right in Post-communist Europe*. London: Routledge.

Hundseder, F. (1993) *Stichwort Rechtsextremismus*. Munich: Heyne.

Irving, R. E. M. and Paterson, W. E. (1991) 'The German General Election', *Parliamentary Affairs* 44(3), 353–72.

Jahresbericht der Bundesregierung (1992) Bonn: Bundeszentrale für Politische Bildung.

Jaide, W. and Veen, H. J. (eds) (1989) *Bilanz der Jugendforschung: Ergebnisse empirischer Analysen der Bundesrepublik von 1975–87*. Paderborn: Schöning.

Kern, H. and Schumann, M. (1984) *Das Ende der Arbeitsteilung?* Frankfurt am Main: Campus.

Kolinsky, E. (1984) *Parties, Opposition and Society in West Germany.* London: Croom Helm.

Kolinsky, E. (1992) 'A Future for Right Extremism in Germany?', in Hainsworth, P. (ed.) *The Extreme Right in Europe and the USA.* London: Pinter.

Kolinsky, E. (1995) 'Foreigners in the New Germany: Attitudes, Expectations, Perceptions', in *Keele German Papers* Research Series, No. 1. Centre for Modern German Studies, University of Keele.

Korfes, G. (1992) 'Seitdem habe ich einen dermaßenen Haß: Rechtsextremistische Jugendliche vor und nach der "Wende", – exemplarische Biographien', in Heinemann, K. H. and Schubarth, W. (eds) *Der antifaschistische Staat enläßt seine Kinder: Jugend und Rechtsextremismus in Ostdeutschland.* Cologne: Pappy Rossa.

Krahulec, R. (1991) 'Besonderheiten des deutschen Nationalismus', in Butterwege, C. and Isola, H. (eds) *Rechtsextremismus im vereinten Deutschland.* Bremen: Steintor.

Kuechler, M. (1994) 'Germans and Others', *German Politics* 3(1), 47–74.

Kühnl, R. (1993) *Gefahr von rechts? Vergangenheit und Gegenwart der extremen Rechte.* Heilbron: Diestel.

Kvistad, G. O. (1985) 'Between State and Society: Green Political Ideology in the Mid 1980s', *Zeitschrift für Parlamentsfragen* 16(3), 211–25.

Leggewie, C. (1989) *Die Republikaner: Phantombild der Neuen Rechten.* Berlin: Rotbuch.

Liepelt, K. (1967) 'Anhänger der neuen Rechtspartei: Ein Beitrag zur Diskussion über das Wählerreservoir der NPD', *Politische Vierteljahresschrift* 8(2), 237–71.

Lipset, S. and Raab, E. (1978) *The Politics of Unreason: Right-Wing Extremism in America 1790–1977.* Chicago: University of Chicago Press.

Lipset, S. and Rokkan, S. (1984) 'Cleavage Structures, Party Systems and Voter Alignments', in Lipset, S. and Rokkan, S. (eds) *Party Systems and Voter Alignments.* New York: Free Press.

Merkl, P. (ed.) (1989) *Germany at Forty.* New York: New York University Press.

Nagle, J. D. (1970) *The National Democratic Party: Right Radicalism in the Federal Republic of Germany.* Berkeley: University of California.

Nolte, E. (1986) 'Vergangenheit, die nicht vergehen will', *Frankfurter Allgemeine Zeitung*, 6 June.

Oesterreich, D. (1993) *Autoritäre Persönlichkeit und Gesellschaftsordnung.* Weinheim: Juventa.

Padgett, S. (1989) 'The Party System', in Smith, G., Paterson, W. E. and Merkl, P. H. (eds) *Developments in West German Politics.* Basingstoke: Macmillan.

Padgett, S. and Burkett, A. (1986) *Political Parties and Elections in West Germany.* London: Hurst.

Paul, G. (ed.) (1989) *Hitlers Schatten verblaßt. Die Normalisierung des Rechtsextremismus.* Berlin/Bonn: Neue Gesellschaft.

Peukert, J. K. and Bajohr, F. (1990) *Rechtsradikalismus in Deutschland.* Hamburg: Ergebnisse Verlag.

Pflüger, F. (1995) *Deutschland driftet: Die Konservative Revolution entdeckt ihre Kinder*. Düsseldorf: Econ Verlag.

Roberts, G. K. (1992) 'Right-Wing Radicalism in the New Germany', *Parliamentary Affairs* 45(3), 335–44.

Roberts, G. K. (1995) '*Superwahljahr* 1994 and Its Effects on the German Party System', *German Politics* 2(2), 4–25.

Roth, D. (1989) 'Sind die Republikaner die fünfte Partei?', *Aus Politik und Zeitgeschichte*, Beilage zur Wochenzeitung 'Das Parlament', B41, 10–20.

Roth, D. (1993) '*Volksparteien* in Crisis: The Electoral Successes of the Extreme Right in Context', *German Politics* 2(1), 1–20.

Roth, R. and Rucht, D. (eds) (1988) *Neue soziale Bewegungen in der Bundesrepublik Deutschland*. Bonn: Bundeszentrale für politische Bildung.

Saalfeld, T. (1993) 'The Politics of National-Populism: Ideology and Policies of the German *Republikaner* Party', *German Politics* 2(2), 177–99.

Schmidt, I. (1992) 'Ausländer in der DDR: Ihre Erfahrungen vor und nach der "Wende", in Heinemann, K. H. and Schubarth, W. (eds) *Der antifaschistische Staat enläßt seine Kinder: Jugend und Rechtsextremismus in Ostdeutschland*. Cologne: Pappy Rossa.

Schönhuber, F. (1981) *Ich war dabei*. Munich: Hanser.

Schubarth, W. (1992) 'Rechtsextremismus: eine subjektive Verarbeitungsform des Umbruchs?', in Heinemann, K. H. and Schubarth, W. (eds) *Der antifaschistische Staat enläßt seine Kinder: Jugend und Rechtsextremismus in Ostdeutschland*. Cologne: Pappy Rossa.

Schubarth, W. and Schmidt, T. (1992) 'Sieger der Geschichte: Verordneter Antifaschismus und die Folgen', in Heinemann, K. H. and Schubarth, W. (eds) *Der antifaschistische Staat enläßt seine Kinder: Jugend und Rechtsextremismus in Ostdeutschland*. Cologne: Pappy Rossa.

Silbermann, A. and Hüser, F. (1995) *Der 'normale Haß' auf die Fremden*. Munich: Quintessenz.

Sinus Institute (1981) *Fünf Millionen Deutsche: Wir wollen wieder einen Führer haben*. Hamburg: Rowolth.

Smith, G. (1996) 'The Party System at the Crossroads', in Smith, G., Paterson, W. E. and Padgett, S. (eds) *Developments in German Politics* 2. London: Macmillan.

Staab, A. (1998) 'Xenophobia, Ethnicity and National Identity in Eastern Germany', *German Politics* 7(2), 31–46.

Staritz, D. (1980) *Das Parteiensystem der Bundesrepublik*. Opladen: Leske.

Stock, M. and Mühlberg, P. (1990) *Die Szene von innen: Skinheads, Grufties, Heavy Metals, Punks*. Berlin: LinksDruck.

Stöss, R. (1983) *Parteienhandbuch: Die Parteien der Bundesrepublik Deutschland*, Vol. 1. Opladen: Westdeutscher Verlag.

Stöss, R. (1988) 'The Problem of Right Extremism in West Germany', *West European Politics* 11(2), 34–46.

Sturm, R. (1992) 'Government at the Centre', in Smith, G., Paterson, W. E., Merkl, P. H. and Padgett, S. (eds) *Developments in German Politics*. Basingstoke: Macmillan.

Süddeutsche Zeitung (1992) 'Bereitschaft zur Gewalt wächst', 16 July, 26.

Süß, W. (1993) 'Zur Wahrnehmung und Interpretation des Rechtsextremismus in der DDR durch das MfA', *Deutschlandarchiv* 26(4), 383–90.

Veen, H. J. (1989) 'Trends in der öffentlichen Meinung im Vorfeld der Europawahl', *Interne Studien* 12. St Augustin: Konrad Adenauer Foundation.

Veen, H. J. and Zelle, C. (1995) 'National Identity and Political Priorities in Eastern and Western Germany', *German Politics* 4(1), 1–26.

Verfassungsschutzbericht (1991–4, 1998) Bonn: Ministry of the Interior.

Wehler, H. U. (1988) *Entsorgung der deutschen Vergangenheit? Ein polemischer Essay zum Historikerstreit*. Munich: Beck.

Weidenfeld, W. and Korte, K. R. (1993) *Handbuch zur deutschen Einheit*. Bonn: Bundeszentrale für Politische Bildung.

Wiesendahl, E. (1990) 'Der Marsch aus den Institutionen: Zur Organisationsschwäche der politischen Parteien in den 80er Jahren', *Aus Politik und Zeitgeschichte*, Beilage zur Wochenzeitung 'Das Parlament', B21, 3–14.

Wiesenthal, H. (1995) 'East Germany as a Unique Case of Societal Transformation: Main Characteristics and Emergent Misconceptions', *German Politics* 4(3), 49–74.

Willems, H. (1993) *Fremdenfeindliche Gewalt: Einstellungen, Täter, Konflikteskalation*. Opladen: Leske Budrich.

Wittenberg, W., Prosch, B. and Martin, A. (1991) 'Antisemitismus in der ehemaligen DDR', *Tribüne* No. 118, 88–102.

Wolf, S. (1991) 'Antifaschismus in der DDR: Versuche einer Bilanz', in Butterwege, C. and Isola, H. (eds) *Rechtsextremismus im vereinten Deutschland*. Bremen: Steintor.

Zelle, C. (1995) 'Candidates, Issues and Party Choice in the Federal Election of 1994', *German Politics* 4(2), 54–74.

Zimmermann, E. and Saalfeld, S. (1993) 'The Three Waves of West German Right Wing Extremism', in Merkl, P. H. and Weinberg, L. (eds) *Encounters with the Contemporary Radical Right*. Boulder, CO: Westview.

CHAPTER SIX

Belgium: explaining the relationship between Vlaams Blok and the city of Antwerp

Marc Swyngedouw

Introduction

Antwerp has earned itself a contradictory reputation during the past decade. In essence, two main items have attracted the attention of the international media: the electoral successes of *Vlaams Blok* (VB), the local extreme right party, and the European City of Culture celebrations, hosted by Antwerp in 1993. By 1996, the only story of any real international interest was the first one. At the 1994 municipal elections, *Vlaams Blok*, a prototype of the New Right parties (Ignazi, 1992: 15–16), set a post-war record by becoming the largest party in the city, polling 28 per cent of the vote. In a country where voting is compulsory and roughly 95 per cent of ballot papers are cast validly, this meant that at least a quarter of the population opted to give its vote to an outspokenly anti-democratic organization, a party which notably does not support the European Convention on Human Rights. This chapter focuses on the city of Antwerp, assessing the context of VB success at this level.

General context

By the 1990s, the ruling City Hall coalition of Christian Democrats (CVP) and Social Democrats (SP) had been in power for a good seventy years. In Antwerp, this degree of continuity is regarded as perfectly normal and typical of politics at all levels. Over the years, power-sharing ratios have been established in virtually all areas of the administration, with these being only minimally adjusted to take account of shifts in the balance of power between the coalition partners, following local elections every six years or because new European, Belgian or Flemish regulations require it. To quote a few examples, since the war, Education has been an SP fiefdom, the Port and Welfare departments have been run by the CVP, and the administrative staffs of these departments have virtually all belonged to the same party. Contract employees (non-tenured officials) who are not members of either the Christian or the Socialist-inspired civil service union, but who are planning to take the examination for tenured appointment, are quietly told to join one of these two organizations. Catholic and Socialist housing organizations have also shared out the areas of the city where they may operate without getting in each other's way.

The advantage of this sharing technique is that both parties know almost to the letter what they can offer to their client networks. For example, city officials are promoted not on the basis of their skills, but because they are regarded as belonging to the right party at the right time. Subsidized housing, jobs, and preferential treatment in numerous organizations and services must be obtained via the party organization, itself controlled by a small elite. In some areas, dynasties have emerged, with central functions in the apparatus passed down from father to son. The elite is to be found not only in City Hall, but also in the Social Democrat (ABVV) and the Christian Democrat (ACV) unions. They too play a key role. The activities of the unions are not limited to a stranglehold on the city's human resources policy, as one might expect. Numerous investment projects and real estate operations, together with physical planning and land use policy, are guided by the unions.

This situation is nothing new. Indeed, it was inherent in the 'pact with the devil', agreed in 1921 between Camille Huysmans (Belgian Workers' Party, the predecessor of the SP) and Frans Van Cauwelaert (Catholic Party, CVP), which laid the foundations for Antwerp's Catholic–Socialist coalition. The system worked well for a considerable period of time. The basic factors in its success were: a solid financial basis combined with economic growth and low unemployment; a strictly compartmentalized population with strong ties to their respective leaders; and a sufficiently broad electoral base for the two credible coalition partners. Moreover, the electoral relationship between the two coalition partners needed to be relatively stable. The two parties had to be capable of holding more than half plus one of all the seats in the municipal council and of operating flexible party machines capable of meeting new social challenges and withstanding new electoral challengers. These basic factors are closely linked. When one of them starts to crumble, the system itself comes under pressure. Nor is pressure on the system anything new. There was, for example, an acute crisis in the depression years prior to World War II (De Wever, 1992). Nevertheless, it is possible to speak of a process of oligopolization of political power in the city of Antwerp, a mixture of long-standing political, social and cultural compartmentalization (pillarization) and relatively recent neo-corporatism, which continued up to the end of the 1980s (Schmitter, 1977;

Van den Brande, 1993). During the 1980s, however, the four preconditions essential for the continuation of this cosy arrangement were exposed to severe pressure. Antwerp became the victim of its own system. The hitherto efficient method of acquiring and maintaining power became counter-productive because of a refusal to abandon outdated practices in a rapidly changing urban environment.

The financial and economic crisis

Prior to 1981 (the year in which Antwerp was merged with surrounding boroughs), Antwerp had the right to borrow money on both the national and international capital markets. This gave the city the ability to finance essential investment in the port. The downside included rather unorthodox accounting practices and a number of prestige projects, which ultimately gave rise to the ballooning of municipal debt. Much of this debt was not necessarily the result of irresponsible management, but due to factors over which the municipal authorities could exercise no short-term control. These included the vacating of the cities by the wealthy, migration from the city centre to the green suburbs, and competition from other ports. It was possible to compensate to some extent for such developments by new borrowing, which made it possible to meet the expectations of the population and redeem promises made to the electorate in a period of relative shortage. More generally speaking, whereas other organizations would have found it essential to take measures to conserve financial resources, municipal borrowing made it possible to put off the day of reckoning in the hope of a future change in fortune. Once the national authorities acted to suppress the right to borrow, Antwerp had to face up to the situation.

Antwerp, like many other large and medium-sized cities, was not alone in facing financial difficulties. Both the federal and the Flemish governments found themselves in a similar position, and both adopted measures aimed at achieving a balanced budget. This had serious consequences in Antwerp; for example, virtually no new public housing was built in the 1980s. Waiting lists indicated that there was still considerable demand for such housing. Antwerp's citizens, accustomed to a system of patronage and clientelism, assumed that the reason that they could not acquire a subsidized home was indifference on the part of the political classes. Government savings had other effects as well. Much-needed infrastructure and maintenance works were spread out over longer periods, postponed or simply dropped. As a result of the economies imposed by the Flemish authorities and of a strict schedule of debt repayment, the city authorities found it impossible to make essential investments. Just as significant, however, spending was concentrated in central Antwerp, and thus residents of outlying districts complained of neglect.

At the same time, Antwerp's economic engine has slowed down. A world port such as Antwerp is engaged in an unremitting, globalized, competitive war. Because of this, unemployment climbed steadily between 1980 and 1995. The decline in employment is clearly visible in the official unemployment statistics. In May 1996, roughly 13.7 per cent of Antwerp's working population was officially unemployed, which was about 2 per cent higher than the Flemish average. Add to this the jobless who are not included in the official statistics (over-55s, the part-time unemployed, etc.), and the very large number, in relative terms, of people dependent on government financial support (welfare payments), and Antwerp's economic situation looked even more grim, especially for the unskilled.

The financial recovery plan of 1990, imposed on the city of Antwerp by the Flemish Minister of Internal Affairs, also implied a reduction in the army of municipal employees and, therefore, a reduced potential for political patronage. Whereas in 1982 the city employed 14,000 people, this figure had fallen to 10,000 by 1994, a reduction of 28.6 per cent. However, it was not just municipal employment which was hit by the immense burden of debt carried by the city of Antwerp. Numerous sacred cows have been sacrificed in order to achieve the targets dictated by the balanced budget objectives. One of these has been financial support to social clubs and associations. As a result of cuts, numerous local social clubs have felt themselves to be abandoned by the city authorities. The pressure to improve returns on city property has meant that traders, private individuals and social clubs who had used their insider contacts to rent premises at extremely low rates or to use them at no cost at all were suddenly confronted with either much higher rents, adjusted to market prices, or the sale of the property. Many people were upset by this step, and some organizations even regarded it as a breach of faith. All in all, the crisis in city finances, combined with a lack of economic growth, meant that significant elements of the patronage demanded by the clientelism of Antwerp's political system were marginalized or disappeared almost entirely. The implicit contract between the coalition parties and voters was broken.

Social, political and cultural decompartmentalization

The dominance of the Church over the population, typical of rural and small-town Flanders, was never so powerful in the cities, including Antwerp. Even so, the Catholic presence in Antwerp was well organized and powerful, and had been traditionally built up around a strong network of parish organizations. Socialist organizations offered a similar picture, albeit in a somewhat less intricate structure. The territorial unit of the Socialists was the (administrative) ward, comprising several different parishes. Whereas the clergy played an essential role for the Catholic organizations, the lack of comparable state-paid workers meant that the Socialists tended to rely on the elected representatives of the party. The counterpart of the parish council, the local co-ordinating body for the Catholic compartment or political family, is the Socialist ward propaganda association. Chaired by the local elected representative, these bodies are the nexus of local activities for the Socialist family. The members include representatives of each organization belonging to the Socialist family, ranging from sports clubs to the local band, and women's organizations. The representatives of such associations in both political families generally form the middle ranks of the respective parties, whether CVP or SP. The parish council and ward propaganda associations were often the recruiting grounds for party cadres. A long period of serving political family and party would make a person eligible for election to the local council, for appointment as a trustee of one of the politicized housing associations, or for nomination to other positions in the party or political family. The system worked almost perfectly until the early 1970s. The social and cultural associations flourished. The authority of the leadership was unquestioned. The passing on of local interests and wishes up to city level via parish priest and political representatives left little to be desired. Moreover, at election time, both political families could efficiently mobilize their networks for the electoral battle (Huyse, 1987).

Such a smoothly running system of compartmentalized political families implies a form of apartheid. Not only were the public arenas in which people operated totally separate, but individuals hardly ever came into contact with persons with other ideologies, nor read the others' newspapers. Furthermore, the apartheid of the different political families was often expressed geographically as well. As a result, all lines of communication tended to remain within the political family.

However, the foundations of the compartmentalization system were to crumble with spectacular speed. In terms of social structures, this has had much to do with the social developments which have transformed the Belgian political landscape (see Swyngedouw, 1992a; b). The general rise in prosperity meant that the large middle class no longer viewed the divide between labour and capital so acutely. The generally higher level of education and training increased individual independence from political families and parties. The decline in church attendance meant that a common faith was no longer such a powerful bond in the Catholic political family. The spread of (commercial) mass communications put an end to the monopoly on information of the political families. The internal vision of the political family was replaced by a more generalized and independent interpretation of information. The decline of traditional industries also meant that the power of the old-style union movement was lost. Individualism and neo-liberalism replaced the philosophy and social-economic ideologies of the Christian and Social Democrats. Or, as Betz (1994: 33) has more broadly formulated it, 'Fragmentation and particularisation have become central features of post-industrial capitalism.' Younger, well-educated people developed post-materialist values (Inglehart, 1990). The fact that Antwerp (although no more than a medium-sized city in international terms) is the largest city in Flanders has facilitated and hastened this process.

An essential structural element in explaining the loss of the hold on the electorate of the traditional parties in the cities is the changing structure of the population. Antwerp has experienced a relatively large change in the composition of its population. In recent decades, the city has seen a flight of its inhabitants to the suburbs. By and large, these have often been young, relatively prosperous families, particularly those who lived in less favoured areas. On the other hand, Antwerp has also attracted new residents. Apart from the foreign labour recruited under official immigration plans, new-comers have included the young and economically vulnerable groups seeking the anonymity and/or excitement of city living. The lifting of the Iron Curtain has meant that East Europeans have flooded into Antwerp, where they often reside legally (on a tourist visa) but work illegally. All these people settle in the newly vacant dwellings. As a result, changing groups of residents of foreign origin and of new Belgian residents have become established, and live side by side with the shrinking and ageing group of original residents. This process has had two particular effects on the functioning of the political family system in Antwerp. First, a large proportion of residents who were formerly the middle managers of the political systems have gone. As a result, both parties and political families have lost militants and active members. Second, many Belgians moving into urban areas are either unfamiliar with the local structures of the political families, or otherwise totally uninterested in being absorbed into them. The ageing of the original inhabitants means that the life of the local parties and other politically tinged organizations has gone into a rapid decline. The age structure of the members means that these organizations and their activities have little attraction for young people, marked as they are by the typical concerns of the older people (Culturele Raad Stad Antwerpen, 1987).

The nature of social and cultural associations is changing rapidly, too. Allegiance to one or other religious, philosophical or ideological grouping is increasingly a thing of the past. The number of Christian and, especially, Socialist organizations has fallen significantly. Pluralist associations (which do not wish to be linked with any of the political families) now represent more than half of all such bodies in Antwerp. The total number of long-term active associations in the town offering their members a permanent social network is falling steadily. Simultaneously, the functions performed by the polarized organizations of the political groupings (ideological networking, communication between leaders and supporters, designation of good and evil, and so on) are dissipating.

The crumbing electoral base of the two coalition partners

Antwerp is the only reasonably large city in Flanders, and it has the most electoral weight in terms of number of electors. Any student of Antwerp's political history will know that there has always been room for political experimentation in the city. Before the war, for instance, Antwerp's voters elected a councillor whose platform included the proposed construction of a canopy over the entire city. The success of the ROSSEM[1] party in 1991 in Antwerp can be viewed as part of the same tradition. More seriously, the Flemish Nationalist Party (VU, founded in 1958), the Greens (Agalev, founded in 1979) and the VB (dating from 1978) were also born in Antwerp.

The post-war period started well for the ruling coalition. Until the early 1960s, the Socialist–Catholic coalition could count on a comfortable electoral majority, ranging from between 74 and 85 per cent of the total poll. The period 1960 to 1975 saw the balance being slowly undermined, and the coalition's share of the poll dropped to about 65 per cent, largely the result of the declining popularity of the Catholic partner. The turning-point came in 1982, when Antwerp merged with its outlying boroughs. In that year's elections, the coalition managed to win only 53.6 per cent of the vote. Agalev (the Green Party, an acronym for *Anders gaan leven* – a different way of life) entered the city council with 7.3 per cent of the vote. However, the VB joined the council as well, having won 5.2 per cent of the vote. The numerous small extreme right groups in Antwerp played an important role in this first success, just as they had in the establishment of the VB in Antwerp. Their existence can be largely explained by the fact that many ex-collaborators sought the anonymity of the only large and uniformly Flemish city during the repression which followed the liberation in 1945. They and their successors were brought together by Karel Dillen in 1978, the founder of the VB, who had played an important role in many of these groups in the post-war period.

Things then went from bad to worse for the ruling coalition. In the municipal elections of 1988, it won only 48.8 per cent of the vote, while in 1994 it could only muster 35.6 per cent of the poll. In the same period, Agalev gained first 9.2 per cent and then 13 per cent of the vote. However, it was the VB which took the majority of the lost votes. From being the smallest party in 1982, it rose to third largest in 1988 (17.7 per cent) and became the largest party of all in 1994 with 28 per cent. The results of municipal elections in Antwerp since 1945 are illustrated in Figure 6.1.

Despite its declining success at the polls, the CVP–SP coalition carried on business as usual until 1992–3. The more or less proportional voting system employed for municipal elections (Imperiali) meant that the large parties win comparatively more seats. Even with only 48.8 per cent of the votes in 1988, the coalition was able to cling on to a narrow majority. The result was

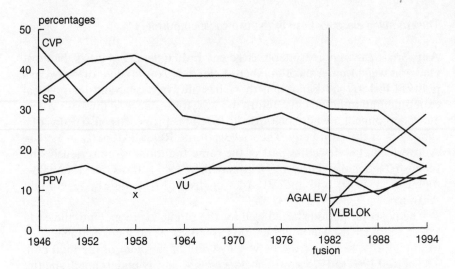

Figure 6.1 Results; Municipal Elections, City of Antwerp 1946–94. CVP: Catholic Party; SP: Social Democrats; Agalev: Green Party; VB: *Vlaams Blok*; PVV: Liberal Party. VU: Flemish Nationalist Party. *x*: merger of lists *Liberale Actie* and *Lilaer-Liberalen*; *: same percentage for CVP and VU because of merger into the list 'ANTW94'.
Source: Official election results.

that the authority of burgomaster (mayor) and aldermen (those, together with the *burgomaster*, elected by the city council into the executive power) tumbled to a historic low. The councillors (members of the city council) and aldermen representing the coalition partners now had the power to hold the coalition to ransom. If a councillor was dissatisfied, even on very personal matters, he or she could threaten not to support the coalition in council. As a result, important matters were delayed for months and sometimes for years. Disputes between the coalition partners – and worse still, within each party – grew apace. Sometimes it was enough for one alderman to be in favour of a proposal for another to oppose it. All forecasters were agreed that the coalition partners would be severely punished at the next round of municipal elections in 1994.

The fallout from the 1991 national elections was, of course, felt in Antwerp as well. At these elections, the VB reaped success by capturing almost 10 per cent of the vote. Spurred on by its party chairman, Guy Verhofstadt, the Liberal Party, or PVV, reinvented itself as the VLD, or Free Liberal Democrats. The name change as such is not significant; what is important is the fact that neo-liberal ideas about society and the economy gained the upper hand in the party. Hitherto, the Liberals had stood for vague liberal views of society and political clientelism, whereas the party's new programme was aimed at cutting back the 'profitariat', seen as the unions, mutual health insurance societies, welfare organizations of the Christian and Socialist parties, or in other words all the organizations making up the formal structure of the compartmentalized political families (Verhofstadt, 1991; 1992). To bring this about, however, the VLD needed to become the largest party in Flanders, which would have guaranteed it a place in the national coalition government. Verhofstadt's initial strategy was an attempt to absorb the VU, itself faced with declining returns over several elections and apparently heading for political extinction. After the failure of this initial strategy, an offensive was launched which was aimed at encouraging individual VU, CVP and SP representatives to join the VLD. Several representatives did in fact take the plunge, including a CVP councillor in Antwerp. Shortly afterwards, an SP councillor in Antwerp moved to the *Vlaams Blok* – to quote him, 'in the footsteps of his electors'. The SP–CVP coalition thus no longer had a working majority in Antwerp after being in power for over seventy years. In December 1992, the VU joined the CVP and SP in a new coalition, which served out the rest of the term until the end of 1994.

As elsewhere in Europe, it appeared that Antwerp's political and union bosses had been deeply involved in corruption, financial malpractice, and other shady business (Hunter, 1996). There was considerable disquiet when some of Antwerp's leading politicians – from the CVP, SP and VLD – were accused, rightly or otherwise, of taking part in a false invoice swindle, which may or may not have had to do with financing their respective parties. The already threadbare credibility of Antwerp's Socialist movement was affected deeply when it turned out that one of the Socialist trade unions had been paying its personnel very significant sums of undeclared money, drawn from the contributions paid by its members. Articles appearing in the press insinuated in the vaguest wording – since, so far, nothing has been proven – that some of the top politicians and members of the Socialist Party were involved in prostitution and financial malpractice. Another affair was linked to an insurance company of the Socialist political family. Also, three top politicians of the SP's French-speaking counterpart, the PS (*Parti Socialiste*), were forced to resign after being accused of corruption. Furthermore, for the first time in Belgium's history, a leading Socialist politician was murdered in the city of Liège. The murder remains unsolved, but it would appear that it was linked to fraud and a settling of accounts within the PS. In addition, a CVP minister in the federal government was accused of corruption in an important and unsuccessful environmental project; the VLD was hit by an armaments purchase scandal; the CVP was involved in a subsidy fraud; and so on.

Whether these insinuations and accusations had any real substance is essentially irrelevant, for, as the October 1994 municipal elections approached, there was a general feeling that at least some of the traditional politicians were either unreliable (switching from one party to another without resigning their seats) or corrupt (an even more startling bribery affair, relating to the purchase of helicopters from Augusta, was to emerge in 1995).

New policy challenges and the ruling parties

In the former ruling coalition parties, the middle tier of membership had virtually ceased to exist. The few remaining representatives of the middle tier are nearly all elderly. The younger generation (below 40) is almost entirely absent. Outreach programmes aimed at the young had a livelier existence on paper than in reality. The formerly smoothly running party propaganda machines, which had made widespread use of volunteer workers, are now struggling. Professional consultants and paid 'volunteers' must now be mobilized to get the electoral message across. Furthermore, there is an overall process of gerontification at work in both the Christian and the Socialist parties. Party congresses called to discuss policy platforms are virtually ignored by ordinary party supporters. The loss of membership on both sides is considerable, although the number of card-carrying supporters remains relatively high because of the many officials and schoolteachers in city and public schools who are obliged to be members if they are to have any chance of promotion. Action groups, and so on, no longer have their roots in the political families. Apart from the absence of party activists, this has much to do with party activities in general, which have entirely failed to keep pace with the needs of the new, better-educated generation. In the past, a sort of unwritten contract existed between party leaders and their supporters, under which the rank and file gave leaders their votes and unqualified support in exchange for the defence of their interests. However, defining exactly what these interests were was the exclusive task and duty of the leaders. The functioning of the SP and CVP in Antwerp is to a large extent still based on this contract. Party positions are worked out behind closed doors, and these will, usually without the explicit approval of the various sections of the party, determine party policy. Critics of this procedure and of the positions adopted are pushed aside. This way of proceeding has little or no attraction for younger, better-educated people. As a result, the social composition of the two parties bears only a minimal resemblance to the social composition of Antwerp's population as a whole. This, in turn, helps to explain why old procedures have survived and why the current generation of party chiefs have remained in office. An ever-diminishing group of party activists, imbued with party tradition, continue to work ever more closely in accordance with these practices.

At this juncture, it is important not to forget a highly relevant aspect specific to the situation in Antwerp: the 1982 merger of the city with the surrounding boroughs. As Antwerp merged with the boroughs of Ekeren, Merksem, Borgerhout, Deurne, Berchem, Wilrijk and Hoboken, an administrative entity of almost half a million inhabitants was created. At a stroke, the population lost seven burgomasters, seven sets of aldermen and seven councils. At the same time, seven centres of political patronage (the seven borough halls) were eliminated as the municipalities merged with the city of Antwerp. Of the 294 council seats prior to the merger, only 55 were left.[2] Whereas in the past, most of the population could say that a councillor lived just round the corner, most of the new councillors were now relatively distant figures. It was not just the general population who had difficulty coming to terms with the merger; the political parties also found it a bitter pill. What came to be known as 'districtism' – that is, the stressing of the specific qualities of the local district (the former boroughs) and the more satisfactory functioning of the independent municipalities compared to the big city – continued to be a subject of lively debate both inside and outside party circles.

All these elements meant that the compartmental political families and the parties lost their hold over the electorate and lost touch with the population. Three crucial problem issues then emerged, against this background: the urban environment and urban renewal; the problems of Belgians and members of ethnic minorities (so-called migrants) living side-by-side; and the law-and-order issue, or the problem of the Antwerp police force.

The municipal authorities had failed to create even a hint of a policy on urban renewal. Nothing at all was done to halt the flight from the city of Antwerp, which, according to the city's own studies, was due largely to the lack of open space and greenery. Those residents who were left behind blamed the authorities for doing little or nothing to help their locality meet existing needs. If there was any urban development policy at all, it was concentrated on isolated operations in the town centre, with streets and squares being spruced up and pedestrianized to attract cafés, restaurants and shops. Residents accused the authorities of allowing buildings to decay, or of simply neglecting to maintain them and, above all, of failing to keep the streets and public spaces clean.

Like many other cities, Antwerp also had to cope with the increasing pressure of traffic. But, unlike some other cities, the city authorities simply provided more space to adapt the city to car traffic. The only achievement in terms of public transport was the construction in the 1970s and 1980s of an extensive underground light-train network. This lay virtually unused until 1994, but the construction works were a constant source of traffic jams and delays. Bus drivers had to go on strike before the authorities were prepared to start fining drivers who parked in the reserved bus lanes, and begin removing their vehicles. Outside the rush hour, travelling from one side of the old town to the other by public transport could easily take an hour or more, while the same trip by car hardly takes fifteen minutes. Bicycle paths were scarce, and those which did exist were often used for uncontrolled illegal parking. Public transport and traffic insecurity were consequently the items near the top of agenda of local meetings with policy-makers.

The total absence of an urban planning and development strategy led a group of Antwerp residents to establish a non-profit organization called *Stad aan de Stroom* (City and the River) with the aim of revitalizing some of the totally neglected urban areas bordering the River Scheldt. The populations of these neighbourhoods, who had been closely consulted during the planning process, came to expect great things of the renovation process. The disappointment was considerable, then, when in mid-1992 it became clear that the city was no longer prepared to support the project and that nothing was to come of the proposed urban renewal plans. This disappointment came on top of the fiasco of the so-called renovation areas. In the period 1982–90, the city authorities had been talking at length with residents in declining areas about the renewal of their districts, but it now turned out that the resources promised by the Flemish authorities were to be minimal.

Population movement to the suburbs, with the neglected central districts slowly being abandoned for the green municipalities in the Greater Antwerp area, had another effect. The relatively cheap homes and low rents available were gradually taken over by migrants from Morocco and Turkey. These people had been attracted to Belgium and to Antwerp in the prosperous 1960s and 1970s as guest workers. Their visibly different lifestyle and demonstrative presence on the streets, the latter in part because the homes occupied by the usually large families were relatively small, gave the impression that they were more numerous than they actually were. In fact, they represented only a small percentage of the population, recently estimated at 6.3 per cent of the total.[3] However, they are concentrated in certain districts, including Borgerhout, central Antwerp and Hoboken. In 1987, the year before the VB breakthrough in Antwerp, they represented respectively 9.2 per cent, 6.6 per cent and 5.2 per cent of the population in these districts, the highest percentages for all eight city districts. Even in the mid-1990s, it was not true to say that there were American or even French-style ghettos in Antwerp. In 1994,[4] Turks and Moroccans represented 15.9 per cent of the total population of Borgherhout, the district with the highest number of Muslim residents. Their demographic profile, consisting of many young children and adolescents, contrasts sharply with that of the Belgians living in the same districts, most of whom are middle-aged or older, a situation which can give rise to age-related conflicts. They compete here with working-class and lower middle-class Belgians for jobs and resources. Unemployment is much higher in these areas than the city average (Marynissen *et al.*, 1988). The difficulty migrants have in renting homes, largely as a result of discrimination, has encouraged them to buy their own houses. Belgians and migrants therefore find themselves competing at the bottom end of the housing market. The pressure from the national authorities to use objective criteria when allocating subsidized housing has meant that migrants, because of their (larger) families, lower wages and higher unemployment (a result of the discriminatory operation of the labour market), tend to qualify for housing before the often childless Belgians. This gives Belgian applicants for subsidized housing the impression that the newcomers are receiving favourable treatment. Other processes to note apply where, with the arrival of migrants in a district, shops, restaurants, tea houses and cafés open to cater for, for example, Turkish and Moroccan tastes. The fall in the number of (native) Belgians has meant too that considerable numbers of 'Belgian' shops, restaurants and cafés have had to shut (see Swyngedouw, 1992c).

Following the 1982 electoral campaign, the Young Socialists warned Antwerp's newly elected burgomaster of the negative attitudes of the population and of SP voters in certain wards towards guest workers. However, coalition policy consisted of ignoring social tensions as much as possible in the hope that they would go away. After all, the VU had grown in size and power, and then started to fade away without affecting the coalition. Had the coalition parties not proved able to see off or to absorb new entrants and their issues? The VB's success in Antwerp in the 1987 national elections served to change attitudes. Apart from a strategic 'low-profile' policy, plus the occasional statement of intent about integration, and the rights and, more particularly, the duties of migrants, this change was marked only by the coalition's introduction of a special corps of police officers trained to resolve friction between migrants and native Belgians – consequently they were instantly dubbed the 'friction police'. In the 1988 local elections, the VB increased its vote by 12.5 per cent in the commune of Antwerp and won 10 of the 55 seats on the city council. This factor, together with the coalition's electoral decline, signalled the start of municipal 'trial and error' policies. Modest investment programmes were implemented for the wards where the coalition lost the most votes. Money from the Flemish authorities was used to establish a social programme. In line with the coalition's habits, the SP and CVP came to an agreement as to how this funding was to be shared out, in order to serve their clientelistic networks. Municipal public initiatives (SP), private Christian Democrat (CVP) initiatives, Freemason (SP) ones and a few pluralist initiatives (private but without links to one of the parties) were launched in order to help integrate underprivileged native Belgians and migrants. No coherent policy was developed in this way. At best, these initiatives would exist in isolation, but in the worst cases the different initiatives became competitors.

After 1988, law and order became a big issue in Antwerp. Year after year, the coalition partners and the VB would dispute the implications of crime statistics. This would typically involve questions concerning the more efficient functioning of the city and state police, and the greater willingness of citizens to report minor offences. The debate would then be wound up usually by speculative questions about whether (young) migrants (albeit second-generation and born in Belgium) were more involved in street crime because of their foreign origin or because of their social status. Of course, the local press gave considerable attention to these debates, and the local population was convinced that urban crime was rising and that migrant and illegal residents were primarily responsible for this. New problems (youth vandalism, racial tensions, petty street crime, and so on) emerged in the more socially deprived districts of the city. The efficiency of the city police in the struggle against crime was closely scrutinized by the press and the public. Significantly, every member of this police force, with only one exception, was a Belgian native. Moreover, it was speculated that a large percentage of the force were either sympathetic to or supporters of the extreme right *Vlaams Blok* party. What is clear is that the morale in the police force was low. Furthermore, with the 1994 municipal elections approaching, the coalition was confronted with the police force partially on strike and a local population dissatisfied with its functioning.

The strategy of the *Vlaams Blok*

The founding of the *Vlaams Blok* in the late 1970s by Karel Dillen was the result of a successful merger of small extreme right-wing groups. Outside the democratic Flemish nationalist party, the *Volksunie* (People's Union), Flemish nationalism of the extreme right-wing variety continued to thrive in numerous small organizations. These ranged from the paramilitary *Vlaamse Militanten Orde* (VMO, Order of Flemish Militants) to the more intellectual and ideological *Were di*, from associations of Eastern Front veterans (soldiers who had fought for the Nazis in Russia) and former collaborators to the *Vlaams Nationalistisch Jeugdverbond*, a youth movement. Most of these organizations were established in the period between 1946 and 1965. Dillen played a leading role in virtually all of these, thus winning their confidence, despite the persistence of internal rivalries. Also important, many of those accused or suspected of wartime collaboration subsequently left the countryside to seek the relative anonymity of the only relatively large monoglot city in Flanders, Antwerp. They provided financial and other support for the *Vlaams Blok* in its early years. Up until the municipal elections of 1982, the *Vlaams Blok* had only one elected representative (Dillen) in the chamber, and in the 1981 national elections had won 1.8 per cent of the votes in Flanders and 4.7 per cent in the canton of Antwerp. *Vlaams Blok* itself was surprised by the 1982 electoral success of its candidates in Antwerp. The two candidates elected to the city council were regarded within the party as second-rate figures. Although the main plank of the VB programme was Flemish nationalism (and the total independence of Flanders), it soon became clear that their modest success was based mainly on their anti-immigration stance, which was then rather marginal to the party's central policy. This situation changed completely with the 1988 municipal elections, when 10 the VB councillors were elected (Husbands, 1992: 137).

By 1988, the party had been restructured, particularly in Antwerp. Filip Dewinter, a leading member of the party, and from 1987 a member of the Belgian parliament, became leader of the VB faction on the Antwerp City Council. Dewinter started his political career as the leader of the *Vlaams Blok* youth. Because of his organizing talent, he was soon chosen by Dillen as a candidate for parliament. He became (and still is) the main organizer of the VB, and represents the hard-line anti-immigrant stance of the party. He organized the party in a Stalinist-like way, promoting small, active core groups in different neighbourhoods and with specialized branches – for instance, for propaganda. The party has two kinds of members, activists and paying members. Until 1989, the party depended financially on gifts from supporters and membership dues. Since 1989, state public financing has become its most important income source.

Dewinter pushed anti-immigration policies to the top of the party's agenda. Electoral support was subsequently won in various phases. At first, until about 1987, the VB aimed its agitprop activities at the most socially deprived neighbourhoods of the city. The presence of local VB activists in these areas ensured the organization of demonstrations against the presence of immigrants, protest actions against the alleged growth of local Muslim prayer houses and mosques, and the systematic blaming of migrants for crime, unemployment, and any other evils. The accusations that the city authorities were unjustly favouring the immigrants, that the traditional parties (CVP, SP, VLD and VU) were untrustworthy and corrupt, and especially that all problems (unemployment, urban decline, criminality, and so on) would be solved once the migrants were deported, were to find a sympathetic ear among the lower-class voters in these districts. Analysis of the national election results for each ward in the inner city and the Borgerhout district for 1985 and 1987 (Swyngedouw, 1989) revealed that the VB was achieving its best results and making the most progress in these underprivileged districts. Indeed, the VB was achieving between 20 and 30 per cent of the vote in these areas. In fact, there is a close relationship between the VB's results and the presence or otherwise of guest workers, but this yardstick cannot be applied to all wards. Old or run-down housing, poor residential amenities, numerous vacancies (untenanted houses), high levels of unemployment among the active population, many people dependent on subsistence payments from social welfare agencies and other government channels: these were characteristics of the wards where the VB now prospered.

The municipal elections of 1988 saw the start of the second phase of the VB activity, with the party notably extending its reach. The party's efforts were transferred, at least in part, to more prosperous areas of Antwerp. The VB still continued to do best in the most deprived wards, although it is striking how areas which were typically Liberal (PVV) now tended to support the VB. The European elections of 1989 saw this trend confirmed, with the VB achieving 20.3 per cent in the city of Antwerp. Compared with 1987 and 1988, the PVV suffered severe losses in its traditional electoral heartlands. Whilst the PVV polled between 26.5 and 31 per cent in 1987, it achieved only between 20.1 and 23.5 per cent in 1989. The losses suffered by the SP were even greater. In typical SP wards, losses rose to between 5 and 10 per cent. Here, too, the VB picked up many votes (Swyngedouw, 1990: 425). Working from its bridgeheads in the poorest wards of the city, the VB was able to build its support systematically in the more prosperous parts of town.

The national elections of 1991 saw the breakthrough of the VB outside Antwerp. From 3 per cent in 1987 and 6.3 per cent in 1989, the VB jumped to 10.3 per cent in 1991 in Flanders overall, going up to 12.2 per cent in 1995. For the city of Antwerp, the corresponding figures were 10.1 per cent (1987), 17.7 per cent (1988 municipal elections) and 25.5 per cent (1991), and 28 per cent in the municipal elections of 1994. In the national elections of 1995, the VB had its first setback in Antwerp, polling 26.7 per cent of the votes in the city. The party's gains were concentrated in the areas around Antwerp and along the long-standing linear concentrations of industry between Antwerp and Brussels and between Antwerp and Ghent, again confirming the above trend. In some of the most deprived wards of Antwerp, the VB received a huge 40 to 50 per cent of the votes.

Since 1989, the VB has used its finances to establish a broad-based propaganda machine (including quarterly regional publications and a monthly party magazine), and to organize conferences and one-day seminars. At these gatherings, party activists expound their vision of society and apply it to virtually every aspect of life, ranging from subjects such as espousing an anti-European Union stance, to anti-abortion viewpoints and to strong law-and-order proposals. In the period 1989-94, the VB and subordinate party organizations, such as the *Vlaams Blok Jongeren* (youth), organized no fewer than thirteen conferences and colloquia, compared to just six in the period from its foundation in 1979 to 1987 (Spruyt, 1995). A coherent neo-corporatist ideology has also been developed and is shared by the hard-core party militants and the leadership.

The VB essentially maintains that people are not the same or equal. The most common distinction between people made by the VB is on the basis of their cultural or ethnic origins. However, the VB rarely allows itself to support a distinction on a purely biological (racial) basis. The racism of the VB is thus primarily cultural. The VB principle of 'fundamental natural inequality between communities' (Principles) implies, however, an ethnic hierarchy in which the Flemings are at the top, with Dutch and Afrikaners (South Africa) immediately below them, as members of the same people, sharing the same language and culture. Next down the hierarchy, and still more or less equal, are the assimilated (French-speaking) Flemings of Brussels, Wallonia and French Flanders (an area in the north of France). These people, according to the VB, live in 'occupied territory'. These groups are followed by European foreigners. At the bottom come the non-European foreigners, who share neither the language, the territory nor the ethnic background of the Flemings.

The social views of the VB are drawn directly from the authoritarian theories of the 1930s and take the form of 'solidarism'. Historically, the solidarism of the VB is linked to the solidaristic corporatism of Mussolini. In the VB's view, society is structured upon an organic solidarism. This implies that whoever 'truly experiences natural ethnic commitment' will reject the class system and the class struggle, and will opt instead for the 'required solidarity of all with all in the community', 'a solidarity between employer and employee, of all occupations with one another' (Principles). For the VB, solidarism is a sort of third way between the exploitative capitalism of liberal economies and coercive communist systems. Consequently, as far as the VB is concerned, the ethnic community takes absolute precedence over the individual.

VB voters are familiar with only a few of the most striking themes of the party: anti-immigration, opposition to the traditional parties and their 'corruption', and an independent Flanders. Moreover, only the first two really influence VB voters. This situation is a result of strategic choices made by the leadership, which presents the VB as a 'new' party without any political past, and avoids any overt association with the 'New Order' of the 1930s, wartime collaboration, or with the extreme right (paramilitary) organizations of the 1960s and 1970s. Even though many VB officials have their roots in such organizations, the public image of the VB politician is now of a respectable, well-dressed individual, who argues for the 'true' interests of the Flemish people.

The peak: the municipal elections of 24 October 1994 in Antwerp

Unsurprisingly, all eyes were on Antwerp during the 1994 municipal elections. The main question was whether the VB would be capable of ousting the existing coalition or if it could be kept out of any new coalition. Unfavourable opinion polls led the traditional parties to try to convince voters that their apparatus had been (at least partly) overhauled. The CVP and VU entered into a pre-election pact under the name 'Antwerpen '94'. Several aldermen and councillors were not included on this electoral list and were replaced, including by a popular former federal minister, and by the controversial but well-known organizer of the 1993 Antwerp Cultural City of Europe event. The Liberal Democrats (VLD) spearheaded their electoral list with the son of a famous Christian Democrat politician from

Antwerp, who was their candidate for burgomaster, and also persuaded a prominent leading businessman to stand for them. The Greens (Agalev) put up one of their national heavyweights as candidate for burgomaster and included candidates who had formerly supported the SP and extreme left parties. The SP decided to stick with its traditional candidates but, like Agalev and Antwerpen '94, added to its list several Belgians of Turkish and Moroccan origin. That the electoral market had been opened up was emphasized by the fact that some eighteen parties now sought election to Antwerp City Council. Significantly, the 1994 elections were the first local elections to be subject to legal limitations on campaign spending. This, of course, had most effect on financially powerful parties such as the VLD, CVP, VU and SP, which all suffered effective limitations on their campaign expenditure. Parties which were able to count on the volunteer services of their supporters thus benefited from the new situation. The campaign focused around two key themes. First, there was the standing of the current burgomaster, a member of the SP. Controversy about his personality and policies was exploited by the VB to explain everything that had gone wrong in Antwerp. As a result, electoral opinion became divided for or against the burgomaster. The other main issue concerned migrants and illegal residents, and was linked to law-and-order matters – the VB's favourite theme, and the big issue of these elections. The VB and Agalev came to represent the two poles, the first standing for 'Migrants go home', the second proclaiming 'Migrants at home here'. The VLD approached the immigration issue in terms of 'compulsory integration' and law and order.

The VB concentrated on Antwerp in the hope of creating a situation in which it would be impossible to construct a coalition without itself, thus lancing the 'cordon sanitaire' which had so far barred its way to office. The VB won 28.5 per cent of the vote and 18 of the 55 seats on Antwerp's city council. The net result was that virtually all the other parties that won seats on the city council (SP, Antwerpen '94, VLD and Agalev) now joined a broad coalition to keep out the VB. As in 1988, the 'quality' of the VB representatives was much improved: the barber being replaced by the lawyer. This is a calculated practice of the VB, which should ensure a pool of expertise and administrative skills in the year 2000, when the next municipal elections are due.

The exit poll carried out by ISPO[5] (N = 2700) on behalf of BRTN Television (the Flemish-language public service broadcaster) made it possible to identify the profile of the VB elector and to determine where the VB votes came from[6]. In short, the VB attracted electors from all sections of the population. Significantly, about 40 per cent of the electors who took part in the 1988 and 1994 municipal elections appear to have changed their voting habits. This is a remarkably high proportion compared to the 33 per cent in the landslide election of 1991, and the 16 per cent in the 1987 elections who changed allegiances (Swyngedouw and Billiet, 1988). The VB was the party with the most faithful voters, retaining 87 per cent of its 1988 electorate. The CVP and VU supporters appeared not to be tempted by the electoral pact offered by Antwerpen '94: only 42 per cent of CVP and VU 1988 voters opted for this. Also, 63 per cent, 66 per cent and 70 per cent of electors who voted for the SP, VLD and Agalev respectively at the last election voted for these parties again in 1994. Consequently, the stability of the VB's support at successive elections is remarkable.

Only the VB and Agalev appear to have any particular attraction for new voters – that is, those voting for the first time in municipal elections in 1994 (aged 18 to 25). The VB attracted roughly 30 per cent of their votes and Agalev 20 per cent. Other parties polled only 12 per cent or less of this cohort. The VB electorate can, therefore, be regarded as being young. Moreover, it appears that the polarization of the VB and Agalev around the immigration theme (VB: immigration bad, Agalev: immigration good) defined the voting patterns of the young.

The VB was able to attract voters from all other parties. As regards new VB voters in 1994, 36 per cent were former supporters of the CVP/VU list, 26 per cent former SP voters, 18 per cent had left their voting papers blank or had voted invalidly in 1988, 9 per cent were former VLD supporters, and 6 per cent had formerly voted Agalev. These results confirmed the trend in evidence at the national elections in 1991: that the CVP and SP, the traditional, mainstream parties with their compartmentalized structures, lost most to the VB, and that the small Flemish nationalist party, the VU, has lost the largest proportion of its vote to the VB. In contrast, the VB lost only a minimum of voters (not even 1 per cent) to other parties.

After controlling for other variables in the voting model, it seems that gender has no influence on the voting patterns of Antwerp voters. As for education, the VB is heavily over-represented among voters with low educational attainments (34.6 per cent)[7], and among voters with an average educational status (30.5 per cent), and severely under-represented among the better educated (17.1 per cent). As regards commitment to a faith or personal philosophy (religion, church attendance), the VB is under-represented among persons who are deeply committed, with 23.6 per cent among Catholics who regularly visit church, and only 12.3 per cent among secular humanists. On the other hand, it is over-represented among those who claim not to be committed to anything in particular (28.3 per cent) and among marginal believers (those who say that they are Catholic but who do not go to church) (30 per cent). To sum up, the lower the level of education, the more likely a person is to vote VB; the more a person is involved in formal networks of faith or philosophical outlook, the less likely he or she is to vote VB. The occupational variable is, however, the one which makes it clear why the VB has become the biggest party in Antwerp. The VB is heavily over-represented among blue-collar workers (33.2 per cent; blue-collar workers represent 22 per cent of the total Antwerp electorate), and is neither over-nor under-represented among the non-active population. This corresponds to earlier findings (Swyngedouw *et al.*, 1992). The VB is only *slightly* under-represented among white-collar workers (23.5 per cent), but is *even less slightly* under-represented among executives, the self-employed and the professions (24.7 per cent). The success of the VB in Antwerp at the 1994 municipal elections is, therefore, the result of the successful extension of its recruiting activities to white collar workers (lower-middle-class employees), and above all to (small) self-employed persons, while its supporters among blue-collar voters have remained faithful.

An explanation for this might be found in the relatively precarious social and economic position occupied by lower-middle-class employees in the 1990s, accentuated here by fear of downward mobility as a result of unemployment. The (small) self-employed person has long been confronted with falling levels of consumption; crucially, domestic (consumer) demand remains depressed because of the sense of economic insecurity among the population, and demand has failed to revive when other economic indicators have improved. Consequently, the number of business failures has steadily increased since the early 1990s. To this should, then, be added the competition (alluded to earlier) from immigrant newcomers in certain areas of Antwerp.

Conclusion

Seventy years of coalition has meant the erosion of the distinction between the centre-right CVP and the centre-left SP. The coalition partners converged with the object of pursuing a pragmatic policy of retaining and exercising power. As a result, there was room for the emergence of new parties, which have fed upon the issues and administrative problems ignored or unrecognized by the ruling coalition. For Agalev, this was the environmental question and urban planning policy; for the VB, it was immigration and law and order. The two parties are in many ways each other's mirror image: universalist versus particularist (Swyngedouw, 1993; Kitschelt, 1991, 1995). This value-orientation can be defined as the culturally normative element of a cleavage: 'a set of values and beliefs which provides a sense of identity' (Bartolini and Mair, 1990: 215). The rise of an anti-immigrant party, drawing upon xenophobic and culturally racial values (Tagüieff, 1990; Mayer and Perrineau, 1992), indicates changed social, economic and political conditions at the end of the 1980s and into the 1990s.

The relatively dramatic effect in political terms is that the clientelistic system of compartmentalized political families, providing work and subsidized housing as its primary rewards, which was for so long the foundation of the CVP–SP coalition in power, has become increasingly counterproductive owing to changes in social and economic conditions. The system can operate successfully only when the key conditions presented above apply, namely that the population is strictly compartmentalized; that the governing authority is financially strong and employment levels are sufficiently high; that flexible party machines are capable of recognizing, exploring and meeting new challenges; and that they have a sufficiently large and loyal electoral base. These key preconditions were undermined by: (a) disappearing traditions and power-sharing arrangements; (b) the false belief by the governing coalition in its power to endure despite a rapidly changing urban environment and population; (c) structural economic recession; (d) the decompartmentalization of the political families; and (e) the emergence of a multicultural society.

The likely losers in this structural transformation are young, unskilled, blue-collar workers, lower-middle-class employees and small self-employed persons. These are the categories which have sought salvation in the VB, which has offered them the simple but misleading illusion that once all the immigrants have gone, the prospects for welfare and the certainties of the past will all come flooding back. Such is the VB response, with its 'positive' message to the frustrated sections of the population. The anti-immigrant slogans, populist anti-(party) political message, combined with a well-organized party apparatus supported by convinced party activists, in the specific political and historical context of the city of Antwerp at a time of difficult social and economic transition, are the threads from which the VB has woven its web of success in Antwerp.[8]

Notes

1. ROSSEM was a populist anti-establishment party named after its founder and leader Jean-Pierre Van Rossem.
2. Calculations based on *Koninklijk Besluit tot wijziging van de rangschikking van de gemeenten, Belgisch Staatsblad*, 26 June 1976: 8591–603, as published in Anon. (1976).
3. In 1994, Antwerp had a total population of 458,725 inhabitants, 58,341 of whom were foreigners (12.7 per cent), of which 21,353 were Moroccans and 7503 were Turks (*Statistisch Jaarboek Stad Antwerpen 1994*).
4. When all foreigners are taken together (including EU subjects), there are only two wards in Antwerp where the population of foreigners approaches one-third of the total. In these wards, Moroccans and Turks alone represent 23 per cent and 27 per cent of the population respectively (*Statistische Jaarboek Stad Antwerpen 1994*).
5. ISPO: Interuniversity Centre for Political Opinion Research, University of Leuven, Department of Sociology. The results of the BRTN Television exit poll were calculated by Marc Swyngedouw and Roeland Beerten.
6. This analysis was made using a multivariate log-linear logit model. The logit parameters were then converted to proportions, using the Kaufman and Schervish (1986) model. The estimated proportions are net effects for the relevant variables after checking the other variables in the model. The dependent variable is voting behaviour (including the blank/invalid option). The independent variables are gender, age, occupation, philosophical commitment,

education, subjective financial situation and trade union membership. The analysis of the shifts in voting behaviour between the municipal elections in 1988 and 1994 was made on the basis of a modified log-linear 'mover–stayer' model on the relevant transition table (see Swyngedouw, 1987).

7. It should be noted that for analytical purposes, and in contrast to the official counting method, blank and invalid votes are regarded as a valid form of voting behaviour (amounting here to 5.4 per cent). This means that in the model, compared to the official results, all the parties have slightly lower results. The result for the VB is then 26.5 per cent.

8. The VB's success continued in June 1999 when – benefiting from issues of state/ political incompetence, corruption and a major food health scandal – the party made significant gains in national, European and regional elections. In elections to the Flemish Regional Council, for instance, the VB won 15.5 per cent (12.3 per cent in 1995) and 20 seats (15 in 1995). In the Euro-elections, the party achieved 9.4 per cent (7.8 per cent in 1994), retaining its 2 MEPs, while in the national legislative elections an increased return (9.9 against 7.8 per cent in 1995) earned it four extra seats (15 against 11 in 1995). In the City of Antwerp, moreover, up to almost 30 per cent of electors were now voting for the *Vlaams Blok*. (Editor's note. Source: Minister of the Interior (Belgium); *The Economist*, 19 June 1999).

References

Anon (1976) 'Nieuwe rangschikking gemeenten na samenvorming: aantal raadsleden en schepenen' *Gemeente en Provincie* 30, 4–5.

Bartolini, S. and Mair, P. (1990) *Identity, Competition and Electoral Availability: The Change of European Electorates 1885–1985*. Cambridge: Cambridge University Press.

Betz, G.-H. (1994) *Radical Right-Wing Populism in Western Europe*. Basingstoke: Macmillan.

Culturele Raad Stad Antwerpen (Antwerp Cultural Council) (1987) *Grondslagen voor een cultuurbeleid*. Antwerpn: CRSA-UIA.

De Wever, B. (1992) 'Vlag, groet en leider: geschiedenis van het Vlaams Nationalistisch Verbond 1933–1945'. Ph.D. thesis, University of Ghent.

Hunter, M. (1996) 'Europe's Reborn Right', *New York Times Magazine*, 21 April 1996.

Husbands, C. (1992) 'Belgium: Flemish Legions on the March', in Hainsworth, P. (ed.) *The Extreme Right in Europe and the USA*. London: Pinter.

Huyse, L. (1987) *De gewapende vrede: politiek in België na 1945*. Leuven: Kritak.

Ignazi, P. (1992) 'The silent counter-revolution: hypotheses on the emergence of extreme right-wing parties in Europe', *European Journal of Political Research* 22(1), 3–34.

Inglehart, R. (1990) *Culture Shift in Advanced Industrial Society*. Princeton, NJ: Princeton University Press.

Kaufman, R. L. and Schervish, P. G. (1986) 'Using adjusted crosstabulation to interpret log-linear relationships', *American Sociological Review* 51, 717–33.

Kitschelt, H. (1991) *The Logics of Party Formation: Ecological Politics in Belgium and West Germany*. Ithaca, NY: Cornell University Press.

Kitschelt, H. (1995) *The Radical Right in Western Europe: A Comparative Analysis*. Ann Arbor: University of Michigan Press.

Marynissen, R., Poppe, E., Jacobs, T. and Van Hove, E. (1988) *Kansarmoede in de grootstad Antwerpen, Deel 2: De bewoners*. Brussels and Antwerpn: Koning Boudewijstichting – UIA.

Mayer, N. and Perrineau, P. (1992) 'Why do they vote for Le Pen?', *European Journal of Political Research* 22, 123–41.

Schmitter, P. (1977) 'Corporatism and policy-making in contemporary Western Europe', *Comparative Political Studies* 10(1), 1–152.

Spruyt, M. (1995) *Grove Borstels: stel dat het Vlaams Blok morgen zijn programma realiseert, hoe zou Vlaanderen er dan uitzien?* Leuven: Uitgeverij Van Halewyck.

Statistisch Jaarboek Stad Antwerpen 1994. Antwerpn: Stad Antwerpen.

Swyngedouw, M. (1987) 'A pilot study of Portuguese electoral shifts 1976–1982', *Quality and Quantity: European – American Journal of Methodology* 21, 153–75.

Swyngedouw, M. (1989) *De keuze van de kiezer: naar een verbetering van schattingen van verschuivingen en partijvoorkeur bij opeenvolgende verkiezingen en peilingen*. Leuven and Rotterdam: SOI/BMG.

Swyngedouw, M. (1990) 'Verkiezingen in Antwerpen: het Vlaams Blok, islamitische minderheden en kansarmoede' *Tijdschrift voor Sociologie*, Special issue. De nieuwe Vlamingen, No. 5–6, 401–30.

Swyngedouw, M. (1992a) 'National Elections in Belgium: The Breakthrough of Extreme Right in Flanders', *Regional Politics and Policy* 2(3), 62–75.

Swyngedouw, M. (1992b) 'L'essor d'Agalev et du *Vlaams Blok*', *Courrier Hebdomadaire du CRISP*, No. 1362, Brussels.

Swyngedouw, M. (1992c) *Waar voor je waarden: de opkomst van Vlaams Blok en Agalev in de jaren tachtig*. Leuven: ISPO/SOI.

Swyngedouw, M. (1993) 'Nieuwe breuklijnen in de vlaamse politiek? De politieke ruimte van de 18 tot 65-jarige Vlaamse Kiezer na de verkiezingen van 24 november 1991', in Swyngedouw, M., Billiet, J., Carton, A. and Beerten, R. (eds) *Kiezen is verliezen: onderzoek naar de politieke oprattingen van Vlamingen*. Leuven and Amersfoort: Acco.

Swyngedouw, M. and Billiet, J. (1988) 'Stemmen in Vlaanderen op 13 december 1987', *Res Publica* 30(1), 20–50.

Swyngedouw, M., Billiet, J. and Carton, A. (eds) (1992) 'Van waar komen ze, wie zijn ze? Stemgedrag en verschuivingen op 24 november 1991', *ISPO-Bulletin* (Leuven), Vol. 1992/3, 45.

Tagüieff, P. A. (1990) *La force du préjugé: essai sur le racisme et ses doubles*. Paris: La Découverte.

Van den Brande, A. (1993) 'Machtslogica's, waardenoriëntatie en kiesgedrag: een poging tot sociologische verklaring', in Swyngedouw, M., Billiet, J., Carton, A. and Beerten, R. (eds) *Kiezen is verliezen: onderzoek naar de politieke opvattingen van Vlamingen*. Leuven and Amersfoort: Acco.

Verhofstadt, G. (1991) *Het Burgermanifest*. Brussels: PVV.

Verhofstadt, G. (1992) *De weg naar de politieke vernieuwing, Het Tweede Burgermanifest*. Antwerpn: Hadewych.

Vlaams Blok (n.d.) *Grondbeginselen* (Principles): *manifest van het rechtse Vlaams nationalisme*. Brussels: Vlaams Blok.

CHAPTER SEVEN

The Netherlands: explaining the limited success of the extreme right

Cas Mudde and Joop Van Holsteyn

Introduction

The third wave of right-wing extremism in West Europe, which started in the early 1980s (von Beyme, 1988), did not pass the Netherlands by. This chapter deals with the Dutch manifestation of extreme right parties, most notably its main representative, the *Centrumdemocraten* (Centre Democrats, CD). In the following three sections, a portrait of this party is presented, describing its history, organization and ideology, and electorate. The last section will discuss the limited success of the extreme right in the Netherlands, compared to that of equivalent parties in countries like Austria, Belgium and France.

History of extreme right parties in the Netherlands

Though the Netherlands has a long history as a (semi-) sovereign state, within its current borders it has existed only since 1830 (see Kossmann, 1978). In that year, the country lost its southern part to the new state of Belgium. Unlike the situation in the Dutch-speaking part of Belgium, this did not give way to a significant 'revanchist' movement in the Netherlands. Aspirations for a Greater Netherlands (or *Diets*) were not strong within the Dutch population. As far as there were any 'nationalist' sentiments, they were focused upon the colonies (such as Surinam and especially Indonesia).

During the inter-war years, the Netherlands experienced a plethora of extreme right organizations (see De Jonge, 1982; Zaal, 1973). Most of these were groups of only a few people, sometimes publishing amateurish-looking papers, but hardly ever with any significant influence on political life. With

144

Mussolini's coup in Italy in 1922, several new groups emerged in the Netherlands, such as the *Verbond van Actualisten* (Association of Actualists, VVA) and the *Algemeene Nederlandsche Fascisten Bond* (General Dutch Fascists' Association, ANFB), openly calling themselves fascist despite their often different ideology, or even lack of fascist ideology. These groups always remained sectarian, and never contested elections with any success. A new impetus to the Dutch extreme right was provided by the rise to power of Hitler's *Nationalsozialistische Deutsche Arbeiter Partei* (German National Socialist Workers' Party, NSDAP) in the 1930s. Many former fascist organizations and activists now transformed themselves into National Socialists. However, the extreme right camp was highly fragmented by internal strife, caused by personal rather than ideological animosities. At one time, there were no fewer than five different organizations with the name *Nationaal-Socialistische Nederlandsche Arbeiders-Partij* (Dutch Nationalist Socialist Workers' Party, NSNAP), none of them with any substantial following (see De Jonge, 1979, 1982).

The only extreme right organization that experienced some electoral success during the inter-war years was the *Nationaal Socialistische Beweging* (National Socialist Movement, NSB), founded in December 1931 (see De Jonge, 1979; Meyers, 1984). Despite the party's name, the NSB founder and leader, Anton Mussert, was not a devoted follower of Hitler. Rather opportunistically, he was attracted to the combination of the terms 'national' and 'socialist', without knowing what the German version of Nazism really meant; he also wanted to avoid the label 'fascist', because there were so many fascist parties already (Meyers, 1984: 63–4). Though in part a translation of the NSDAP programme, the NSB programme did not contain some of the more typical National Socialist features, most notably racism and anti-semitism, and therefore rather resembled the other (non-Nazi) fascist programmes of that time. Unlike the other extreme right *groupuscules*, however, the NSB was able to attract both members and voters. Within three years it had 21,000 members, and two years later it reached its peak of 52,000. Moreover, the first time it contested an election, in the provincial election of April 1935, the party secured an average of almost 8 per cent of the votes (with significant regional differences; see Kooy, 1964; Von der Dunk, 1982). Nevertheless, the success evaporated quickly: in the parliamentary election of 1937, the NSB gained only 4.2 per cent of the votes. This was followed by a severe drop in membership, which fell back to less than 30,000 before the German invasion of the Netherlands in May 1940.

Under the German occupation, the NSB became, in 1941, the only legal political party in the Netherlands, and its membership increased to around 100,000 at its height. The Germans rewarded the party with most positions of mayor as well as offices in the police, judicial system and media. Thousands of NSB members joined the *Nederlandsche SS* (Dutch SS), mainly fighting in the *Westland* division (alongside Flemish volunteers) on the Eastern Front. At the same time, the party itself was internally divided between the *Diets* camp of Mussert and the *Deutsch* camp of Meinoud Rost van Tonningen. Whereas Mussert had hoped for a sovereign Greater Netherlands within a National Socialist Europe dominated by Germany, Rost van Tonningen fully supported the Netherlands' inclusion in the Greater German Reich. This internal strife was noted by the German Nazi leadership, which generally supported Rost van Tonningen (who was especially backed by Himmler), though without ousting Mussert.

After World War II, most people in the Netherlands were determined that fascism and Nazism should never return. The exiled Dutch queen, Wilhelmina, had made it clear that there would be no place for traitors in the future, referring primarily to NSB members. In the post-war climate, therefore, it was very hard for people with extreme right sympathies or opinions to organize or speak out openly. Only a few such organizations emerged, but all were minuscule and tried to pose as social rather than political organizations.[1] When, in the early 1950s, a political party was founded that resembled the pre-war NSB in ideology and even in name (*Nationaal Europese Sociale Beweging*, National European Social Movement, NESB), it was banned (Van Donselaar, 1991: 51–79).

Not until the early 1970s was the extreme right able to make its comeback on the Dutch political stage. In March 1971, the *Nederlandse Volks-Unie* (Dutch People's Union, NVU) was founded (see Bouw *et al.*, 1981). In its first three years of existence, the party was unknown to the general public and preoccupied with internal struggles. In 1974, though, Joop Glimmerveen's openly racist, aggressive local election campaign in The Hague provoked much negative publicity. The NVU did not win a seat on the city council, but its name was firmly established, as was the position of Glimmerveen as new party leader. However, the NVU had to pay a price for its radical, aggressive campaign and for later provocative actions. In fact, legal action was taken against the party, which subsequently lost most of its electoral support.[2]

The radicalization of the NVU even went too far for some of its own members. They left the party and founded other, relatively more moderate, though still extreme right-wing, parties. One of these was the short-lived *Nationale Centrumpartij* (National Centre Party, NCP), born in December 1979. After a meeting in February 1980 – the first official meeting of the party – some of the younger members raided an Amsterdam church in which 'illegal' foreigners were sheltering against expulsion. This led to a storm of protest and negative publicity, and one week later the NCP dissolved itself. The next day, though, a new party – the *Centrumpartij* (Centre Party, CP) – was set up by some of the NCP members; the most significant, Henry Brookman, had also been a prominent member of the NVU.

The CP was the first 'successful' post-war extreme right party in the Netherlands (see Brants and Hogendoorn, 1983). It won 1 seat (out of 150) in the parliamentary election of 1982, which was taken by Hans Janmaat, a political wanderer who was one of the first CP members.[3] Subsequently, the party developed: it claimed over 3000 members in 1984, and at the 1983 local by-election in the new city of Almere, the CP won almost 10 per cent of the votes. Success, however, had its drawbacks. Problems arose between the party leadership (chairman Konst and vice-chairman De Wijer) and the parliamentary party, i.e. Janmaat. The internal tensions, which were as much of a personal as of a political nature, finally led to a split: the party leadership expelled Janmaat and some of his followers in October 1984. Janmaat refused to give up his seat in the Second Chamber and he joined the *Centrumdemocraten* (Centre Democrats, CD) in December 1984. Hence, this new party, founded on 7 November 1984 by former aides of Janmaat, had a good start: it had a member of parliament right from the beginning, and this brought advantages such as publicity and state subsidies.

The CP, on the other hand, soon faced serious difficulty. The internal struggle received a great deal of media attention, and both Konst and De Wijer were pressed by their employers to choose between the CP and their professions as teachers. They chose the latter. The CP's membership was also badly depleted, as some former members left politics, and others joined Janmaat and 'his' CD. A further blow to the CP came in 1986: after winning a mere 6 seats in the March local elections, the party won no seats in the parliamentary election of May 1986. Furthermore, the CP was convicted of electoral fraud and subsequently declared bankrupt. Only a few days after this verdict, on 20 May, the *Centrumpartij '86* (Centre Party '86, CP'86) was created.

After almost a decade of internal strife and splits, therefore, two very small parties competed on the political fringe over the legacy of the once moderately successful CP. Whereas CP'86 was the legal heir to the old CP, the real continuation in membership (especially cadres) and ideology was with the CD. In 1989, the CD won a seat in the Second Chamber, which was taken again by Janmaat, but CP'86 was in too much disarray to contest the parliamentary election. The 'victory' of the CD here surprised most observers of the extreme right; after the internal problems of the mid-1980s, it was thought that these parties would simply disintegrate. The 1990 local election caused an even greater shock, as the so-called *centrumstroming* (centre movement)[4] won a total of 15 seats (CD 11, CP'86 4), mostly in the bigger cities in the *Randstad*, the highly urbanized western part of the Netherlands. In the provincial election the following year, the CD was again successful in this area, winning a total of 3 seats in the provinces of North and South Holland and Utrecht (see Husbands, 1992b).

Nineteen ninety-four was an election 'super' year, with elections for the local councils on 2 March, for the Second Chamber on 3 May and for the European Parliament on 9 June. Both parties were very successful in the local election, gaining a total of 85 seats, 77 for the CD and 8 for CP'86 – as well as one seat for the CD splinter *Nederlands Blok* (Dutch Block, NB) in Utrecht (see Mudde and Van Holsteyn, 1994; Van Holsteyn, 1995). In almost all municipalities where the CD stood, it gained representation. CP'86, on the other hand, was primarily successful in municipalities that were not contested by the CD. In the few municipalities where the extreme right did not win a seat, especially the big cities in the northern provinces, this was (partly) due to internal competition. All in all, the extreme right parties had submitted candidates in only 50 of the more than 600 municipalities and received approximately 200,000 votes, an average of 7.4 per cent in the constituencies that they contested (Buijs and Van Donselaar, 1994: 117).

At the same time, and in part as a consequence of this success, the CD in particular encountered problems, as Janmaat and other prominent party members received much bad publicity. This led to defections from the CD, including several newly elected council members. Some left the party and politics altogether, others founded their own party, or kept their seats on the local council as independent representatives.[5] These setbacks were accentuated by the impact of stories from three undercover journalists during the campaign for the parliamentary election, portraying the CD as 'a party of fascists, criminals and scum' (see Rensen, 1994a; see also Kooiman, 1994; Van Hout, 1994). Arguably, most damaging was a television programme about a newly elected council member in Amsterdam, who bragged that, in the early 1980s, he had started several fires in centres providing services for foreigners. This was screened less than a week before the parliamentary election, and may well have contributed to the disappointing (from the party's viewpoint) result of 2.5 per cent. One month later, the party polled under 1 per cent in the European election. Within four months, therefore, the CD had gone from a record high to a score which was only marginally higher than the CP's 1982 electoral returns. This downward trend was continued in the provincial election of 1995, in which the CD lost 1 seat (in Utrecht) in comparison to the 1991 provincial election.

Moreover, the CD lost members, and returned to a shadowy existence. Perhaps this prompted its short-lived overtures to CP'86. Despite the fact that this party had renamed itself the *Nationale Volkspartij/CP'86* (National People's Party/CP'86) in November 1995, to make apparent its difference from the CD, the two parties held joint demonstrations and intensified merger negotiations in 1996. However, when the CP'86 party conference rejected fusion, CD leader Janmaat returned to public allegations of extremism and anti-semitism against his former ally. CP'86, in turn, purged its leadership of the merger protagonists, most notably party leader Henk Ruitenberg. His successor, party veteran Wim Beaux, openly denounced the half-hearted politics of Janmaat's CD.[6] Both parties also became subject to increasing legal pressure. Janmaat, Schuurman and the CD were convicted for incitement to racial hatred in May 1994 and, after some appeals, were finally fined in December 1996 (the criminal proceedings were based on statements made in 1989 and 1990). Penalties varied from Dfl. 1000 for Janmaat himself to Dfl. 5000 for the (executive) committee of the CD. Among a host of court cases against individual members of the party, in May 1995, an Amsterdam court found CP'86 guilty of being a criminal organization intent on insulting behaviour and inciting racial hatred (AWR, 1996). On top of that, almost the entire leadership was given a month's suspended sentence and a fine of Dfl. 5000; half of it was suspended. On 18 November 1998, the Amsterdam court banned and dissolved the party, which by then amounted to just a handful of members after continuous splits (Van den Brink, 1996).

Organization and ideology of the CD

Extreme right parties in the Netherlands have always suffered from a shortage of membership, cadres and organizational stability. The CD is no exception to this rule. Its membership figures are kept secret or are, at best, vague: for years, Janmaat claimed that the party had a membership of 3000 that was increasing rapidly. Journalists and scholars see this as an exaggeration, generally placing the number between 1000 and 1500 (Buijs and Van Donselaar, 1994: 8; Van den Brink, 1994: 211–12; 1996: 178), although Rensen puts it at 2700 (Rensen, 1994b: 122, 126). However, only a small part of the membership is active within the party, at most 100 members. Not surprisingly, these are mainly party delegates on the various representative bodies, as the CD is first and foremost an electoral party, believing that electoral victory is the only way to exercise political influence (Mudde, 1996: 271).

At first glance, the party statutes of 1991 present a democratic, formal structure. The CD is organized through four party organs: the congress (conference), the council, the executive and the committee (*Dagelijks Bestuur*, DB: art. 14). The first of these layers, formally the most important, is constituted by all paying members (who ask the party secretary for permission to attend), yet it is convened only once a year. The DB, which has fewer formal powers, and only a few members, runs the party on a daily basis. On closer scrutiny, the many exceptions to this formal hierarchy point to a far stronger formal position for the DB *vis-à-vis* other party organs and branches (see Esser, 1996: 11–12); for instance, article 34.2 states that the DB is qualified to allocate tasks or competencies from the congress to the council whenever it is deemed to be in the interest of the party. There is no appeal possible against such decisions. Moreover, the old DB nominates its successor to congress, which then either elects it for seven years or rejects it – the latter is only possible with a two-thirds majority (art. 16.2e).

Despite the reasonably democratic formal structure, Janmaat has dominated the CD completely from the moment he joined the party. This has been possible for two reasons: the inactivity of the party membership and the accumulation of party positions. Janmaat is party leader, leader of the parliamentary party (and from 1989 to 1994 he was the *only* member), chairman of most party foundations, and 'adviser' in almost every other party structure. Moreover, two of his most loyal supporters, party secretary Wil Schuurman (his wife) and party treasurer Wim Elsthout, also hold several party offices at the national, regional and local levels. Therefore, Janmaat is either directly or indirectly involved in every major (and often even minor) decision of the party. Because of the pivotal position of Janmaat in both the formal and the informal party structures, he is also able to suppress internal opposition. At the same time, Janmaat's character – 'tormenting and resentful' as one psychologist put it (Van Ginneken, 1994: 146) – and his authoritarian style of leadership have always been a source of frustration for many ambitious or talented party members.

Ideologically, the CD has remained loyal to the moderate and superficial brand of ethnocentric nationalism of the CP (Halbertsma-Wiardi Beckman, 1993; Mudde, 1998). In short, the ideology of the CD is almost exclusively focused on the immigration issue and can be summarized as offering a choice between assimilation and repatriation. This is clearly stated in the second chapter of the 1989 party programme. Point 2 of this chapter states this very concisely: 'Foreigners and minorities either adjust to the Dutch ways and customs or leave the country.' In the 1990s, this policy nucleus was embedded increasingly within broad, populist anti-party propaganda (Mudde, 1996). This is not to say that the CD is an ideological party or even that it is active in distributing propaganda. In fact, the party rarely issues statements (they are generally ignored by the press anyway), distributes pamphlets or demonstrates on the streets. 'Ideology' is propagated mainly through a limited number of election programmes and party papers.

Since its foundation at the end of 1984, the CD has contested four parliamentary elections. The 1994 election programme was entitled *Oost West, Thuis Best* (East West, Home Best), and contained 22 themes (policy areas) elaborating on the 1989 programme. The elaboration was largely an optical illusion, however, caused by a different lay-out, rather than proof of ideological development. The core of the self-proclaimed 'centre democratic ideology', as stated in the preamble of both programmes, remained:

[On] the one hand, the quest for the preservation and development of Dutch political and cultural identity and, on the other hand, the promotion of national solidarity in our country; either by trying to prevent unwanted divergences between distinctive sections of Dutch society or by coming to a harmonious solution to these divergences (p.1).

The programme was no more than a muddled collection of only slightly interrelated policy demands. The party itself summarized the programme in ten points (a tradition dating back to the beginning of the CP):

1. stop discrimination against the Dutch;
2. introduction of the death penalty;
3. lower the costs of living;
4. promotion of Dutch products;
5. petrol for Dfl. 1.50 per litre;
6. place asylum seekers in labour camps;
7. a cleaner environment without raising taxes;
8. stop the destruction of Dutch culture;
9. control the movement of travellers at the border;
10. the Netherlands is not an immigration country.

In this top ten of political goals, the ethocentrist themes of 'the Dutch first' and 'stop the anti-Dutch policy' figure prominently in points (1), (4), (9) and (10), but also in points (6) and (8). The other points are vague indications of a conservative (2), social (3) and environmentalist (7) outlook. The rather peculiar point (5), the desire for the price of petrol to be lowered, is a good example of the superficial, 'populist' nature of the party's demands and programme.

Compared to the old programme, the 1994 version contained some new policy statements, which can be classified into four different groups. First, there are demands that could be labelled as culturally conservative (e.g. a ban on televised pornography, restrictions on divorce). Second, there are proposals of a protectionist nature, especially in the field of economics (e.g. pleas for partial autarky of the Dutch defence apparatus and agriculture). The bulk of the new demands, however, fall into one of two non-ideological categories: issues that made headlines in the period before the election (e.g. strengthening of dykes, and increasing their height; protection of the status of elderly people) or mere details (e.g. moving fog lamps from the left to the middle rear of cars). The term 'ideology' should thus be very loosely applied to the CD, conjuring up more a collection of unrelated thoughts on different topics than a consistent and comprehensive theory of how society should be organized. This can also be seen in the 'ideological' content of the party papers (see Mudde, 2000).

The most important of the party papers is *CD-Info*, a seven-page pamphlet sent to all members (and donors) on a monthly (or bi-monthly) basis since January 1988. In this paper, the party discusses current political and social themes superficially, primarily applauding the activities of its own member(s) of parliament, Janmaat in particular, and criticizing those of all other parties.[7] For a more 'elaborate' position, the scientific bureau of the CD, since 1992 called the *Thomas Hobbes Stichting* (Foundation) after Janmaat's favourite philosopher (see Fennema, 1992), publishes *CD-Actueel*, nominally quarterly but in practice a very irregularly distributed journal of some twenty pages. The journal carries longer articles, primarily from the few academics in the party, but even these 'intellectuals' seldom present a sophisticated view on the issues they discuss.

The articles in the CD party papers have even less ideological content, focusing mainly on four, often interlinked, themes: opposition to multiculturalism; populist anti-party sentiments; the allegedly undemocratic struggle against the CD; and crime prevention. Opposition to multicultural society is omnipresent and linked to almost every other issue that is discussed in the party papers. Though the CD's discourse is openly xenophobic, its opposition is based principally on demographic (the Netherlands are full) and economic arguments (foreigners take away jobs and cost money). In the eyes of the CD, the main culprit in creating a multicultural society is not 'the foreigner', but the 'clique' of established parties, which started the disastrous immigration and which later tried to cover it up by placing a taboo on discussing the issue. This also explains why 'they' fight every righteous force (i.e. the CD) that tries to defend with every fibre the Dutch people. Not totally without foundation, Janmaat believes that he is the victim of an unprecedented smear campaign (or conspiracy), led by the 'Socialists' of the *Partij van de Arbeid* (PvdA, Labour Party) and its 'subsidized vassals' (i.e. anti-racist and anti-fascist movements).

The electoral basis: protest or xenophobia?

For the past twenty years, Dutch extreme right parties have appealed to the voter with varying success in European, national, provincial and (sub)-local elections. We shall concentrate our analysis on the first-order elections for the Second Chamber. In 1982 and 1989, the CP and the CD respectively were able to return 1 member of parliament, while in 1994, the CD gained enough votes to send 3 representatives to parliament (see Table 7.1). In 1998, however, all three lost their seats – to add to the near-total loss of the CD's 77 local seats in March.

As already intimated, the extreme right parties traditionally have their electoral strongholds in the *Randstad*, as well as in the strongly urbanized parts of the rest of the country (see Husbands, 1992b). In the 1980s, the extreme right parties' electoral success was mainly in the three biggest cities of the Netherlands: Amsterdam, Rotterdam and The Hague. In the parliamentary election of 1982, more than 40 per cent of all votes for the CP were cast in these cities; in 1986, 38 per cent (for the CP and the CD); and in 1989, 45 per cent (for the CD). In that period, the extreme right parties also had

Table 7.1 Support for Dutch extreme right parties in parliamentary elections, 1977–98

Year	Party	Number of voters	Percentage of all voters	Seats in Second Chamber
1977	NVU	33,434	0.4	—
1981	NVU	10,641	0.1	—
	CP	12,242	0.1	—
1982	NVU	1,632	0.0	—
	CP	68,423	0.8	1
1986	CP	36,741	0.4	—
	CD	12,277	0.1	—
1989	CD	81,472	0.9	1
1994	CD	220,621	2.5	3
	CP'86	32,311	0.4	—
1998	List Janmaat/CD	52,226	0.6	—

Source: Netherlands Central Bureau of Statistics, *Election Statistics* for 1977, 1981, 1982, 1986, 1989, 1994, 1998.

moderate success in some of the strongly urbanized medium-sized cities in the *Randstad*. This picture changed only slightly in the 1980s, yet did so dramatically in 1994 (Table 7.2). In the parliamentary election of 3 May, the CD won just 17 per cent of its total number of votes in the biggest cities. However, the drop in the party's vote in the West was accompanied by electoral penetration of the southern provinces and, rather surprisingly, of smaller communities. So, in the period 1981–94, electoral support for the CD shifted geographically from the West to the South, as well as from the biggest cities to the smaller cities and communities.

The electoral rise of the NVU, and especially the national breakthrough of the CP in 1982, raised questions about the motivations of extreme right voters. Did they vote principally as a protest against foreigners and ethnic minorities? Or were they rather people who voted CP as a protest against the established political parties or politics in general? Which element was the more important: support for the extreme right party, or protest against the established parties? In this section, the electoral basis of the extreme right in the Netherlands will be examined in this context, situating the discussion within one of the prevailing controversies of the international research on the extreme right (see Hainsworth, 1992; Stöss, 1994; Billiet and De Witte, 1995).

In the early 1980s, a choice for the NVU or CP was seen primarily as a consequence of racist convictions. The term 'racist electorate' was used widely to describe the group of (potential) voters of extreme right parties

Table 7.2 Support for Centre Party (CP) and Centre Democrats (CD) by region and degree of urbanization, 1981–98

	1981 (CP)	1982 (CP)	1986 (CP)	1989 (CD)	1994 (CD)	1998 (CD)
The Netherlands (%)	0.1	0.8	0.4	0.9	2.5	0.6
Average percentage by region						
The *Randstad*	0.23	1.0	0.6	1.4	2.8	0.67
The rest of the country	0.06	0.29	0.18	0.52	2.0	0.58
Coefficient *Randstad*/rest	3.7	3.4	3.3	2.7	1.4	1.2
Average percentage by degree of urbanization						
Non-urban	—	0.3	0.1	0.4	1.8	0.4
Weakly urban	—	0.2	0.2	0.5	2.0	0.5
Moderately urban	0.1	0.7	0.3	0.7	2.3	0.6
Strongly urban	0.1	0.7	0.3	0.8	2.4	0.8
Very strongly urban	0.4	1.8	0.9	2.0	4.1	0.9

Note: The *Randstad* consists of the Western provinces of North and South Holland and Utrecht; the rest of the country consists of all the other provinces. The division and labelling of degrees of urbanization changed somewhat over the years, but this does not influence the trend. In 1988, the CD did not participate in the province of Drenthe.

Source: Daalder *et al.* (1998).

(Van Donselaar, 1982: 134; Brants and Hogendoorn, 1983: 42). At the same time, it was clear that it was not only racist sentiment that led people to opt for an extreme right party. The voters also felt abandoned by the major political parties and 'the system', and a vote for the extreme right could be viewed as 'a powerless protest' against these forces (Bovenkerk *et al.*, 1980: 118).

The debate on the nature of support for extreme right parties was fuelled by the entrance of Janmaat into the Second Chamber. Commentators looked increasingly at the possible difference between the ideology of extreme right politicians and their voters' motivations, as well as at the importance of dissatisfaction with and distrust of traditional parties and politics (Van Schendelen, 1983; De Jong *et al.*, 1984). However, a satisfactory or convincing answer as to the relative importance of the various voters' motivations was not found in the results of empirical analyses. One examination of the two main explanations of a choice for the CP, for instance, led to ambiguous results and to disagreement among the researchers. In fact, it was argued that a choice for the CP was primarily inspired 'by two sorts of motives: protest against minorities and protest against established politics in general' (Van Donselaar and Van Praag, 1983: 103).

The authors disagreed, though, with Van Donselaar seeing xenophobia as the dominant motivation, while according to Van Praag, it was a more general political protest.

Research into support for the extreme right was impeded significantly by the fact that almost no data at the individual level were available. In virtually all research, aggregated data (election results, unemployment figures, age structure, number of ethnic minorities in a certain geographical area and so on) were used, and this made the search for individual voting motives difficult. Opinion polls, however, shed some light on the phenomenon. Comparatively, the electorate consisted of more men then women, relatively poorly educated voters, people living in the big cities of the *Randstad*, persons with low incomes and those claiming social benefits, individuals without religious convictions, and those who did not read a newspaper (De Hond, 1983). Subjectively, CP voters were relatively dissatisfied with their personal housing conditions, and generally dissatisfied with their personal situation, past and present, and with the state of the country as a whole. They combined a rather gloomy view of the future with an expectation of an (unwelcome) increase in their neighbourhood in the number of foreigners, already too numerous in their view. The CP voters supported the opinion that unemployed Dutch people should take over the jobs of foreigners and that all unemployed foreigners should be expelled. With respect to development aid and the death penalty, they held very conservative opinions. According to this extensive opinion poll, two groups of extreme right voters could be distinguished: the victims of society and the ultra-conservatives (De Hond, 1983: 6). In conclusion, aversion to foreigners and protest against established politics were both seen as important, though the former seemed to be of slightly more importance. A second and more limited study emphasized predominantly the importance of the 'victims of society' subjective factor (Stapel, 1984). CP voters could be seen as people in a difficult socio-economic position, who believed that non-Dutch groups were being disproportionately supported by the state. Individuals living in the same neighbourhood as 'foreigners' and who harboured this idea were particularly inclined to vote CP.

This pattern of negative opinions towards 'foreigners' and ethnic minorities, combined with feelings of dissatisfaction and protest against established political parties and processes, characterized the 1980s. There was, however, a shift in interpretation of the motives of extreme right voters, towards defining the protest variable as the more determinant factor. Thus, it was suggested that there was a small hard core of extreme right voters, but that the bulk of extreme right voters consisted of protest voters (Van Holsteyn, 1990). For these protest voters, the immigration question still played an important role, but the 'political class' was especially blamed for allowing too much immigration.

Research into the extreme right received a new impetus in the run-up to

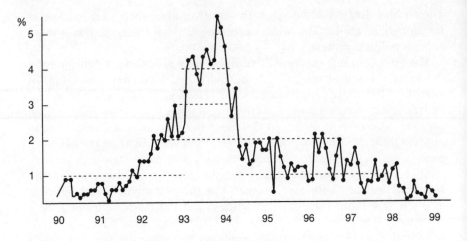

Figure 7.1 Centre Democrats in the polls, January 1990–January 1999
Source: (NIPO-Dutch Gallup; monthly averages).

super election year, 1994. In the opinion polls, support for the CD increased dramatically in the period 1991–3; in 1993, the CD stood consistently above 4 per cent and reached a peak in November with a monthly average of 5.5 per cent (see Figure 7.1). In a sequel to the 1983 opinion research, evidence was again found for the thesis that the CD profited both from supporters of its ideas and from dissatisfied protesting citizens (Van der Veen and Dicke, 1993). With regard to socio-demographic characteristics, there was not much change since 1983,[8] although there had been a shift towards the average income among extreme right supporters. Subjectively, CD voters in 1993 were still more dissatisfied with life than were other voters, but less so than CP voters had been in 1983; the CD voters saw themselves less as 'victims of society' in 1993. The ambivalence in the relationship between the CD and its voters showed up most clearly in the attitudes of the voters towards certain political issues and towards the CD as a political party (see Table 7.3). In 1993, as in 1983, the extreme right voters shared the party's 'tough' viewpoint on development aid and capital punishment, and they also showed a negative attitude towards foreigners – that is, they tended to believe that foreigners should not be allowed to enter the country, and that those already present should be sent back to their own country or ought to adjust fully to Dutch customs and society. However, these voters were hardly convinced and loyal adherents: only a minority thought that the CD had the best proposals for solving problems concerning foreigners, a third did *not* know that Janmaat was 'their' representative in the Second Chamber, and very few had much faith in him as a member of parliament. In 1993, one out of ten CD voters even hoped that their party (that is, the party they once voted for or intended to vote for) would *not* be represented in

Table 7.3 Some political attitudes of extreme right voters,
1983 and 1993 (%)

	CP voters 1983	Other voters 1983	CD voters 1993	Other voters 1993
Development aid should be stopped	37	10	30	6
Capital punishment should be restored for serious crimes	70	35	72	36
We should allow people from developing countries to enter our country	5	21	11	31
All unemployed foreigners should be sent back to their own country	76	29	72	32
Unemployed Dutchmen should take over the jobs of foreigners, who should then be sent to their own country	57	15	52	24
Foreigners who stay in the Netherlands should accommodate themselves more	—	—	93	69
Trust in none of the major traditional political parties	39	19	30	12
The party with the best proposals for solving the problems with foreigners is:				
• the CD	—	—	40	3
• no party at all	—	—	14	6
• don't know	—	—	26	53
People who do *not* know the name of the CD member of Parliament (Janmaat)	32	48	31	45
Faith in Janmaat as member of Parliament				
• (very) much faith	34	5	18	2
• some faith	43	6	38	16
• (almost) no faith at all	23	89	44	81
Wants *no* representation of CP/ CD in the Second Chamber after the next elections	3	73	11	66
Wants CP/CD *not* to participate in government	23	82	34	85
	N = 231	N = 207	N = 207	N = 267

Source: Van der Veen and Dicke (1993); CP (Centre Party) and CD (Centre Democrat) voters
are people who said they have voted for the party in the past or are intending to vote for the
party in the future.

parliament after the next elections, and about one-third did *not* want their party to participate in government.

In the media, which covered the scandals of extreme right parties and politicians extensively, the dissatisfied (potential) protest voter was highlighted as the classic example of an extreme right elector in the run-up to the elections of 1994 (Van Holsteyn, 1995). The daily and weekly press featured articles on the electoral basis of the CD, and dissatisfaction and political protest were portrayed as the voters' main motivations. The idea of protest as the dominant driving force for the majority of extreme right voters can be substantiated by employing the so-called 'elaborated theory on second-order elections' (Oppenhuis *et al.*, 1996). Second-order elections – that is, elections where national political power is not at stake (in the eyes of the voters, at least) – can function as markers of party strength, depending on the timing of the parliamentary (i.e. first-order) election. When such power is not really at stake, voters perceive local, provincial and European elections as some sort of super opinion poll. When the second-order election is held shortly before the first-order election, some voters will use it to voice their protest:

> The tactical situation in such a 'marker-setting election' is characterised by an apparent lack of consequences for the allocation of power on the one hand and by the attentiveness of politicians and media on the other. In this circumstance, strategic voting may take the form of what is generally referred to as 'protest voting', benefiting small radical parties in particular. Knowing that politicians are attentive to the results, while no actual power is at stake, some voters apparently take the opportunity (in the phrase of the British football hooligans) to 'put in the boot' (Oppenhuis *et al.*, 1996: 302).

However, when second-order elections are held shortly after the first-order election, they are largely ignored. As they neither involve the question of power nor provide the occasion for a significant national protest vote, the same authors speak of 'throw-away elections'. So, whereas the first second-order election gives the voter the opportunity to vote 'with the boot', the second will particularly attract voters who vote 'with the heart'. In the Dutch elections of 1994, this meant that the approximately 7.4 per cent of the votes gained by the CD in the local election, two months before the parliamentary election, were mainly from 'protesters', whereas the real core of support was revealed in the following month's European election, and stood at a mere 1 per cent (Mudde and Van Holsteyn, 1994; Van Holsteyn, 1995). Subsequently, the CD polled generally under 2 per cent, dropping to 0.6 per cent in the May 1998 parliamentary election (see Table 7.1), and 0.5 per cent in the June 1999 European election.

Explaining the limited success of the Dutch extreme right

The Dutch extreme right can be considered to be one of the least successful representatives of the current West European extreme right. Even their electoral high point, 2.5 per cent of the votes in 1994, is only half of the electoral support that extreme right parties averaged in twelve West European countries in the 1980s and 1990s (Weinberg *et al.*, 1995: 42). To further illustrate the limited success of the Dutch extreme right, a brief comparison with the Flemish *Vlaams Blok* (VB), (Flemish Bloc) is illuminating. In 1982, these two parties were the only extreme right parties of the third wave in Western Europe represented in parliament, both parties scoring around 1 per cent of the votes (see Swyngedouw, Chapter 6). More than ten years later, the VB polled 12.5 per cent in the European election of 1994, whereas the CD won a mere 1 per cent.

How could the Dutch extreme right be one of the first successful representatives of the third wave in the early 1980s and yet be one of the least successful in the 1990s? In this section, the limited success of the CD in particular, and of the extreme right in the Netherlands in general, will be discussed. As almost all studies turn to 'external' factors to explain the *success* of extreme right parties, we will start our discussion by finding out whether the absence of these factors can explain the lack of success in the Dutch case. Most of the studies on the success of extreme right parties focus on mapping their objectively favourable circumstances. This implies that the prime reason for the parties' success is external – that is, located outside the parties. Following this argument, we might expect that the breeding-ground of extreme right parties is not as favourable in the Netherlands as in other West European countries.

In general, two different, yet interlinked, favourable conditions are identified in the literature: anti-politics sentiment and xenophobia (Betz, 1994). Anti-politics sentiment contains a wide range of resentments against 'the political' – that is, the system, the parties, the politicians, and so on. The importance of these sentiments for the party system is clearly visible in the recent political turmoil in Italy, where years of growing frustration with the corrupt political system led to the creation of the Second Republic, in which not only was the system changed in several respects, but most key players (politicians and parties) were ousted, and several individuals were even convicted (see Morlino, 1996; Rosenthal, 1996). Admittedly, Italy is an exception, but growing and destabilizing forms of anti-politics sentiment have been identified in other West European countries, such as Austria (see Chapter 3) and Belgium (Chapter 6). When we look at comparative data, we see that the Dutch are traditionally one of the most satisfied people in the European Union and that there is no decline in the level of overall life satisfaction in the period 1974–94 (see Eurobarometer, 1995; SCP, 1996). On the other hand, the Dutch National Election Studies show that a substantial part of the Dutch electorate, over 20 per cent, can be classified as politically (very) cynical.[9] Although this figure has not really increased in the past decade or so, it shows that there is at least some fertile soil for parties trying to capitalize on political protest.

Apart from survey data at the individual level, there are various other indicators of anti-politics sentiment. One of the most often used is low voter turnout (Andeweg, 1996; Betz, 1994; Poguntke, 1996). The Netherlands is no exception to the general trend of decreasing voter turnout. Even though turnout in parliamentary elections is still rather high, comparatively, it is nonetheless declining slightly: 1998 saw the lowest turnout (73.3 per cent) at parliamentary elections, since the abolition of compulsory voting in 1970. This trend of declining turnout is most apparent in second-order elections, especially the provincial and European elections. At the 1994 European election, turnout was lowest in the Netherlands (and Portugal and the United Kingdom), where a mere 35 per cent voted. In the 1999 Euro-election, the abstention rate in the Netherlands was 70 per cent, not far behind the United Kingdom's 77 per cent. So, even when we accept that anti-politics sentiment in the Netherlands is less widespread than in many other West European countries, it is clear that the extreme right mobilizes only a small part of it.

The second aspect of a generally favourable breeding-ground for extreme right parties is xenophobia, or rather strong dissatisfaction with the presence of large and/or growing numbers of immigrants. If the extreme right of the third wave has been identified with one issue, it is with the issue of immigration (von Beyme, 1988; Husbands, 1992a). The explanation follows the same pattern as the anti-politics argument: the limited success of the Dutch extreme right can be explained by the limited spread of xenophobia in the Netherlands. Again, empirical evidence rejects, or at least undermines, this line of reasoning. Several surveys show that substantial groups of the Dutch population think that there are too many foreigners in the Netherlands, that they should leave the country (after finishing their employment), or that the number of asylum seekers is too high (Moors and Beets, 1991; SCP, 1996). In 1994, 'immigration and ethnic minorities' were perceived by most voters as the main national problem in the Netherlands (Aarts, 1995). Compared to countries with successful extreme right parties, like Belgium and France, the percentage of people who see the number of 'foreigners' in their country as too high is not that much lower (57, 55 and 47 per cent respectively in 1994; see Melich, 1995). Even though the differences are relatively bigger in the case of the acceptance of foreigners (especially from the Southern Mediterranean) and asylum seekers, and in the case of a more general 'index of xenophobia' (Melich, 1995), the fact remains that the extreme right in the Netherlands is far less successful in profiting from the existing circumstances.

We can conclude that the breeding-ground, as far as attitudes to politics and immigrants are concerned, is only slightly less favourable in the Nether-lands than in other West European countries. This factor thus cannot explain the relatively poor electoral results of the Dutch extreme right parties. Again, we look to other countries for possible other explanations. One of the few cases of unsuccessful extreme right electoral mobilization that has received serious scholarly interest is that of England. In the English case, the failure of the extreme right is generally explained by two external factors: the electoral system (Elbers and Fennema, 1993; Van Donselaar, 1995), and the fact that the Conservative Party under the leadership of Margaret Thatcher took the issue of immigration away from the extreme right (Eatwell, 1992; Taylor, 1993).

The first explanation sounds plausible, as the first-past-the-post system allows for only one winner in each constituency (but see Eatwell, Chapter 8). However, this kind of reasoning cannot be used for the Dutch case with its system of extreme proportional representation, which is considered to be one of the most open political systems in the world (Andeweg and Irwin, 1993). Moreover, Dutch politics has a tradition of party pluralism which is considered valuable by politicians of both small and large parties, and by voters as well. Voting for small parties is not considered a wasted vote in the Netherlands. Indeed, in 1994, 80 per cent of the electorate disagreed with the statement that people who vote for a small party are wasting their vote, and 49 per cent disagreed with the statement that only big parties really meant something in politics (Anker and Oppenhuis, 1995: 64). As a political party requires no more than 0.67 per cent of the votes to get a seat in parliament, new parties enter the political arena quite often (see Lucardie, 1996). The only possible negative side of the electoral system for the Dutch extreme right might be that the voter has a very wide variety of parties to choose from, thereby diluting potential support. Still, the fact that it was not so much the extreme right that profited from the substantial loss of votes by the established Christian Democratic and Social Democratic parties in the 1994 parliamentary election, as was generally expected, but some other established parties and two rather 'new' parties – the *Socialistische Partij* (Socialist Party, SP) and the *Algemeen Ouderen Verbond* (General League of the Elderly, AOV) (see Irwin, 1995) – once again proves that the Dutch extreme right performs very poorly despite generally favourable circum-stances.

The second explanation, as regards the English case, has also recently been employed in the Netherlands. Thus the surprisingly poor result of the CD in the 1994 parliamentary election has been explained in part by the victory of the conservative-liberal *Volkspartij voor Vrijheid en Democratie* (People's Party for Freedom and Democracy, VVD) (see Brill, 1994; Fennema, 1995). It is argued that this latter party has won over voters on the immigration issue, on which its party leader, Frits Bolkestein, spoke out on several occasions in recent years. It should be noted that this contention was largely 'created' by strong, somewhat exaggerated reactions in the media and by reactions from other politicians to the (occasional) remarks by Bolkestein. However, more important than the VVD leader speaking out on immigration was the fact that he was generally linked with this issue in the media (Kleinnijenhuis and Pennings, 1995). In the Dutch case, the evidence is far from convincing to support the argument that the traditional right appropriated the issue and thereby the voters of the extreme right. First and foremost, the 'evidence' is based primarily on voter shifts at the aggregate level. Information about the motives of new VVD voters shows that the immigration issue did not play an important role in their party choice (Schmeets *et al.*, 1996; Irwin and Van Holsteyn, 1997). It may also be the case that if there was any effect on the electoral support for the VVD, the issue may have won some but lost other voters for the party (Kleinnijenhuis *et al.*, 1995: 140). In addition, we have no proof that these (attracted) voters even considered voting for an extreme right party. There is also a theoretical problem: the same argument is used in a completely different way in the case of some other countries. In France and Belgium (i.e. Flanders), for instance, it is generally argued that, as the traditional right became more preoccupied with the immigration issue, this only increased support for the extreme right, as it gave legitimacy and salience to the issue and consequently to the extreme right party (Fitzmaurice, 1992; Kühnl, 1992). In the often-quoted words of *Front National* (FN) leader, Jean-Marie Le Pen, the people like the original better than the copy. Hence, again the question is why the Dutch case was different, i.e. why in the Netherlands the original is weaker than the copy – if there was any real copy at all.

The answer to this question must be found in internal factors. The propitious breeding-ground has to be utilized by a political entrepreneur (Ignazi, 1996), but not every entrepreneur is equally successful. If there is one common theme in the history of the extreme right in the Netherlands, it is that it is simply too weak (organizationally, electorally, ideologically) to become a real political force. Whereas the CP and VB had almost the same level of electoral support in the early 1980s, the VB was able to expand its support considerably. The VB profited from the fact that the *Vlaamse Liberalen en Democraten* (Flemish Liberals and Democrats, VLD) adopted 'its' issues of immigration and law and order, and, as a result, the VB dominated the political campaign for the 1991 parliamentary election (Maddens, 1994). In sharp contrast, the CD remained an outsider, even when the VVD made immigration one of the topics of the 1994 electoral campaign.

One reason why the CP and its successor parties never used their opportunities to the full is that they are all badly organized parties, lacking both cadres and members. In addition, and in part because of this, the Dutch extreme right has always been plagued by scandals and splits. Therefore, it has never been able to present successfully to the voter its potentially 'attractive product'.[10] In comparison to well-organized and professional parties like the VB and the *Freiheitliche Partei Österreichs* (Austrian Freedom Party, FPÖ), the CD failed to convince the voter that it was a viable alternative to the established parties. The data on voters presented above, for instance, clearly show the ambivalent relationship of many CD voters with 'their' party. Also, the simple fact that the CD and the CP'86 contested the same election in effect kept both out of various local councils, whereas together they would have gained enough votes for at least 1 seat.

This explanation, however, brings in another question: why are extreme right parties in the Netherlands such weak organizations? A commonplace explanation for both the organizational and electoral weakness of the Dutch extreme right is the character of Hans Janmaat.[11] According to most observers, he lacks the political skills (of a Dewinter or Haider) necessary to build a good organization and fully exploit the grievances of the electorate. Should Janmaat, therefore, be replaced by a person of higher calibre, then the Dutch extreme right arguably would enjoy success, like its Flemish or Austrian counterparts. However plausible this might sound, the thesis has several shortcomings. It is undeniably true that Janmaat has had a negative impact on the organizational capacity of the Dutch extreme right. Since his expulsion from the CP in 1984, he has made certain that this kind of coup would be impossible in his new party, the CD. Also, the fusion talks between the CD and other extreme right parties (most notably CP'86) have often been frustrated by Janmaat or deadlocked by the aversion of leaders of the other parties towards him. This notwithstanding, Janmaat is the only leader of the post-war extreme right in the Netherlands who has been able to get his party (and himself) into parliament. One can even argue that it is his personal name as much as (or even more so than) that of the political party that has enabled this success. Surveys show that Janmaat is one of the best-known politicians in the Netherlands: his name is known by over 90 per cent of the eligible voters (Anker, 1995: 206–7). Significantly, too, in 1993 only one-quarter of Dutch voters were of the opinion that the CD would be a more attractive party without Janmaat (Van der Veen and Dicke, 1993: 21). Of course, the 1998 parliamentary election result and Janmaat's loss of seat was a personal and party blow, but did not fundamentally disturb his leadership of the CD.

An alternative interpretation has been suggested by Van Donselaar, who explains the weakness of the Dutch extreme right by pointing to the repressive social and legal climate in the Netherlands. This leads to a so-called adjustment dilemma for the extreme right: on the one hand, they have to moderate their stand because of the threat of criminalization and legal action but, on the other hand, they cannot be too moderate because they might offer too vague a political profile and thereby lose core members and voters (Van Donselaar, 1995: 13). Though plausible, this thesis has some empirical snags. First, it cannot be tested, as the social and legal climate has always been repressive and thus the independent variable is a constant.

Second, it seems to presuppose that the extreme right is voted for primarily on the basis of support rather than protest, which contradicts the dominant interpretation as presented above. Finally, the case of the former *Communistische Partij [van] Nederland* (Communist Party [of the] Netherlands, CPN) shows that it is possible to build a well-organized political party under conditions of extreme repression in the Netherlands (see Verrips, 1995).

So, though we accept the fact that the repressive social and legal climate in the Netherlands creates organizational problems for the Dutch extreme right, the case of the CPN shows that these can be overcome, especially with support from others. As in many other West European countries, the Communists in the Netherlands had to live under strong repression, particularly in the 1950s. Still, they had two advantages while building and maintaining a strong party apparatus. First and foremost, they had the backing of the communist world, notably the Soviet Union. Not only were they supported financially, but the Soviet Union also provided for the schooling of cadres – a necessity in order to maintain an organization, yet almost an impossibility in a situation of strong repression. Second, the Communists had sufficient of a shared ideological and organizational history with the Social Democrats to enable them to link their political struggle to themes that were accepted by large parts of the political establishment. Even though the leadership of the social democratic *Partij van de Arbeid* (Labour Party, PvdA) was among the main opponents of the CPN, and vice-versa, activists at the regional and local level from both parties were less rigorously separated, and often worked together in various front organizations of the Communist Party.

This brings us to the most specific problem of the Dutch extreme right parties: unlike kindred parties in some other countries, they do not benefit from the existence of an organized nationalist subculture (Mudde, 1994). In the case of the VB, this party escaped the political fringe only after introducing so-called 'Operation Rejuvenation', in which various young VB members, mostly ex-leaders of nationalist youth and student bodies, were integrated into the party leadership (Mudde, 1995). Also, parties like the Austrian FPÖ profit from the broad German-national *Lager*, and Le Pen's FN attracts highly educated cadres from networks like the *Club de l'Horloge* and various New Right channels. In sharp contrast, the Dutch extreme right has had to do virtually everything on its own, in almost complete isolation and under strong social and legal pressure as well.

The lack of a Dutch nationalist subculture is caused by the fact that in the Netherlands, unlike in countries such as Belgium (Flanders) and Austria, the so-called national question does not play any significant role at all. One reason for this may be the long tradition of the Netherlands as a trading nation, with an international orientation that does not allow for narrow-minded nationalism. Also, though a reasonably young country within its current borders, the Netherlands has never been threatened in its national identity or integrity, except for the five years of German Nazi occupation. This persistent feeling of 'national security' may explain the absence of the national question from the political agenda.[12] As a consequence, almost every form of Dutch nationalism is directly linked to the extreme right – and kept largely separate from the 'democratic' camp. Related issues such as ethnic or cultural identity are similarly suspect and do not figure centrally in the political debate. Hence, extreme right parties have little or no possibility of linking up usefully with more widely supported themes and organizations, and are consequently forced into a role on the fringe.

Notes

A preliminary version of this chapter was presented as a paper entitled 'Small and Struggling: Some Thoughts on the Limited Success of the Dutch Extreme Right' at the International Conference on Political Extremism, Hostility and Violence towards Foreigners and Other Marginalised Groups, Ljubljana, 22–24 March 1996. In rewriting, we benefited from comments by Paul Hainsworth and Jaap Van Donselaar.

1. Most notably, the *Stichting Oud Politieke Delinquenten* (Foundation for Former Political Criminals, SOPD) and the *Werkgemeenschap Europa in de Lage Landen* (Working Community Europe in the Low Countries, WELL) – the Dutch section of the Malmö-based European Social Movement. For a general history of the early post-war extreme right, see Van Donselaar (1991, 1993), Iddekinge and Paape (1970), and Hirl (1987).

2. After several years of discussion, the NVU was named a 'criminal association' by the Amsterdam court on 8 March 1978. Because of legal technicalities and flaws, this meant that the party was not banned, and was thus still legal, but it was excluded from contesting elections. This bizarre verdict was repealed by the Supreme Court in 1979, which ruled that as long as the party was not banned, it could not and should not be obstructed in functioning as a political party in any way (see Eskes, 1988; Van Donselaar, 1991: 165–7).

3. J. G. H. (Hans) Janmaat, born on 3 November 1934 in Gouda. After studying aircraft construction for two years, he had to stop because his father went bankrupt. After several more or less unsuccessful jobs, including two years as a 'guest worker' in Germany, he decided to return to university. He completed his political science study at the University of Amsterdam at the age of 40 and became increasingly active in various political parties. He claims to have presented a radio speech on the 'foreigner issue' in the late 1970s for *Democratische Socialisten '70* (Democratic Socialists '70, DS'70), a conservative splinter from the Social Democratic PvdA. According to Janmaat, he was then thrown out of DS'70 because the party leader had become jealous and afraid after the enthusiastic reactions to the speech. Janmaat joined the CP, as its seventh member, after reading an article in the left-wing journal *Vrij Nederland* (see Van Ginneken, 1994: 146–54; Van Holsteyn, 1998: 47–60).

4. The term *centrumstroming* is used as the collective noun for the CP and its successor parties. The term originated in the CP, where Janmaat, especially, uses it, and has since become integrated into media and scholarly discourse.

5. On 12 June 1996, the Dutch newspaper *Trouw* reported that 26 of the 78 seats won by the CD at the local election of 1994 were no longer held by the party. Eight seats had never been taken up at all, nine people had left the party but kept their seats as independents, and nine of the elected persons had joined (or founded) other extreme right parties such as CP'86, the NB and the *Burgerpartij Nederland* (Citizen's Party of the Netherlands, BPN). Van Riel (1997: 20–1), in research on the extreme right local councillors elected in 1994, claims that, by 1 May 1996, there were only 41 CD representatives left (in 26 municipalities). The others had voluntarily left the party, were expelled or suspended by it, or had left the council. CP'86 also lost several seats (especially in *deelgemeenten*, city districts) through defections and expulsions.

6. In November 1996, the NVP/CP'86 was again plagued by internal strife, this time leading to the expulsion of the neo-Nazi wing around Martijn Freling (council member in Rotterdam) and Stewart Mordaunt (local councillor in The Hague and vice-chairman of the party). After a lengthy legal battle, this 50- to 100-member strong section acquired the official right to the party name and changed it back to CP'86. The 'moderate' wing was left without the party name and most of its leading members (who left politics altogether), and has since tried to survive under various different party labels.

7. These articles are often contributed by Janmaat himself, though often under an obvious alias like W. Leidsman (which translates roughly as W. Leader).

8. For other analyses of support for extreme right parties over a ten-year period, see Scheepers *et al.* (1993, 1994) and Eisinga *et al.* (1998). Using opinion poll data, extreme right voters are described here in terms of sociological characteristics, and several hypotheses are tested that are derived from theories concerning the electoral support of former fascist parties.

9. In 1994, almost 90 per cent of the respondents of the Dutch Parliamentary Election Study (fully) agreed with the statement that politicians promise more than they can deliver, 34 per cent with the statement that ministers and secretaries of state are primarily concerned about their own personal interests, and 40 per cent with the statement that one is more likely to become a member of parliament because of one's political friends than because of one's abilities. All in all, almost 20 per cent were very cynical – that is, they agreed with all three statements (Anker and Oppenhuis, 1995: 175–6).

10. See, for a similar argument in the English case, Husbands (1988); for the German case, see Stöss (1994).

11. Some non-Dutch scholars hold another view, placing Janmaat alongside successful extreme right leaders such as Le Pen and Haider (Hafeneger, 1994; Ignazi, 1996).

12. This is in contrast to, for instance, Flanders, where a broad nationalist subculture (the 'Flemish Movement') developed as a consequence of years of oppression of the Dutch-speaking population by the French-speaking elite (see Willemsen, 1969). Through its various mouthpieces, among which are political parties like the VB and the *Volksunie* (People's Union, VU), the Flemish national question has almost always been on the political agenda.

References

Aarts, K. (1995) 'Nationale politieke problemen, partijcompetentie en stemgedrag', in Van Holsteyn, J. J. M. and Niemöller, B. (eds) *De Nederlandse kiezer 1994*. Leiden: DSWO Press.

Andeweg, R .B. (1996) 'Elite–Mass Linkages in Europe: Legitimacy Crisis or Party Crisis?', in Hayward, J. (ed.) *Elitism, Populism and European Politics*. Oxford: Clarendon Press.

Andeweg, R. B. and Irwin, G. A. (1993) *Dutch Government and Politics*. Basingstoke: Macmillan.

Anker, H. (1995) 'Kiezers, politici, en partijkeuze', in Van Holsteyn, J. J. M. and Niemöller, B. (eds) *De Nederlandse kiezer 1994*. Leiden: DSWO Press.

Anker, H. and Oppenhuis, E. V. (1995) *Dutch Parliamentary Election Study 1994*. Amsterdam: Steinmetz Archive/SWIDOC/SKON.

AWR (1996) *Anti-Semitism World Report 1996*. London and New York: Institute for Jewish Policy Research/American Jewish Committee.

Betz, H.-G. (1994) *Radical Right-Wing Populism in Western Europe*. Basingstoke: Macmillan.

Beyme, K. von (1988) 'Right-wing Extremism in Post-war Europe', *West European European Politics* 11(2), 1–18.

Billiet, J. and De Witte, H. (1995) 'Attitudinal Dispositions to Vote for a "New" Extreme Right-Wing Party: The Case of *"Vlaams Blok"* ', *European Journal of Political Research* 27(2), 181–202.

Bouw, C., Van Donselaar, J. and Nelissen, C. (1981) *De Nederlandse Volks-Unie: portret van een racistische splinterpartij*. Bussum: Het Wereldvenster.

Bovenkerk, F., Doeuwes, A., Gloudi, M. and Van Velzen, J. (1980) 'De verkiezingsaanhang van de Nederlandse Volksunie', in Bovenkerk, F. (ed.) *Omdat zij anders zijn: patronen van rasdiscriminatie in Nederland*, 4th edition. Meppel: Boom.

Brants, K. and Hogendoorn, W. (1983) *Van vreemde smetten vrij: opkomst van de Centrumpartij*. Bussum: De Haan/Unieboek.

Brill, P. (1994) 'Bolkesteins perceptie', *De Volkskrant*, 16 March.

Buijs, F. J. and Van Donselaar, J. (1998) *Extreem-rechts*. Leiden: LISWO.

Daalder, H., Dittrich, K. L. L. M. and Gosman, J. G. (1998) 'Verkiezingsuitslagen', in *Compendium voor politiek en samenleving in Nederland* Samsom. Alphen aan den Rijn: H.D. Tjeenk Willink.

De Hond, M. (1983) *De opkomst van de Centrumpartij*. Amsterdam: Inter/View.

De Jong, J., Krijnsen, H. and Te Velde, R. (1984) 'Stemmen op de Centrumpartij? Een verkenning van politiek wantrouwen en sociale jaloezie', *Beleid en Maatschappij* 11(4), 109–15.

De Jonge, A. A. (1979) *Het Nationaal-Socialisme in Nederland: voorgeschiedenis, ontstaan en ontwikkeling*. The Hague: Kruseman.

De Jonge, A. A. (1982) *Crisis en critiek der democratie: anti-democratische stromingen en de daarin levende denkbeelden over de staat in Nederland tussen de wereldoorlogen*. Utrecht: H&S.

Eatwell, R. (1992) 'Why Has the Extreme Right Failed in Britain?', in Hainsworth, P. (ed.) *The Extreme Right in Europe and the USA*. London: Pinter.

Eisinga, R., Lammers, J., Lubbers, M. and Scheepers, P. (1998) 'Het electoraat van extreem-rechtse partijen: individuele en contextuele kenmerken, 1982–1996', in Van Holsteyn, J. and Mudde, C. (eds) *Extreem-rechts in Nederland*. The Hague: Sdu.

Elbers, F. and Fennema, M. (1993) *Racistische partijen in West-Europa: tussen nationale traditie en Europese samenwerking*. Leiden: Stichting Burgerschapskunde.

Eskes, J. A. O. (1988) *Repressie van politieke bewegingen in Nederland: een juridisch-historische studie over het Nederlandse publiekrechtelijke verenigingsrecht gedurende het tijdvak 1798–1988*. Zwolle: Tjeenk Willink.

Esser, M. (1996) *De lijstenmakerij van extreem-rechts: de kandidaatstelling van Centrumdemocraten, Nationale Volkspartij/CP'86 en Vlaams Blok*. Leiden: Vakgroep Politieke Wetenschappen.

Eurobarometer (1995) *Trends 1974–1994*. Brussels: Office for Official Publications of the European Communities.

Fennema, M. (1992) 'Vergeleken met het Vlaams Blok is Janmaat liberaal', *De Volkskrant*, 4 February.

Fennema, M. (1995) 'Some Theoretical Problems and Issues in the Comparison of Racist Parties in Europe', paper presented at the ECPR Joint Sessions, Bordeaux, April–May.

Fitzmaurice, J. (1992) 'The Extreme Right in Belgium: Recent Developments', *Parliamentary Affairs* 45(3), 300–8.

Hafeneger, B. (1994) 'Rechtsextreme Europabilder', in Kowalsky, W. and Schroeder, W. (eds) *Rechtsextremismus: Einführung und Forschungsbilanz*. Opladen: Westdeutscher Verlag.

Hainsworth, P. (1992) 'Introduction. The Cutting Edge: The Extreme Right in Postwar Western Europe and the USA', in Hainsworth, P. (ed.) *The Extreme Right in Europe and the USA*. London: Pinter.

Halbertsma-Wiardi Beckman, M. (1993) 'De ideologische achtergrond van Centrumpartij en Centrumdemocraten', *Socialisme en Democratie* 50(12), 518–25.

Hirl, L. (1987) 'Der organisierte Rechtsextremismus in den Niederlanden nach 1945 unter besonderer Berücksichtigung seiner Tradition', dissertation at the University of Vienna.

Husbands, C. T. (1988) 'Extreme Right-Wing Politics in Great Britain: The Recent Marginalisation of the National Front', *West European Politics* 11(2), 65–79.

Husbands, C. T. (1992a) 'The Other Face of 1992: The Extreme-Right Explosion in Western Europe', *Parliamentary Affairs* 45(3), 267–84.

Husbands, C. T. (1992b) 'The Netherlands: Irritants on the Body Politic', in Hainsworth, P. (ed.) *The Extreme Right in Europe and the USA*. London: Pinter.

Iddekinge, P. R. A. and Paape, A. H. (1970) *Ze zijn er nog*. Amsterdam: De Bezige Bij.

Ignazi, P. (1996) 'The Crisis of Parties and the Rise of New Political Parties', *Party Politics* 2(4), 549–66.

Irwin, G. A. (1995) 'The Dutch Parliamentary Election of 1994', *Electoral Studies* 14(1), 72–6.

Irwin, G. and Van Holsteyn, J. (1997) 'Where to from Here? Revamping Electoral Politics in the Netherlands', *West European Politics* 20(2), 93–118.

Kleinnijenhuis, J. and Pennings, P. (1995) 'Campagnes en berichtgeving', in Van Holsteyn, J. J. M. and Niemöller, B. (eds) *De Nederlandse kiezer 1994*. Leiden: DSWO Press. 27–41.

Kleinnijenhuis, J., Oegema, D., de Ridder, J. and Bos, H. (1995) *De democratie op drift: een evaluatie van de verkiezingscampagne van 1994*. Amsterdam: VU Uitgeverij.

Kooiman, K. (1994) 'Undercover in de CD', *De Groene Amsterdammer* 118(12), 23 March, 6–11.

Kooy, G. A. (1964) *Het echec van een 'volkse' beweging; nazificatie en denazificatie in Nederland*. Assen: Van Gorcum.

Kossmann, E. H. (1978) *The Low Countries 1780–1940*. Oxford: Oxford University Press.

Kühnl, R. (1992) 'Der Aufstieg der extremen Rechten in Europa', *Blätter für deutsche und internationale Politik* 37(6), 730–41.

Lucardie, P. (1996) 'Prophets, Prolocutors and Pyromaniacs: New Parties in the Netherlands'. Paper presented at the ECPR Joint Sessions, Oslo, March–April.

Maddens, B. (1994) 'Kiesgedrag en partijstrategie: de samenhang tussen de beleids-matige profilering van de partijen en het kiesgedrag van de Vlamingen op 24 november 1991'. Dissertation at the University of Leuven, Leuven.

Melich, A. (1995) 'Comparative European Trend Survey Data on Racism and Xenophobia', paper presented at the ECPR Joint Sessions, Bordeaux, April–May.

Meyers, J. (1984) *Mussert, een politiek leven*. Amsterdam: De Arbeiderspers.

Moors, H. and Beets, G. (1991) 'Opvattingen over buitenlanders sterk bepaald door politieke kleur', *Demos* 7(7), 55–6.

Morlino, L. (1996) 'Crisis of Parties and Change of Party System in Italy', *Party Politics* 2(1), 5–30.

Mudde, C. (1994) 'Janmaat is het beste wat extreem-rechts in Nederland te bieden heeft', *De Volkskrant*, 4 November.

Mudde, C. (1995) 'One against All, All against One! A Portrait of the *Vlaams Blok*', *Patterns of Prejudice* 29(1), 5–28.

Mudde, C. (1996) 'The Paradox of the Anti-party Party: Insights from the Extreme Right', *Party Politics* 2(2), 287–98.

Mudde, C. (1998) 'Het programma van de Centrumstroming', in Van Holsteyn, J. and Mudde, C. (eds) *Extreem-rechts in Nederland*. The Hague: Sdu.

Mudde, C. (2000) *The Extreme Right Party Family: Fact or Fiction?* Manchester: Manchester University Press.

Mudde, C. E. and Van Holsteyn, J. J. M. (1994) 'Over the Top: Dutch Right-Wing Extremist Parties in the Elections of 1994', *Politics* 14(3), 127–34.

Oppenhuis, E., Van der Eijk, C. and Franklin, M. (1996) 'The Party Context: Outcomes', in Van der Eijk, C. and Franklin, M. (eds) *Choosing Europe? The European Electorate and National Politics in the Face of Union*. Ann Arbor: University of Michigan Press.

Poguntke, T. (1996) 'Anti-party sentiment – conceptual thoughts and empirical evidence: explorations into a minefield', *European Journal of Political Research* 29(3), 319–44.

Rensen, P. (1994a) 'Een partij van fascisten, criminelen en tuig', *Nieuwe Revu*, 2–9 February, 41–58.

Rensen, P. (1994b) *Dansen met de duivel: undercover bij de Centrumdemocraten*. Amsterdam: L.J. Veen.

Rosenthal, L. (1996) 'Dateline Rome: the new face of Western democracy', *Foreign Policy* No. 104, 155–68.

Scheepers, P., Eisinga, R. and Lammers, J. (1993) 'Het electoraat van de Centrum Partij/Centrum Democraten in de periode 1982–1992', *Mens en Maatschappij* 68(4), 362–85.

Scheepers, P., Eisinga, R. and Lammers, J. (1994) 'Het electoraat van extreem-rechts in Nederland: contemporaine geschiedschrijving vanuit een sociologisch perspectief', in Voerman, G. (ed.) *Jaarboek Documentatiecentrum Nederlandse Politieke Partijen 1993*. Groningen: Rijksuniversiteit Groningen.

Schmeets, J. J. G., Scheepers, P. L. H. and Felling, A. J. A. (1996) 'Het minderhedenvraagstuk en de partijkeuze in 1994', *Mens en Maatschappij* 71(2), 131–41.

SCP (1996) *Sociaal en Cultureel Rapport 1996*. Rijswijk: Sociaal en Cultureel Planbureau.

Stapel, J. (1984) 'De profiteurs van positieve discriminatie', *Beleid en Maatschappij* 11(4), 102–8.

Stöss, R. (1994) 'Forschungs-und Erklürungsansätze: Ein Überblick', in Kowalsky, W. and Schroeder W. (eds) *Rechtsextremismus: Einführung und Forschungsbilanz*. Opladen: Westdeutscher Verlag.

Taylor, S. (1993) 'The radical right in Britain', in Merkl, P.H. and Weinberg, L. (eds) *Encounters with the Contemporary Radical Right*. Boulder, CO.: Westview Press.

Van den Brink, R. (1994) *De internationale van de haat: extreem-rechts in West-Europa*. Amsterdam: SUA.

Van den Brink, R. (1996) 'The Netherlands', in *Extremism from the Atlantic to the Urals*. Paris: European Center for Research and Action on Racism and Anti-semitism.

Van der Veen, A. and Dicke, O. (1993) *CD-stemmers anno 1993*. Amsterdam: Interview.

Van Donselaar, J. (1982) 'Racistische partijen in drie Europese landen', in Van Amersfoort, J.M.M. and Entzinger, H.B. (eds) *Immigrant en samenleving*. Deventer: Van Loghum Slaterus.

Van Donselaar, J. (1991) *Fout na de oorlog: fascistische en racistische organisaties in Nederland', 1950–1990*. Amsterdam: Bert Bakker.

Van Donselaar, J. (1993) 'Post-war fascism in the Netherlands', *Crime, Law and Social Change* 19(1), 87–100.

Van Donselaar, J. (1995) *De staat paraat? De bestrijding van extreem-rechts in West-Europa*. Amsterdam: Babylon-De Geus.

Van Donselaar, J. and Van Praag, C. (1983) *Stemmen op de Centrumpartij: de opkomst van anti-vreemdelingen partijen in Nederland*. Leiden: Centrum voor Onderzoek van Maatschappelijke Tegenstellingen.

Van Ginneken, J. (1994) *Den Haag op de divan: een psychologische analyse van onze politieke top*. Haarlem: Aramith.

Van Holsteyn, J. (1990) 'En wij dan? De kiezers van de Centrumdemocraten', *Socialisme en Democratie* 47(6), 158–61.

Van Holsteyn, J. (1995) 'Groeistuipen of stuiptrekkingen: extreem-rechts en de verkiezingen van 1994', *Socialisme en Democratie* 52(2), 75–85.

Van Holsteyn, J. (1998) 'Hans Janmaat, kamerlid', in Van Holsteyn, J. and Mudde, C. (eds) *Extreem-rechts in Nederland*. The Hague: Sdu.

Van Hout, B. (1994) 'De dodenlijst van de Centrum Democraten', *Panorama*, 17–24 March, 12, 15, 17.

Van Riel, C. (1997) *Doen of laten? Het functioneren van gemeenteraadsleden van extreem-rechts*. Leiden: Vakgroep Politieke Wetenschappen.

Van Schendelen, M. P. C. M. (1983) 'De Centrumpartij: karakter, voedingsbodem, toekomst', *Beleid en Maatschappij* 10(11), 298–305.

Verrips, G. (1995) *Dwars, duivels, dromend: de geschiedenis van de CPN 1938–1991*. Amsterdam: Balans.

Von der Dunk, H. W. (ed.) (1982) *In de schaduw van de depressie: de NSB en de verkiezingen in de jaren dertig*. Alphen aan den Rijn: A.W. Sijthoff.

Weinberg, L. B., Eubank, W. L. and Wilcox, A. R. (1995) 'A brief analysis of the extreme right in Western Europe', *Italian Politics and Society* 43(1), 41–8.

Willemsen, A. W. (1969) *Het Vlaams-nationalisme: de geschiedenis van de jaren 1914–1940*. Utrecht: Ambo.

Zaal, W. (1973) *De Nederlandse fascisten*. Amsterdam: Wetenschappelijke Uitgeverij.

CHAPTER EIGHT

The extreme right and British exceptionalism: the primacy of politics

Roger Eatwell

British exceptionalism

During the inter-war years, the extreme right was less successful in Britain than in virtually any other West European state. Its most important group, Sir Oswald Mosley's British Union of Fascists, was so weak that it did not contest the 1935 general election, and made little impact in local elections. Briefly aided by the support of the mass-circulation newspaper the *Daily Mail*, it attracted 50,000 members during early 1934, but 5000–10,000 was its norm (Skidelsky, 1975; Thurlow, 1998). Thus in the post-war era there have been no major pockets of ageing extreme right supporters of the type which emerged especially in Italy and West Germany during the late 1940s and early 1950s. Nor has there been the major electoral breakthrough among new supporters of the sort achieved by the *Front National* in France during the 1980s.

The largest of the British post-war extreme right groups, the National Front (NF), was formed in 1967 and has always rejected the 'fascist' tag. Yet in spite of stressing its British credentials, the NF has proved incapable of winning any form of election, though in some local elections it attracted a notable minority following. Its membership peaked at an unimpressive 14,000 back in 1972 (curiously, a time when extremist parties were doing poorly in most European countries). By the mid-1990s, the NF was little more than a dwindling band of activists, though in 1995 the core of the party sought to revive its fortunes by adopting the name 'National Democrats'. The main leader of the NF during the 1970s was John Tyndall, who went on in 1982 to form the British National Party (BNP). Tyndall had been an overt Nazi in the past, which allowed opponents to label the BNP, like the NF before it, 'Nazi'. But on a minority vote, the BNP won a much-publicized local election victory in 1993 on London's Isle of Dogs. However, its

Table 8.1 National Front (NF) and British National Party (BNP) general election performances

Year	UK total constituencies	NF cands.	NF average[a]/ highest % vote	BNP cands.	BNP average[a]/ highest % vote
1970	630	10	3.6/5.6	—	—
1974 (Feb.)	635	54	3.3/7.8	—	—
1974 (Oct.)	635	90	3.1/9.4	—	—
1979	635	303	1.4/7.6	—	—
1983	650	60	1.1/2.4	54[b]	0.6/1.3
1987	650	1[c]	0.6/0.6	2[c]	0.5/0.6
1992	651	14	0.7/1.2	13	1.2/3.6
1997	659	6[d]	1.2/1.0	56	1.4/7.5

Notes:

[a] For seats contested.

[b] The BNP claims this number, but only 50 seem to have adopted the BNP label, and another 4 ran under similar titles. In most cases these candidates made no attempt to campaign locally (whereas in 1997 all BNP candidates seem to have put out election propaganda, though serious campaigning was concentrated in a handful of localities).

[c] Unofficial candidates. The increase in 1985 of the deposit for each candidate from £150 to £500 made the cost of fighting elections significant for fringe parties like the NF and BNP (though the threshold necessary for the return of the deposit was lowered to 5 per cent).

[d] Plus 21 candidates from the National Democrats: average vote 1.2 per cent, highest vote 11.39 per cent (the seat of the Speaker of the House of Commons, which is traditionally uncontested by the main parties).

membership has never been more than 3000, often young working-class 'toughs'. And while there have been a few localities where it could attract 5–20 per cent of the vote, in general its electoral success has been minimal, as Table 8.1 shows. (For an overview of British extremism, see Eatwell, 1996a.)

These opening comments and statistics clearly highlight the exceptionalism of the British extreme right, and seem to point to its essential marginality to the wider study of extremism. However, closer analysis reveals that the British experience is highly relevant to three major questions central to comparative analyses of extremism.

One concerns the very usage of the term 'extreme right', which is all too often taken as an unproblematic ascription covering different types of fascist and non-fascist groups in both the pre and post-1945 periods. Yet Mosley's post-1945 philosophical policy writings, and the little-studied debates within the NF during the 1980s, underline crucial problems about the placement of fascism on the left–right spectrum (Eatwell, 1996b). Similarities with the policies of some Conservatives raise the further question of whether a neat line can be drawn between the 'extreme' and 'moderate' rights. Thus it has been argued that there is a pervasive 'new racism' which cuts across the right (Barker, 1980). This does not articulate the older type of racism, based on ideas of inferiority and superiority among racial groups. Rather it stresses 'natural' group solidarity and exclusiveness. However, questions of typology fall outside the remit of the national chapters in this book: as a result, this theme is not pursued further here (on conceptualizing the right, see Eatwell and O'Sullivan, 1989; Eatwell, 1992, 1996c; Mudde, 1996).

A second area of considerable comparative interest concerns the relationship between extremist groups and racially motivated attacks. There are considerable problems in measuring the level of such violence across countries, as states collect their statistics in different ways (Björgo and Witte, 1993). There are also problems in terms of collecting statistics within individual countries: in Britain, police statistics indicate a level well below the 1990s' average Crime Survey's figure of 100,000-plus racially motivated incidents (which includes verbal abuse). Nevertheless, the apparently high figure for Britain raises the hypothesis that where extremist parties are not successful electorally, activists' attention is diverted towards other areas. Certainly some of the pressure to form the Combat 18–National Socialist Alliance grouping, which largely grew out of the BNP in the early 1990s, seems to have reflected such pressure. But most racial attacks are carried out by young males who are not members of extremist groups, though they may have been influenced by local activists or racist propaganda (Husbands, 1989; Virdee, 1995). Indeed, the whole issue of proof is elusive and requires a detailed micro-perspective – a task too specialized for this book.

The problem of extreme right support

The main focus of what follows, therefore, is on a third question: namely, how to explain the low levels of extremist voting. Has the British extreme right failed because of a basic lack of support within the land? Or has the extreme right been blessed with a more fertile soil to till? Certainly there have been many developments which should have favoured racist or extreme nationalist politics, including the arrival of notable ethnic minorities in some areas (there were 3.5 million non-whites, making up 5.5 per cent of the population, according to the 1991 census); rising unemployment, especially among young, less-skilled males; a variety of problems relating to inner-city decline, such as poor housing, and crime; and last – but by no means least – the strong antipathy towards the growing integration of Europe which has been revealed by many opinion polls.

Surveys undertaken during the 1960s and 1970s revealed extensive support for principles commonly associated with the extreme right, such as the desire for strong leadership, or nationalism. Studies in the 1970s found that over a quarter of respondents agreed with the main policy plank of the NF – namely, the compulsory repatriation of non-white immigrants (Särlvik and Crewe, 1983: 243); 21 per cent thought it would be 'good for Britain' if the NF was represented in the House of Commons; and a quarter of respondents thought that the NF expressed the views of 'ordinary working people' (Harrop *et al.*, 1980: 281). The potential for extremism seems to be underlined by poll evidence from the European Community's journal *Eurobarometer*. The December 1985 issue revealed that 6 per cent of UK respondents self-located as polar 'extreme right' on a 10-point scale, the second highest number in the Community. The December 1988 issue found 11 per cent who were completely, or to some extent, in favour of racist movements, the fifth highest in the Community. The November 1989 issue divided national populations into five categories in terms of attitudes to democracy and race. The fourth category included those who rejected democracy as a good idea: 20 per cent of UK respondents came in this group, the fourth highest in the Community.

It is important not to overstate the import of this information. Opposition to 'Europe' has to be judged in the light of a basic scepticism about alternative scenarios, not least the NF's plan to re-create a primarily white-dominated Empire-based trade and political grouping. A yearning for strong leadership, or holding nationalist – even racist – views, does not necessarily lead to conversion to the extreme right. Moreover, the validity of some polls' findings can be challenged, especially those done on small samples, or involving potentially misleading categories. For example, the self-ascription 'extreme right' in the 1985 poll could encompass many positions, including *laissez-faire*/libertarian, or it could simply reflect a sense of alienation. The same point could be made about actually voting for the extreme right. Thus, it has been argued that the key to NF voting was whether an alternative protest 'vehicle' was available, notably a Liberal candidate (Steed, 1974: 336). The same author has sought to show that there was a relatively constant 2–4 per cent of the vote 'available' to extreme right candidates in certain areas, with variations above this figure mainly reflect-ing factors such as differential turnout (see also Taylor, 1982: 116ff.).

On the other hand, there is evidence that people are less willing to admit to supporting extremist parties. People may also tend to explain their vote to pollsters in terms of everyday factors, such as economic prosperity, rather than more diffuse ones like nationalism, let alone admit 'illegitimate' influences such as racism. Moreover, the exact factors which influence voting may remain obscured by aggregate data analysis. This is not simply the statistical point that if enough correlations are run it would be surprising if some apparently significant relationships did not emerge (Sanders, 1987, sought to demonstrate the importance of economics in voting after the 1982 Falklands War by using 26 factors, each lagged from one to twelve months, a total of 338 possible effects!). There is also more specific evidence.

Correlating the NF vote with the presence of an alternative 'protest' candidate may produce an apparent relationship, but evidence from detailed local studies suggests that the simple protest explanation may be misleading. In particular, the Liberals at the local level, contrary to their national platform, were sometimes perceived as 'hard' on race. Finally, the argument that NF voting is largely explained by factors such as differential turnout out confuses as much as it enlightens. For example, it does not fully explain the particularly high NF votes in some areas, notably parts of London's East End, or Leicester. And where did this constant reservoir go in the 1980s, when voting for extremist parties largely disappeared for a time?

The potential for significant extreme right support can be illustrated by a hypothetical case. The prominent Conservative MP Enoch Powell gained considerable publicity and popularity after 1968 on account of his statements predicting racial violence, and trumpeting the 'voluntary' repatriation of the non-white community. In 1974, he broke with the Conservatives over their acceptance of membership of the European Community, and of continued non-white immigration into Britain (Schoen, 1977). What if he had joined the NF at this point, giving the party added legitimacy? In general, the European extreme right has prospered where it has charismatic, media-attractive leaders – a marked contrast to the ageing A. K. Chesterton, who led the early NF, or the bombastic and pompous Tyndall, who was its leader for most of the 1970s (on Chesterton, see Baker, 1996). And what if elections to the European Parliament, held under proportional representation, had taken place during one of the NF's 1970s peaks? It could be countered that this scenario glosses over important objections. First, there were notable ideological differences between Powell and the NF: in particular, Powell was a great defender of parliamentary democracy and *laissez-faire* economics. Certainly, it is not being claimed here that Powell almost joined the NF, though many other Conservatives who were in no way fascist entered the NF in the 1970s. Second, Taylor has argued that the electoral system had little to do with the NF's failure, citing a single survey where only 5 per cent said that they would be likely to vote NF if they thought it could do well (Taylor, 1982: 179–80). Yet other polls cited above tend to indicate a greater NF potential.

This Powell–proportional representation scenario is meant not just to illustrate the potential for extreme right groups, but also to underline a point about the study of the extreme right. Most analyses of extremist support have played down factors such as the activities of individual politicians, or the operation of the party system, in favour of more sociological and structural explanations. Most typically, Britain is seen as not having experienced a sufficiently severe economic depression to promote extremism (cf. Germany in 1932), and/or its pattern of immigration has not seen the sudden peak which arrived in some countries (e.g. asylum seekers in Germany during 1991–2). The argument here is not that socio-economic factors are unimportant. The point is more to retrieve the relevance of a political dimension – especially the activities of mainstream political elites, the electoral system, and the nature of extremist leadership and ideology.

Put more theoretically, extremist parties tend to break through when there is (Eatwell, 1998a) insurgent group *legitimacy* + rising personal *efficacy* + declining system *trust*. Unpopular governments are not enough: this could simply lead to voting for mainstream opposition parties. There has to be a general loss of faith in mainstream politics. Insurgent parties too need to be seen as not completely beyond the pale. And their potential voters need to believe they can have an effect (otherwise, why bother to vote?). Put another way, the argument here supports a rational choice rather than blind protest theory of voting. Extremist voters are certainly protesting, but their acts in general are not random: they vote for extremist parties when they believe such acts are likely to have an impact. An individual's perception of this is determined more by political than by purely socio-economic factors.

Who voted for and joined the NF in the 1970s?

Opinion poll or aggregate data analyses of NF voting in the 1970s have produced remarkably inconsistent results. The main area of agreement is that NF support tended to be male, was negatively correlated with turnout, and was primarily English. (In Wales and Scotland, moderate, catch-all nationalist parties grew dramatically after the mid-1960s, while Northern Ireland exhibited its own unique pattern of nationalist and regional politics.) The two main areas of disagreement concern the class and age base of the NF. Many have argued that the bulk of NF support came from an 'authoritarian' working-class (Whiteley, 1979), but when Husbands divided NF supporters into 'strong' and 'moderate', he found that while the former were heavily working class, overall there was no significant class factor. Husbands found that the main area of relative NF support was among the 'marginal' self-employed – that is, those without formal qualifications, who tended to employ no one outside the family (Husbands, 1983: 136ff.). He explained this mainly by reference to the precarious economic position of many in this group. He also argued that when his two groups were combined, there was no strong age correlation, challenging the views of many others who have stressed the appeal of the NF to an alienated youth, which was experiencing growing unemployment.

The main focus of Husbands's work was on the locational side of NF support. He argued that there were two main types of environment where NF support was greatest. These were post-1945 boom areas which were experiencing economic difficulties in the 1970s (e.g. Coventry, Slough), and declining traditional industrial areas (e.g. Bradford, Leicester). The NF thus had little support in rural or suburban areas, but was mainly a feature of parts of London, the Midlands and northern England. However, a problem with this approach is that there is no necessary connection: not all areas in these categories showed significant NF support, and it had pockets of 'deviant' support, such as seaside Blackpool. Alternative locational approaches have, therefore, focused on the correlation between NF voting and the immediate presence of ethnic communities, versus 'invasion' approaches which hold that racist voting is likely to be greater in areas on the periphery of ethnic settlement. In Britain, the former seems to offer the best explanation at the local level. Nevertheless, it is important to note that the two NF voting peaks in the 1970s came shortly after well-publicized new waves of immigration by the expelled Ugandan Asians in 1972–3 and Malawian Asians in 1976–7, which raised distinct 'invasion' fears (Taylor, 1979).

A study of the NF's leadership and activists underlines the problems involved in producing a model of support. Most of the leadership tended to be middle class, but it was a mixed bag. There were a small number, especially in the early days, from relatively wealthy backgrounds, individuals who were often important financial props of the party. There was a larger group, typified by Tyndall and Martin Webster, who can best be described as 'marginal' middle class: they tended to be travelling salesmen, or to have some form of self-employed occupation. There was even a group with degree-level education, including the author of the 1974 Holocaust denial pamphlet *Did Six Million Really Die*? – which has been repeatedly reprinted around the world (on the appeal of the Holocaust denial and extremist groups, see Eatwell, 1995). The main linking strands at the top seem to have been a distinct lack of charismatic leadership potential, administrative incompetence, and a tendency to ideological schism! At the grassroots level, studies have stressed the difficulties of generalizing about activists (Billig, 1978; Scott, 1975). The main factor linking local members seems to have been hostility to 'immigrants' rather than socio-economic background.

However, the main centres of NF voting occurred within working-class communities. Husbands's division of NF supporters into 'strong' and 'moderate' is important to an understanding of the *potential* for the NF, but actual NF voting is better understood within the former category. The existence of a clearly demarcated, traditional working-class 'community' seems to have been particularly important in provoking anti-immigrant resentment, and in influencing non-working class groups within that community. It was especially a feature of areas with older extreme right traditions, or weak Labour traditions, for example London's East End. Resentment also stemmed from socio-economic fears: for example, possible falling house prices in areas of immigrant settlement; job competition as the labour market tightened; or the quality of schooling in areas of growing ethnic families. As such, a variety of motives were involved in NF voting. There was unquestionably an element of racism, but there was also an element of financial self-interest. There was even a defence of traditional working-class values such as a stress on 'respectability'. At the turn of the century, opprobrium was vented on those (whites) who left their houses dirty, or drank too much; now, the targets were more overcrowded ethnic minority homes, or the stereotypical view of immigrants as sexually immoral and prone to laziness.

The failure of the NF and the British political tradition

This focus on factors such as community and particular traditions illustrates the importance of not assuming that all significant explanatory factors can be found contemporaneously. Lipset and Rokkan, in their classic study of party systems, argued that, with few exceptions, post-war divisions were based on the cleavages of the 1920s (Lipset and Rokkan, 1967: 50). Thus a crucial question at the macro-historical level is why the extreme right in Britain has failed to make a significant impact at any point in the twentieth century.

One common social science explanation of this lacuna revolves around an analysis of political culture (Benewick, 1969). This analysis sees Britain as a 'civic culture', a country whose democratic institutions are held in high esteem, possessing a unique blend of modernity and tradition. Pervasive, consensual, deferential and non-violent traits, encouraging a deep-rooted civility, seemed to militate against radical and activist philosophies (Almond and Verba, 1963). This approach offers important insights, but it glosses over complex definitional and historical questions (Eatwell, 1997). Arguably, its major problem is that it sees Britain as having been an easy country to govern because of its civic culture. A more fruitful approach is to reverse the causality (though this still leaves unanswered causal and definitional questions). The argument thus becomes the claim that the civic culture, especially deference, has been a result of good government.

The problem about what constitutes 'good government' can be seen in a very specific context by considering a debate about the role of both extreme right and 'anti-fascist' street demonstrations. One of the main legacies of the inter-war era has been the left-wing myth that fascism in Britain was stopped by street violence. Many have claimed that demonstrations, especially those by the Anti-Nazi League, furthered the decline of the NF (Messina, 1989: 121). It could be countered that the League began activity only after the beginning of the NF's demise. But the main point being made here is that the 'state' has on the whole handled such demonstrations well. Another legacy of the inter-war extreme right is the 1936 Public Order Act, which allows the banning of demonstrations. This has been invoked relatively few times since 1945 to ban extremist activities, and critics have argued that this reflects a certain complicity in extreme right politics. Certainly, there has been some worrying antipathy within the police to the ethnic minority population, a situation which has encouraged left-wing commentators to claim that racism is pervasive within the police (Scraton, 1985: 104). However, the British forces of law and order have not shown the connivance, or tendency to turn a blind eye, towards the extreme right that was often a feature of its rise in other countries (Thurlow, 1994). Indeed, although difficult to prove (and thus hardly researched), it is possible that police and anti-fascist penetration of extremist groups has been an important factor in their failure (Hill and Bell, 1988, stress the activities of the anti-fascist magazine *Searchlight*). Permission to hold extreme right demonstrations seems to have been based mainly on the weighing of the interests of public order versus those of free association and speech – and probably ultimately on the belief that such demonstrations diminished rather than increased extreme right support. Certainly the NF was ill-advised to engage in marches during the late 1970s if it was seeking to court more mainstream support (it appears to have hoped for favourable publicity!).

More generally, the question of 'good government' raises debates about elites, and the party system. A party system has many facets. First, the British first-past-the-post electoral system militates against insurgent parties, especially in terms of initial take-off (although there is a level at around the 30 per cent plus point where the system can actually help in a multi-party situation: it is worth noting here that the Nazis in 1932 would probably have gained even greater representation had Germany used the British electoral system). Second, there is the very structure of parties. Britain's major parties have undoubtedly been well organized, both locally and nationally, in comparison with their often cadre-based continental counterparts – and in contrast to the small extreme right groups, which have been unable to mount serious campaigns outside a handful of 'homelands', unless they can bus activists in for single by-elections. Third, there is the relationship between the national and local political system. Britain's unitary state and developed communications helped 'nationalize' issues at an early stage. The extreme right on the Continent was helped by local structures in which different messages could be disseminated by relatively well-organized extremist parties. A fourth relevant aspect of party systems is the nature of the relationship between voters and parties. Are there close ties of partisanship, based on, say, class? Or do voters seem more influenced by certain issues, thereby encouraging volatile behaviour?

The British party system from the 1920s to the 1960s exhibited strong alignment along predominantly class lines but, at the same time, the Conservative and Labour parties were also archetypal programmatic parties. Purely sociological analyses have failed to see that class politics were intimately tied to a particular ideological form. And the central ideological problem of British fascism in the inter-war period was its inability to delineate policies perceived as salient. This has also been true, though less so, during the post-war period, when the growth of an 'immigrant' population has provided extremism with an obvious target for scapegoating.

Labour ideology has included aspects such as the rejection of class analysis by its national leadership, and espousal of a form of corporatism. A vital factor has been its sense of 'movement' which helped tide it through crises, such as after the major split of 1931, and which remained strong even after 1945 (note the decline on the Continent of terms such as *Bewegung* or *movimento*). Labour has also at times exhibited a form of nationalism, and while the Labour leadership in the post-war era could not be considered racist in the classic sense of legitimizing hierarchies, it could be considered racist in other senses. In particular, it has supported 'state racism' in areas such as immigration policy (see Reeves, 1983, for a discussion of racial party ideology), though this has been countered by a more positive support for protective race relations laws (a Labour government passed the first Race Relations Act in 1965). The leadership's hostility during the 1980s and 1990s to 'black sections' in a party which already has women's and other sections reflects a fear that growing ethnic political activity might damage the party, especially in working-class eyes. White votes come before positive discrimination, though the leadership has to balance this with a desire to maintain its predominant vote among the ethnic communities. Finally, it is important to distinguish between the local and national level: at the under-researched local level, there was sometimes a cruder racism, especially in the trade unions.

Conservative ideology historically has served even more to defuse extreme right appeals. One important aspect of its ideology has been its strong nationalism, though, because Britain is a multinational state, this has never taken a specifically racial form. Another important aspect of conservatism is its organicism, which has been linked to concepts such as its own form of corporatism and welfarism. It has also not been anti-working class; indeed, British Conservatism has shown a remarkable understanding of, and appeal to, the working class. Turning more specifically to defusing extremism, it was the Conservatives who passed the first, restrictive, Commonwealth Immigrants Act of 1962, and it was the Conservatives who increasingly came to be viewed by electors as the party most opposed to 'immigration'. Whereas a 1964 poll gave the Conservatives a narrow 21 to 19 per cent lead over Labour on the issue of which party would be most likely to keep immigrants out, by 1970 the respective figures were 57 to 4 per cent (Layton-Henry, 1978: 272; see also Layton-Henry, 1992). As government policy on race tended to be bi-partisan, much of the 'credit' for this dramatic change must go to the activities of Enoch Powell, the right-wing Conservative ginger group the Monday Club, and local campaigning (it is interesting to note that Powell received more column inches in the national press during the 1970 general election campaign than were accorded to the entire Liberal Party). After the two Conservative general election defeats in 1974, anti-immigrant themes resurfaced more visibly. For example, the moderate William Whitelaw made a notable set of speeches on immigration during 1974–5, and during the late 1970s Margaret Thatcher sought to consolidate support among the authoritarian-nationalist constituency, most notably in her well-publicized 1978 reference to Britain being 'swamped' by alien cultures, a comment which was followed by notable Conservative gains in polls and evidence that many people viewed race issues as more important than economic ones (Hall and Jacques, 1981; Studlar, 1985).

Party ideology also has to be understood within the context of media coverage, especially as the decline of street campaigning since 1945 has accorded the media an even greater role in political communication. The nature of the NF coverage in the media is complex. Sections of the media, notably the tabloid market-leader *The Sun*, have undoubtedly exhibited forms of racism and redneck nationalism (Hartmann and Husband, 1974; Murray, 1986; Troyna, 1981). There has also been some tendency to see the extreme right as a 'feature' (*Yorkshire Post*, 3 September 1970; *Observer* colour magazine, 16 June 1991), or to play up the NF's electoral potential (*Guardian*, 5 July 1977). However, the extreme right has received little in the way of direct media sympathy. In general it has simply been ignored, though in the late 1970s there was extensive publicity of the NF's links with Nazism, and its marches were often portrayed as provocative (*Daily Mirror*, 4 April and 19 July 1977). Even the under-researched local press often took up the anti-fascist attack (*South East London and Kentish Mercury*, 5 May 1977; *Western Mail*, 27 April 1978). Such reporting has led to a common view on the extreme right that the mass media were its 'biggest single enemy' (*National Front News*, No. 95, September 1987: 2).

These points about mainstream ideology and the media are not meant to deny the importance of other factors in the NF's decline. This had begun before Thatcher's clear appeal to actual and potential NF supporters (though it could be argued that there has been a universal tendency among commentators to concentrate too much on Thatcher, rather than other Conservatives who anticipated these themes, and campaigning at the local level also needs to be studied). A full discussion of the demise of the NF during and after the late 1970s would have to look too at factors such as its ideological and personality splits: in particular, notable elements in the party became addicted to the most esoteric strands of ideology (Eatwell, 1996b). By the 1980s, some factions within the party openly accepted political violence, and more generally there was an adoption of continental-inspired ideologies which had clear affinities with the fascist tradition – much to the disgust of the 'purer' British nationalists. The role of anti-fascist groups and the widespread tagging of the NF with the 'fascist' label would also have to be considered: while there were notable strands of extreme right-oriented opinion within the electorate, fascism (especially Nazism) was seen as beyond the pale, and aspects of anti-fascism were central to national identity (Britain alone in 1940, the Battle of Britain, and so on).

During the 1980s, the Conservatives continued to benefit from nationalist sentiment, though their ascendancy owed more to divisions and weaknesses within the opposition. This sentiment involved much more than the fact that the Falklands War helped transform Mrs Thatcher from the most unpopular prime minister since Gallup polls began, to the landslide election victor of 1983 and 1987. Even before the Falklands, Thatcher's rhetoric had stressed the communist menace, and the Labour opposition's unilateral nuclear disarmament commitment. There was also a recurring nationalism in Conservative rhetoric on European unity, for example over the publicly conducted demands for British budget rebates in the early 1980s. Anti-Europeanism was formulated more cogently in Thatcher's 1988 Bruges speech, which criticized the growing federalist approach of the European Community. Anti-immigration politics also continued to emerge periodically, most notably in 1981 with the passing of a new Nationality Act, in 1986 with the tightening of regulations for visitors from some New Commonwealth countries, and in 1992 with scare stories about a wave of asylum seekers should Labour win the general election (a theme widely picked up in the Conservative tabloid press as John Major seemed to be staggering towards defeat). Law and order too has continued to be a concern, exhibiting a strong anti-ethnic aspect in the wake of inner-city riots in 1981, 1985 and 1991, and with growing problems such as the spread of addictive drugs.

The BNP: the same old story?

By the early 1990s, the main extremist group was John Tyndall's BNP. Tyndall had part left, part been pushed out of the NF in 1980, mainly as a result of pressures from two factions. One group of radical fascists sought to redefine the creed; another faction of British nationalists believed that Tyndall's overt Nazi past made it impossible to extend the party's appeal outside an alienated fringe. The BNP was in many ways a re-run of the 1970s NF. However, before the early 1990s, it never achieved the high national profile of its predecessor, as it was incapable of mounting major marches, or running serious election campaigns outside a handful of areas (Copsey, 1996; Eatwell, 1998b; Kushner, 1994). Although it put up over 50 candidates in the 1983 general election, this was mainly a shadow exercise in an attempt to gain publicity and attract members (*Members Bulletin*, February 1984) – tasks in which it signally failed.

Tyndall tried initially to prevent the BNP from acquiring the alienated young male fringe which had helped delegitimize the NF, but the party soon acquired a similar visage (on female support for the NF and BNP, see Durham, 1995). Tyndall's efforts to distance himself from the Nazi past also remained somewhat half-hearted. His private monthly journal, *Spearhead*, continued periodically to let the mask slip; in particular, in spite of divisions within the party over the issue, *Spearhead* continued to advertise Holocaust denial material (e.g. *Spearhead*, June 1995). In spite of this continued dalliance with fascism, Tyndall still believed that the best way forward lay in attracting disillusioned Conservative voters – a long-standing belief which helps explain the NF's failure to exploit disarray in the Labour ranks during the 1970s. However, there were some changes in BNP policies *vis-à-vis* the NF. In particular, by the mid-1990s, there were growing doubts about the old commitment to highly statist, corporatist economics designed to provide full employment and welfare (for whites). Indeed, in 1995, Tyndall accused the former Conservative Cabinet free marketeer John Redwood, who had just challenged John Major for the leadership of the party, of stealing the BNP's clothes (*Spearhead*, August 1995).

In spite of the claims of 'supply-side' theorists, notably Herbert Kitschelt, of extremist support, these changes were not important to the sensational local election victory which the BNP achieved in the Millwall district of London's Isle of Dogs in 1993 (Kitschelt, 1995). Although Kitschelt argues that only if such groups choose free-market appeals combined with authoritarian, ethnocentric messages can they attract a broad audience, the BNP in this area in no way stressed free-market policies, though it strongly attacked 'immigrants'. However, the BNP's victory did owe much to other supply-side factors. Although there were various problems in the area, such as high unemployment and competition for good council housing, Millwall was not significantly different in basic socio-economic terms from many other areas in which the BNP came nowhere near to winning an election. But on the Isle of Dogs three factors came together to help the BNP. First, this was an area with a strong sense of white community, 'threatened' by periodic waves of immigration historically, and most recently by 'yuppie' development. This meant that there were local coteries who kept an extreme right tradition alive. Second, the BNP commenced its activities in the area under the name 'Rights for Whites', which focused on specific local grievances, such as the apparently racially motivated killing of a white youth. This helped it to extend its support within the local community, and even gain non-hostile local media coverage: by 1992, the BNP had 20 per cent of the vote in Millwall. Third, the area was historically a Labour stronghold, but during the 1980s the Liberals had begun to exploit racist sentiment among the white community. By the early 1990s, sections of local Labour too were seeking to pander to exclusionist white sentiment. In 1993, in an attempt to squeeze the Liberal Democrat vote, the local Labour Party released canvass returns which seemed to show that the BNP had a serious chance of winning.

Another major academic attempt to explain the BNP's securing victory on 34 per cent of the vote has used Juan Linz's fertile concept of 'political space' (Copsey, 1996; Lunn, 1996; note too that an important part of Kitschelt's approach stresses the need for a favourable 'political opportunity structure'). However, while it is true that local mainstream parties had failed to 'deliver' significantly in terms of cutting the immigrant population, some policies – such as housing allocation – had in general favoured whites. Moreover, there were many inner-city areas where the mainstream parties had left far more ideological space for the extremists to enter, but this rarely produced a significant extremist vote. It is difficult to be precise about exactly who voted for the BNP in Millwall, or why, as there is remarkably little opinion poll evidence. It appears that the overall socio-economic profile was very similar to that of the NF in the 1970s, though a particularly notable feature in Millwall was that 60 per cent of BNP supporters had lived in the area for more than 21 years, although this group made up only 30 per cent of the local population. Motive-wise, there was an element of protest, but it seems that there was also a more positive side to voting – a genuine choice of the BNP as a party whose nationalist policies could stop the rot and which had a chance of winning. It succeeded, therefore, not so much from space as from efficacy and legitimation.

The following year, the BNP lost the seat. Its candidate was inarticulate and had achieved nothing in terms of policy change, while a major anti-fascist campaign by the main parties, local groups and the media once again highlighted the BNP's Nazi pedigree (e.g. *Daily Mirror*, 18 September 1993: 'SIEG HEIL . . . and Now He's a British Councillor'). By this time, the BNP was also troubled by internal splits, and especially tensions with Combat 18 and the National Socialist Alliance (Gable, 1995). There is some evidence that these groups were manipulated by the forces of 'law and order', and it is interesting to note that these tensions – which even led to violence between the factions – became especially intense after the BNP had made such a spectacular breakthrough. However, penetration of these groups was probably designed to elicit information on criminal activity, such as drug dealing, rather than to break extremism. Regardless of manipulation, tensions were inevitable as victory in Millwall strengthened the hand of those in the party who sought to pursue a relatively respectable electoral path, a development which angered the more street-fighting wing. Such problems continued to plague the extreme right in the late 1990s.

During 1995, the BNP sought to revive its flagging fortunes by announcing that it would contest at least 50 seats in the next general election. It also launched its first site on the Internet, offering a choice of articles from its journals and links to various other sites around the world of interest to white nationalists. In the October 1995 issue of *Spearhead*, the Net was described as the most important media development since television. Like the NF, the BNP was obsessed with the media, which was seen as dominated by Jews and/or totally opposed to its cause (BNP, 1993?). The Net offered the opportunity of by-passing the mainstream media, and of giving often isolated members a sense of belonging (Eatwell, 1996d). But initially the site was not always kept up to date, and it was of low graphical sophistication. By the 1997 elections, things had improved, but it is doubtful if many potential voters saw it, let alone were influenced by it. Certainly, the weak performance by BNP candidates in the 1997 general election offers no grounds for thinking that the party's message was reaching receptive new audiences, as it retained its deposit in only 3 seats.

Conclusion

An opinion poll published in the *Daily Express* on 8 August 1995 – and much trumpeted by the BNP on its Net site – highlights a question which was raised near the beginning of this chapter, but which has not fully been answered: namely, to what extent has the failure of the extreme right stemmed from fundamental lack of support? The *Daily Express* poll indicated that 9 per cent of respondents would vote for a Le Pen-type *Front National*, and another 17 per cent said they would seriously consider doing so. As polls typically underestimate the support for extremist parties, these results are hard to square with BNP electoral performances. Possibly the poll was seriously flawed; but, unlike some polls on the NF in the 1970s, it was carried out by a professional polling organization (ICM) on a sample of over a thousand people. As it appears to be the only poll which has probed this issue, there is no way of checking results, and there are dangers of drawing excessive conclusions from one poll. Nevertheless, the fact that extremist parties have on occasion done relatively well, together with other poll evidence indicating the existence of nationalist and racist attitudes, points to the need to examine the *Daily Express* poll more carefully.

As British people might not be aware of the *Front National*, the ICM pollsters adapted four points from its programme to ascertain potential support: (a) whether priority should be given to British citizens on jobs, housing, social security and health; (b) whether organized repatriation should be commenced for groups of immigrants like the unemployed and convicted criminals; (c) whether there should be a tightening of asylum conditions; and (d) whether there should be an expulsion of illegal immigrants and a gradual working towards the repatriation of all migrants. The fact that a significant minority supported a party with such views is a powerful counter to myths of British tolerance, or immunity to extremism – especially as the ICM approach measures only affinity of programme and makes no allowance for the appeal of a charismatic leader like Le Pen. There is considerable evidence from general poll surveys that charismatic leaders appeal to those who are less educated, or to the politically less interested groups, which in recent years have often been the bedrocks of European extremist parties. It is also interesting to note that polls have indicated that one of the key reasons for the loss of Conservative support after the 1992 general election was Major's generally lacklustre leadership. Indeed, it seems that for some time there has been a major strand in working-class opinion which has sought strong leadership (Nordlinger, 1967: 17) – and this trait should not be ignored among sections of middle-class opinion.

As pointed out earlier, a desire for strong leadership – or other desires such as expulsion of illegal immigrants – should not *necessarily* be equated with serious extremist potential. It is also important not to ignore polls which show the growth of racial tolerance and multiculturalism. Nevertheless, there seem good grounds for believing that, since the 1960s, a notable minority of voters have become open to the supply of 'extremist' messages, especially exclusionist anti-'immigrant' and radical nationalist appeals. So why has this potential not been converted into extremist votes? The answer has already largely been provided in the preceding argument, but three points are highlighted here – underlining the crucial political dimension of failure, though picking up other points in passing. To them is appended a brief discussion of the extent to which these factors will remain powerful in the future.

First, the mainstream parties have been based historically on strong bonds of loyalty and have at crucial moments defused extremist potential. Radical critics sometimes talk of the main British parties, especially the Conservatives, as if they had caused racism (Sivanandan, 1976). It has even been argued that, 'Although the British state is still a long way from embracing fascism, it is the case that the development of state racism has helped prepare the ground for the emergence of neo-fascism as a political force in Britain' (Miles and Phizacklea, 1984: 118). While it is true that there has been an unpleasant face to Conservatism, notably in groups such as the Monday Club, and even more so in the secretive Tory Action, assertions such as this involve a serious misconception of what has happened at the party system level, and an inability to discern the complexities of Conservative policy. What the Conservatives, and to a lesser extent the Labour Party, have done is to *manage* racism. In doing so, they have legitimized forms of racism, but the general impact has been to defuse the issue as a potential extreme right clarion call.

However, affective allegiance to the mainstream parties appears to be in long-run decline and is unlikely to increase, given the decline of class identity and the loss of faith in traditional ideologies. The Conservatives are more divided over the issue of further European integration than over any issue since the turn of the century. Although in 1992 the Conservatives used fear of asylum seekers as a late election scare, many liberal Conservatives are unhappy about such tactics – not least as they fear the loss of both tolerant white votes and growing support among the Asian community. Indeed, in 1997, John Major seems to have told some leading Conservatives not to use immigration as a key campaign theme. Subsequently, the weak leadership of William Hague seems to have opened a notable gap for a party led by a suitably charismatic leadership. The Labour Party too may soon face problems in spite of its 1997 landslide (and increase in membership) – as illustrated by the party's poor Euro-election performance in 1999. The middle-class, at times conservative, leadership of Tony Blair could alienate many traditional working-class supporters. They have no obvious alternative home, though it is pertinent to note that the UK Independence Party performed well in the 1999 European election (see below) and that some polls showed that James Goldsmith's Euro-referendum party attracted former Labour as well as Conservative support in the 1997 election (Goldsmith's party will presumably die with its rich leader, who passed away shortly after the 1997 election). Labour is also faced with potential problems over ethnic assertiveness within the party, as it remains the main party of non-white voters.

Second, the election system has had several notable effects. Most obviously, it makes it difficult for new entrants to gather momentum, unless they can concentrate their vote very locally (in the way that Welsh and Scottish nationalists have done). As the 1993 Millwall election shows, the system can help parties once they reach a crucial size in multi-party contested elections, but as this is over 30 per cent it has been difficult for the extremists to reach this level. The electoral system has also had two other, less noticed effects. First, it encourages the different factions in the mainstream parties to stay together. If Britain had a list form of proportional representation, the Conservatives might well have split already over Europe. Second, it makes it less likely that local, or even national, deals will be struck with extremists – tendencies which in France and Italy especially have helped give the *Front National* and *Alleanza Nazionale* added legitimacy and profile (see Chapters 2 and 4).

With the election of a constitutionally reforming New Labour government, the issue of electoral reform is now on the agenda. Britain will not introduce a list system for parliamentary elections, but such a system was introduced for the 1999 European elections, and some form of proportional representation is a distinct possibility in the next decade for parliamentary and especially local elections. The BNP was too weak to benefit from the Euro changes in 1999, its 79 candidates achieving just 1 per cent of the vote (well behind the UK Independence Party's 7 per cent). But a new party in the future might be able to take advantage of such institutional change. Even if there is no change, a major split in a mainstream party could still occur: the formation of the Social Democratic Party by leading Labour members and others in 1981 shows that the present system does not guarantee that there will be no splits. A major breakaway by more radical nationalist Conservatives could provide a powerful force, though they may have problems defining a viable economic policy. Autarchic nationalism is clearly a thing of the past, as is reviving the Commonwealth. Free-market views have often been popular when linked to nationalism in other European countries, but there are signs that their appeal is waning. The forces of globalization make the market dangerous, and public support for the provision of extensive welfare remains relatively strong. There are also splits on the right about whether to adopt an English rather than British nationalist stance in response to the rise of Welsh and Scottish nationalism (which helped lead to these nations/regions being given their own elected assemblies from 1999). There certainly seems some potential for an English backlash, but historically the Conservatives have defended the Union.

The third problem concerns the extremist parties themselves. British extremism has far too clearly been tainted with the brush of fascism, a movement which has no legitimacy (unlike in Italy, where there are notable signs of a rehabilitation of aspects of Fascism). When Mosley re-entered politics after 1945, even many anti-semites would not join him as they thought he was beyond the pale (and he alienated many nationalists through his pro-European position). For all their protestations, both the NF and BNP have all too clearly been tagged with the Nazi label. Leadership too has been weak. A more charismatic leadership might have been better able to exploit limited media opportunities. There may be widespread media opposition to extremism, but there are media paradigms which make strong leaders attractive. The media's fascination with conflict and crime could also help set an agenda which might suit extremism – for example, news or feature coverage of black rioting or drug dealing.

It seems highly unlikely that the existing extremist parties can make a major breakthrough, but a new BNP leadership and influx of more politically educated members (of the type that helped the NF in the early 1970s) could provide a new impetus. In 1999, the rising star of the BNP was Nick Griffin, a Cambridge-educated graduate who for the 1999 Euro-elections helped push the BNP towards a more moderate stance – for instance, by repudiating the policy of compulsory repatriation and seeking allies among specific aggrieved groups, such as small farmers. Moreover, the violent side of extremism could encourage an ethnic backlash or further ethnic assertiveness in a way which might alienate white voters. It is not clear whether a member of an extremist group planted the bombs which might have killed dozens in London in April 1999 (the extreme right strategy of 'leaderless resistance' is targeted at lone assassins), but there seems little doubt that some activists are not averse to bombing suitable targets. Indeed, there are some violent activists who pursue this as a deliberate strategy: they believe that this is the way to shake complacent whites from their apathy. The problem for such extremists will be how to prevent their street presence/violence delegitimizing them (or other extremist groups) as an electoral force.

Clearly, at this point, the argument is becoming ever more speculative, and unduly concerned with the macro-political. A full analysis of the potential for the extreme right would require more detail on socio-economic change than has been possible here. For instance, is a white under-class emerging, and could it be the basis of a new extremism? It would also require a more localized perspective to assess whether race relations really were deteriorating after a period of improvement since the 1960s. However, it should be clear from the preceding arguments that the potential for a British Le Pen-type party has never been greater – especially if it emerges from the Conservatives rather than the ranks of British fascism.

The author would like to thank the British Academy for two grants to study the contemporary British extreme right.

References

Almond, G. and Verba, S. (1963) *The Civic Culture*. Princeton, NJ: Princeton University Press.

Baker, D. (1996) *A. K. Chesterton and British Fascism*. London: I. B. Tauris.

Barker, M. (1980) *The New Racism*. London: Junction Books.

Benewick, R. (1969) *Political Violence and Public Order*. London: Allen Lane.

Billig, M. (1978) *Fascists*. London: Harcourt Brace Jovanovich.

Björgo, T. and Witte, R. (eds) (1993) *Racial Violence in Europe*. Basingstoke: Macmillan.

British National Party (n.d. 1993?) *The Enemy Within: How TV Brainwashes a Nation.?* BNP.

Copsey, N. (1996) 'Contemporary Fascism in the Local Arena: The British National Party and "Rights for Whites" ', in Cronin, M. (ed.) *The Failure of British Fascism*. Basingstoke: Macmillan.

Durham, M. (1995) 'Women and the British Extreme Right', in Cheles, L. *et al.* (eds) *The Far Right in Western and Eastern Europe*. Harlow: Longman.

Eatwell, R. (1992) 'Towards a New Model of Generic Fascism', *Journal of Theoretical Politics* 4, 161–94.

Eatwell, R. (1995) 'How to Revise History and Influence People: Neo-Fascist Style', in Cheles, L. *et al.* (eds) *The Far Right in Western and Eastern Europe*. Harlow: Longman.

Eatwell, R. (1996a) *Fascism: A History*. London: Viking.

Eatwell, R. (1996b) 'The Esoteric Ideology of the National Front in the 1980s', in Cronin, M. (ed.) *The Failure of British Fascism*. Basingstoke: Macmillan.

Eatwell, R. (1996c) 'On Defining the "Fascist Minimum": The Centrality of Ideology' *Journal of Political Ideologies* 1, 303–19.

Eatwell, R. (1996d) 'Surfing the Great White Wave: The Internet, Extremism and the Problem of Control', *Patterns of Prejudice* 30, 61–71.

Eatwell, R. (1997) 'Britain', in Eatwell, R. (ed.) *European Political Cultures*. London: Routledge.

Eatwell, R. (1998a) 'The Dynamics of Extreme Right Electoral Breakthrough', *Patterns of Prejudice* 32, 3–31.

Eatwell, R. (1998b) 'The BNP', in Betz, H.-G. and Immerfall, S. (eds) *New Party Politics of the Right*. New York: St Martin's.

Eatwell, R. and O'Sullivan, N. (eds) (1989) *The Nature of the Right*. London: Pinter.

Gable, G. (1995) 'Britain's Nazi Underground', in Cheles, L. *et al.* (eds) *The Far Right in Western and Eastern Europe*. Harlow: Longman.

Hall, S. and Jacques, M. (1981) *The Politics of Thatcherism*. London: Verso.

Harrop, M., England, J. and Husbands, C. T. (1980) 'The Bases of National Front Support', *Political Studies* 28, 271–83.

Hartmann, P. and Husband, C. (1974) *Racism and the Mass Media*. London: Davis-Poynter.

Hill, R. and Bell, A. (1988) *The Other Face of Terror*. London: Grafton.

Husbands, C. T. (1983) *Racial Exclusionism and the City*. London: Allen & Unwin.

Husbands, C. T. (1989) 'Racial Attacks: The Persistence of Racial Vigilantism in British Cities', in Kushner, T. and Lunn, A. (eds) *Traditions of Intolerance*. Manchester: Manchester University Press.

Kitschelt, H. (1995) *The Radical Right in Western Europe*. Ann Arbor: University of Michigan Press.

Kushner, A. (1994) 'The Fascist as "Other"? Racism and Neo-Nazism in Contemporary Britain', *Patterns of Prejudice* 28, 27–45.

Layton-Henry, Z. (1978) 'Race, Electoral Strategy and the Major Parties', *Parliamentary Affairs* 31, 270–9.

Layton-Henry, Z. (1992) *The Politics of Immigration*. Oxford: Blackwell.

Lipset, S. M. and Rokkan, S. (1967) *Party Systems and Voter Alignments*. New York: Free Press.

Lunn, K. (1996) 'British Fascism Revisited: a Failure of Imagination', in M. Cronin (ed.) *The Failure of British Fascism*. Basingstoke: Macmillan.

Messina, A. (1989) *Race and Party Competition in Britain*. Oxford: Clarendon Press.

Miles, R. and Phizacklea, A. (1984) *White Man's Country*. London: Pluto Press.

Mudde, C. (1996) 'Right-Wing Extremism Analyzed', *European Journal of Political Research* 27, 203–24.

Murray, N. (1986) 'The Press and Ideology in Thatcher's Britain', *Race and Class* 27, 1–19.

Nordlinger, E. (1967) *The Working Class Tories*. London: MacGibbon & Kee.

Reeves, F. (1983) *British Racial Discourse*. Cambridge: Cambridge University Press.

Sanders, D. (1987) 'Government Popularity and the Falklands War: A Reappraisal', *British Journal of Political Science* 17, 281–313.

Särlvik, B. and Crewe, I. (1983) *Decade of Dealignment*. Cambridge: Cambridge University Press.

Schoen, D. (1977) *Enoch Powell and the Powellites*. London: Macmillan.

Scott, D. (1975) 'The National Front in Local Politics', in Crewe, I. (ed.) *British Political Sociology Yearbook*. London: Croom Helm.

Scraton, P. (1985) *The State of the Police*. London: Pluto.

Sivanandan, A. (1976) *Race, Class and the State*. London: Institute of Race Relations.

Skidelsky, R. (1975) *Oswald Mosley*. London: Macmillan.

Steed, M. (1974) 'The Results Analysed', in Butler, D. E. and Kavanagh, D. (eds) *The British General Election of February 1974*. London: Macmillan.

Studlar, D. (1985) ' "Waiting for Catastrophe": Race and the Political Agenda in Britain', *Patterns of Prejudice* 19, 3–15.

Taylor, S. (1979) 'The Incidence of Coloured Populations and Support for the National Front', *British Journal of Political Science* 9, 250–6.

Taylor, S. (1982) *The National Front in English Politics*. Basingstoke: Macmillan.

Thurlow, R. (1994) *The Secret State*. Oxford: Blackwell.

Thurlow, R. (1998) *Fascism in Britain*. London: I. B. Tauris.

Troyna, B. (1981) *Public Awareness and the Media*. London: Commission for Racial Equality.

Virdee, S. (1995) 'Racial Violence and Harassment: A Case for a National Survey?', *Policy Studies* 16, 45–51.

Whiteley, P. (1979) 'The National Front Vote in the 1977 GLC Elections: An Aggregate Data Analysis', *British Journal of Political Science* 9, 370–80.

CHAPTER NINE

Radical right-wing populism in Scandinavia: from tax revolt to neo-liberalism and xenophobia

Jørgen Goul Andersen and Tor Bjørklund

Introduction

Modern right-wing extremist parties in Scandinavia are not rooted in any historical traditions of right-wing extremism, and it is questionable whether the label 'extremist' is at all appropriate. But the parties exhibit important likenesses to right-wing extremist parties elsewhere and seem to draw upon similar social forces. They belong to a family of modern, radical, right-wing populist parties (Betz, 1994), a somewhat broader concept under which contemporary extreme right-wing parties may also be subsumed. By 1999, three parties belonging to this family were represented in Scandinavian parliaments: the Progress parties in Denmark and Norway, and the Danish People's Party, which was formed in 1995 as a breakaway from the Progress Party, but has now become its main successor.

The story of modern right-wing populism in Scandinavia commenced in 1972 when Mogens Glistrup, in Denmark, launched his anti-tax Progress Party. This inspired Anders Lange to establish a similar party in Norway in 1973.[1] Without any notable inspiration from abroad, a Swedish sister party had emerged by 1990, when Ian Wachtmeister and Bert Karlsson met up in an airport and decided to form a party, New Democracy (*Ny Demokrati*). These three sister parties were all conceived by persons outside the networks of the old party system, as a protest against the other parties. We might also perhaps add a Finnish predecessor, the Finnish Rural Party, which was created in 1958 by a well-known politician (Veikko Vennamo) as a splinter from the Farmers' Party (the Centre Party), and originally named the Smallholders' Party. The party made its electoral breakthrough in 1970 with 10.5 per cent of the votes cast.

However, although the Finnish Rural Party eventually came to adopt some of the issues characteristic of modern right-wing populism, it emerged as another type of party, which basically represented a traditional populist protest against modernization (Sänkiaho, 1971). After a turbulent history, the Finnish Rural Party then evaporated in the 1990s. It gained only 1.3 per cent of the votes and a single parliamentary seat in 1995 and, by 1997, the party no longer existed. The issues and the electorate of the Swedish party, on the other hand, were more close to those of the Danish and Norwegian Progress parties, but unlike these two parties it turned out to be a flash party, which did not succeed in mobilizing after its initial breakthrough, with 6.7 per cent of the votes in 1991. Therefore, our emphasis below is on the Danish and Norwegian parties, although we shall seek to explain why an apparently quite similar party was unsuccessful in Sweden.

To begin with, the different success stories do not rest upon any difference in historical traditions. There have been antecedents of the extreme right wing in Denmark and Norway, but these were parties and movements of another kind. As in other countries, Denmark and Norway had their Nazi parties in the 1930s and the 1940s. Both of these parties were certainly extremist, but voter support remained low. The Danish party peaked with 2.1 per cent of the votes in 1943 (Djursaa, 1981). By the same token, the Norwegian party, led by Vidkun Quisling, was a party without political significance until it collaborated with the German Nazis. The party's best election result was in 1933, with 2.2 per cent of the votes.

From 1953 to 1968, a small Independent Party ran for elections in Denmark and typically obtained 2 to 3 per cent of the votes. Although far to the right, it was by no means extremist; it was founded by a former Liberal prime minister as a reaction against a 1953 constitutional change that abolished the bi-cameral system, and the new party simply advocated more orthodox liberal and non-socialist policies (Eriksen, 1978).[2] In Norway, there were no new parties on the right from 1945 to 1973 but, unlike Mogens Glistrup, who was a successful tax lawyer without any previous political activity, the founder of the Norwegian party, Anders Lange, was a long-standing right-wing activist. Before the Nazi occupation, he had been connected to right-wing organizations sympathetic to fascism. However, he was unquestionably against the Nazi regime and participated actively in the resistance to the occupation. In the post-war period, he emerged as a rather strange political propagandist, on the fringe of the established right wing.

The breakthrough of new parties

The emergence and consolidation of new parties are rare phenomena in Scandinavia. Until 1973 in Denmark and Norway, and until 1988 in Sweden, the three countries had very stable party systems which were basically frozen around 1920 (Lipset and Rokkan, 1967). The few new parties which emerged were typically breakaways from established parties, and were most frequently short-lived.

Several prerequisites are required in order to establish successfully a new party. A crucial factor is whether the new party is linked to basic changes in the party cleavage structure, which we believe is the case with the Progress parties. However, this applies also to the Swedish sister party. The significant questions are: why did a Swedish sister party not emerge in the 1970s, as in the two other countries, and why did it turn out to be a flash party when finally it did emerge? We believe that cleavage transformation is a necessary but by no means sufficient condition here. Even changes in cleavage structures infrequently crystallize into new parties. Among other preconditions, we distinguish between: (a) the preconditions for the breakthrough of a new party, and (b) the circumstances which are favourable to its consolidation. Among the breakthrough conditions, general turbulence in the party system thus seems to be an important factor. Established parties will normally be able to absorb or suppress new conflicts; they have strong defence mechanisms which normally preclude the emergence of new parties. The 1973 Danish and Norwegian elections were 'earthquake elections', and this label applies also to the 1991 Swedish elections. Both the 1973 elections came in the aftermath of European Community (EC) referendum campaigns, with widespread grassroots activity and considerable polarization between voters and party elites, especially in Norway. Although this had no immediate impact on support for the Progress parties, which mobilized voters on the issue of taxation, the prevalent mood of political distrust and deteriorating bonds between voters and their parties undoubtedly facilitated the formation of new parties. In 1973, this precondition was not present in Sweden, which had not yet applied for EC membership.

As regards the issue of taxation, the successful tax revolts of Mogens Glistrup and Anders Lange were also related to two other conditions. First, the end of the 1960s/early 1970s had been the most expansive period for the welfare state, followed by an unprecedented increase in taxes (Sejersted, 1982; Wilensky, 1975). Second, in this period, non-socialist coalition governments were in office in Denmark and Norway (Denmark, 1968–71; Norway, 1965–71, 1972–3). This aroused frustration among non-socialist voters, who had hoped for a change of regime. In Sweden, this second precondition was absent, as the Social Democrats remained in office until 1976, during the most expansive growth period of the welfare state. Accordingly, Sweden did not experience such a sudden increase in political distrust as the two other countries (Andersen, 1992). Rather, distrust of politicians and dissatisfaction with welfare and taxes built up gradually from the mid-1970s (Gilljam and Holmberg, 1995).

However, although public-sector expansion was slower at that time, the non-socialist government in Sweden (1976–82) also failed to control public expenditure growth. But at the same time, the political agenda had changed significantly. The government fell apart because of a division over the nuclear power issue, which was put to a referendum in 1980. After the 1979 election, a broad non-socialist government was reconstructed but, in 1981, the Conservatives left the coalition in protest against a tax reform package. For disillusioned right-wing voters, there was thus a non-socialist alternative outside government. Also, there was growing disillusionment among voters, who saw little difference between the Social Democrat and non-socialist governments.[3] Moreover, the weakening of loyalty bonds was accelerated by the collapse of communism and the end of the Cold War, developments which served to question long-standing doctrines in Swedish politics. Finally, in 1991, a new issue was put on the agenda: the immigration question.

To sum up, the cleavage structures of the Scandinavian countries were alike, but the factors that could serve as a catalyst for the formation of new parties were delayed in Sweden until the late 1980s. But in the elections of 1988 and 1991, for the first time in more than sixty years, Sweden experienced the electoral breakthrough of a new party. Furthermore, and in line with our emphasis on general turbulence in the party system, not one but three new parties emerged almost simultaneously: the Greens in 1988, and the Christian Democrats and New Democracy in 1991.

Leadership as a condition for consolidation

How can we explain, then, that New Democracy was simply a flash party, which disappeared as suddenly as it had emerged? At this point, we suggest that *leadership* is a decisive factor, especially in the early stages of the life cycle of a new party, when it is most vulnerable. This applies to all new parties, but perhaps in particular to right-wing populist parties. The leadership of the Swedish New Democracy was split between its two founding fathers: Bert Karlsson and Ian Wachtmeister.[4] What started as a strong political alliance between two different leaders ended with conflict and controversies. They were ultimately unable to co-operate, and neither of them wished to remain in charge of the party. Although rivalry and internal conflicts are the rule for most newly established parties, the Swedish party was exceptional, as both publicly recognized leaders retired.

In Norway, the party was in an equally critical situation when the founder of the party, Anders Lange, suddenly died in 1974. For some years afterwards, the party was in a state of chaos and it seemed destined to fall apart. Even the subsequent leader, Carl I. Hagen, had belonged to a faction that had defected, and he had tried to establish a new party prior to the death of Lange. After replacing the latter as MP, however, he rejoined the party, which was later renamed from Anders Lange's Party for a Strong Reduction in Taxes, Duties and Public Intervention to the Progress Party. Since 1978, Carl I. Hagen has been the chairman and undisputed leader of the party. He has even been described as the owner of the party. This has not prevented quarrels and controversies, and several vice-chairmen and aspiring leaders have dropped out in protest. But none of them has seriously tried to launch a new party.

The counterpart Danish party was effectively consolidated in the 1970s under the leadership of Mogens Glistrup. But it has experienced chronic turbulence in leadership ever since. While Glistrup was imprisoned for tax evasion in the early 1980s, electoral support declined to a critical level, but when Pia Kjaersgaard took over his seat in parliament, she soon managed to capture *de facto* leadership of the party. When Glistrup returned from prison, he had become increasingly extreme and isolated. He was re-elected to parliament in 1987 but found himself without much influence in the party, and finally defected just before the 1990 election, when he tried to launch a new party, the Party of Well-Being. Because of a shortage of time in which to collect the necessary supporting signatures, the party fielded candidates on the lists of a populist party of the extreme left (Common Course), which had been represented in parliament from 1987 to 1988. But only about 0.5 per cent of the voters followed Glistrup, and the Common Course party failed to pass the 2 per cent threshold necessary for representation.

Later in the 1990s, personal conflicts accumulated within the Progress Party parliamentary group, where the majority sought to prevent a concentration of power in the hands of Pia Kjaersgaard. She eventually left the party in 1995, and along with three other MPs and about one-third of the party members, she launched yet another new party, the Danish People's Party (DPP). The Progress Party elected Kirsten Jacobsen as its new leader. She has represented the party in parliament since 1973, and has gained a positive public reputation owing to her talents in uncovering political/ bureaucratic scandals. Ideologically, the differences between the parties are small. But as die-hard economic liberals are concentrated in the Progress Party, which coincidentally has few effective spokespersons on immigration policy, a sort of division of labour is taking place, with the Danish People's Party becoming the strongest anti-immigration party and the Progress Party becoming the party with the strongest anti-state regulation profile. However, the difference is only a matter of degree, and in the 1998 general election campaign, the Progress Party also sought to mobilize on the issue of immigration. Moreover, according to the 1998 election study (see below), the policy stances of the two parties remain very close in the eyes of voters.

In the 1998 election, the Progress Party survived the 2 per cent threshold of representation for the Danish parliament only because of Kirsten Jacobsen's personal popularity, which secured 10.4 per cent of the votes for the party in her own constituency (the county of Northern Jutland). In the rest of the country, the party won less than 2 per cent, and as Kirsten Jacobsen (for personal reasons) has given up formal leadership and become much less active, the future of the party is uncertain. In the 1998 election, the party obtained only 4 seats, while the Danish People's Party won 13 seats.

Electoral support

The Swedish party, New Democracy, experienced short-lived success as its electoral support fell sharply from 6.7 per cent in 1991 to 1.2 per cent in 1994. Despite objectively favourable conditions in terms of economic crisis and extremely high immigration figures, the party suffered a failure in leadership at a critical stage and there is little sign of recovery. Besides, the Swedish threshold of 4 per cent continues to work against efforts to secure parliamentary representation. In fact, the party has nearly disappeared. In the 1998 general election, it gained only 0.2 per cent of the votes, and made no impact at all on the June 1999 Euro-election.

The Norwegian counterpart was voted out of parliament in 1977, and few commentators believed that it would recover. However, the aspiring party leader, Carl I. Hagen, proved such assessments wrong. From 1978, he quickly consolidated the party, in terms of both organization and electoral support. As indicated in Table 9.1, the party has had fluctuating results, but in the 1987 local election it exceeded 10 per cent for the first time. This success was clearly influenced by the immigration question, which was raised as a consequence of the sudden growth in the number of asylum seekers (Table 9.2). In the subsequent parliamentary election in 1989, the party won 13 per cent. However, an internal party conflict between economic neo-liberals and populists soon emerged, culminating in 1994 with a split: four out of the ten MPs left the party, along with the strongly neo-liberal youth organization. Nevertheless, the 1995 local election turned out to be a victory, as immigration again emerged as a central issue on the voters' agenda. According to the 1995 Local Election Survey, nearly half of Progress Party voters pointed to immigration as their most important issue. For many voters, the party appeared as a single-issue party: 93 per cent of those electors who regarded immigration as the most important issue voted for the Progress Party.

Despite the fact that the immigration question was not especially salient in the 1997 parliamentary election campaign, the Progress Party obtained its best result ever. With 15.3 per cent of the votes, the party became the second largest. The campaign focus was on 'public health' and 'care for the elderly', and both the Progress Party and the Social Democrats concentrated on these two issues. Carl I. Hagen claimed that the incumbent Social Democrats were responsible for the inadequacies of the public (national) health service, and that in spite of oil revenues, the waiting lists were growing. His advice was: spend more public money and reorganize the health service. Paradoxically, Carl I. Hagen, who at the beginning of the 1970s had been an ardent defender of welfare cuts, had now become a spokesman for increased public expenditure. Indeed, there was widespread support for his call to allocate more money to sick and elderly people. In light of the party's history, it was surprising that welfare issues were now the rallying platform,

Table 9.1 Voter support for radical right-wing populist parties in Scandinavia (%)

Year of election	Denmark[a]		Norway[b]	Sweden[c]
	PP	DPP	PP	ND
1973	15.9		5.0 (P)	
1975	13.6		1.4 (L)	
1977	14.6		1.9 (P)	
1979	11.0		2.5 (L)	
1981	8.9		4.5 (P)	
1983			6.3 (L)	
1984	3.6			
1985			3.7 (P)	
1987	4.8		12.3 (L)	
1988	9.0			
1989			13.0 (P)	
1990	6.4			
1991			7.0 (L)	6.7
1993			6.3 (P)	
			12.1 (L)	
1994	6.4			1.2
1997			15.3 (P)	
1998	2.4	7.4		0.2
1999			13.5(L)	

Source: Statistical Yearbooks.

Notes:
[a] PP = Progress Party; DPP = Danish People's Party.
[b] PP = Progress Party. P = parliamentary election; L = Local elections.
[c] ND = New Democracy.

although the immigration question and the fight against crime were also highlighted. But the most important issue for recruiting *new* voters was welfare. For example, nearly half of the voters who defected from the Social Democrats to the Progress Party mentioned 'public health' and 'care for the elderly' as the most important issues determining their choice of party.[5] However, the immigration question was again not entirely absent from the campaign, and among those who pointed to this issue as the most important, two out of three voted for the Progress Party, a group that comprised 20 per cent of the party's voters.

The Danish Progress Party was the most successful of the above parties in the 1970s: it won 15.9 per cent in the breakthrough election of 1973, and maintained the most stable share of the votes among all Danish parties in the three subsequent parliamentary elections. In the mid-1980s, support for

Table 9.2 Number of asylum-seekers in the Nordic countries, 1983–94

Year	Denmark	Norway	Sweden	Finland
1983	800	200	3,000	–
1984	4,300	300	12,000	–
1985	8,700	900	14,500	–
1986	9,300	2,700	14,600	–
1987	2,800	6,600	18,100	50
1988	4,700	6,670	19,800	50
1990	5,300	4,000	29,000	2,500
1992	13,884	5,236	84,018	2,834
1994	6,551	3,397	18,640	849

Source: IGC (International Governmental Conference), Geneva.

it almost evaporated, but under the leadership of Kjaersgaard the party recovered and, in the 1990s, support stabilized with 6.4 per cent in the two elections of 1990 and 1994. Even the subsequent split did not finish off the two parties; on the contrary, their joint support increased from 1997, when immigration became among the most important issues on the voters' agenda, and in the 1998 election they jointly obtained nearly 10 per cent. At the same time, the Danish People's Party emerged as the main successor to the Progress Party, which survived the 2 per cent threshold for representation only because of its popular leader, Kirsten Jacobsen. In 1999, however, Jacobsen announced that she would not contest the next election – and, in October, all the MPs left the party, following the disruptive return of Mogens Glistrup after several years of exclusion.

Ideology and political style

We have characterized the Progress parties (and New Democracy) as radical right-wing populist parties. This refers mainly to their ideology and political style, but it also corresponds with a particular social composition of voters and certain issue positions and preferences among these voters. Without (for reasons of space) embarking upon a full theoretical discussion of the concept of populism, we concentrate below on a presentation of the ideology and political style of the parties, in order to spell out in what sense the parties may be labelled populist – and in what sense they may *not* so be labelled.

Not so much populism in style

The Progress parties (and the Danish People's Party) cannot be considered genuinely *extremist*, either in ideology or in political style. They have a *populist* legacy, but also have become increasingly conventional under the leadership of Carl I. Hagen and Pia Kjaersgaard/Kirsten Jakobsen, respectively. The populist legacy in the Danish party derives from Mogens Glistrup, who, in his first television appearance in 1971, compared tax evaders with railway saboteurs during the German occupation. But almost from the beginning, there was a conflict between the adherents of Glistrup's expressive radicalism and adherents of a more conventional line – a conflict between 'slackeners' and 'tighteners', which continued until Glistrup left the party. However, in the 1980s, the softer approach came to dominate the party, not least as a consequence of the ambition of Kjaersgaard and others to become respectable coalition partners for the Conservatives and the Liberals.

Characteristically, populist movements are frequently loosely organized and built around charismatic leaders. Indeed, both Anders Lange and Mogens Glistrup strongly resisted those who wanted a traditional party organization. They wanted their parties to be movements rather than parties (in order to maintain their personal control; see Larsen, 1977). Glistrup and Lange secured for themselves a position as lifelong honorary members of their party's executive committees but, after Lange's death, Hagen established a purely conventional party organization. Even the Danish party was gradually transformed into a more regular party organization, although certain irregularities remained, such as the right of local branches to send an unlimited number of delegates to the annual congress. Because of such irregularities, the Norwegian party refused to have official contacts with the Danish equivalent.

Another aspect of populist style is the notion of the 'people against the elites'. Thus we encounter a classic definition in Shils (1956: 68): 'Populism proclaims that the will of the people as such is supreme over every other standard ... populism identifies the will of the people with justice and morality.' This sort of explicit disregard for legal principles could be found, for instance, in the arguments of the Danish Progress Party when the Minister of Justice was forced to resign in 1988 (he was eventually impeached and convicted in a state trial in 1994)[6] because of his abuse of power in the administration of refugee policy. Whereas supporters from the government parties argued that the Minister's conduct did not violate the law, the Progress Party did not consider the legal arguments at all, but explicitly supported the Minister's course of action on the grounds that it was in accordance with the attitudes of the majority of the population, as expressed in opinion polls. However, such instances are rare, even in the case of the Danish party.

By the same token, the Progress parties have rarely supported any sort of illegal or violent behaviour. Again, the Danish party has been the most radical. Even among 'slackeners', there were – in the 1970s and early 1980s – a few instances of civil disobedience by MPs against what was considered to be excessive regulation by the state (e.g. speed limits and the regulation of telecommunications). Glistrup has made overtly racist statements but, unlike France's Pierre Poujade, the parties have never urged people not to pay taxes, not even when Glistrup was at his zenith. Furthermore, the parties have never adhered to a conspiratorial view of society and, apart from Glistrup in the 1980s, the parties have never adopted an aggressive, passionate or bitter rhetoric. Rather, they have skilfully employed a good sense of humour (especially Glistrup and Lange in the 1970s), the language of common sense (Kjaersgaard), or critical (and competent) scrutiny of scandals (Jakobsen). Carl I. Hagen is the most ordinary, professional politician, gifted with verbal and tactical skills. In parliament, he strictly follows the formal rules of the political game.

The conflicts within the Norwegian party have often been described as ideological conflicts between neo-liberals and 'populists'. Hagen sought to balance the two camps. In the early 1980s, he was regarded mainly as an exponent of the liberal economic faction, but ten years later he turned his back on the neo-liberals and was seen as a spokesperson for the 'populists'. However, populism is a concept with many meanings (Canovan, 1981). In this case, a 'populist' means a politician who speaks a plain and under-standable streetwise language and who feels free to express attitudes, such as on immigration, which are not 'politically correct', but which enjoy strong support among 'the common people'. Although this sort of populism may also reduce the party's respectability among potential coalition partners, it is a criterion that does not distinguish very clearly between 'populists' and other, more mainstream politicians.

The notion of 'the people against the elites' is prevalent in both Progress parties' preference for more direct democracy. Once again, however, this is not exclusively a populist issue. Increasingly, too, both parties are present-ing themselves less as being in simple opposition to all other parties; on the contrary, they have to a large degree sought co-operation and practical compromises. In short, what characterizes their populist political style is the appeal to the common people, a preference for direct democracy, and the disregard for political correctness as well as for experts and other elites. This may imply a notion of the people against the elites, as in the field of immigration policy, but this is most of what was left of the populist legacy in policy style in the 1990s.

No traditional populist ideology

Turning to the ideological aspects of populism, there is little resemblance at all to the conventional picture of populism. Lipset (1981) and others have frequently summarized 'populism', 'petty bourgeois protest' and 'fascism' under the heading 'revolt against modernity'. However, this is clearly inapplicable to the Progress parties. There has never been any nostalgia for the past or any reaction against 'permissiveness'. The parties are authoritarian on most law-and-order issues but they are not intolerant of diversity in life-styles as long as the taxpayers' money is not affected. This holds also for their supporters (as well as for their Swedish counterparts; see Gilljam and Holmberg, 1993: 149). Unlike the Christian Democrats, the radical right-wing populists are clearly 'modern'. In this respect, the parties differ significantly from, for instance, the American 'New Right' (Andersen and Bjørklund, 1990).

Second, whereas nationalism is a core principle in fascism (Linz, 1978: 25), and frequently also in populism, the Progress Party in Denmark originally appeared to be less nationalist than other parties. In some of his most quoted statements, Mogens Glistrup proposed to abolish the Danish defence forces (in favour of an automatic telephone answering in Russian: 'We surrender'!), and to sell off Greenland and the Faeroe Islands to the highest bidder. Although the Progress Party never adopted such ideas, but rather pursued conventional defence and foreign policies, apart from being hostile to the United Nations and to foreign aid, it did not project a strongly nationalist profile. More recently, immigration policies and the Danish parties' rejection of the Maastricht Treaty in the 1992 and 1993 referenda, as well as the Amsterdam Treaty in the 1998 referendum, may imply a more nationalist position. This has become increasingly pronounced in the case of the Danish People's Party; still, it is questionable how much it means to voters. The Scandinavian parties and their voters may perhaps be accused of xenophobic sentiments, welfare chauvinism and parochialism but, until recent changes in the Danish People's Party they could not be described as genuinely nationalist. Moreover, classic petty bourgeois anti-capitalism, which has been traditionally a core ingredient in populist parties, is completely absent from the two Progress parties. On the contrary, the parties have consistently demanded that all existing measures designed to protect small producers against 'big capital' should be abolished.

Neo-liberalism

The demand for the abolition of such protective measures is consistent with a general conception of the state which has no commonality with any sort of fascist or (traditional) populist ideology. The core principle is simply the neo-liberal belief in the forces of the market. This also means that the parties' policies are somewhat less eclectic than they might appear at first glance. Still, the ideology of the Progress parties cannot be equated with mainstream neo-liberalism. It is not the neo-liberalism of the upper strata. This is particularly evident from the concrete policies pursued by the parties. In the first place, the parties have always demanded higher expenditure on the health sector and on state pensions – that is, for the two areas which are given highest priority among the lower strata in particular. The preferred areas for expenditure cuts are culture, refugees and foreigners, foreign aid and state bureaucracy. This approach also corresponds with the preferences of the lower strata (Andersen, 1995). A closer inspection of the parties' budget proposals reveals support for public expenditure cuts (in particular in the Danish case), which would certainly not satisfy the preferences of the lower strata (Gooskens, 1993). However, like some extreme ideological positions in the party programmes, these stances are hardly visible to the voters. In addition, at least in Norway, the party leader has displayed a relaxed attitude to the letter of the party manifesto.

The Norwegian and Danish parties diverge on the taxation issue, as the former demands lower marginal taxes and a gradual move towards proportional taxes, whereas the latter has traditionally assigned priority to a higher basic allowance rather than lower marginal taxes. Some of the *redistributive* aspects of the Danish party's taxation policy bear more resemblance to Social Democrat policies than to mainstream neo-liberalism.[7] This helps to explain why the Progress parties have frequently presented themselves as the true successors of the Social Democrats from their heydays in the 1930s (Denmark) and 1950s (Norway). In Norway, the relationship to the working class is further underlined by the location of party headquarters next to the Social Democrats' Oslo office, and with windows facing Youngstorget – the old square where the working class has traditionally assembled, ever since the start of the labour movement.

Immigration

Since the second half of the 1980s, refugee and immigration policies have become the most important issues of the Progress parties. Originally, the parties paid little attention to immigration, and the 1973 party pamphlets of the two parties did not even mention the issue. Instead, the parties criticized the abuse of social security by people who were 'unwilling to work'. In Denmark, the issue of immigration did not appear until 1979, when a local representative, A. Th. Riemann (a veterinarian), was charged (and later fined) for writing that immigrants were 'multiplying like rats'. He was supported by Glistrup, who gradually became involved with groups that were hostile to immigrants. But at that time, the statement only contributed to the declining support for the party (in particular, large numbers of better-educated people left the party in the 1979 election), and in the early 1980s the party became virtually isolated among the population at large (Glans, 1986).The immigration issue almost evaporated, and in the first half of the 1980s it was nearly absent from the political agenda, and also from the statements of the Progress parties. However, following a dramatic increase in the number of asylum-seeking refugees (in Denmark in 1984–6, in Norway in 1986–7; see Table 9.2), the rising number of foreigners again received public attention (Tonsgaard, 1989), and in 1987–8, this became one of the most important themes in the election campaigns of the Progress parties (Bjørklund, 1988; Siune, 1989: 118–19).

Characteristically, Glistrup was the first to see the potential of the issue. Immediately on his release from prison in March 1985, he launched an aggressive attack on immigrants, phrased in much the same language as Riemann's. However; unlike Riemann, he was not prosecuted for his statements. The anti-immigrant stance initially did not contribute to the popularity of the party: the issue was not on the voters' agenda, and support for the Danish Progress Party in opinion polls continued to decline until February 1986, when it reached a low point of 1.7 per cent (Andersen, 1988). But the party had acquired a clear image on the issue. Subsequently, Glistrup's statements became increasingly radical, as reflected in the slogan 'Make Denmark a Muslim Free Zone', which was also articulated in a speech by Jane Oksen MP in the opening session of the 1990/1 Danish parliament. Oksen, like Glistrup, left the Progress Party in 1990, and statements such as the above were far beyond the line of social acceptability in Denmark. The slogan was publicly condemned by Kjaersgaard. Kjaersgaard and Carl I. Hagen, in contrast, managed to keep their criticism of immigration and refugee policies within socially acceptable limits. In the beginning, their parties' attack on immigration used to be justified mainly on economic grounds, and the arguments may be summarized here as a sort of 'welfare state chauvinism', albeit with xenophobic undertones. However, it is likely that, among many voters, the economic arguments have also lent legitimacy to more outrightly hostile attitudes towards foreigners. Besides, the Danish and Norwegian publics are quite receptive to arguments against fundamentalist religion in general and Islam in particular, and in the 1990s, the parties, especially the Danish People's Party, became explicitly critical of the idea of 'multiculturalism'.

In order to emphasize the economic aspects of immigration, the Norwegian Progress Party has proposed that national and local authorities should put a price tag on immigrants, based on a cost–benefit analysis accounting mechanism. The proposal aroused widespread criticism, which the Progress Party interpreted as a fear of confronting harsh realities. Significantly, the discussion about 'immigrant accounts' did not create internal divisions, since the defection of the neo-liberal faction in 1994 had left the party, at least temporarily, more united on the immigration question. Also, the youth organization, which split off from the party, was dominated by young neo-liberals who, in principle, were not against immigration, provided that immigrants did not depend upon the state social security system. They even managed to put their imprint on the party manifesto.[8] However, this had little practical importance for the party's image, as Carl I. Hagen was free to mobilize on the immigration issue when the neo-liberals had departed. His arguments then changed from being predominantly economic to become more cultural: ethnic homogeneity was seen as ensuring a calm and peaceful society, whereas different religious, ethnic and cultural minorities allegedly generated problems. Following this new emphasis, at the 1995 party convention, Carl I. Hagen focused on internal problems within Muslim society in Norway. He talked about intolerant Muslim fundamentalists who fought against integration with Norwegian society and who violated basic human rights. Accused of racism, Hagen replied that he had only quoted from a book written by an Oslo-based Iraqi immigrant.

Despite the Norwegian Progress Party's relative unity, some small activist groups regard the party as being too soft on the immigration issue. Thus two minor parties were launched and tried, unsuccessfully, to win support at the most recent elections, advocating an extremely hostile attitude towards immigrants. However, as with Glistrup's extreme statements around 1990, such groups have probably been advantageous to the Progress Party, as they receive public attention and thus contribute to keeping the immigration issue on the agenda. At the same time, they give the Progress Party the opportunity to dissociate itself from a socially unacceptable racism. In addition, the new parties function as a convenient siphon for the most outspoken racists and xenophobes.

Conclusions

In terms of political style and ideology, the Progress parties bear relatively little resemblance to traditional populist (let alone extremist) movements. They do seek to mobilize the people against elites, advocate increased use of direct democracy, and sometimes proclaim the will of the people as the supreme standard. On the other hand, the parties have become increasingly domesticated, and the standard ideological elements of populism – nationalism and anti-capitalism – until recently, have been virtually absent from their ideologies. Rather, the core elements today are a particular variant of neo-liberalism, especially in Denmark, directed at the lower strata; and a significant emphasis on immigration, which has replaced taxation as the rallying issue of the parties. Welfare issues, such as care for the elderly, are also important – as was especially evident in the 1997 Norwegian election and to some extent in the Danish 1998 election campaign. The ideology of the parties is discussed further in the next section, along with an analysis of the political attitudes of their supporters.

Political attitudes

General left–right position

Unlike the extreme left, extreme or radical right-wing movements are rarely labelled 'extreme' because they are extreme on *conventional* left–right issues. It is other issues, and/or the parties' political style, that endow them with such labels. Although the Progress parties are quite ideologically consistent in terms of their extreme liberalism (in principle), their position on conventional aspects of the left–right dimension, such as welfare and economic redistribution, is more ambiguous. This also applies to their supporters. However, we must distinguish between subjective and objective left–right position. The latter is defined by the voters' location on an economic left–right scale as indicated by particular left–right questions, whereas the former is defined by the respondents themselves.[9]

In both countries, the supporters of the Progress parties on average consider themselves further to the right than the supporters of any other party. Table 9.3 and subsequent tables present data from the mid-1990s but, unless otherwise indicated, the figures from the 1997 and 1998 elections, respectively, do not indicate any significant change, and the profiles of the Danish People's Party and the Progress Party in Denmark reveal only negligible differences. As far as left–right position is concerned, figures are basically stable, although the ranking of the three right-wing populist parties and 'conventional' conservative parties sometimes reverse. For example, in the 1997 Norwegian election study the Progress Party voters situated themselves just to the left of the Conservatives. However, standard deviations (figures not presented) indicate that the supporters of the three parties are more heterogeneous than the supporters of most other parties. This self-placement seems to derive from a sort of weighting of 'old politics' and 'new politics' issues (Borre and Andersen, 1997).

On the economic left–right scale, the position of Progress Party voters is clearly to the right, but not extreme. Surveys have consistently shown that Progress Party voters are located more to the left than the Conservatives (Norway, Denmark) and the Liberals (Denmark). This holds, in particular, for the issue of equality, where Progress Party voters in Denmark occupy a centrist position, even a bit to the left of the centrist parties. In summary, the supporters of the Progress Party are not unambiguously to the right, and certainly not extremely to the right. They perceive themselves as being a little more to the right than conservative/liberal voters (or at about the same position), but on basic left–right questions, they are not. When it comes to equality, the Danish Progress Party voters rather occupy a centrist position.[10] Thus, a consistently rightist ideological position is not what distinguishes Progress Party voters.

General distrust

The Progress parties have frequently been described as 'protest parties' and 'discontent parties' (Lane and Ersson, 1994). Indeed, there is no doubt that they represent protest and discontent against the established parties, and at the aggregate level it is also likely that support for the Progress parties is related to the degree of frustration with non-socialist governments or with the non-socialist opposition alternative. If we take as our point of departure

Table 9.3 Position on left–right self-placement scale[a], on economic left–right index and on equality issue, by party choice. Index values and PDIs (percentage difference index)

	Denmark				Norway		
Party	L-R self-placement, 1994	Economic inequality, 1994[b] (PDI)	S-E LR position, 1994[c]	Party	L-R self-placement, 1995	Economic inequality, 1993 (PDI)[c]	S-E LR position 1989[3]
Progress P.	7.50	−6	32	Progress P.	6.75	23	43
Liberals	7.49	27	43				
Conservatives	7.37	38	49	Conservatives	6.72	39	50
Centrist parties	5.93	1	16	Centrist parties	5.16	−8	21
Social Dem.	4.94	−35	−4	Labour	4.70	−8	4
Left-wing	3.48	−65	−35	Left-wing	3.37	−45	−17
Population	5.94	−9	15		5.40	−2	19

Source: Election Surveys, Danish (1994) and Norwegian (1989, 1993) Electoral Programmes, 1995 Local Election Survey 1995.

Notes:
[a] Measured on self-placement scale from 0 to 10.
[b] Wording: 'Next, a question about living standards and incomes. A says: "The differences in incomes and living standards are still too great in our country, so people with smaller incomes should have a faster improvement of living standards than those with larger incomes." B says: "The levelling of incomes has gone far enough. Those income differences that still remain should largely be maintained.' (PDI = B−A.)
[c] Socio-economic left–right position: Composite index of four items including the above-mentioned. The others are: maintenance or cuts in social expenditure; state regulation of business; and nationalization. All items coded −1; 0; +1 (0 = neutral/don't know). Values are summarized and divided by 4, and the index scores may thus be read as average PDIs.
[d] Wording: 'In Norway, the economic differences between people have been reduced so much that further reduction is not necessary.' (PDI = agree – disagree.)
[e] Composite index of four items including the above-mentioned. The others comprise state regulation of business; nationalization; and 'market forces ought to a larger degree determine economic development' (i.e. one of four items deviates from the Danish index). All items coded −1; 0; +1 (0 = neutral/don't know). Values are summarized and divided by 4, and the index scores may thus be read as average PDIs.

the concept of political cynicism, we may also observe that Progress Party voters are consistently the most cynical among those on the right-wing side of the political spectrum (Andersen, 1992).

Recent data on political distrust show that Progress Party voters in both countries exhibit by far the highest level of political distrust among all voters (see Table 9.4), and the same was found for New Democracy voters in Sweden in 1991 (Gilljam and Holmberg, 1993: 173). Historically, however, cynicism among Progress Party voters has been very dependent on government composition, relations of co-operation, and policies. There is no doubt that cynicism is a highly relevant factor, but it is an insufficient explanation;

Table 9.4 Cynicism, by party. PDI (percentage difference index)

	Denmark 1994	Norway 1995
Progress Party	−58	−16
Liberals/Conservatives	21	22
Centrist parties	18	5
Social Democrats	20	42
Left-wing	−3	21
Population	8	19

Sources: Election Survey, Danish (1994) and Norwegian (1995) Local Election Survey.
Wording: Denmark: 'How much trust do you have in Danish politicians in general?' (PDI = great or some − not much or very little.)
Norway: 'How much trust do you have in Norwegian MPs in general?' (PDI = great or some − not much or very little).

in part, it is an independent or catalysing factor (Glans, 1986), but to a large extent, it is also an intervening variable which summarizes policy dissatisfaction. Thus we have to look too at the policy sources of discontent.

Taxation and welfare

Dissatisfaction with taxation and the public sector would be an obvious possibility for discontent as both parties emerged as tax protest parties. Taxation was the most salient issue among the electorate in both countries in 1973, and surveys revealed that the Progress parties clearly deviated from the others on the tax issue (Glans, 1986). However, in the 1980s and 1990s, taxation was not very salient at all – and not more salient among Progress Party voters than among others.[11]

A majority of Progress Party voters in Norway are against a lowering of taxes on high salaries, and a majority of supporters of the Danish party even declare themselves in favour of imposing higher taxes on high-income groups. These figures, of course, depend on the wording of the questions, but it is remarkable that Progress Party supporters in Denmark are located alongside the Social Democrats on this issue – and far to the left of any other non-socialist party. The Norwegian Progress Party voters are a little more to the right, but still less inclined than Conservative voters to support reduced taxation of high salaries.

This does not mean that Progress Party voters look very favourably on the welfare state: on general questions concerning maintenance of welfare provision or adoption of cuts in social spending, or about preference for either more welfare or tax relief, they are located to the right alongside Conservative (Norway, at least before the 1997 election, and Denmark) and

Liberal (Denmark) voters. To some extent, this represents a change from the situation in the 1980s, when Progress Party supporters in Denmark were more centrist, even on welfare issues (Andersen and Bjørklund, 1990). But it certainly also marks a change in attitude from the breakthrough period, where Progress Party voters were distinguished significantly from other non-socialist voters on exactly these issues. Furthermore, unlike the situation – at least in Denmark – in the mid-1970s, the populations – including Progress Party voters – are generally favourable to welfare: according to the 1993 election survey, only 20 per cent of the supporters of the Norwegian party wanted cuts in social security and even fewer among the 1997 voters (11 per cent); and a small majority of the Danish party's supporters want to maintain existing welfare provision and disagree with the view that welfare spending has gone too far.

To sum up, it is not on welfare and taxation issues that Progress Party supporters differ from other non-socialist voters any more. From time to time, they are more centrist than the Conservatives/Liberals, at least on issues that relate to economic redistribution. As already mentioned, Progress Party voters also differ according to issues: on basic welfare issues such as health, care for old people and pensions, they tend to be more 'lavish' than other non-socialist voters, whereas they are very critical of all sorts of 'luxury' expenditure such as on culture.[12]

Immigration, aid to developing countries

As noted above, the issue of immigration did not have much saliency among the voters until the second half of the 1980s. At first, immigration still did not become a permanently salient issue. As Tonsgaard (1989) has demonstrated, it tended to be a flash issue which disappeared as soon as media attention declined. Or, according to Aardal and Valen (1995), the immigration question was an undercurrent in public opinion, one which could easily be brought to the surface by a dramatic event. However, in the 1990s, the immigration question became a more permanently salient issue among the voters.[13] This holds in particular for the Danish 1998 election, where immigration was the most salient issue next to welfare policies. More than one-third of the voters indicated that they regarded immigration as one of the 'most important problems that politicians should take care of' (Andersen, 1999). However, for quite a large minority of these voters, this expressed a positive attitude towards immigrants, and it does not seem that the Progress parties and the Danish People's Party managed to benefit from this issue in the campaign as such. Still, there is no doubt that in a long-term perspective, the issue of immigration is the most important single issue in a new dimension of cleavage in the Danish party system.

It is noteworthy that attitudes towards foreigners are so strongly correlated with attitudes towards foreign aid to developing countries that they in

Table 9.5 Attitudes towards taxation and welfare, by party, 1993/1994. Percentages and PDIs (percentage difference index)

	Denmark 1994				Norway 1993		
Party	Increase tax on high incomes (PDI)[a]	Welfare should be maintained (PDI)[b]	Prefer more welfare rather than tax relief (PDI)[c]	Party	Reduce tax on high incomes (PDI)[d]	Cut social security (%)[e]	Prefer public services rather than tax relief (PDI)[f]
Progress P.	26	4	−36	Progress P.	−33	20	−2
Cons/ Liberals	−34	2	−36	Conservatives	−23	19	−15
Centrist parties	−9	51	−1	Centrist parties	−59	9	48
Social Dem.	31	62	26	Social Dem.	−59	9	59
Left-wing	43	80	45	Left-wing	−73	5	76
Population	5	35	−3		−53	11	42

Source: Elections surveys, Danish (1994) and Norwegian (1993) Electoral Programmes.

Wordings:
[a] 'High incomes ought to be taxed more heavily than they are today' (PDI = agree − disagree).
[b] 'A question about social expenditure. A says: "Social reforms have gone too far in this country. People should to a greater extent manage without social security and support from the state." B says: "Those social reforms that have been made in our country should be maintained at least to the same extent as now" '. (PDI = agree with B − agree with A.)
[c] 'If it becomes possible to lower taxes in the long run, which would you prefer: lower taxes or improved public services?' (PDI = public services − lower taxes).
[d] 'Reduce tax on high incomes'. (PDI = agree − disagree.)
[e] 'What is your opinion about social security expenditures; should they be (a) reduced in the future, or should we (b) maintain them at the present level, or should they be (c) extended further?' Category (a) is shown in the table.
[f] 'It is more important to expand public services than to cut taxes.' (PDI = agree − disagree.)

fact constitute a common dimension (Andersen, 1992). Even here, the economic argument that foreign aid does not help much, as most of the money is wasted anyway, may be mainly a legitimizing device – that is, other arguments would be invented if the economic argument was seriously contradicted.

At any rate, these are the issues where Progress Party voters deviate most significantly from the voters of all other parties. As demonstrated by Table 9.6, their supporters are strongly opposed to immigration, which is seen as a threat to national identity, and a huge majority favour cuts in foreign aid. On these points, they are clearly at odds with other non-socialist voters. Exactly the same pattern was found in Sweden in 1991 (Gilljam and Holmberg, 1993: 155). Essentially, such 'new politics' issues are also con-

Table 9.6 Attitudes toward immigration, foreign aid and the environment, by party, 1993/94. Percentages and PDIs

	Denmark 1994				Norway 1993		
Party	Immigrants a threat to our national identity (PDI)[a]	Cut aid to foreign countries (% agreeing)	Econ. growth v. environment (PDI)[b]	Party	Immigrants a threat to our national identity (PDI)[d]	Aid to foreign countries should be cut (per cent agree)	Reduce environmental demands (PDI)[c]
Progress P.	74	79	−9	Progress P.	49	68	9
Cons/ Liberals	8	48	−22	Conservatives	−6	30	−22
Centrist parties	−43	21	−60	Centrist parties	2	21	−39
Social Dem.	−1	41	−47	Social Dem.	−7	27	−24
Left-wing	−55	21	−85	Left-wing	−51	11	−70
Population	−1	42	−41		−6	26	−31

Source: Election surveys, Danish (1994) and Norwegian (1993) Electoral Programmes.
Wordings:
[a] 'Immigration constitutes a serious threat to our national culture' (agree − disagree).
[b] 'Economic growth should be ensured by means of industrial buildup, even though this may be in conflict with environmental interests' (agree − disagree).
[c] 'In the present economic situation in Norway, one ought to reduce environmental demands' (agree − disagree).

sidered left–right items and may help explain why the Progress Party is considered as being so far to the right.

In sum, there is little doubt that immigration is the core issue that distinguishes Progress Party voters from other non-socialist voters. It is, moreover, an issue that is strongly related to political cynicism (Andersen, 1992), and ethnic politics has become increasingly salient and indeed is likely to remain so (Gaasholt and Togeby, 1996), a situation thought unlikely by many commentators until recently.

A small note of caution is needed, however. What we have demonstrated is that a negative attitude towards foreigners, perhaps even xenophobia, is fundamental in explaining who does and does not vote for the Progress parties. But strictly speaking, we cannot rule out the possibility that the figures may also reflect who *abstains* from voting for the Progress parties – that is, that there may also be a *negative* identification involved. This is important for the conclusions that may be derived at the aggregate level: we have not demonstrated that the incidence of hostility towards foreigners is the only important determinant of aggregate electoral support for the Progress parties. It is possible that, besides this explanation, the degree of confidence in other non-socialist parties may also be an important factor.[14]

The environment and 'new politics'

The emphasis on immigration control does not necessarily make the Progress parties single issue parties. Their main issue has changed since 1973, but even at that time, they could not properly be described as single issue parties against taxes, and the subsequent attitudes on immigration also do not stand in isolation. Rather, they are related not only to foreign aid attitudes, but to a wider syndrome of 'new politics' issues, including authoritarian values and (most frequently) the environment. Moreover, on a number of indicators of authoritarian attitudes, Progress Party voters are consistently the most authoritarian. Progress Party voters in both countries also tend to be among the least 'green' voters (see Table 9.6). In a purely descriptive sense, these issues may be summarized as constituting a 'new politics' dimension. This dimension has given birth to 'New Left parties' and 'New Right parties' (Inglehart and Rabier, 1986), respectively characterized as 'the legitimate and the unwanted children of the New Politics' (Ignazi, 1992: 6). 'New Left parties', such as the Greens, are legitimate children since they expose new politics issues. 'New Right parties', on the other hand, are unwanted since they are a reaction to 'new politics' and emerge as an unexpected consequence.

The Progress parties, in a sense, do mobilize on 'new politics' issues. But they cannot simply be conceived as a counter-reaction to the 'new left'. In the first place, the parties differ from the American 'New Right' in not stressing traditional and religious values – this is a concern of the Christian Democrats.[15] Second, although the Progress parties may be diametrically opposed to the new left, the new politics issues on which they mobilize cannot simply be conceived as a *reaction* to the post-materialist left. The parties are, though, certainly linked to basic changes in the post-industrial cleavage structure in society.

European integration

It would be tempting to relate the Progress parties to changing cleavages and to broad historical changes in yet another respect. Lipset and Rokkan (1967) described the stability of cleavages and the 'freezing' of party systems in fully mobilized, industrial *nation-states*. But nation-states are also in transition, not least among the members of the European Union (EU). One could thus imagine that the Progress parties would be parties in favour of the defence of the nation-state. However, the parties – as well as their supporters – have, until recently, been cross-pressured by the perception that the EU means more market and less state. Thus, the Norwegian party ended up recommending EU membership in the 1994 referendum, although with an (arguably inconsistent) argument favouring the internal market but not the union. The same standpoint was adopted by the Danish parties, which – more consistently – advocated a 'yes' to the European Single Act in the 1986 campaign, but a 'no' to subsequent amendment through the Treaty on European Union in 1992, 1993 and 1998 (in 1993, as the only anti-European Union party in parliament).

Until recently, this Euro-scepticism did not have much impact on the parties' support. Although it was the only party favouring a 'no' in 1993, and while some 43 per cent voted no, the Danish party did not benefit from this. On the contrary, there were some party grassroots objections to the decision of the leadership, while in both countries the parties' supporters were divided. In Denmark, a small majority supported the official party line and voted no (Andersen, 1994). In Norway, a small majority voted yes (Bjørklund, 1996).[16] In the 1998 Danish referendum, however, nearly all supporters of the Danish People's Party and a huge majority of Progress Party voters followed the official recommendations of the parties and voted no (Andersen, 1998).

In the 1994 Norwegian EU referendum, the voters rejected membership for the second time, by more or less the same margin (52.2 per cent) as in the 1972 referendum (53.3 per cent). Again, as in 1972, the 1994 referendum result settled the EU question as a central political issue for some years to come. Consequently, the various party standpoints on membership seem to be of little practical political significance. Carl I. Hagen, in the 1997 election campaign, even announced that he had changed his opinion and was now an opponent of membership. But he also added that this standpoint had no political implications, as Norwegian EU membership, for the time being, was not a realistic option.

Nevertheless, in Denmark, the EU question is politically potent. According to a survey conducted in the autumn of 1997, the supporters of the Progress Party and the DPP had already at that time taken overwhelmingly negative stands on the issue of EU integration, and the combined effect of EU attitudes and attitudes towards immigration was very substantial. Among voters favouring liberal refugee policies, support for the two parties was negligible, regardless of attitudes to the EU. Among voters with a critical attitude to refugee policy, but with neutral or positive attitudes to European integration, support was at 5 per cent. But among voters who were also critical of European integration, support was up to 24 per cent (see Table 9.7). At the same time, the survey revealed quite an impressive party shift among voters exhibiting this critical combination. Of 1994 socialist voters, 11 per cent now voted for the Progress Party or the DPP; for non-socialists, the figure was 15 per cent. The first-mentioned pattern was largely confirmed by the 1998 election survey, but the 1997 survey is perhaps a stronger indication that the direction of causality is not only from party choice to attitudes, but probably also to quite some extent the other way around. There used to be a zero correlation between attitudes to immigration and attitudes to the EU. Although the correlation has become positive,

Table 9.7 Percentage of voters intending to vote for the Danish People's Party or Progress Party, by combination of attitude to European integration and attitude to refugee policy, 1997

	Attitudes to refugee policy: Denmark should receive more/the same/fewer refugees		*N*	
Attitudes to European integration	More/the same	Fewer		
Faster EU integration/same as now	1	5	269	439
Less integration/out of the EU	1	24	124	206

Source: Nation-wide representative survey of 1518 voters aged 18 or more, conducted by Jørgen Goul Andersen and A.C. Nielsen AIM for 'Ugebrevet Mandag Morgen', Aug./Sep. 1997. Respondents were asked which party they would vote for if an election was called for tomorrow.

it remains weak (Andersen, 1998); it is a case of two factors operating rather independently in changing the political adherences among Danish voters.

Conclusion: ideological profile

Progress Party supporters are not extreme right-wing supporters on traditional right–left issues, but consider themselves far to the right because of their position on 'new politics'. On these issues the Progress parties are more xenophobic, more authoritarian and less green than the supporters of any other party. The original issues of taxation and welfarism play a minor role – in fact, in Norway, welfare has been turned into a rallying issue – and distrust is to *some* degree an epiphenomenon of the policy positions of the supporters.

Social profile

Gender and age profile

In spite of the fact that the DPP and (informally) also Denmark's Progress Party are led by women, the Progress Party has always been a male-dominated party at the electoral level, and the same holds for the

Norwegian party (as well as for the Swedish; see Gilljam and Holmberg, 1993: 187). In fact, this is the most constant element in the social composition of party supporters. In Denmark, the proportion of men has varied between 55 and 67 per cent in elections since 1973, and in Norway, the figures are between 59 and 67 per cent, respectively, according to the election surveys.[17]

The age composition, on the other hand, has been more varied, depending on the success of the parties. In the 1990s, the age distribution in Denmark is slightly skewed towards older voters. The Norwegian Party, on the other hand, up to the mid-1990s, clearly had its best foothold in the youngest age group (like the Swedish New Democracy in 1991; see Gilljam and Holmberg, 1993: 193). However, since the 1995 Norwegian election the age distribution has become more even. In the 1997 election, there were no age differences among female Progress Party voters. But the party still had its core supporters among young men. Consequently, the earlier difference between the Norwegian and Danish parties seems gradually to have disappeared.

Class profile: a working-class party

The most surprising aspect of the social composition of the Progress parties is the class composition. From the beginning, the Danish party had a social profile which attracted much attention. In the light of classic theories of populism and petty bourgeois protest, the significant over-representation of the self-employed was heavily debated (Fryklund and Peterson, 1981). Yet the self-employed have always been a minority among party supporters. More remarkable, in both Denmark and Norway, the Progress Party was the first non-socialist party which was not under-represented among manual workers (Tables 9.8 and 9.9). The Norwegian party, in its first election in 1973, had a more traditional right-wing social profile. However, the proportion of workers among Progress Party supporters has increased in nearly every election in Denmark since 1973, and in Norway the renaissance of the Progress Party was also accompanied by a significant increase in the number of workers (see Table 9.9). A similar profile was evident in Sweden in 1991 (Gilljam and Holmberg, 1993: 198, 200). In the 1990s, the two Progress parties even obtained a higher proportion of workers among their electorate than any other party, including the Social Democrats.[18]

The increasing proportion of workers in the Progress Party corresponds with an equally significant protracted decline in the proportion of manual workers among the left-wing parties. This unusual social composition is perhaps the strongest indicator of a changing cleavage structure and of the classification of the Progress parties as belonging to a genuinely new party type. From the description of party ideology and voters' attitudes above, it is perhaps not so surprising. Xenophobia and authoritarianism are classic

Table 9.8 Proportion of workers among the supporters of various party groups *in Denmark*. Deviations from sample means (percentage points)

Party	1966	1973	1977	1979	1981	1984	1987	1988	1990	1994	1998
Progress Party	−4	−1	+2	+6	+9	+4	+14	+15	+16	+18	+15
Non-socialist parties	−26	−15	−20	−17	−15	−12	−12	−15	−16	−11	−10
Social Democrats	+27	+26	+20	+15	+18	+20	+19	+16	+16	+13	+9
Left-wing parties	+26	+17	+6	+3	+4	0	+2	+4	+1	−3	−3
Normal	40	37	35	36	36	32	32	36	31	34	35

Source: 1966–98 Election Surveys, Danish Election Programme. Owing to slight variation in delineations between workers and non-workers, the 'normal' distribution of all voters exhibits minor fluctuations, which does not affect the figures of the table significantly, however.

Notes: Entries are deviations between the proportion of manual workers among the supporters of various party groups and the proportion in the entire sample ('normal'). Only voters belonging to the labour force are included (1966–88: including housewives classified according to husband's position, but this does not affect the figures significantly).
In the 1998 election survey, the figures on over-representation of workers was +13 and +15 for the Danish People's Party and the Progress Party, respectively.

Table 9.9 Proportion of workers among the supporters of various party groups in Norway. Deviations from sample means (percentage points)

Party	1965	1973	1977	1981	1985	1989	1993[a]	1995[a]	1997[b]
Progress Party	—	−5	+15	+9	+3	+7	+3	+8	+5
Conservatives	−29	−29	−25	−19	−13	−15	−16	−10	−7
Centrist parties	−17	−12	−9	−8	−12	−8	+1	+1	−1
Social Democrats	+21	+19	+18	+20	+16	+13	+7	+6	+2
Left-wing parties	+21	+16	0	−6	−2	−3	−10	−9	−2
Normal	43	43	41	35	32	32	22	19	19

Source: 1965–93 Election Surveys, Norwegian Electoral Programme, 1995 Local Election Survey. 1997 MMI Election panel.

Notes: Entries are deviations between the proportion of manual workers among the supporters of various party groups and the proportion in the entire sample ('normal').
[a] Based on a narrower classification of workers by Statistics Norway.
[b] Unskilled workers.

aspects of working-class values, along with a dichotomous world-view. But, as pointed out by Lipset (1981), these aspects were of little significance while workers voted for socialist parties which defended the class interests of workers, and these parties were tolerant and anti-authoritarian. Within the well-organized working classes of Europe – not least in Scandinavia – such ideologies could spread downwards to the grassroots. However, if the bonds between individual workers and the working-class organizations, including labour parties, are seriously weakened, such elements of spontaneous class consciousness are likely to become decisive in the party choice of workers. We are not able to test these propositions systematically here. But we shall briefly comment on two alternative interpretations that might be put forward.

Marginalized working class or decline of solidarity

At least two competing interpretations might be suggested in order to explain the attraction of workers to radical right-wing populist or extremist parties. In the first place, several scholars have suggested that the support among workers for the Progress parties, or New Right parties in general, reflects some sort of post-industrial/post-modern marginalization of the working class, equivalent to the former marginalization of the old middle class. Second, it might be suggested that, because of its increasing wealth, the working class is losing its bonds of solidarity, and consequently shows less support for the welfare state. At least at the individual level, there is no convincing support for any of these suggestions. Collectively, the working class may be marginalized in post-industrial information society. But just as it has always been difficult to find much support for the 'marginalized middle class' interpretation of fascism or populism at the individual level, there is little to suggest an equivalent relationship when it comes to the Progress parties.

In Denmark, it is *not* the case that the two 'Progress parties' recruit disproportionately from the ranks of unemployed or early retirement pensioners. In Norway, however, where the unemployment rate is significantly lower, the Progress Party has had a higher proportion of unemployed among its voters than have other parties.[19] But since the Progress Party is a rather small party, the overwhelming majority of the unemployed vote for other parties.

The working-class support for the Progress parties may in some sense reflect the decline of the working class as a class (in terms of both size and organization). However, if this is the case, the relationship between marginalization and voter support is a subtle one. Finally, we have no evidence concerning the association between personal well-being (or feeling of decline) and support for the Progress parties, but there is not much to suggest that we should look in this direction. The opposite assumption of decline of solidarity (which may be derived from, for example, rational choice theory) is equally implausible. Progress Party supporters are no longer exceptional on issues of taxation or the welfare state.

Thus, we are more inclined to see working-class support for the Progress parties as a quite 'natural' phenomenon that is in accordance with the values and preferences actually found among workers in present-day society. Focus should perhaps rather be directed towards the factors that modify such sentiments. Among these, education is an obvious variable, and the association between Progress Party support and education (which was zero in 1973) has become increasingly important. The Progress parties disproportionately recruit among voters with low educational attainment. In Norway, this is especially pronounced among young and middle-aged voters, and appears to be the main explanation for the over-representation of workers. One might, of course, feel tempted to interpret this in terms of Lipset's assertion of the relationship between education and a 'complex frame of reference', in accordance with an interpretation of party ideology that stresses 'primitivism' or similar aspects in the ideologies of the parties. However, this is hardly a fair interpretation of party ideologies, at least if measured by comparative standards, and it seems more plausible that education involves a socialization into a set of values that are not very compatible with Progress Party ideas. Again, this is in line with a 'spontaneous consciousness' interpretation.

Conclusion

At the time of writing, there are radical right-wing populist parties of some importance in only two of the Scandinavian countries. To a large degree, this seems to be a matter of historical accident, as the Swedish party failed at a decisive stage of the party's life cycle. In the case of Finland, the picture is more uncertain, although the very small number of immigrants and refugees may help to explain why there may have been little scope for mobilization on the immigration issue. Institutional rules that discriminate against small parties may add to the explanation of the absence of a radical right-wing populist party in Sweden, but this is partly contradicted by the absence of such a party in Finland (which has no threshold of representation) and the presence of one in Norway (where there is a relatively high effective threshold – 4.0 per cent – except for parties that are geographically concentrated).

Ultimately, then, we are left with right-wing populist parties in only two Scandinavian countries: the Progress parties and the Danish People's Party. It is unlikely that these parties will disappear, since they are well institutionalized. It is also significant that even in the context of the serious splits in the Progress Party in Denmark in 1994–5, the combined support of the two

Danish parties soon recovered, and the DPP, at least, seems to have some chance of survival. Although these three parties may deviate from ideal-type extreme-right parties elsewhere in Western Europe, they nevertheless seem to feed from the same sources – in particular, immigration and the deterioration of working-class organizations. From the analysis above, we suggest that the Scandinavian parties and other extreme right-wing parties such as the French *Front National* are family-related in much the same way as are Social Democrats and Communists, which must both be characterized as labour parties. Moreover, it is perhaps only to be expected that, in social democratic Scandinavia, we find less extreme (or more 'social democratic') variants of this new type of party.

Notes

1. During most of their lifetime, there has been little or no direct contact between the Danish and Norwegian parties. The Norwegian party regarded the role of Mogens Glistrup as democratically dubious and avoided close formal relations. After Glistrup left the party, this obstacle disappeared, but without resulting in any significant co-operation. However, in the initial phase, there was some collaboration as Glistrup joined Anders Lange in Norwegian election campaigning.
2. In the 1973 election, an agreement allowed the Independent Party to put up a few candidates on the list of the Progress Party. One of these candidates was elected and, in accordance with the agreement, immediately broke with the Progress Party and declared herself a representative of the Independent Party.
3. Some accused the non-socialist governments of pursuing social democratic policies from 1976 to 1982, and the Social Democrat government was accused of pursuing a non-socialist policy, not least via reform which lowered the marginal tax rates.
4. Bert Karlsson was a successful and unconventional businessman with an image as 'a man of the people'. Ian Wachtmeister, on the other hand, had more of an upper-class image, having the title of count, and a background as leader of various companies in the industrial sector. Wachtmeister was also known among the general public, however, especially as a writer of two (fairly successful) satirical books.
5. According to a panel study conducted by MMI (Markeds og Mediainstituttet). Approximately 5000 were interviewed just before the election day and re-interviewed on election day. There were only minor deviances between the election result and the party distribution in the panel study (0.6 per cent or smaller).
6. Because of accusations of misleading parliament on this question, Prime Minister Poul Schlüter resigned in January 1993 and paved the way for a Social Democratic government.
7. In fact, the demand for a higher basic allowance was echoed by the Danish Communist Party in the mid-1970s.

8. According to the party manifesto of 1993, as well as in 1983 and 1989, the party was in favour of immigration, in principle. But as the Norwegian system (like the Danish) gives immigrants access to the social security system on nearly the same terms as Norwegians, the party opposes it.

9. Left–right self-placement may involve a weighting of various dimensions (e.g. 'old' and 'new' politics), or it may even be a dependent variable if people see themselves as being to the right because they vote for a party which is usually considered a right-wing party. The Progress Party is indeed considered to be much further to the right than any other party among the voters at large. In 1994, Danish voters on average assigned the Progress Party to a position of 8.86, as compared to 7.91 for the Liberals and 7.56 for the Conservatives. The corresponding Norwegian figures are, with reference to the 1993 parliamentary election, 9.03 (Progress Party) and 8.62 (Conservatives).

10. In the 1970s, the Danish Progress Party supporters were more unambiguously to the right, except on the issue of equality (Andersen, 1978; Glans, 1986).

11. In Norway, marginal taxes and taxes on capital income have been lowered very significantly, whereas income taxes in Denmark have remained far above the 1973 level for both higher and lower incomes. Thus, it is questionable whether the changes in the tax system are responsible for the lower levels of interest among voters. Furthermore, in the 1990 Danish election, when the conservative coalition government called for an election on the issue of taxation and promised to lower income taxes, it was heavily defeated by the voters (Andersen, 1994).

12. In the 1989 Norwegian Election Survey, the voters were asked how they perceived support from the welfare state to various groups. Regarding support to the unemployed, the elderly and the disabled, the Progress Party voters had a profile which resembled that of left-wing voters and Social Democrats – that is, they favoured greater support. This was definitely not the case as regards support for refugees and asylum seekers. Not surprisingly, the Progress Party voters wanted to cut social security for this sector. On a more general question, the Progress Party voters often refused to give support to people in trouble if the recipients could be blamed for causing their own problems.

13. In Denmark, it was mentioned spontaneously by 4 per cent in 1987 (first appearance), 1 per cent in 1988, 2 per cent in 1990, and 8 per cent in 1994 (Andersen, 1996: 5).

14. There may even be some self-validating elements here, as non-socialist parties, in particular in Norway, tend to become confused when confronted with increasing support for the Progress parties. The Norwegian party is regarded as an unrealistic partner, and the illustrating example is the 1986 occasion when the Progress Party voted down a non-socialist government.

15. Also, on this point, Swedish findings from the 1991 election are entirely consistent with the Danish and Norwegian results (Gilljam and Holmberg, 1993: 149).

16. The supporters of the Swedish New Democracy in 1991 were overwhelmingly favourable to the EU, but this was before opposition was mobilized in Sweden.

In the 1991 election survey, only 16 per cent were against Swedish membership. In the referendum in 1994, only a small majority voted yes.

17. The Danish 1998 Election Survey indicates that only 47 per cent of the 1998 electorate of the Progress Party were males (N = 73).

18. According to the Danish polls from 1996 and 1997, the two Danish parties achieved a genuinely proletarian profile, as some two-thirds of the parties' adherents were workers (*Ugebrevet Mandag Morgen*, 32/1996 and based on samples of about 7000 and 6000 respondents, respectively).

19. That was the case in the 1989, 1993 and 1995 elections, but not in the 1997 election. However, at that time, the rate of unemployment was insignificant.

References

Aardal, B. and Valen, H. (1995) *Konflikt og opinion.* Oslo: NKS-Forlaget.

Andersen, J. G. (1978) 'Nogle bemærkninger om Fremskridtspartiet og arbejder-klassen', *Politica* 9(3–4), 95–114.

Andersen, J. G. (1988) *Vælgermosaik.* Working Paper No. 19, Centre of Cultural Research, University of Aarhus.

Andersen, J. G. (1992) 'Politikerleden – myte eller realitet' and 'Årsaker til mis-tillid', in Andersen, J. G., Nielsen, I. J., Thomsen, N. and Westerståhl, J. *Vi og vore politikere.* Copenhagen: Spektrum.

Andersen, J. G. (1994) 'Samfundsøkonomi, interesser og politisk atfærd', in Petersen, E. *et al.* (eds) *Livskvalitet og holdninger i det variable nichesamfund.* Aarhus: Department of Psychology, Aarhus University Press.

Andersen, J. G. (1995) 'Vælferdsstatens folkelige opbakning', in *Social forskning: temanummer om velfærdssamfundets fremtid august 1995.* Copenhagen: Danish National Institute of Social Research.

Andersen, J. G. (1996) *Socialdemokratiets vælgertilslutning 1971–1994.* Working Paper Series 1996: 2. Department of Economics, Politics and Public Admin-istration, University of Aalborg.

Andersen, J. G. (1998) *Danskerne og Europa.* Copenhagen: Ugebrevet Mandag Morgen.

Andersen, J. G. (1999) 'Vælgernes politiske dagsorden', in Andersen, J., Borre, O., Andersen, J. G. and Nielsen, H. J. (eds) *Vælgere der tænker.* Aarhus: Systime.

Andersen, J. G. and Bjørklund, T. (1990) 'Structural Changes and New Cleavages: The Progress Parties in Denmark and Norway', *Acta Sociologica* 33(3), 195–217.

Betz, H.-G. (1994) *Radical Right-Wing Populism in Western Europe.* Basingstoke: Macmillan.

Bjørklund, T. (1988) 'The 1987 Norwegian Local Elections: A Protest Election with a Swing to the Right', *Scandinavian Political Studies* 11, 211–34.

Bjørklund, T. (1996) 'The Three Nordic 1994 Referenda Concerning Membership in the EU', *Co-operation and Conflict* 31, 11–36.

Borre, O. and Andersen, J. G. (1997) *Voting and Political Attitudes in Denmark.* Aarhus: Aarhus University Press.

Canovan, M. (1981) *Populism.* New York: Harcourt Brace Jovanovich.

Djursaa, M. (1981) *DNSAP: danske Nazister, 1–2*. Copenhagen: Gyldendal.
Eriksen, H. (1978) *Partiet de uafhængige 1953–1960*. Odense: Odense University Press.
Fryklund, B. and Peterson, T. (1981) *Populism och missnöjespartier i Norden*. Lund: Arkiv.
Gaasholt, Ø. and Togeby, L. (1996) *I syv sind*. Aarhus: Politica.
Gilljam, M. and Holmberg, S. (1993) *Väljarna inför 90-talet*. Stockholm: Norstedts Juridik.
Gilljam, M. and Holmberg, S. (1995) *Väljarnas val*. Stockholm: Norstedts Juridik/ Fritzes Förlag.
Glans, I. (1986) 'Fremskridtspartiet: småborgerlig revolt, högerreaktion eller generell protest?', in Eklit, J. and Tonsgaard, O. (eds) *Valg of vælgeradfærd*. Aarhus: Politica.
Gooskens, M. (1993) 'How Extreme Are the Extreme Right-wing Parties in Scandinavia? Three Approaches for Measuring Party Distance', MA thesis, Political Science Department, Leiden University.
Ignazi, P. (1992) 'The Silent Counter-revolution: Hypotheses on the Emergence of Extreme Right-Wing Parties in Europe', *European Journal of Political Research* 22, 3–34.
Inglehart, R. and Rabier, J. J. (1986) 'Political Realignment in Advanced Industrial Society: From Class-Based Politics to Quality of Life Politics', *Government and Opposition* 21, 456–79.
Lane, J.-E. and Ersson, S. O. (1994) *Politics and Society in Western Europe*. London: Sage.
Larsen, B. V. (1977) 'Fremskridtspartiets organisation', MA thesis, Department of Political Science, University of Aarhus.
Linz, J. (1978) 'Some Notes toward a Comparative Study of Fascism in Historical Perspective', in Laqueur, W. (ed.) *Fascism: A Reader's Guide*. Harmondsworth: Penguin.
Lipset, S. M. (1981) *Political Man*, expanded and updated edition. Baltimore: Johns Hopkins University Press.
Lipset, S. M. and Rokkan, S. (1967) 'Cleavage Structure, Party Systems and Voter Alignments: An Introduction', in Lipset, S. M. and Rokkan, S. (eds) *Party Systems and Voter Alignments*. New York: Free Press.
Sänkiaho, R. (1971) 'A Model of the Rise of Populism and Support for the Finnish Rural Party', *Scandinavian Political Studies* 6, 27–47.
Sejersted, F. (1982) *Opposisjon og posisjon 1945–1981: høyres historie*, 3 bind. Oslo: Cappelen Forlag.
Shils, E. (1956) *The Torment of Secrecy*. New York: Free Press.
Siune, K. (1989) 'Valgkampene og vælgerne', in Eklit, J. and Tonsgaard, O. (eds) *To Folketingsvalg*. Aarhus: Politica.
Tonsgaard, O. (1989) 'Flyktninge og indvandrere – et politisk spørgsmål', in Eklit, J. and Tonsgaard, O. (eds) *To Folketingsvalg*. Aarhus: Politica.
Wilensky, H. D. (1975) *The Welfare State and Equality*. Berkeley: University of California Press.

CHAPTER TEN

After the fall: nationalist extremism in post-communist Russia

Michael Cox and Peter Shearman

Introduction

In 1985, Mikhail Gorbachev set out to reform the Soviet Union and make it a more effective 'socialist' superpower. Yet in just over four years, Soviet control over Eastern Europe had effectively disintegrated; and within six, the Soviet Union had broken up altogether. Though these momentous, and quite unexpected, events generated some alarm in the West (especially over the disposition and control of the Soviet Union's large nuclear arsenal), the overwhelming mood abroad was one of triumphalism tinged with a sense of genuine optimism about Russia's future. Indeed, such was the sense of euphoria in those early days that many hoped – and most assumed – that having won the Cold War, the West would now proceed to win the peace by helping to build a stable capitalist democracy on the remains of the former Communist empire. This optimism derived from three basic assumptions. The first was that the events of 1991 constituted a 'new Russian revolution' which had swept away the old Soviet system and with it most of the barriers to fundamental reform. The second was that, although there were still obstacles standing in the way of change, Russia could quickly and relatively painlessly exit its Communist past if there were strong political leadership, radical economic policies and sufficient Western support. And the third was that reform within Russia would lay the basis for an entirely new relationship between Russia and the West (Cohen, 1993). From this perspective, it was essential for the United States in particular to intervene energetically into Russian affairs; not just to accelerate Russia's transformation but also to defend the reformers against so-called 'reactionary and conservative' opponents who had nothing to gain and much to lose if the reforms were successful. Not that there was much to fear from such quarters. The forces of opposition, it was argued, were too much tainted with a failed Soviet past.

Also, they had no credible programme and, perhaps most important of all, they had no support in the West.

The analysis presented here looks in some detail at those whom the West initially dismissed as being of no real political significance: the 'reactionaries and the conservatives' with apparently nothing to offer the Russian people – political figures like Vladimir Zhirinovsky, leader of the ill-named Liberal Democratic Party of Russia (LDPR). Seen by many as a chauvinist clown with only limited support, his reasonable showing in the Russian presidential elections of 1991, followed two years later by his 23 per cent vote in the elections to the Russian parliament (Duma), not only cast a large cloud over the nascent transition to Western-style capitalist democracy in Russia, but sent a major shock wave around Western capitals – one which was especially felt in Washington, where the Clinton administration had set so much store by what it had hoped would one day become a close strategic alliance with Russian reform (Cox, 1994). Admittedly, the vote for the Liberal Democrats did not translate itself into a serious threat to Yeltsin. Moreover, support for the party did not hold up in the years thereafter. Nonetheless, many of its anti-Western and less than democratic ideas (albeit in a more sanitized form) were to find a new home in the increasingly influential and much better organized Communist Party of the Russian Federation led by Gennady Zyuganov. Building upon genuine popular discontent caused on the one hand by the humiliating collapse of Russian power and influence, and on the other by the high social and economic costs involved in the reforms themselves, Zyuganov articulated a distinctly chauvinist, but also populist, programme which expressed the fears and discontents of many ordinary people. Certainly, to many Russians there seemed to be a good deal of truth in what both he and, before him, Zhirinovsky, had to say. After all, far from creating a 'normal' society, the leap-to-capitalism experiment endorsed and supported by the West, had managed to fulfil hardly any of its promises. Instead, it had brought skyrocketing consumer prices, growing inequality, impoverishment for most Russian families and plummeting industrial production – perfect conditions for leaders like Zyuganov and Zhirinovsky to find a ready-made audience for their diatribes against those who, they claimed, were seeking to destroy Mother Russia.

But how should we characterize this new opposition? Certainly it would be highly misleading to equate the Zhirinovsky (even more so, the Zyuganov) phenomenon with classical fascism. Fascism, after all, was a specific response to a genuine crisis of inter-war capitalism, when communism seriously threatened the established order, with Benito Mussolini as perhaps its first genuine theorist (Gregor, 1979). In Russia, the conditions were, and remain, quite different; and even if they were not, one would still be extremely wary of using a term that has been so loosely deployed as to rob it of any objective value. Moreover, as Vladimir Pribylovsky has pointed out, political discourse in modern Russia in particular has become so debased that one has to take great care in distinguishing the everyday language of politics from scientific analysis. He cites a simple, but telling, example. In 1995, there were at least four 'anti-fascist' centres in Moscow. These had originally been set up by the self-styled 'democrat' Yevgeny Prosheckin, the 'communist' Boris Gunko, the 'radical national-patriots' Sergei Zharikov and Andrei Arkhipov, and the 'patriot' Sergei Baburin. Since being created, however, each of the four organizations seems to have spent a good deal, if not most, of its time denouncing the others as 'fascist' rather than analysing the phenomenon! In Russia it would seem that a fascist 'can be anyone I don't like' (Pribylovsky, 1995). Furthermore, though some very small groups in Russia are happy to label themselves as fascists or neo-Nazis (for instance, Alexander Barkashov's Russian National Union), most organizations are deeply opposed to being characterized in this way; in part, one suspects, because of the critical importance which World War II and the defeat of Nazi Germany played in the country's history (Dunlop, 1996). Zhirinovsky, no less, has successfully taken newspapers and individuals to court for calling him a fascist, including one famous case against Yegor Gaidar, Yeltsin's former Acting, later Deputy, Prime Minister. In the end, Gaidar was instructed to pay the LDPR leader compensation for besmirching his name.

Finding an adequate term to define Russian nationalist extremism is thus not an easy task, especially in a country where traditional political labels seem to have lost all meaning – where, indeed, the ostensibly 'liberal' Yeltsin disposed of the Russian parliament in 1993 by bombing it, where Zyuganov, the 'Communist', rarely if ever refers to Marx, and Zhirinovsky, the anti-semite, was once a co-founder of a Jewish cultural organization known as *Shalom* (Clark, 1995: 283). In reality, there is no precise definition we can use to characterize those who have loosely been defined as the 'new right' in Russia. In this chapter, therefore, we will avoid the pitfalls of trying to put a label on this powerful tendency, and instead seek to understand the origins, strength and views of those various groups or individuals that espouse an ideology which is stridently nationalist in tone, deeply suspicious of the West, hostile to Western capitalism, more likely to favour a strong state than democracy, and inclined to indulge in the most rabid forms of attacks upon 'Jews' (Mudde, 1995). Those who fall into this camp also tend to view the world around them in a highly paranoid fashion, assuming that Russia is surrounded by enemies whose prime goal is to destroy the country. They also have little or no sympathy for the rights of other non-Russian nations. Viewing the breakup of the Soviet Union in 1991 as 'one of the greatest tragedies to affect us in recent years' (to quote Zyuganov's deputy, Valentin Kuptsov), most, if not all, nationalist extremists favour the reconstitution of some form of traditional Russian empire with Russia standing once again at its heart (Simonsen, 1997: 53).

In what follows, we shall look first at the intellectual origins of modern Russian extremist nationalism. The thesis that will be advanced here is that many of the arguments deployed by the 'new' nationalist opponents of reform have, in effect, been borrowed or plundered from the intellectual armoury of the old Communist regime. In other words, the views of key figures like Zhirinovsky and Zyuganov are not original at all but, rather, only latter-day reformulations of the ideology (or at least parts of the ideology) of the previous Soviet system (Shearman, 2000). In this very specific, but important sense, there is nothing particularly 'new' about the new nationalist opposition in post-Communist Russia. We shall then look in turn at the rise of the Liberal Democratic Party of Russia, the emergence of Zyuganov and the Communist Party of the Russian Federation, the constitutional crisis of October 1993 and the subsequent parliamentary elections of 1993 and 1995. Finally, we will examine the presidential contest of 1996 and conclude with a few general remarks about Russia's political prospects and the likely trajectory of Russian nationalism.

The decomposition of Stalinism

Although the Communist Party of the Soviet Union (CPSU) espoused a universal doctrine, contained within official Marxist–Leninist ideology were other strains, distinctly non-Marxist and specifically Russian in character. Among these, one can readily identify a messianic nationalism, a denigration of other foreign cultures, a partly submerged anti-semitism, an abiding suspicion of all things 'Western', a ready acceptance of a powerful state, and a justification for Russia's civilizing and progressive role among the 'family' of Soviet nations. The sources of this cannot be traced back to Marx, of course, but derive from Stalin's invention and defence of the concept of socialism in one country in his struggle against the 'cosmopolitan' and internationalist Trotsky. Historically, the result of Stalin's victory was to leave the Soviet Union formally 'socialist' in appearance, but 'nationalist' in theory and practice (Laqueur, 1993). Indeed, during World War II and the early years of the Cold War, the 'socialist' component of Soviet ideology virtually disappeared altogether, to be replaced by a celebration of all things Russian and a denunciation of everything that was not. Following Stalin's death, there was, it is true, a partial modification of this extraordinarily crude (but one suspects highly effective) propaganda campaign which succeeded in both isolating Russia from the outside world and giving Russians a highly inflated view of their own worth. Unfortunately, the very uneven process of ideological de-Stalinization did not go as far as some might have hoped for – a significant indication of which was the fate of Alexander Yakovlev, one of the key architects of Gorbachev's programme of reform (*perestroika*). An important figure in the Soviet elite, he was in effect 'exiled' to become Soviet ambassador to Canada after his article 'Against Anti-historicism' was published in the newspaper *Literaturnaya Gazeta* in November 1972. Yakovlev was, at the time, acting head of the ideological department of the CPSU Central Committee, and his piece (published without permission from the Party leadership and attacked because it 'reeked of Zionism and Freemasonry'!) was a comprehensive critique of Russophilism, an ideology dominant in such journals as *Molodaya Gvardiya* and *Nash Sovremennik* and prevalent in the arts more generally (Pankin, 1996: 22). Significantly, the person most responsible for both encouraging and protecting this tendency was Mikhail Suslov, chief party ideologist in the Brezhnev era. Suslov was a critical figure in the late Soviet system. Immensely influential and deeply suspicious of any moves to reform that system, his role basically was not so much to develop Marxism as to provide the elite with a functionally useful doctrine which could be employed to legitimize the regime and its various activities at home and abroad. As one commentator astutely observed, Suslov seemed to sense 'the weakness of traditional Marxism among the masses' and hence 'experimented with a form of national Bolshevism based on an alliance between Party conservatives and Russian nationalists' (Carter, 1990: 87).

This ideological amalgam of formal communism and Russian nationalism was something which aroused a good deal of comment among analysts of the Soviet Union. Yet it also contained within it a potential for further development, as was noted in a study that was widely criticized when it first appeared in 1987. Writing at a time when Gorbachev was enjoying great popularity at home – and even more abroad – Alexander Yanov predicted that by the turn of the century the agenda in Russia would be set not by liberals (let alone reform socialists like Gorbachev and Yakovlev), but by others, who would mix communism and nationalism into a dangerous brew that would be both aggressively anti-Western and anti-democratic (Yanov, 1987). Yanov's prediction was to come true much earlier than even he could have anticipated, for one of the most visible and publicized results of Gorbachev's political reforms was the emergence of a previously submerged Russian nationalism – the most significant organized expression of which was the small but highly aggressive group *Pamyat* (Memory). *Pamyat* was a very loose coalition of 'patriotic' groups that had evolved and developed in the late 1970s with the ostensible purpose of protecting Russia's ancient monuments and churches (Nove, 1989: 38). Its original cultural focus gradually gave way to political activism, however, and in December 1987 the organization issued an *Appeal to the Russian People*. This set out its basic views (*Arkhiv Samizdata*: 1 February 1988). The document was hyper-nationalist, overtly racist and riddled with hostile comments about Jews, who were said to be part of a deliberate conspiracy to undermine the great Russian state. One *Pamyat* group in Novosibirsk, concerned about the ecology of Lake Baikal, even accused Jews of organizing an anti-Russian plot to deliberately pollute the lake (Devlin, 1995: 76) The best known of *Pamyat*'s political leaders, Dmitry Vasilyev, also made a name for himself in the early months of the Gorbachev era when he gave a public reading of The Protocols of the Elders of Zion, a nineteenth-century piece of official propaganda which claimed that Jews were attempting to take over the world (Cox, 1992: 270–4).

The actual 'programme' of *Pamyat* was an interesting blend of blind prejudice and genuine insight into the Soviet condition. The party was never intellectually consistent, however. Thus, though it opposed democracy as a political form of organization, it also seemed to support Gorbachev's attempt to reform the Soviet Union. In one document, it even endorsed the idea of referendums to decide country-wide issues. In some of its statements, it seemed to favour economic collectivism. In others, though, it strongly supported the idea of the private ownership of the land. It was certainly highly vociferous in its condemnation of Soviet urban reality and attacked what it (and, no doubt, many people) saw as the 'unnatural' life many people in the Soviet Union were forced to lead, living in communal apartments in huge impersonal buildings in giant, featureless cities. Not surprisingly, it raised environmental concerns and spoke passionately, and in many ways accurately, against the ecological catastrophe which had been visited upon the country by Soviet communism. More generally, it saw hardly anything of worth coming out of seventy years of Soviet rule. The revolution, in its view, had been an unmitigated disaster for Russia. Lenin, according to one spokesman, 'hated Russia', as did his 'Jewish Bolshevik' colleagues, who had destroyed a once great country and replaced it with an historical abomination in the shape of the Soviet Union – a political system run by those inspired by the credo of Marxism, an evil doctrine that was part of a larger world-wide Zionist–Masonic conspiracy designed to undermine Russia and keep it weak.

On foreign affairs, *Pamyat* had relatively little to say, though, significantly perhaps, it generally favoured what might loosely be described as a 'strictly isolationist and pacifist line'. Basically, Russia, in its view, should be playing less, rather than more, of an international role: in part because Soviet foreign policy had traditionally been guided by what it saw as the dubious and dangerous ideology of Marxism–Leninism, and partly because it feared that if the nation continued along its adventurist international path, it would continue to be drawn into tragic adventures such as the one in Afghanistan, where Russian blood had been spilt in a 'criminal' conflict in which Russia had no interest. *Pamyat*, however, managed to weave its critique of Soviet foreign policy into a more general attack on two of its great hate figures: the Jewish revolutionary Leon Trotsky, and international 'Zionist capital'. In one memorable statement, redolent of classical Stalinism, it decried both Zionism and 'imperialism' and their agents inside the country who, in *Pamyat*'s words, reanimated 'Trotskyism in order to discredit socialism, to sow chaos and to open the country's gates to Western capital and Western ideology' (Krasnov, 1993: 118).

There is little doubting the fact that those in and around Gorbachev were highly embarrassed by the antics of *Pamyat*, especially when it attacked a number of the reformers for either being or at least 'harbouring' 'Jews and Freemasons'. That said, the authorities were noticeably reluctant to deal with *Pamyat*'s increasingly aggressive activities. For example, in 1987, when 1500 of its supporters gathered outside the newspaper offices of the reformist newspaper *Moscow News* and chanted anti-semitic slogans at those within, the then chief of the Moscow Communist Party, Boris Yeltsin, did not have them arrested but instead arranged a meeting to discuss their grievances (Spier, 1989: 51)! Later, following an attempt by members of the organization to break up a meeting of liberal writers in Moscow in January 1990, little was done. Furthermore, when rumours of a *Pamyat*-inspired pogrom against Russian Jews were rife, it was, in the end, international opinion rather than determined action by the authorities themselves which finally led to the arrest and imprisonment of one (but only one) of the more extreme members of *Pamyat*. Even then, the accused was sentenced only to two years and not the maximum five. Moreover, as the public prosecutor at the time pointed out, 'the case came about not because of the state and law enforcement bodies but in spite of them' (Boulton, 1990).

The official tolerance displayed towards *Pamyat* led a number of commentators to the not illogical conclusion that the movement was not some spontaneous or autonomous manifestation of popular opinion (though it clearly did tap into some grievances), but a distorted expression of the views of at least a section of the Soviet elite itself. Certainly, *Pamyat* had its defenders at the highest level of Soviet life. For instance, in 1987, Vadim Kozhinov, a prominent literary critic, though critical of what he termed the organization's 'infantilism' and 'ignorance', urged that the positive aspects of its activities not be overlooked. In 1988, Valentin Rasputin, who later went on to join Gorbachev's presidential council, not only denounced what he called the 'left-wing' bias of the Soviet press for labelling all Russian patriots like *Pamyat* as 'Black Hundreds', but attacked those who indiscriminately vilified its followers (Krasnov, 1993: 120). Even the more liberal Gavril Popov (later Mayor of Moscow) was more than a little indulgent towards the organization. While accepting that there were good reasons to be concerned about some of its more malign features, he believed that among the *Pamyat* membership there were many honest and sincere patriots. Indeed, he went so far as to suggest that *Pamyat* should be regarded as less of a threat, and more a legitimate protest against Soviet rule; in particular, against the debasement of Russian life and the transformation of the Russian people into slaves and 'brutes', willing to 'carry out the role that the administrative system [had] assigned to them' (Popov and Adzhubei, 1988).

There was never much chance of *Pamyat* evolving into a mass movement; even less of its challenging Soviet rule (Pribylovsky, 1992: 60–4). But the importance of *Pamyat* lay not in its size but, first, in its ideas – many of which were later to find a home in other, more significant parties – and, second, in the fact that it reflected, in a more extreme form, the beliefs and attitudes of those within the larger and far more powerful Russian establishment. Indeed, given the hierarchical and controlled nature of the Soviet system (even in its last chaotic years), one must assume that *Pamyat* could have manifested itself only if people at the very top of the Soviet power structure had, in the words of one commentator, 'smiled on the enterprise' and smoothed its path; and one must also assume that they did so not simply because *Pamyat* was a useful vehicle for countering the reformers, but because its underlying anti-Westernism and extreme nationalism were positions with which they themselves happened to agree. In this, perhaps, lay *Pamyat*'s true historic significance (Clark, 1995).

Zhirinovsky and the Liberal Democratic Party of Russia

The Liberal Democratic Party of the Soviet Union (later the Liberal Democratic Party of Russia [LDPR]) was to become the organized voice of extreme nationalism in the transitional period from the Soviet to the post-Soviet eras. The organization was founded in March 1990 and was the first opposition party to the ruling Communist Party of the Soviet Union to gain official registration (in April 1991). Yet as was pointed out at the time, the rise of Zhirinovsky and the LDPR was, according to its liberal opponents, 'suspiciously smooth' (*Moscow News*, No. 4, 31 January 1994). Certainly, in comparison to some of the other fledgling political movements that were being publicly vilified in the state-controlled media, the LDPR was provided with easy access to television and official party organs such as *Pravda*. Representatives of the party also gained what to many seemed like easy access to leading political figures such as Prime Minister Nikolai Ryzhkov and the Chairman of the Supreme Soviet, Anatoly Lukyanov. It even received an official invitation to attend the Revolutionary Day celebrations and military parade in Moscow in 1990 (Lester, 1994: 17–30). Rumours spread that Zhirinovsky was a creation of the KGB (which he denied), and the original founder of the party, Vladimir Bogachev, tried to expel him for allegedly collaborating with the secret police. Whether or not the party was originally a product of the security services or was simply manipulated by them remains an open question. The fact remains, Zhirinovsky struck back and purged Bogachev from the party's ranks. Thereafter, he effectively dominated and controlled the organization. He also changed its orientation and, under his direction (and almost certainly encouraged by elements within the secret police), the LDPR abandoned its original support for a market economy, multi-partyism, a law-governed state and the 'de-ideologization' of society, and, following its Second Congress in October 1990, began to articulate a far more aggressive ideology.

The programme adopted by the Liberal Democrats included four broad demands: to reconstitute the Russian Empire; to defend the position of ethnic Russians throughout the former Soviet Union; to enhance state power with an authoritarian executive structure at its core; and to limit both the extent of privatization and the degree of foreign ownership of the Russian economy. But the party's appeal probably owed less to its detailed arguments about the structure of the Russian economy or the future shape of the political system than to Zhirinovsky's ability to speak for those many millions fearful of change and concerned that there was really no place for them in the new market-oriented Russia. Moreover, though wild and outlandish in many ways – he at one point demanded that the United States return Alaska to Russia – Zhirinovsky did at least speak to the masses in terms which they could understand. He also tended to promise them the world: higher pensions for the old, guaranteed full employment for the workers, more opportunities for the young, and (most important of all, perhaps) greater respect for the Russian people. Zhirinovsky was especially adept in tapping into a bruised and battered Russian psyche by painting a picture of 'poor Russia' being misused and abused by its numerous enemies, among which he included the other nationalities, the International Monetary Fund, Muslims and the Islamic faith in general. Zhirinovsky was very vitriolic indeed in his denunciations of the non-Christian countries of Turkey, Iran and Afghanistan. These bastions of Islam in his opinion should be either subjugated or dismembered; and, as long as the United States did not stand in Russia's way, there was no need for conflict between the two powers over the issue!

While advocating an aggressive policy towards the other nations of the former Soviet Union (he believed that the new Russian Empire should be a unitary state), Zhirinovsky thought it had been a mistake for the old Soviet Union to waste money in the Third World on useless revolutionary adventures in places like Africa or Latin America. His vision, therefore, was not of Russia as a world power, but of Russia as a classic empire: in effect, a Greater Russia divided into various regions organized not along ethnic or 'national' lines but along purely administrative ones. Zhirinovsky was at pains, however, to point out that his vision was not racially exclusive. Nonetheless, there were very strong racial overtones in what he had to say, notably in his diatribes against Muslims inside and outside Russia. And, though careful not to sound too anti-semitic, the fact that he constantly denied that he was a 'Jew' himself, and claimed that there was 'not a drop' of Jewish blood in his veins, did imply an attitude towards the larger 'Jewish question'. Certainly, he was not above exploiting anti-semitism when it served his political purposes.

Zhirinovsky's rabble-rousing and racially charged speeches obviously tapped into something in the wider Russian public. But there is reason to believe that his articulated views on domestic and foreign affairs (like those previously of *Pamyat*) also reflected the outlook of a section of the Russian elite. It is certainly the case that Zhirinovsky (in the same way as *Pamyat*) was protected by those in power. Even Yeltsin seemed to indulge him while borrowing some of his less aggressive nationalist rhetoric to maintain his own grip on power. Indeed, there is a good deal of evidence to support the thesis that Zhirinovsky's stance on a number of issues was but a popularized version of views held by some in the Russian establishment itself. Thus his argument about the need to rebuild the Russian Empire after the disintegration of the Soviet Union was not at all dissimilar to the position accepted by several leading strategists in and around the Russian President. His views on the Islamic threat were hardly original either. In fact, there were many at the highest level who took it for granted that radical Islam was one of the greatest dangers facing Russia in the late twentieth century. Furthermore, while his musings about Russia fighting 'the corner for the white race in Asia' may have sounded like 'demented raving' to some in the West, as has been suggested, this was 'only a slight distortion of the serious thinking that was going on in the heart of the Russian establishment' – an establishment that had no liking for the United States, but still felt that a deal could be struck with the Americans in which Russia would be allowed to shape the fate of its own sphere of influence, in exchange for allowing the United States to do what it liked in the rest of the world (Clark, 1995: 285).

Constitutional crisis

Zhirinovsky was the first candidate to register for the Russian Republic's presidential elections in May 1991. This provided him with a very effective platform from which to publicize and test his views among the Russian electorate. Yeltsin was always firm favourite to win, on a simple slogan of opposing the 'centre' in the name of democracy. However, Zhirinovsky's third place and 6.2 million votes (8.1 per cent of those cast) demonstrated that there was clearly a market for his particular brand of extremism – a perception reinforced by the 3 million votes also cast for the neo-Stalinist candidate, General Albert Makashov. Yeltsin also was prepared to flirt with nationalism during the election, arguing that Russia had for too long 'suffered' at the expense of the other republics in the old Soviet Union. A new consensus was thus already beginning to emerge, and once the Soviet empire fell apart completely – with all its attendant problems for Russia and Russians – strident nationalism would assume an increasingly virulent form.

The first indication of the increasing strength of the extremists was to come during the crisis between the executive and the legislature in September and October 1993. Hitherto, Yeltsin had pursued a twin-track strategy of radical market reforms at home (advocated by the International Monetary Fund and Acting Prime Minister Yegor Gaidar) and a pro-Western foreign policy abroad (strongly endorsed by the United States and supported by Foreign Minister Andrey Kozyrev). The strategy, though, had many critics, especially within the partially reformed old Soviet parliament, the Congress of People's Deputies, which effectively became the focus of what the Russian media termed an 'irreconcilable opposition' to both the government's economic policies and what it saw as its slavish approach to the West in general, and the United States in particular. The leaders of the opposition were Yeltsin's own vice-president, Alexander Rutskoi, and the chairman of the Supreme Soviet, Ruslan Khasbulatov. Yeltsin issued a presidential decree disbanding the parliament on 21 September. The opposition refused to comply and, from their redoubt in the parliament building, announced the establishment of an alternative government with Rutskoi as acting president (Dunlop, 1993: 283–326). The parliament was stormed in dramatic fashion to remove what Yeltsin called the 'fascist–communist' conspirators inside. Then, having succeeded, he called elections for a new parliament for the following December, no doubt hoping that this would both eliminate the opposition and provide democratic endorsement for his policies.

The storming of the Russian parliament, however, was unlikely to deal a political death blow to an opposition combining both nationalists and communists in an alliance determined to re-create a new Russian empire and hostile to what it regarded as the democratic reformists' subordination of Russia to the West. Already, in September 1992, the conservative newspaper *Sovietskaya Rossiya* had published a *Political Declaration of the Left and Right Opposition*. The following month, it then issued *An Appeal to the Citizens of Russia*, the platform of the newly created extra-parliamentary bloc the National Salvation Front (NSF), which claimed to have established local branches in nearly 900 Russian cities (*Sovetskaya Rossiya*, 22 September 1992; 1 October 1992). The NSF's declaration squarely placed the blame for the problems besetting Russia on Yeltsin and 'anti-nationalists' who, in their view, were seeking unbridled power in order to weaken the Russian state. Yeltsin was also attacked for being 'slavishly dependent on the West', especially the United States. Interestingly, the NSF traced this policy directly back to Gorbachev, Yakovlev and their Western conspirators. The declaration finally called for the re-creation of a new union, the establishment of a strong unitary state, and the resignation of Gaidar and Yeltsin.

One of the more significant features of the NSF's declaration was the list of individuals who put their signature to the document. Basically, the statement brought together a pot-pourri of monarchists, communists and anti-Marxist nationalists; though among the most prominent signatories were Gennady Zyuganov, Richard Kosolapov (the former editor of the CPSU's theoretical journal *Kommunist*), the ultra-nationalist Aleksander Prokhanov, KGB general Alexander Sterligov, a few prominent military figures (including Makashov), and several Russian writers, notably Valentin Rasputin. Though divided on many issues, the Front was united at least in its fierce opposition to Yeltsin, who attempted, but in the end failed, to ban it. But he need not have bothered, for within a matter of months the organization was no longer the force it had once been. However, things did not stand still and, in November 1992, the ban that had originally been placed on the Communist Party was lifted by the Constitutional Court and Zyuganov was to become the head of the newly established Communist Party of the Russian Federation (CPRF).

Zyuganov and the Communist Party of the Russian Federation

Before becoming leader of the CPRF, Zyuganov had been among those within the old CPSU who had been most vehemently opposed to Gorbachev's domestic and foreign policy reforms. In July 1991, he thus joined forces with a group of nationalists, conservative military leaders and writers, including Prokhanov and Rasputin, and published the highly significant *Word to the People*. This warned against the imminent disintegration of the Soviet Union and the onset of civil war (*Moskovskaya Pravda*, 23 July 1991). The statement also called for a broad coalition of forces, including the Orthodox Church, the military and true Russian communists, to reverse the nation's slide into chaos. Zyuganov was active on many fronts. He had, for example, been a member of the editorial board of Prokhanov's ultra-nationalist, neo-national, Bolshevik newspaper *Den* (Today). This later reappeared as *Zavtra* (Tomorrow), after having been banned by Yeltsin. Moreover, prior to the formation of the NSF, he had been instrumental in bringing together various groups of communists and nationalists in what came to be referred to as the 'red–brown' alliance. In January 1991, he had also helped organize the Co-ordination Council of Patriotic Movements, later renamed the Council for Patriotic Forces. The following December, he then joined the All-Russian People's Union, successor to the conservative *Soyuz* group in the Soviet parliament. This had been established by the extremist activist Sergei Baburin in an attempt to unite opposition forces.

Zyuganov's long-term aim, clearly, was to build an effective opposition to Yeltsin; and, while prepared to work with more extreme elements – he had, for example, written for the 'notoriously anti-semitic newspaper' *Al-Kods* (Simonsen, 1995: 60–3) – he basically sought to use the extremists without necessarily endorsing their position or using their language. Zyuganov's more respectable form of what Yegor Gaidar has more bluntly called

'National Socialism' was the amalgamation of a number of ideological currents (Clark, 1996). One of these was the quasi-biological theory of history espoused by Lev Gumilyov, the son of the famous Russian poets Anna Akhmatova and Nikolai Gumilyov (1991). Gumilyov had developed a thesis about nations which described the rise and fall of civilizations in essentially Darwinian terms. The fundamental unit of life, he argued, was the 'ethnos', or nation, two or more of which might unite or fuse together to form what he termed a 'superethnos'. Russia was one such entity; Western Europe another. The two, however, were not just different but bound to compete. Yet Russia was not just opposed to – and by – the West, but threatened by it: first, and in particular, by what Gumilyov saw as the various 'parasite' states, the United States being the most important of these, feeding off the resources of others – including Russia; and, second, from other 'parasite' ethnoses (especially Jews) who had lost their territory. The latter were seen as especially dangerous. Indeed, according to Gumilyov, Bolshevism itself was nothing more than an alien Jewish (and Western) import which had done enormous damage to the country precisely because it did not reflect indigenous Russian values.

In ideological terms, Gumilyov certainly had an influence on Zyuganov's thinking, as his ideas did on many within the Russian elite and on what has been aptly termed the wider 'red–brown family' (Clark, 1995: 170). Nevertheless, Zyuganov's world-view probably owed less to Gumilyov and more to his time in the CPSU. Here he had been employed in the ideological department during the party's last years. Always a bitter opponent of Yakovlev and Gorbachev, he had first worked towards his candidate degree in philosophy from the Academy of Social Sciences of the CPSU, before going on to take his doctorate in history in Moscow. As the old system began to fall apart in the second half of the 1980s (it was reported that the CPSU's ideological machine had stopped printing official Soviet propaganda in 1988), Zyuganov began to construct an ideology which combined elements of traditional Soviet communism with classic Russian nationalism. According to this amended form of standard Soviet theory, the West had always been – and was bound to remain – opposed to Russian civilization. The coming of communism might have given new shape to the conflict, but the Cold War itself was only a moment in a longer-term and more deeply rooted historical antagonism which had been going on for at least two hundred years. Hence, when it ended on Western terms after 1989, this did not mean that the underlying struggle between Russia and the West had come to a conclusion. Far from it. Indeed, having defeated and dismantled the Soviet Union, the West's next goal, according to Zyuganov, was to subordinate Russia completely and turn it into a Third World dependency. Russia, therefore, had to oppose this 'conspiracy' (on occasions, Zyuganov referred to the malevolent part being played by Jews in all this) and prevent itself being turned into a raw materials appendage of the advanced Western capitalist countries (Zyuganov, 1995).

Zyuganov's deeply rooted antipathy to the West, and his desire to prevent what he saw as the transformation of Russia into a supplier of raw materials for the advanced capitalist world, were in turn supplemented by a strong opposition to Western liberalism. Liberalism, he believed, was essentially 'un-Russian'. Russians, he felt, yearned for something much deeper than the 'anything goes' mentality of the West. He even repeated the old argument that Soviet rule (once shorn of its earlier alien excesses) reflected the Russian collectivist tradition, one that pre-dated the revolution of 1917 and still lived on in spite of the collapse of Soviet power. This restatement of the importance of an essential 'Russianness' also influenced Zyuganov's attitude toward the Orthodox Church. The Church, he argued, had once been, and should now be reaffirmed as, the guardian of Russia's spiritual life. But he also favoured the Church for more political reasons. The Church, after all, was no great supporter of democracy. As Zyuganov was well aware, the Russian Orthodox Church emphasized both the subordination of the individual to the collective and of the citizen to the all-powerful state. Thus it had been before the Russian Revolution of 1917. So it would be once again now that the Soviet era was over.

Zyuganov therefore managed to weave together a doctrine that was ostensibly communist, without in any way being egalitarian; anti-Western, without in any sense being revolutionary; and anti-imperialist, without being Marxist. More shrewd, less overtly racist and a good deal more stable than Zhirinovsky, Zyuganov would in time emerge as a powerful figure in Russian politics. But not before Zhirinovsky had had his moment.

The 1993 Duma elections

Following the crisis of October 1993, the expectation was that elections to the new parliament would legitimize Yeltsin's course of economic reform and Western-oriented foreign policy. In the event, the elections produced a parliament as hostile to the government as the one that had recently been disbanded by tanks; and this in spite of the fact that a number of conservative newspapers were temporarily suspended from publication (including *Pravda* and *Sovetskaya Rossiya*), that some political blocs were banned (including the NSF), and that the state-controlled media was strongly biased in favour of Gaidar's Russia's Choice. The main victors in the election, however, were not the reformers, but Zhirinovsky's Liberal Democrats, the Communist Party of the Russian Federation, the 'left-leaning' Agrarian Party and Women of Russia. Together they polled over 50 per cent of the vote. Zhirinovsky's party received the largest percentage of votes in that half of the ballot where people voted on a nation-wide party list system based on proportional representation. Half of the seats in the Duma were filled from this list, with the other half being elected in single-member territorial constituencies based upon a simple plurality. The Liberal Democrats did particularly well in the former ballot, where Zhirinovsky's broad nationalist appeals were clearly attractive to large numbers of Russians. In the constituency vote, however, bread-and-butter issues were more salient, and voters seemed to opt for more local candidates. The largest number of candidates elected in the constituency ballots were independent of any bloc (White *et al.*, 1997).

Some observers have attempted to explain the vote for Zhirinovsky by stressing contingent factors: the divided nature of the opposition, the proliferation of political parties and blocs, the reaction against the negative portrayal of Zhirinovsky in the media, and the absence of a coherent and well-established moderate opposition to Yeltsin. Zhirinovsky was also in a good position, according to some pundits, because he had never been a member of the old *nomenklatura* (or even a member of the CPSU). Moreover, he had also taken a neutral position in the stand-off between parliament and president in the October crisis. Finally, according to surveys done at the time, a substantial portion of LDPR voters made up their minds only at the last minute – up to one-third of the voters on the actual day of the election (*Izvestiya*, 30 December 1993).

Though there is clearly something to the argument that support for the Liberal Democrats was not that stable, it ignores one irrefutable fact: the deteriorating situation in Russia and the ability of the Liberal Democrats to provide a crude, but credible, explanation as to why things had gone so badly wrong. By the end of 1993, Russians were faced with all sorts of novel and disturbing threats: to their living standards, to their right to work and to their everyday security. Under such circumstances, it was hardly surprising that so many were prepared to accept Zhirinovsky's paranoid theories. As he himself earlier acknowledged in an interview, 'in a rich nation my programme would not go over very well. But in a poor embittered country like Russia, this is my golden hour' (*Boston Globe*, 21 October 1993). Furthermore, though his programme in 1993 might have been eccentric and inconsistent, it was in many respects more readily comprehensible to ordinary Russians than those offered by his more moderate opponents. It also spoke to their problems and addressed their fears about the present and the future – including those to do with the fate of the 25 million ethnic Russians living in the 'near abroad'. Significantly, a poll of Russian attitudes found that fully two-thirds regretted the disintegration of the Soviet Union. Moreover, when asked what society needed most, only 8 per cent said 'democracy', while 83 per cent plumped for security and law and order (*Moscow News*, No. 15, 9 April 1993).

If the twin issues of law and order and the plight facing ethnic Russians outside Russia were major concerns of the ordinary Russian people, so too was the deteriorating material situation in Russia itself. Naturally enough, Zhirinovsky was keen to heap the blame for Russia's difficulties upon the West and the West's various Russian allies. His thesis was not without some logic. According to Zhirinovsky (and indeed many others), having imposed a painful programme of economic reform upon the country, the West had then singularly failed to provide Russia with sufficient aid to cushion the impact of the reforms. At least one Western observer seemed to concur, noting, more in sorrow than in anger, that 'unfortunately some western policies designed to prevent a Weimar scenario from unfolding in Russia' actually appeared to be having the opposite effect (Snyder, 1993). However, it was not just the West that was to blame. The Jews too, it was now regularly argued, bore some of the responsibility for the current crisis. According to one poll conducted in 1992, nearly 20 per cent of all Muscovites thought there was a 'global Jewish conspiracy' to undermine the Russian state. Another 24 per cent remained undecided (Bryn and Deytyanev, 1992). A prominent member of the Orthodox clergy – Metropolitan Ioann of St Petersburg and Ladoga – agreed (*Sovetskaya Rossiya*, 20 February 1993). In fact, in a series of well-publicized interviews, he not only argued that there was a conspiracy, but explained it in the crude anti-semitic terms outlined in the infamous Protocols of the Elders of Zion (*Den*, 21–27 February 1993). The leader of the LDPR was equally forthright, and in another outburst asserted that Jews were 'trying to destroy Russia' because they were 'aggressive, cruel, and hate everything that is Russian'.

The programme of the Liberal Democrats was not just an anti-semitic rant, however, and contained (among other things) discussions on the economy, social policy, foreign policy, the environment and defence (Shearman, 1997). It had a good deal to say as well about the wider political system and called, not surprisingly, for a strong executive authority, a unitary state and the abolition of ethnic republics. In addition, it offered a quick fix to deal with the breakdown in law and order. It also promised to purge the economy of corrupt elements and to reassert state controls over all but a small private sector. It even called for a halt to the demilitarization of the Russian economy and for Russia to become far more competitive and aggressive in the international arms market. It is, therefore, not so surprising that, against all expectation, Zhirinovsky attracted a much larger vote than had originally been anticipated; though significantly, many of those who voted for the Liberal Democrats were not simply impoverished, elderly members of the old Soviet working class (much of this vote went to the CPRF), nor indeed the lumpenproletariat, but younger, well-educated, skilled males in urban areas in Russia's heartland who were deeply concerned about their own material future and the country's more general decline. The party also did especially well in the Russian Far East, regions dominated by the military-industrial complex, and some areas of Central Russia (Wyman *et al.*, 1995).

The 1995 Duma elections

The elections of 1995 were different from those of 1993 in a number of ways. For instance, in 1993, eight out of the thirteen parties standing were elected. In 1995, however, only four out of forty-three participating parties passed the 5 per cent hurdle. There also appeared to be a higher degree of public interest, with 64 per cent of the registered electorate turning out in 1995, as opposed to 54 per cent in 1993. In 1995, moreover, fewer independents were elected from the single-member constituencies (77 as compared to 141). Finally, many more 'patriotic' parties stood in 1995, including Russian National Union, the bloc of Stanislav Govorukhin, Rutskoi's Derzhava movement, the Russian All-People's Movement (led by Alexander Bazhanov), the National Bolshevik Party, the National-Republican Party of Russia and the more moderate nationalist bloc, the Congress of Russian Communities (with Alexander Lebed running on its ticket).

But neither these smaller organizations nor the Liberal Democrats fared especially well, although the LDPR did manage to climb comfortably over the 5 per cent barrier, and thus come second overall. On the other hand, its percentage of the vote fell by over half, from more than 23 to only 11.4 per cent: and it only won 1 single-member constituency, compared to 5 in 1993. The showing of the other far right parties was almost derisory. The National Bolshevik Party, for instance, gained minimal support. For example, Alexander Dubin won less than 1 per cent of the vote in a St Petersburg district – despite having supportive concerts hosted by the rock star Sergei Koryakhin. Fellow party member Eduard Limonov (whose meetings were attended by youths wearing swastikas) amassed less than 2 per cent in one of Moscow's electoral districts. Alexander Barkashov, head of the Russian National Union, did even worse. A former member of *Pamyat* and once referred to as the 'leader of domestic fascism' by the newspaper *Nezavisimaya Gazeta*, his party's support for laws restricting mixed marriages between Russians and other ethnic groups, and the promise to keep Russia free from 'democrats, communists, Jews, pacifists, ecumenical Christians and humanists', did little to enhance its electoral fortunes (*Moskovskiie Novostii*, 10–17 April 1994).

The decline of the Liberal Democrats and the poor showing of the minor parties on the far right was compensated for, to some extent, by a surge of support for Zyuganov's Communist Party. The figures speak for themselves. In 1993, 6.6 million had voted for the latter party; by 1995, the number had more than doubled to 15.4 million. In the process, it had acquired 22.3 per cent of the party list vote and captured a further 58 single-member seats. All told, this gave it a total of 157 seats in a Duma of 450. Significantly, too, in 62 of the Russian Federation's 89 regions, the CPRF led the party list voting.

How do we account for the ability of the Communists to attract many of the votes which had previously gone to the LDPR? There are many explanations. One, obviously, is the degree of support which the Communist Party was able to call upon from other significant nationalist forces in Russia. Another critical element was organization and, in particular, the party's ability to draw upon the old structures and cadres of the CPSU. Of equal importance was Zhirinovsky himself, whose antics did a great deal to undermine the credibility of the LDPR. Also central was the Communists' readiness to put across what amounted to a nationalist line in a more effective, less demonic way than the Liberal Democrats. The Communists did not even oppose a market economy. What they did insist upon, though, was that the economy remain in Russian hands – for only Russian capital (they asserted) would strengthen, rather than weaken, the Russian state. In good Zhirinovsky fashion, Zyuganov also denounced Yeltsin in no uncertain terms for having betrayed Russia to foreign interests. The Yeltsin leadership, he argued, had 'surrendered everything' to the West, first by allowing the union to be 'illegally torn apart' and then by permitting Russia to be subordinated to Western interests. The Communist Party, he promised, would be altogether more assertive and would fight for both 'the honour and dignity of the Russian state' and the reunification of 'the great Russian people' (*International Affairs*, 1996).

The success of the Communist Party of Russia in 1995 could, of course, be interpreted (and indeed has been) as signifying a massive endorsement for a reconstituted Russian left – and, by implication, a major defeat for the far right. The argument cannot be dismissed entirely. Certainly, many Western observers, in particular those keen to applaud anything opposed to the drive for capitalism in Russia, seemed to be heartened by the revival of something that looked, or at least formally sounded like, communism in the former Soviet Union. But the notion that there was a genuine swing to the left, or that the Zyuganov vote reflected a serious socialist revival in Russia, ignores at least two critical points: the ideological orientation of many of the organizations and individuals who actually backed the Communist Party in 1995; and the similarity in public rhetoric and programmatic promise between the Communists and the Liberal Democrats. Viewed in this way, what in fact happened in 1995 was less a swing from right to left, more a redistribution of support between two parties articulating the same nationalist themes in an attempt to win over the same discontented, alienated Russian voter.

The 1996 presidential elections

In his ultimately unsuccessful run for the Russian presidency in 1996, Zyuganov once again put himself forward as the public voice of the 'national-patriotic bloc'. The nature of his appeal is perhaps best illustrated by a brief look at those who endorsed his candidacy. Among these were several leading clergymen from the Russian Orthodox Church, extremist communists, self-defined 'patriotic forces', trade unions, *Pamyat* organizations, the National Republican Party, Stanislav Terekhov's Union of Officers, Valentin Chikin (the chief editor of *Sovetskaya Rossiya*), Prokhanov, Rutskoi and Ryzhkov. Zyuganov's political message in 1996 was very much the same as it had been in the previous year. The country's troubles he laid at the political door of Yeltsin for having allowed Russia to be 'pillaged' by a Western-inspired programme of economic privatization. He also attacked the Russian President for supporting the breakup of the former Soviet Union back in 1991 and called for the creation of a new union (with Russia as its core), and the defence of those 25 million Russians living in the near abroad, whose human rights were being 'totally violated'. In addition, he demanded the creation of a 'special council' composed of respected public figures, with the clear objective of defending traditional Russian culture against the 'onslaught of Western trash' on Russian television and in the arts. At one point, he even went so far as to call for censorship and a limit to be placed on the importation of all foreign material, in general, and foreign films, in particular (*New Perspectives Quarterly*, 1996).

Fighting the presidential elections on such a programme, Zyuganov did remarkably well. Indeed, during the first round he polled nearly a third of the vote, only 3 percentage points behind Yeltsin, though 17 ahead of General Alexander Lebed, the tough former paratrooper, who had earlier fought in Afghanistan and later played a significant military role in forcibly curbing separatist tendencies in the republic of Moldova (those 'fascists' who had no right to rule, in his opinion). Fortunately for Yeltsin, Lebed – the scourge of independent Moldova – threw his support behind the President, and in the second round Yeltsin won a decisive victory, winning 53 per cent of the vote against Zyuganov's 40. But significantly, he was only able to do so not by confronting his opponents, but by incorporating them; this meant in effect conceding to a number of their demands and, according to certain critics, making himself their political prisoner. It has been suggested that the 1996 election represented a clear and unambiguous contest between two competing visions, one leading back towards some nebulous and mythical past and the other leading forward to an uncertain, but real, democratic future. Moreover, because Yeltsin won so convincingly in the second round, it has also been assumed that the future now belonged to democracy. To use the words of the then British prime minister, John Major, the outcome in 1996 proved conclusively that democracy had finally 'taken root in Russia'. This somewhat upbeat view should not be allowed to pass without comment, however. Most obviously, it ignores the simple fact that the elections were not completely democratic or open. Zyuganov, for example, had little access to the state-controlled television service. Nor was any reference made during the course of the election to the critical fact that Yeltsin was actually seriously ill. Far more worrying, though, was the fact that the opposition managed to win over 30 million votes on a platform which mixed legitimate concerns for social justice and law and order with manifestly illiberal demands directed in turn against the liberal democratic West, non-Russians and a variety of scapegoats from Jews through to the International Monetary Fund. Of course, one might be more confident about the future if Yeltsin himself had stood on a genuinely liberal platform. However, this was not the case, and far from projecting a totally different vision for Russia, during the course of the elections he constantly conceded the ideological high ground to his chauvinist opponents. In fact, one of the more remarkable things about the 1996 election was the extent to which he felt politically impelled to use much of the same rhetoric as his enemies in order to win a majority. This hardly boded well for Russia's future or its longer-term relations with the West.

Conclusion

It is worth emphasizing here that the period after the 1996 election was characterized by continuing problems, with the economy in crisis, the President resorting to short-term government reshuffles (in an attempt to retain authority and help redress socio-economic deficiencies) and reports of widespread corruption. Indeed, as regards the latter, the new prosecutor general, Yury Chaika, in early 1999 ranked Russia as among the ten most corrupt countries in the world and interpreted corruption as one of the country's most destructive forces. In these circumstances, and with liberal democratic institutions and practices still resting on shaky foundations, the potential for resort to extremist, populist and ultra-nationalist solutions remains strong. In November 1998, for instance, Galina Starovoitova – a prominent human rights activist and a deputy in the State Duma – had been shot dead in St Petersburg. Earlier, she had condemned the Duma for failing to censure anti-semitic remarks by Albert Makashov (KPRF, and a Russian presidential candidate in 1991). Makashov had blamed all Russia's ills on the Jews; moreover, he appeared to have the support of his party leader, Zyuganov. Furthermore, May to July 1999 witnessed several bomb attacks on Moscow synagogues and the vicious stabbing of the director of the city's Jewish arts centre by an extreme right sympathizer. According to one report (Engel, 1999), 'The sight of swaggering Jew-hating skinheads has been one of the most startling images of the post-Soviet era.' Unsurprisingly, Jewish requests for emigration visas rocketed during 1998–9. These developments provided telling illustrations of the socio-political climate in the new Russia.

As we have argued, conditions in Russia following the disintegration of the Soviet Union have created an environment in which extreme Russian nationalists and Russian nationalism have been able to flourish by appealing to the vainglorious, the dispossessed, the frightened and the insecure. If the crisis was merely economic, one might be more sanguine. But the crisis has shaken all institutions and beliefs to the core. No doubt, apologists for the current regime would argue that it takes time to build democratic forms, and that much has been achieved in a short space of time – and that given more time, Russia will become a 'normal' country. There is little, however, to support such an argument. Nor should one have expected it to be otherwise. After all, in the period since the collapse of the Soviet Union, ordinary Russians have been forced to deal with several major challenges, including the retreat from empire, a collapse in societal norms and the unedifying sight of the new elite accumulating vast wealth while the overwhelming majority suffer. Any one of these factors would have been damaging enough to Russian democracy. Taken together, they have proved cancerous. What is so extraordinary is not that strident nationalism and chauvinism have done so well, but that they have not done better.

But what if the new 'Russian right' were to come to power? What would happen? Certainly, it is unlikely that Russia would 'go fascist'. As we suggested at the very beginning, conditions in Russia in the 1990s are not comparable to those in Europe in the 1930s, when capitalism was menaced by communism. Today, in Russia, the threat is not communism so much as a resurgent nationalism that has been able to amass votes by appealing to all those whose lives have been turned upside down by economic reform and imperial disintegration. What the new nationalists would actually do if they were to come to power remains unclear. It is hardly likely that they would restore the old Soviet system. Much more probable would be the emergence of an authoritarian regime, perhaps similar in character to those once common in Latin America – with the obvious difference that a nationalist and authoritarian government in Russia would be neither sympathetic to the United States nor willing to listen to its democratic entreaties to improve its ways. Hence, should the democratic process give power to a party or presidential candidate from the new communist–nationalist alliance – for that is the most likely source of the challenge to the reformers – then, on the basis of our analysis, democratic development could easily be reversed and relations with the Western world would deteriorate significantly. As Russia enters the new millennium, there is little ground for optimism.

Editor's postscript: President Yeltsin resigned on the last day of the twentieth century.

Acknowledgements

Thanks to Professor Stephen White of the University of Glasgow and Dr Judith Devlin of University College Dublin for reading an earlier draft.

References

Arkhiv Samizdata (1988) No. 6138, 1 February.

Boulton, L. (1990) 'A Survival of the Past: Anti-semitism is Back', *Financial Times*, 20 February.

Bryn, R.J. and Deytyanev, A. (1992) 'Anti-Semitism in Moscow: Results of an October 1992 Survey', *Slavic Review* 51(1), 1–12.

Carter, S.K. (1990) *Russian Nationalism: Yesterday, Today, Tomorrow*. London: Pinter.

Clark, B. (1995) *An Empire's New Clothes: The End of Russia's Liberal Dream*. London: Vintage.

Clark, B. (1996) 'Nationalist Ideas Move from the Margins', *The World Today* 52(5), 119–21.

Cohen, S. F. (1993) 'U.S. Policy toward Post-communist Russia: Fallacies, Failures, Possibilities', *Prepared Testimony to the Committee on Foreign Affairs, Congress of the United States, House of Representatives*, 24 February, 453–79.

Cox, M. (1992) 'After Stalinism: The Extreme Right in Russia, East Germany and Eastern Europe', in Hainsworth, P. (ed.) *The Extreme Right in Europe and the USA*. London: Pinter.

Cox, M. (1994) 'The Necessary Partnership? The Clinton Presidency and Post-Soviet Russia', *International Affairs* 70(4), 635–58.

Devlin, J. (1995) *The Rise of the Russian Democrats: The Causes and Consequences of the Elite Revolution*. Aldershot: Edward Elgar.

Dunlop, J. B. (1993) *The Rise of Russia and the Fall of the Soviet Empire*. Princeton, NJ: Princeton University Press.

Dunlop, J. B. (1996) 'Alexander Barkashov and the Rise of National Socialism in Russia', *Demokratizasiya* 4(4), 519–30.

Engel, M. (1999) 'A History of Hate', *The Guardian*, 16 August.

Gregor, A. J. (1979) *The Young Mussolini and the Intellectual Origins of Fascism*. Berkeley: University of California Press.

Gumilyov, L. (1991) 'Menya nazivayut Evarzitsyem', *Nash Sovremennik*, No. 1.

International Affairs (Moscow) (1996) No. 1, 6–9, (in English).

Krasnov, V. (1993) '*Pamiat*: Russian Right-Wing Radicalism', in Merkl, P. H. and Weinberg, L. (eds) *Encounters with the Contemporary Radical Right*. Boulder, CO: Westview Press.

Laqueur, W. (1993) *Black Hundred: The Rise of the Extreme Right in Russia*. New York: HarperCollins.

Lester, J. (1994) 'Zhirinovsky's Liberal Democratic Party: A Profile', *Labour Focus on Eastern Europe* No. 47, 17–30.

Mudde, C. (1995) 'Right-Wing Extremism Analyzed', *European Journal of Political Research* 27(2), 203–24.

New Perspectives Quarterly (1996) Spring, 4–7.

Nove, A. (1989) *Glasnost in Action: Cultural Renaissance in Russia*. Boston: Unwin Hyman.

Pankin, B. (1996) *The Last Hundred Days of the Soviet Union*. London: Pinter.

Popov, G. Kh. and Adzhubei, N. (1988) 'Pamiat' i Pamiat'', *Znamia* No. 1 (January), 188–203.

Pribylovsky, V. (1992) *Dictionary of Political Parties and Organizations in Russia*. Washington, DC: Center for Strategic and International Studies.

Pribylovsky, V. (1995) 'What Awaits Russia: Fascism or Latin-Style Dictatorship?', *Transition*, 23 June, 6–7.

Shearman, P. (1997) 'Defining the National Interest: Russian Foreign Policy and Domestic Politics', in Kanet, R. and Kozhemiakin, A. (eds) *The Foreign Policy of the Russian Federation*. Houndmills and London: Macmillan, 1–27.

Shearman, P. (2000) 'The Collapse of Communism in the USSR, Nationalism and the State', in Vandersiluis, S. O. (ed.) *The State and Identity Construction in International Relations*. Houndmills and London: Macmillan, 76–106.

Simonsen, S. G. (1995) 'Leading the Communists through the '90s', *Transition*, 14 July, 60–3.

Simonsen, S. G. (1997) 'Still Favouring the Power of the Workers', *Transition*, December, 52–6.

Snyder, J. (1993) 'Nationalism and the Crisis of the Post-Soviet State', *Survival* 35(1), 5–26.

Spier, H. (1989) 'Soviet Anti-Semitism Unchained: The Rise of the "Historical and Patriotic Association" Pamyat', in Freedman, R. O. (ed.) *The Politics of Anti-semitism*. Durham, NC: Duke University Press.

White, S., Rose, R. and McAllister, I. (1997) *How Russia Votes*. Chatham, NJ: Chatham House Publishers.

Wyman, M., Miller, W. L. and Heywood, P. (1995) in Lentini, P. (ed.) *Elections and Political Order in Russia*, Budapest: Central European University Press, 124–42.

Yanov, A. (1987) *The Russian Challenge and the Year 2000*. Oxford: Blackwell.

Zyuganov, G. (1995) *Veryu v Rossiyu*. Moscow: Voronezh.

CHAPTER ELEVEN

Marginalization or mainstream? The extreme right in post-communist Romania

Michael Shafir

Five main factors appear to have combined to help the re-emergence of the extreme right in post-communist Romania. Of these, two may be considered to be of a historic nature. The first is the rich legacy of an extreme right that had not only successfully managed to mobilize large strata of Romanian society in the inter-war period (Heinen, 1986), but has also produced an outstanding intellectual elite comparable only to that of its Italian and French proto-fascist and fascist peers (Sternhell, 1978; 1983; Sternhell, *et al.*, 1989). The roots of this elite can be traced back to the nineteenth century and to the dispute between the partisans of Western emulation in political and social development, and the 'autochthonous' search for a model alleged better to suit Romanian society's specific features (Volovici, 1991; Ornea, 1995). The values of 'Romanianism', on which this elite constructed its argument, were eventually blended (and this is the second factor explaining the re-emergence of the extreme right) with those of Marxism, producing the Romanian version of 'national communism', on which I shall say more below. By then, however, the 'generation of Angst and adventure', as it has been aptly dubbed by Tismaneanu and Pavel (1994), had been liquidated in prison or had been forced into exile by the country's Communist rulers. Paradoxical as this may sound, the destruction of the extreme nationalist elite had been a condition for the successful resurrection of its values by the Communist counter-elites in what Jowitt (1971) termed the 'breaking-through' process.

The ousting of the Nicolae Ceauşescu regime in December 1989 meant, among other things, that a half-lifted curtain could now be fully raised. Before the eyes of a disoriented political audience (on the one hand, the inter-war Iron Guard and its associates had been branded to the end as 'enemies' and 'traitors to the nation', and on the other hand its credo had been turned into one indistinguishable from that of the regime itself), two main 'stage directors' now stepped in, in an attempt to reap political capital. The first was the few remnants of the League of the Archangel Michael (or the Legion, as the Iron Guard was also known), operating from exile, and their even fewer survivors in the country (Shafir, 1991a: 22; 1994a: 368; 1994b; Vago, 1995: 6). The second 'stage director', whose role has been much more central, was the 'Forces of Old', embodied by the former secret police, the notorious *Securitate*, now in search of a new role to justify its existence. Personalities linked to both the *Securitate* and its new institutional version, the Romanian Intelligence Service (SRI), are behind attempts to bring about the rehabilitation of Romania's wartime leader, Marshal Ion Antonescu, and either were involved in the launching of chauvinistic publications (for instance, the journal *Europa*) or are closely involved with the activities of extremist political parties such as the Greater Romania Party, discussed later in the chapter (Shafir, 1997). Finally, the fifth and last factor contributing to the re-emergence of the extreme right has been the nature of the main ruling party. Under its different names (National Salvation Front, Democratic National Salvation Front and Party of Social Democracy in Romania), this political formation has adopted a 'utilitarian' approach in its relations with the emerging organized extremism. Though its leader in all but name, former president Ion Iliescu, cannot be suspected of pro-extremist sympathies, the party has been willing to condone extremism and went so far as to set up a coalition with extremist parties, in order to ensure its dominance over post-communist political life (Shafir, 1996c).

The conceptual approach

Before we proceed to analyse the post-communist Romanian extreme right, an elucidation of concepts is warranted, as this may heuristically serve comparative purposes. Defining the extreme right, it has been observed, is no easy endeavour (Hainsworth, 1992: 3–7). The many varieties of the species not only defy taxonomy but, some claim, even resist chronology. Sabrina Ramet has made a powerful argument in favour of the phenomenon's transhistoricity. According to Ramet (1999), fascism, Nazism, the radical right and the extreme right are all different facets of 'organized intolerance', whose roots go back in history, well beyond the modern (industrial and post-industrial) age. Those (including this author) who are persuaded that the phenomenon should be confined within parameters which did *not* pre-date the modern age (such as, notably, mass mobilization and the technological capacity needed to induce that mobilization and control it) have been faced with an additional difficulty in the wake of the overthrow of communist regimes. The 'blurred edges between the categories' of different shades of right-wing politics had been complicated enough even before that dramatic development (Eatwell, 1989: 74), but they have now become especially complicated by the emergence, in several former communist countries, of so-called 'red–brown' alliances and political amalgams.

While history had already witnessed political conversions from one extreme to the other, never before had the two 'deadly enemies', the extreme left and the extreme right, overtly joined mind and might in the common (but hitherto separate) struggle against their shared foe: individualism and democracy. Not even the Hitler–Stalin pact of 1939 had dared openly to acknowledge a community not just of temporary interests, but of core political values. To witness demonstrators now carrying Stalin's portraits marching alongside partisans of the 'Black Hundred', and octogenarians of the civil war alongside monarchists, is still not easily comprehensible.

Some commentators may be inclined to 'explain' the phenomenon, too hastily, through a familiar enough historic cliché. The truism of the 'extremes' touching one another is an avenue leading to a dead end, however, unless accompanied by 'hows' and 'whys'. In other words, historic evidence (the 'hows') and cultural (in the anthropological sense of the term) insight must combine to produce a convincing pattern. Hainsworth argues (1992: 1) that political culture may be one of the keys to understanding the electoral successes and failures of the extreme right wing. While the argument is produced in connection with post-war Western Europe, it is applicable to post-communist East and Central Europe as well. Indeed, the legacy of authoritarianism, of exacerbated nationalism and of the centrality of communitarian (as opposed to individualist) values has been emphasized by many scholars. This is not to say that the political cultures of the former communist states are identical. For example, the distinction between the inheritors of the Byzantine legacy of the Orthodox Church, on the one hand, and the legacy of the Western Churches, on the other hand, is one important difference. In the latter case, the 'dual submission' (to God and Caesar) induces dual competition (between God and Caesar) and, at the end of the day, undermines absolute authority. And is it not absolute authority (or its more benign form, state paternalism) that the 'reds-cum-browns' are missing, among other things?

Cultural similarities may explain the 'whys' of the emerging 'red–brown' alliances, but they do not fully explain the 'hows', unless one further aspect is taken into account: the legacy of 'national communism'. With the possible exception of the now-defunct Czechoslovakia, all former communist states in East-Central Europe have had a 'national communist' phase, although its intensity was by no means equal everywhere. 'Socialism in one country' can be considered to have been the first instance of 'national communism', followed by 'Titoism' and then by many other varieties. To a lesser or greater extent, 'national communism' was based on incitement to hatred of the 'historic enemy' (internal, external or both) as part and parcel of the search for an alternative 'legitimizing formula'. It was on this basis that radical right and radical left could meet. Reminiscing on his research work in Romania in 1970–1, Daniel Chirot recalls how Traian Herseni, a 'major propagandist for the Iron Guard', told him after liberation from prison and reinstatement as a university professor, 'I used to write things praising "The Captain" [Corneliu Codreanu, the putative Romanian Führer] and now I write pretty much the same thing, but praising Ceauşescu. I'm not a Marxist, you understand, but I have to admit that I like what he is doing' (Chirot, 1994: 239). And what Ceauşescu was doing was precisely to blend the radical left and the radical right discourse.

The demise of communism has made the 'natural' separation of the two discourses again possible. Paradoxically, however, it was exactly at this point in time that the two discourses were blended into one another, to such an extent that it becomes difficult to distinguish between them. Yet the distinction is still necessary, if only because of the possibility that the future might again see a parting of ways. Under discussion here are two distinct, and yet interrelated, types of political formations, both displaying a 'radical mind' mentality (Shafir, 1999). Parties of a 'genuine' radical right nature are, for the time being, still relatively few and unrepresentative in East-Central Europe. Yet the 'radical mind' mentality is found not only among those political formations that I define as parties of 'radical continuity,' distinguishing them from parties of 'radical return', but also in mainstream political formations. It is this diffuseness that provides food for thought when considering the dangers, or prospects, of a take-over by right-wing extremism.

The distinction between 'radical continuity' and 'radical return' serves to indicate *which* 'past' is chosen as the chief frame of reference. 'Radical continuity' partisans are inheritors of 'national communism'. They may, and usually do, exacerbate the xenophobic aspects of national communism, but are also linked to it by choice, by the personal histories of their leaders, or via electoral needs. There is usually a combination of all three of these variables, but this is not always the case. Sometimes, overt reference is made in positive terms to 'socialist achievements', though in most cases 'socialist' is dropped adjectively in favour of 'national', 'people's', or another such term. Moreover, 'conspiracy theories', as Ramet (1999) points out, are always part and parcel of the 'radical continuity' discourse. These theories are closely linked to the mechanism of 'externalization of guilt', which makes it possible to deflect the blame for any, and often all, wrongs done throughout history by one's own nation on to 'the Other' (Shafir, 1991c; Karnoouh, 1990: 157–8). The discourse emphasizes both international and local conspiracies bent, allegedly, upon undermining the future of one's own community. Combinations are manifold and sometimes strange. The KGB is said to be in league with the CIA, with both seen as unconscious tools of the Israeli equivalent, the Mossad, and the Jew, in one way or another, is always depicted as at the centre of mischief. In the Jew's alleged bid to secure world domination, he or she is acting in consort with whosoever happens to be the perceived 'historic enemy' and hides behind such deviously constructed concepts as 'human rights', and international organizations such as the World Bank, the European Union and many others. This is one, but not the only, trait 'radical continuity' partisans share with the partisans of 'radical return'. The common bond is not surprising. After all, national communism, particularly in its *avant-la-fin* stage of the 1980s, adopted the extreme nationalist inter-war *content* (but not its *form*) as its own legitimizing device. 'Radical return' formations are distinguished from 'radical continuity' parties mainly by their open advocacy of a return to values that motivated the far right in the inter-war years, including proto-fascism, fascism and even Nazism. They find 'models' in leaders such as Tiso, Hlinka, Antonescu, Codreanu, Horthy, Szálasi, and Pavelić. But again, and because of the same reasons, they may be joined in this pursuit of 'role models' by some partisans of 'radical continuity'.

Before we turn to Romania proper, it will be useful to illustrate the above distinction with some examples from other countries. The 'radical continuity' category would certainly include individuals such as Slobodan Milošević or Franjo Tuđman. On the other hand, leaders such as Vojislav Šešelj of the Serbian Radical Party (see Chapter 12) or the Croatian Party of Historic Right's Ante Djapić should be viewed as belonging to the 'radical return' category. Bulgaria's Socialist Party is a party of 'radical continuity', whereas its Revival Movement, led by Father Gelemenov (a self-professed admirer of Nazism), belongs to the 'radical return' part of the spectrum, as do the obscure '*Shturm*' Patriotic Movement and the Bulgarian National Socialist Party. The latter parties are non-parliamentary, a trait that (for the time being?) unifies many (but not all) parties belonging to the 'radical return' category. In Poland and the Czech Republic, there are no parties of 'radical continuity' to speak of, with the possible exception of the insignificant Polish National Front (that is, the *Polski Front Narodowy* led by Janusz Bryczkowski, the general secretary of the Grunwald Patriotic Association, and *not* the *Narodowy Front Polski*, led by Wojciech Podjacki and Wojciech Bela – the latter is another Polish example of a 'radical return' formation). In Hungary, István Csurka's Hungarian Justice and Life Party fits the 'radical continuity' category, while Albert Szabó personifies the 'radical return' neo-Arrow Cross revival. To the same category belong in Poland and in the Czech Republic, respectively, formations such as Bolesław Tejkowski's National Community–Polish National Party and Miroslav Sládek's Republican Party, as well as a plethora of other, smaller organizations. In Slovakia, Vladimir Mečiar, whose evolution is intricate, started off as an anti-communist reformer, eventually adopted 'radical continuity' postures, only to later move into a populist mixture of central and radical ideas after the elections of 1994; on the Slovak 'radical return' side are formations such as the Christian Social Union, the Slovak People's Party and the Slovak National Unity (Institute of Jewish Affairs, 1994: 78-81, 117–30; Jelinek, 1994; Karsai, 1999). Finally, Russia provides perhaps the most interesting case, inasmuch as the one leader who is most renowned for his extremist postures, Vladimir Zhirinovsky, is perhaps the least significant of the contenders. Zhirinovsky is probably not a 'radical continuer' and neither is he a partisan of 'radical return'. The Russian Liberal Democratic (*sic*) Party leader is just a 'radical clown' or, more probably, a 'radical puppet' serving to deflect attention from where real danger lies. On the 'radical continuity' side, the best Russian example is perhaps provided by Viktor Anpilov's Russian Communist Workers' Party, while prominent examples of 'radical return' partisanship are embodied in Aleksandr Barkashov's Russian National Unity and in Nikolai Lysenko's National Republican Party; but Gennady Zyuganov (see Chapter 10), the leader of the Russian Communist Party, should also be placed in the 'radical continuity' category.[1]

It should be emphasized, however, that the 'radical continuity'–'radical return' continuum is an 'ideal type' rather than a 'model'. Many formations probably have features of each of them.

Parties of 'radical continuity'

Against the background discussed above, it is difficult to provide a clear-cut answer as to the locus of Romania's post-communist extreme right parties. There are two main obstacles. The first concerns the 'departure point'. Since 'national communism' has both marginalized and centralized right-wing political discourse, it is 'in the eye of the beholder' to determine whether the extremists had moved from marginalization to mainstream, or whether they had been part of the mainstream from the very beginning. The second difficulty rests in political fluidity. Since the overthrow of the communist regime, there have been three rounds of parliamentary elections in Romania (in 1990, 1992 and 1996), and each round produced a somewhat different political map. Three 'radical continuity' parties were represented in the 1992 parliament, and two in the legislature elected in 1996. Although one 'radical return' formation was also present for a brief period in the former parliament, it did not owe its presence there to the electorate's choice. The three are the Greater Romania Party (*Partidul România Mare*, PRM), the Socialist Labour Party (*Partidul Socialist al Muncii*, PSM), and the Party of Romanian National Unity (*Partidul Unității Naționale Române*, PUNR).

In the general elections of 1992, the PRM obtained 3.89 per cent of the vote for the Chamber of Deputies and 3.85 per cent of the vote for the Senate, as a result of which it was represented by 16 deputies and 6 senators. (Romania has a bi-cameral system: parliament was composed of 341 deputies in 1992 and 343 in 1996; and of 143 senators.) Membership of the PRM rose dramatically, most likely as a result of its joining the government in January 1995, and being thus in a position to 'distribute goods'. After an actual drop from 28,000 in 1992 to 20,000 in 1993, membership rose in 1995 to a significant 32,000 and reached nearly 35,000 by the end of that year. Membership of the party's youth organization (which has 138 local branches) also rose, from 2500 in 1993 to over 5000 in 1995 (Shafir, 1995; *România mare*, No. 305, 10 May 1996). The party was set up in November 1990 by two ultranationalist writers, Eugen Barbu (who died in late 1993), and Corneliu Vadim Tudor, a former Ceauşescu 'court poet' (Shafir, 1991b). From the start, the PRM adopted anti-semitic and xenophobic postures, targeting not only Jews, but also Hungarians and Roma. It deplored, at first in hints and later openly, the departure of Ceauşescu from the political scene, seeing in him a national hero who, like Antonescu, had fought for the country's independence, seeking to deliver it from the plight of Jewish, Hungarian and other international conspirators and from its predatory neighbours, all of whom were put in one basket. By early 1996, the 'open secret' of Tudor's former connections with Ceauşescu's secret police was officially disclosed by none other than Virgil Măgureanu, the director of the SRI, whose removal Tudor had demanded precisely for having earlier hinted at such connections. Măgureanu, whom Tudor accused of being a Hungarian ethnic, had obviously been acting in concert with President Ion Iliescu. The incumbent president and Tudor had been political allies, but once the alliance broke down, Tudor accused Iliescu of being a 'Gypsy', a former KGB agent, one who had been put in power and kept there by Jews, and an atheist who did not hesitate to order Ceauşescu's execution on the 'holy day of Christmas' (Shafir, 1996a).

The breakdown of the alliance of the PRM with the ruling Party of Social Democracy in Romania (PDSR) had been triggered by electoral calculations (on both sides), but also by Tudor's tempestuous personality. Having insulted Iliescu, he played into the hands of his many political adversaries on the democratic side of Romania's political spectrum, who were only too happy to help lift his parliamentary immunity. He was a candidate in the 1996 presidential elections (which is one reason for his unrestrained attack on Iliescu), winning 4.72 per cent of the votes, and was again elected a senator, which restored parliamentary immunity to him. The PRM as a whole did better in 1996 than in 1992, securing 4.46 per cent (and 19 seats) in the Chamber of Deputies ballot, and 4.54 per cent in the ballot for the Senate (where it now had 8 senators) (*Cronica română*, 8 November 1996).

The PSM, led by Ilie Verdeţ, a former premier under Ceauşescu, was set up in November 1990 and was registered with the Bucharest Tribunal in January 1992. After the 1992 elections, the PRM and the PSM founded, in the Senate, the National Bloc faction. Verdeţ aside, the most prominent member of the PSM is Adrian Păunescu, who, like Tudor, is a former 'court poet' of the Ceauşescu family. Păunescu owned both the weekly *Totuşi iubirea* and the daily Vremea, both of which often carried nationalist articles, sometimes under Păunescu's signature. In February 1996, Păunescu was chosen by the PSM to run against Iliescu in the next presidential contest. He performed very poorly, and gained the support of only 0.69 per cent of the electorate. The parliamentary elections of 1996 turned out to be a débâcle for the PSM. In the former parliament, the party (no official membership figures are available) had obtained 3.03 per cent of the votes for the Chamber of Deputies and 3.18 per cent of those for the Senate. In 1996, however, it failed to pass the 3 per cent electoral hurdle, winning 2.16 per cent in the vote for the Senate and 2.15 per cent in that cast for the Chamber of Deputies (*Cronica romană*, 8 November 1996). The débâcle can be attributed in part to the polarization of the electorate. Supporters of the left had opted for the PDSR, and those of the centre-right for the umbrella organization of the democratic opposition, the Democratic Convention of Romania (CDR), which emerged as the strongest faction in parliament, and whose candidate, Emil Constantinescu, won the presidential contest.

Both the PRM and the PSM are close to the Romanian Cradle (*Vatra românească*), an extremist anti-Hungarian organization founded in early 1990, whose political arm is the PUNR. The honorary president of Romanian Cradle, Iosif Constantin Drăgan, who has an Iron Guardist past is reputed to have amassed a fortune in the West, and is known for his close links with the former regime. According to files made public by a Romanian weekly in early 1995, Drăgan had been an agent for the *Securitate*, having been blackmailed into collaboration by a threat to reveal the fraudulent sources of his wealth. Drăgan also heads the Marshal Antonescu League and the Marshal Antonescu Foundation, while Tudor and other leading figures of his party are prominent members in both. He was the main sponsor of the first statue of Antonescu, erected in Slobozia in 1993. Since then, two more statues have been erected to the memory of the Marshal, and a fourth one is being planned in the main Transylvanian town of Cluj. The initiative was generated by the PUNR chairman, Cluj mayor Gheorghe Funar, and Drăgan is, once more, to be the main provider of funding (Shafir, 1997).

Funar took over the chairmanship of the PUNR in 1992, and has since acquired an international reputation for his provocative actions and pronouncements against Romania's Hungarian minority, which makes up close to a quarter of the population of Cluj (Gallagher, 1995: 168, 203, 208–9 and *passim*; Shafir, 2000). In 1998, following internal disputes in the PUNR that led to his ousting from the chairperson's position, he joined the PRM, becoming General Secretary of that party. His politics are apparently in tune with the Romanian ethnic majority, a considerable part of which had been transferred to Cluj by Ceauşescu as part of the effort to 'Romanianize' the city. Funar was one of the few mayors to be elected (in his case, re-elected) in the local elections of 1996 on the first ballot, securing more than 50 per cent of the poll (Radio Bucharest, 6 June 1996). However, running for president of the country turned out to be another matter. In 1992, he had achieved a respectable 10.87 per cent of the vote, coming third after the two main contenders, Ion Iliescu and the CDR's Emil Constantinescu. In 1996, though, he managed to gain the support of only 3.22 per cent of the electorate. Much of the loss can be attributed to the signing on 16 September 1996, after years of contention, of the long-pending Hungarian–Romanian basic treaty. The PUNR had opposed the step, claiming that it amounted to a 'sell-out' of Romania's national interest and that it would bring about Transylvania's incorporation into Hungary. The claims, however, were discredited more than anything else by the similar negative attitude to the document displayed in Hungary by the centre-right opposition. Since the PUNR is, above all, a 'one-issue' anti-Hungarian party and, moreover, since Funar's formation was also plagued by internal rivalries on the eve of the elections, the party chairman's and the party's own electoral performance of 1996 were incomparably less impressive than those of 1992. The PUNR, which in 1993 had 49,000 members (Eskenasy, 1996), had obtained 7.71 per cent of the votes for the Chamber of Deputies and 8.12 per cent of the votes for the Senate in 1992. This had translated into a parliamentary representation of 30 deputies and 14 senators. In 1996, though, the PUNR was one of the main losers of the elections, along with the PDSR and the PSM. Its parliamentary representation decreased to 18 deputies and 7 senators, reflecting a drop to 4.36 per cent in the share of the vote for the Chamber and 4.22 per cent in that cast for the Senate (*Cronica română*, 8 November 1996). With the exception of the PRM, which probably picked up some of the PUNR losses, the other three members of the coalition that had ruled the country for most of the time after the 1992 elections[2] had thus paid a heavy price for the country's economic mismanagement and deterioration in living standards. It is in this light, rather than one signifying a rejection by the electorate of extremist policies, that the outcome of the 1996 ballot must be judged.

Parties of 'radical return'

As already mentioned, only one 'radical return' party was represented in parliament in 1995, and that representation was very brief. The Party of National Right (*Partidul Dreapta Naţională*, PDN) did not sit in the legislature as a result of electoral choice. Cornel Brahaş, a former vice-chairman of the PUNR, defected from his party after quarrelling with Funar and joined the PDN, which had polled less than 0.1 per cent in the 1992 elections. When he joined, the party had a membership of some 5800 and branches in 10 out of Romania's 41 counties (interview with Brahaş in *Adevărul*, 2 June 1995). One of his first acts was to print and distribute in parliament a book written by a former general in Ceauşescu's secret police. It accused Hungarians and Jews of all the evils that had ever affected Romania, especially concentrating on their alleged joint guilt for having brought about the country's 'bolshevization'. It should be pointed out that this is but one out of thousands of examples of the Romanian variant of the aforementioned 'conspiracy theories'. The author, Neagu Cosma, branded Jews and Hungarians as 'traitors' and as 'Romania's grave-diggers', claiming that 74 out of a total of 484 senators and deputies in parliament were closet Jews (*Cronica română*, 16 November 1995; *Buletin informativ UDMR*, 16 and 23 November 1995).

The PDN had been launched in April 1992 by the young journalist Radu Sorescu. The party's 'Manifesto to the country' was published in 1993, in the first issue of *Noua dreaptă* (The New Right), a publication which later changed its name to *Dreapta naţională* (The National Right). The manifesto stated that the PDN promotes an 'ethnocratic state' which 'excludes [national] minorities from its midst as long as they refuse to be assimilated into the Romanian nation'. This construct was posed against democracy, for the latter was seen to be based on individual rights, 'regardless of race and religion'. The foundations of the ethnocratic state, instead, rested on 'the will of the Romanian nation'. Public office, therefore, was to be the preserve of 'genuine Romanians' alone. Members of national minorities who proved 'disloyal' to the ethnocratic state would be deported. The manifesto went on to state that mankind could fulfil itself only 'within the framework of the state' and that, consequently, 'human rights' were but a fiction 'of the cowardly and the weak'. A special subchapter in the manifesto dealt with the problems of national minorities. Romas were said to be 'at war with the Romanian nation', and the manifesto proposed to set up 'reservations for their isolation' as a 'final solution'. Hungarians were deemed to be 'cruel, vengeful and irredentist' and 'if one million Hungarians refuse to abide by the state order, [then] one million Hungarians must be expelled [from the country]'. The same fate applies to all 'immigrants' who had come to Romania (particularly from the Middle East) after the overthrow of the former regime and who were said to be running 'organized crime' in the country. As regards foreign policy, the party did 'not recognize the legitimacy of European forums (i.e. the European Union and its institutions) set up during the Cold War' because they promote an 'international world order' that does not 'take into consideration the will of nations'. Instead, the PDN advocated a Romanian 'military and economic orientation towards Germany and Japan'. In other words, what was envisaged was a revival of the World War II 'Axis', minus Rome.

Unlike the Romas and the Hungarians, Jews were not specifically mentioned in the manifesto. But the PDN's attitude towards them could be derived from the manifesto's description of the 'offensive of Romanianism', where it was stated that the Romanians' Latin 'national spirit' was incompatible with 'Judaeo-Masonic mercantilism'. The latter was seen to be the foundation of democracy, which transformed nations into 'slaves of big international finance' (*Noua dreaptă*, No. 1, 1993). *Noua dreaptă* interpreted negative reactions to the PDN's manifesto in the independent media as tantamount to 'selling out' to the 'Judaeo-Masonic occult'. The authors of attacks on the PDN were defined as 'notorious mercenaries, who take salaries straight from the synagogue's cashier' (*Noua dreaptă*, No. 2, 1993).

The editorial in the April 1993 issue of *Noua dreaptă* was signed by Sorescu, who wished to assure his readers that, 'We are not what we seem to be' – that is, legionnaires or fascists. But the issue's front page carried an article, written in 1937, by the Iron Guardist politician Alexandru Cantacuzino, the title of which (reproduced on the cover) read, 'Pull out your guns, you lazy bums'. Like other legionnaires of the time (Emil Cioran, for example), Cantacuzino was calling on his fellow Romanians to take up arms and impose their will on history. Whether by accident or not, *Noua dreaptă* announced (in the same issue) the setting up of a paramilitary organization, called 'The Civic Guards'. The front-page article was accompanied by a photo showing Codreanu decorating Cantacuzino who, as an introduction to his tract put it, 'had grasped that violence was necessary for the purification of the nation'.

Furthermore, the PDN's statutes, which somehow were leaked to the press and published in a Bucharest daily, clearly adopted the Legionary Movement (as the Iron Guard was also called) organizational structure as a blueprint. PDN members had to take an oath abhorring 'democratic chaos' and placing the interests of the 'movement' above their own interests. Once taken, the oath would turn them into 'brothers' (those aspiring to join the Legionary Movement, were known as 'Cross Brothers'). The statutes further stated that the PDN's 'ten commandments' were 'inspired by the six commandments of the Legionary Movement' and that members saluted each other with a raised arm 'identical with the Legionary salute'. Like the legionnaires, they call one another *camarad* (comrade), and the official uniform is identical to that of the Legion: green shirts with leather trim and black trousers (*Ora*, 9 November 1993, as cited in *Dimineaţa*, 29 December 1995). The leader of the movement ('Commander', the title of Codreanu's successor, Horia Sima) heads a six-member Grand Council, which Brahaş joined upon his defection from the PUNR. As an official bulletin of the PDN indicated in 1995, Brahaş was put in charge of reorganizing the movement, which had apparently suffered from Sorescu's sudden decision in 1994 to retire from politics and his replacement by an arts and law student, Aurelian Pavelescu (*Punctul nostru de vedere*, No. 4, 7 June 1995).

More importantly, perhaps, Brahaş, a businessman, had apparently pumped funds into the PDN's coffers as the party braced itself for the 1996 elections. Ironically enough, this is precisely what put an end to Brahaş's membership of the PDN and hence to that party's presence in parliament, for in January 1996 he was accused of having embezzled party funds, and therefore left the party (*Evenimentul zilei*, 1 June 1995; *Cronica română*, 20 and 22 January 1996 and 6 March 1996; *România liberă*, 5 March 1996; *Ziua*, 6 March 1996; and *Jurnalul naţional*, 9 March 1996).

But the PDN, in fact, did not contest the 1996 general elections. A new law on political parties, passed by parliament earlier in the year, increased the number of supporting signatures necessary for a party to be legally registered, from 251 to 10,000. The PDN was not among the 43 political formations that had managed to register by September 1996 (*Jurnalul naţional*, 29 October 1996). Running in the local elections held in June 1996, before the new law had applied, the PDN managed to collect, right across the country, only 135 votes in the elections of mayors and 192 votes in those for the local councils (*Monitorul oficial al României*, Part I, No. 132, 25 June 1996).

Several other 'radical return' formations acted outside parliament before the passing of the new party law. One of the most important was the Movement for Romania (*Mişcarea pentru România*, MPR), which had been set up in late 1991. Like the PDN, the MPR did not re-register as a political formation. Since the MPR movement has been covered extensively elsewhere (Shafir, 1994b), I will not deal with it here, apart from emphasizing that it was the first political movement in Romania to openly (or nearly so) acknowledge its descent from the Iron Guard. The PDN, in fact, emulated the MPR, as does a new organization set up in 1995, the Brâncoveanu Eagle Association (Schröder, 1995). All three movements target youth in particular and, at least in so far as the MPR is concerned, apparently with some success.

While the PDN and the MPR claim that the Iron Guard legacy must be adapted to new times' and circumstances, 1994 saw the emergence of an attempt to wholeheartedly embrace that legacy. Şerban Suru, a teacher in his early thirties at a Bucharest high school, had set up in November 1992, on Codreanu's birthday, a movement with a declared Iron Guardist orientation called New Christian Romania (Noua Românie Creştină). Precisely for this reason, the Bucharest Municipal Tribunal refused to register his movement in November 1993. Suru eventually renounced the attempt, and the party was said by a Timişoara pro-Iron Guard publication in 1994 to be 'for the time being dispersed, but not forgotten' (*Tineretul liber*, 1–2 December 1992; *România mare*, No. 136, 29 January 1993; *Jurnalul naţional*, 7 August 1995; *Gazeta de vest*, No. 114, October 1995). Suru and his 'nests', (the basic organizational cells in Codreanu's movement), figured prominently in the media in 1995. In 1994, he had set up the 'Horia Sima nest', so named after

Codreanu's successor as leader of the Iron Guard (*Adevărul*, 29 October 1994; *Evenimentul zilei*, 29-30 October 1994); this was followed in 1995 by the setting up of several other 'nests', in Craiova, Braşov, Sibiu, Constanţa and in the capital of the Republic of Moldova, Chişinău (*România liberă*, 17 November 1995; *Evenimentul zilei*, 9 December 1995). Members of the latter were involved in demonstrations against the government of Moldova, organized by partisans of reunion with Romania, and were eventually arrested and accused of preparing 'extremist actions', the nature of which was not specified (BASA-Press, 15 May 1996). Also in 1995, Suru, who one year earlier had inaugurated in Bucharest a library providing documentation on the Iron Guard, attempted officially to register an association called *Legiunea Creştină* (the Christian Legion), the declared purpose of which was the 'dissemination of historic truth' about the Iron Guard. The Notary General refused registration, however, and the Bucharest Tribunal, before which the decision was appealed, upheld the ruling, viewing the *Legiunea Creştină* as unconstitutional (*Evenimentul zilei*, 22, 23 and 24 June 1995; *Adevărul*, 23 June 1995; *România liberă*, 24 June 1995). Just as controversial was a summer labour legionary camp, organized by Suru at Padina, in the Carpathian Mountains, on the model and on the spot of one of the inter-war legion's camps. Participants wore the green shirts of the Legionary Movement and were supposed to divide activities between work, indoctrination and prayer (*Curierul naţional*, 17 June 1995; *România liberă*, 17 November 1995). The two dozen or so young participators, however, did not enjoy the backing of all the elderly generation of Iron Guardists or even of all their younger successors, for that matter. *Gazeta de vest*, a monthly printed in Timişoara by Horia Sima's followers, for instance, criticized Suru for 'showing-off', for not really 'internalizing' the values of the Legionary Movement and, by provoking the authorities into reaction, for possibly endangering the movement's post-communist 'achievements' (*Gazeta de vest*, No. 113, September 1995, and No. 115, November 1995).

The older Iron Guardists, in fact, had set up their own party in May 1993. It was called the 'For the Fatherland' Party (*Partidul 'Pentru Patrie'*, PPP). The party ran in the local elections, as well as in the general election, of 1996. It did very poorly in both. In the local elections, only 71 people voted for a PPP mayor across the entire country, and the party received only 119 votes for local councillors, again country-wide (*Monitorul oficial al României*, Part 1, 25 June 1996). In the general election, the PPP garnered 0.17 per cent of the vote for the Senate and 0.15 per cent of the ballot cast for the Chamber of Deputies (*Cronica română*, 8 November 1996).

MICHAEL SHAFIR

Right-wing extremism in mainstream formations

A superficial comparison between the 1992 and the 1996 election results might conclude that political extremism finds itself on a course leading to marginalization. After all, the parliamentary representation of 'radical continuity' parties dropped from 59 to 37 seats in the Chamber of Deputies, and from 25 to 15 in the Senate. Also, the 'radical return' parties did not enter either legislature. However, radicalism of an extreme right nature is far from being limited to the two categories of parties surveyed above. The web of ideas crosses political boundaries and makes strange bedfellows. Take, for instance, the Romanian Democratic Agrarian Party (*Partidul Democrat Agrar Român*, PDAR). Set up as a satellite of the ruling party in February 1990, mainly to counter the opposition National Peasant Party Christian Democratic, the party was a member of the coalition up to 1994 and a strong supporter of the government. In the 1992 parliamentary elections, the PDAR failed to clear the 3 per cent electoral hurdle in the Chamber of Deputies, but managed to achieve 3.31 per cent in the elections to the Senate, enough to gain a foothold there. Miscalculating through opportunism rather than demonstrating any ideological transformation, the PDAR then moved into opposition. By that time, significantly, it had been joined by several ultra-nationalists.

One of these was Radu Theodoru, who became the party's vice-chairman, replacing Oliviu Tocaciu. Tocaciu himself had discovered that engaging in extreme right activities could be a lucrative affair, and in 1993 he financed the first Romanian translation of Adolf Hitler's *Mein Kampf*. Theodoru, perhaps the most vicious of Romania's anti-semites, had been a founding member of the PRM but, having quarrelled with Tudor in late 1992, he joined the Party of Social Democratic Unity, and soon became its chairman. Eventually, he moved again, this time to the PDAR. His credo, however, did not change with the shift in political colours. No one else in Romania cites the infamous Protocols of the Elders of Zion as 'proof' of the international Jewish conspiracy as often as Theodoru does (the protocols have been printed on several occasions – the latest, in 1995, by the 'respectable' Moldova publishing house). In 1995, he serialized in the anti-semitic Bucharest weekly *Europa* (whose editor-in-chief, Ilie Neacşu, is close to Tudor and in 1996 became a member of the PRM's Steering Committee) (*Politica*, No. 219, 11 May 1996), a tract which was eventually put on sale as a 300-page volume, entitled *Romania, the World and the Jews*.

A prominent colleague of Theodoru in the PDAR was, until recently, senator Ion Coja. Like Theodoru, Coja was both a vice-chairman of the PDAR and a political migrant. He started off his political career in parliament representing the National Salvation Front, as the PDSR was then called, and was also a founding member of *Vatra românească*, becoming its first vice-chairman. Coja then moved to the PUNR and, after quarrelling with Funar, to the PDAR. In March 1966, he was elected as the PDAR's candidate in the presidential elections scheduled for the fall (Radio Bucharest, 3 March 1996). But then the PDAR struck an alliance with two other formations, the New Romania Party and the Romanian Ecological Movement, setting up an electoral alliance called the National Centrist Union (UNC). The UNC decided to have a joint candidate in the presidential elections and Coja lost out in the contest to Ion Pop de Popa. Remorseful, he moved back to the PUNR, failing, however, to be elected to parliament.

Coja's never-ending political migration saga did not stop him from collaborating with the PDN and with the MPR. He used to be a regular contributor to *Noua dreaptă* (where he explained to readers that 'the right is God's', since one made the sign of the cross with that hand, whereas 'the left' was the hand and the mind 'of sin', among which he counted democracy and human rights (*Noua dreaptă*, No. 1, 1993)), then to the MPR publication *Mişcarea*. His attempts to bring about a unification of the PDN and the MPR failed, but Coja remained one of the chief apologists of the Iron Guard which, he claimed, had never committed the crimes attributed to it and had allegedly been cleared of any suspicion by the Nuremberg War Crimes Tribunal. The claim was so absurd that the weekly *Dilema* refused to publish his contribution. It is illustrative of the Romanian intertwining of 'radical return' and 'radical continuity' that Coja (undoubtedly a representative of the former stream) eventually had the tract published in Păunescu's *Vremea* (25–26 May 1996).

Prejudice based on religious fundamentalism is part of the mind-set of the radical right. In Europe and in the United States, the main target are the Jews, although Romas, as well as gays and lesbians, also figure prominently (Shafir, 1999). Concluding a survey on anti-semitism in Europe since the Holocaust, Robert S. Wistrich wrote that, in all former communist societies, 'Ancient prejudices embedded in the popular psyche have come to the fore ... even where there are scarcely any Jews left'. In some cases, he added, these prejudices are 'intensified ... by the very abstractness of anti-Jewish stereotypes in their protean nature, which can be readily transformed and adapted to new situations' (Wistrich, 1993: 19). Yet as the world approaches the third millennium of the modern era, one would have expected the end of such hoaxes as the Middle Ages Jewish blood libel, according to which Jews kill Gentile children and use their blood for preparing the unleavened Passover bread. Yet in late 1995, *Baricada*, a weekly published in Bucharest by the Meridian press trust and owned by the then chairman of the Romanian Ecologist Movement, Victor Eduard Gugui, resurrected the calumny. Following the discovery and arrest of a ring of baby smugglers in which two Israelis had been involved, Gugui's publication wrote, 'As is well known, the Jewish unleavened bread requires *kosher* fresh Christian blood.' Proof, however, was unlikely to emerge 'as long as the Jewish Mafia practice of chasing after *kosher* meat is covered up by the Mossad' (*Baricada*, No. 46, 14 November 1995). Even the PRM weekly *România mare*, in its coverage of the same story, had not ventured that far. According to the latter publication, the Israeli embassy in Bucharest was likely to 'hush up' the story because 'when the Jews are engaging in slave-trading Christian children in order to sell off their body-parts to hospitals, this is called being humane, and when the Christians protest ... this is said to be anti-semitism, xenophobia, extremism' (*România mare*, No. 282, 1 December 1995). But, significantly, the PRM is considered to be extremist, and rightly so, while Gugui's party is supposed to be 'mainstream'.

The mainstream label applies also to the pre-1996 major political party, Iliescu's PDSR. However, as has been shown, this did not stop it from forging an alliance with the PRM, to whose publications some of its parliamentarians (Gheorghe Dumitraşcu, for example) are regular contributors. The display of 'indignation' that the PDSR professed to show when Iliescu was attacked by Tudor (see above) prompted Andrei Pleşu, a former anti-Ceauşescu dissident and a former minister of culture in the first post-communist government, to note sarcastically:

> One cannot but be amazed by the fact that the government party discovers the vices of its partner only at the end of three years of cohabitation. Vadim Tudor's record of anti-semitic publications dates back to well before [the anti-Ceauşescu uprising of] 1989. Assiduously anti-Magyar and anti-Romanian (since he insulted without hesitation three quarters of the country's intellectual elite), he never hid his idiosyncrasies, his vulgarity, his spiritual degeneration. He was no better when they [the Greater Romania Party and the Party of Social Democracy in Romania] wed than when they were divorced. Striking an alliance with such a specimen could have just a single, seriously reprehensible justification: the [PDSR] determination to stay in power at whatever price, without a trace of moral or civic scruples. ... It was only after [Tudor] threw coarse insults at Ion Iliescu that the chiefs of the governmental coalition discovered with astonishment, as it were, his rudeness and his anti-semitism. As if Romania's president were the first 'Jew' that Vadim insulted, after years of cosmopolitan smiles. ... In other words, one lives in a brothel for three long years and suddenly one comes up with the announcement that one is surrounded by prostitutes, from whom one wishes to distance oneself (*Dilema*, No. 146, 27 October–2 November 1995).

Furthermore, during the presidential electoral campaign, Iliescu himself did not hesitate to appeal to anti-semitic prejudice. Addressing an electoral meeting on 21 October, Iliescu said that former prime minister Petre Roman, who was one of his rivals in the race, had 'no real roots in our people'. This was a gross allusion to the fact that the father of the former premier had been a Jew. Earlier, the manager of the PDSR electoral campaign, Ovidiu Șincai, accused Roman's father, a former communist official, of having intended to set up an independent state in Transylvania. The accusation fell in line with allegations that Roman represented 'Judaeo-Communism', which had been repeatedly aired by extremist formations of the like of the PRM (*Adevărul*, 23 and 16 October 1996, respectively).

'Marginalization of the mainstream'

At first sight, the above heading might appear to be a contradiction in terms. If 'mainstream' politics is to be understood as 'sane democratic politics', however, its marginalization is clearly possible. It is particularly so in societies where the dominant trends in political culture and opportunist 'politicking' on the part of those who may be pursuing immediate interests, at the expense of their own and society's long-term interests, combine to undermine democracy. Incipient democracies, such as those of Eastern and Central Europe, are particularly fragile for, as Ramet observes, 'an intolerant society is more threatening to the preservation of personal autonomy than is an intolerant state' (1995: 454). Without personal autonomy, of course, democracy is just a farce.

Partly under pressure from Western influences, a process that could bear fruit if Romania decided to pursue integration into Atlantic and European structures, the PDSR began to move away from its extremist partners. But, as Iliescu's anti-semitic remark indicates, there was no guarantee that extremist postures would not be embraced again if required. Voted out of power in November 1996, the PDSR is unlikely to forgo its 'utilitarian' approach to political extremism. On the contrary, it needs its former coalition allies (the PRM and the PUNR) represented in the new parliament more than it ever did in the past. The presence of extremists within its own ranks is also conducive to a *rapprochement* with the former allies. A large question mark loomed over the major party in the new coalition, formed by the CDR, the Democratic Party–National Salvation Front (PD–FSN) and the Hungarian Democratic Federation of Romania (UDMR). The PD–FSN is led by Roman and the UDMR, of course, represents the interests of the Hungarian minority. At first sight, this may appear to guarantee the absence of extreme nationalist tones in the new leadership team. However, within the CDR, which is a heterogeneous organization of competing ideological outlooks, there are personalities known to have taken positions which are in many respects closer to those of the PUNR than to those of the UDMR. Some members of the new coalition are also known to be closet (or open) anti-semites. Indeed, the CDR included the leader of the Brâncoveanu Eagle Association, Radu-Mihai Chesaru, on its lists of councillors elected in the local elections of 1996 in Bucharest.

Furthermore, opinion surveys seem to indicate that Romanian democracy is far from being entrenched, and 'red–brown' extremism or extremism of a 'radical return' nature might profit from this in the long term. As in other former communist countries, the two institutions that seem to enjoy public confidence are the Church and the Army, neither of which is known as the most solid pillar of tolerance. The CDR is particularly keen on cultivating them both. Other key institutions, and above all parliament and the judiciary, are held in low esteem.[3] A not insignificant minority of 11 per cent, in a poll conducted by Gallup at the end of December 1995, were of the opinion that 'in order for the situation to improve, political parties must be abolished'. About the same proportion (10 per cent) thought political life would improve if parliament were to be abolished, and nearly one in three respondents (33 per cent) supported the temporary suspension of some civic rights (*Evenimentul zilei*, 4 January 1996). The legislature's image may temporarily improve in the wake of the enthusiasm triggered by the change of November 1996 (Lieven, 1997). But if the CDR fails to deliver on its promise of improved living standards, as is likely to happen, those who viewing democratic institutions with distrust may conclude that the radicals of one shade or the other were right, after all.

Earlier polls had indicated the presence of a substantial minority that has no use for democratic values. For example, a survey conducted in 1993 by the Romanian Institute for Public Opinion Surveys (IRSOP) found that more than one in four Romanians (27 per cent) would support 'an authoritarian, iron hand leadership' (*Libertatea*, 16–17 March 1993). In late February 1996, there were indications that this minority had already grown significantly. A Gallup poll had about one in three Romanians (33.5 per cent) displaying support for an 'iron hand government, even if this means limiting democracy'. On the other hand, 37.5 per cent of those questioned said the Romanian parliament included 'extremist parties' that should not be in the legislature; 32.6 per cent of those so persuaded named the PRM, 8 per cent the PSM and 12.2 per cent the PUNR. Yet the highest score here was the UDMR's (39.1 per cent), which indicated that extreme nationalist propaganda was successful (*Evenimentul zilei* and *România liberă*, 29 March 1996). The specific threat of 'a dictatorship' seemed to worry the Romanian respondents least, with 'prices', 'a war in the region' and 'illness' heading the list of main concerns in 1995 and in 1996. In this connection, it may be worth noting that, in a survey conducted by IRSOP in 1995, no less than 62 per cent of the respondents replied that they had 'a good opinion' of Antonescu. On the other hand, only 5 per cent approved of (in a survey conducted by the same institute in December 1994) the prospect of a revival of the Iron Guard movement (*Adevărul*, 9 May 1995 and Romanian Television, 22 December 1994). In his bid for success in the presidential elections, Tudor promised to be 'a new Antonescu', and to 'make order' by resorting to 'two years of an authoritarian regime' (*Politica*, No. 176, 15 July

1995; *România mare*, No. 272, 22 September 1995). The electorate did not provide him with the chance. But what about the year 2000, when the next elections are due? Or 2004, or 2008, for that matter?

Notes

1. I am indebted to the following colleagues at the now defunct Open Media Research Institute in Prague for providing information included in this paragraph: Robert Orttung and Peter Rutland (Russia); Stan Markotich and Patrick Moore (Croatia and Serbia); Sharon Fischer (Slovakia); Stefan Krause (Bulgaria); and Jakub Karpinski (Poland).
2. That coalition was headed by the PDSR and included the PUNR, the PRM and the PSM.
3. These returns are valid for the entire period since the overthrow of the communist regime. The economy of this article does not allow a detailed presentation, however. Suffice it to mention that in the quarterly surveys conducted in 1995 and 1996 for the Soros Foundation by the Bucharest Institute for Research on the Quality of Life and the Centre for Urban Sociology, the Church's lowest rate of approval was 82 per cent and its highest 91 per cent, while the Army had an approval rate fluctuating between a low of 76 per cent and a high of 92 per cent. By comparison, parliament's *disapproval* rates fluctuated between a low of 71 per cent and a high of 78 per cent, and the disapproval rate of the judiciary between 47 per cent at lowest and 56 per cent at highest (*Evenimentul zilei*, 21 March 1995, 20 June 1995, 7 October 1995; *Adevărul*, 20 December 1995; *Jurnalul naţional*, 23 October 1996; *Cotidianul*, 23 October 1996).

References

Chirot, D. (1994) *Modern Tyrants: The Power and Prevalence of Evil in Our Age.* New York: Free Press.

Eatwell, R. (1989) 'Right or Rights? The Rise of the "New Right" ', in Eatwell, R. and O'Sullivan, N. (eds) *The Nature of the Right.* London: Pinter.

Eskenasy, V. (1996) 'Roumanie', in J.-V. Camus (ed.) *Les extrémismes, de l'Atlantique à l'Oural.* Paris: Éditions de l'Aube/CERA.

Gallagher, T. (1995) *Romania after Ceauşescu.* Edinburgh: Edinburgh University Press.

Hainsworth, P. (1992) 'Introduction. The Cutting Edge: The Extreme Right in Postwar Western Europe and the USA', in Hainsworth, P. (ed.) *The Extreme Right in Europe and the USA.* London: Pinter.

Heinen, A. (1986) 'Die Legion "Erzengel Michael" ', in *Rumänien. Soziale Bewegung und politische Organisation: Ein Beitrag zum Problem des internationalen Faschismus.* Munich: Südosteuropäische Arbeiten.

Institute of Jewish Affairs (1994) *Political Extremism and the Threat to Democracy in Europe.* London: Institute of Jewish Affairs.

Jelinek, Y. A. (1994) 'A Whitewash in Colour: Revisionist Historiography in Slovakia', *East European Jewish Affairs* 24(2), 117–130.

Jowitt, K. (1971) *Revolutionary Breakthroughs and National Development: The Case of Romania, 1944–1965.* Berkeley and Los Angeles: University of California Press.

Karnoouh, C. (1990) *L'Invention du peuple: chroniques de Roumanie.* Paris: Éditions Arcantère.

Karsai, L. (1999) 'The Radical Right in Hungary', in Ramet, S. P. (ed.) *The Radical Right in Central and Eastern Europe since 1989.* University Park: University of Pennsylvania Press.

Ornea, Z. (1995) *Anii treizeci: extrema dreaptă românească.* Bucharest: Editura Fundaţiei culturale române.

Ramet, S. P. (1995) *Social Currents in Eastern Europe: The Sources and Consequences of the Great Transformation*, 2nd edition. Durham, NC: Duke University Press.

Ramet, S. P. (1999) 'Defining the Radical Right: The Values and Behaviours of Organized Intolerance', in Ramet, S. P. (ed.) *The Radical Right in Central and Eastern Europe since 1989.* University Park, PA: Pennsylvania University Press.

Schröder, H. (1995) 'Dumpfe Parolen als letzte Zuflucht', *Süddeutsche Zeitung*, 12 January.

Shafir, M. (1991a) 'Anti-semitism without Jews in Romania', *Report on Eastern Europe* 2(26), 20–32.

Shafir, M. (1991b) 'The Greater Romania Party', *Report on Eastern Europe* 2(46), 25–30.

Shafir, M. (1991c) 'Political Culture and the Romanian Revolution of December 1989: Who Failed Whom?', paper presented at an international colloquium on political culture organized by the Centre Français d'Études et Recherches Internationales, Paris, March.

Shafir, M. (1994a) 'Anti-semitism in the Postcommunist Era', in Braham, R. L. (ed.) *The Tragedy of Romanian Jewry.* New York: Columbia University Press.

Shafir, M. (1994b) 'The Inheritors: The Romanian Radical Right since 1989', *East European Jewish Affairs* 24(1), 71–90.

Shafir, M. (1995) 'Romania', in Spier, H. (ed.) *Antisemitism World Report 1995.* London: Institute of Jewish Affairs.

Shafir, M. (1996a) 'Anatomy of a Pre-elections Political Divorce', *Transition* 2(2), 45–9.

Shafir, M. (1997) 'Marshal Antonescu's Post-communist Rehabilitation: *Cui Bono?*', in Braham, R. L. (ed.) *The Destruction of Romanian and Ukrainian Jews During the Antonescu Era.* New York: Columbia University Press.

Shafir, M. (1999) 'The Mind of Romania's Radical Right', in Ramet, S. P. (ed.) *The Radical Right in Central and Eastern Europe since 1989.* Seattle: University of Washington Press.

Shafir, M. (2000) 'The Hungarian Democratic Federation of Romania: Actions, Reactions, Factions', in Mickey, R. (ed.) *Ethnicity Unbound: The Politics of Minority Participation in Post-communist Europe.* New York: St Martin's Press.

Sternhell, Z. (1978) *La droite révolutionnaire: les origines françaises du fascisme 1885–1914.* Paris: Éditions du Seuil.

Sternhell, Z. (1983) *Ni droite, ni gauche: l'idéologie fasciste en France*. Paris: Éditions Complexe.

Sternhell, Z., Sznajder, M. and Asheri, M. (1989) *Naissance de l'idéologie fasciste*. Paris: Fayard.

Tismaneanu, V. and Pavel, D. (1994) 'Romania's Mystical Revolutionaries: The Generation of Angst and Adventure', *East European Politics and Societies* 8(3), 402–38.

Vago, R. (1995) 'Anti-semitism in Romania 1989–1992', Project for the Study of Anti-Semitism, Tel Aviv University.

Volovici, L. (1991) *National Ideology and Antisemitism: The Case of Romanian Intellectuals in the 1930s*. Oxford: Pergamon Press.

Wistrich, R.S. (1993) 'Anti-semitism in Europe since the Holocaust: The American Jewish Committee', New York: Working Papers on Contemporary Anti-Semitism.

CHAPTER TWELVE

Serbia: extremism from the top and a blurring of right into left

Stan Markotich

Introduction

A central theme in this chapter is that in contemporary Serbia, as in other parts of post-communist Europe, distinctions between left and right have broken down. In Serbia, in recent years, Slobodan Milošević has not been fettered by ideology in his ruthlessly exercised endeavour to maintain and consolidate power. Using the medium of Serbian nationalism, Milošević has pursued what Misha Glenny (1999) defined as his 'basic instinct': 'the cold will to survive'. That Milošević has been able to do so is bound up with Serbian self-identification (and experiences) as a vulnerable and victimized people historically. The chapter begins with a discussion of Serbian extremism in the context of political culture and this is followed by sections that focus upon the ideological question, Milošević's ascent to power, and the way intellectuals have figured in Milošević's Machiavellian equations, while the final sections assess his recent ideological and political trajectory leading into the 1999 Kosovo crisis.

The face of Serbian extremism

Serbian extremism or ultra-nationalism defies an easy definition, and any attempt to codify it beyond accounting for its main ingredients fails to come to terms with its fundamental essence – namely, that it is a commodity constantly in flux, tailored and changed by political elites to meet their ambitions or expedient aims. Over-simplified portrayals see it, in part, as a cultural phenomenon, developed over centuries by the southern Slavs. These people identify strongly with Christian Orthodox religion, and with cultural traditions drawing upon epic poetry, that extols the virtues of heroism in the face of overwhelming military odds. Serbs also have a tradition of defining themselves against other neighbouring groups, especially against the Catholic Croats.

Serbian extremism's dominant characteristic is its highly and integrally parochial nature, a quality common to immoderate politics throughout the Balkan region (Halpern, 1958: 284–306; *NIN*, 20 August 1993). There is nothing in Serbian extremism's make-up that renders it exportable to other groups, nations or societies. In its ugliest form, ultra-nationalism – manifested in Serbian war crimes and atrocities – it has won over apologists throughout the Balkans. Notable here have been Greek journalists and politicians, arguably the most stalwart defenders of Serbian aggression during the recent wars throughout the former Yugoslavia, which broke out in 1991 and drew to a formal close with the signing of the Dayton Peace Accord in December 1995, only to re-ignite dramatically in Kosovo in 1998–9. But rarely do the Serbs' defenders condone acts of genocide, opting instead for the Belgrade-sanctioned position that Serbs are to be supported and sympathized with because allegedly, they have been (and continue to be) the victims of war. Some superficially identical, shared, cultural variables, such as a common belief system rooted in Orthodox Christianity, have undoubtedly predisposed a broader regional public opinion to favour the Serbs. Ultimately, though, common geostrategic and economic interests may be the most compelling variable drawing together capitals such as Belgrade and Athens (Krause, 1995: 50–5).

To explain how right-wing extremism emerged as the dominant political form of expression in Serbia, one needs to recall the history of Yugoslavia, and Serbia's experience within the framework of that state. The Yugoslavian state, from its inception following World War I, had failed to adopt or invent a system of values agreeable or acceptable to the whole population (Jelavich, 1983: 143–57). The forces promoting inter-ethnic social cohesion were absent, but this was not due to a lack of effort, especially on the part of the post-World War II socialist authorities. The League of Communists of Yugoslavia had embarked on policies of Yugoslavianization, nurturing 'brotherhood and unity' and specifically encouraging the public acceptance and adoption of identity and nationality as Yugoslav (Burg and Berbaum, 1984). However, Yugoslavia was a state which, according to one author,

had been beset with problems from the time of its establishment in 1918, and no sooner was the multiethnic state constituted than it started to fall apart. Over the course of its history, Yugoslavia lurched from crisis to crisis, abandoning one unstable formula for another (Ramet, 1996: 37–8).

The borders of socialist Yugoslavia have now been erased by a process beginning in 1991 and after a series of events that prompted Slovenia,

Croatia, Bosnia and Herzegovina, and Macedonia to seek independence (Glenny, 1992; Thompson, 1992; Bennett, 1995; Cohen, 1995; Woodward, 1995). The 1998–9 crisis in Kosovo needs to be seen in this light. Without the parameters or constraints laid out by President Josip Broz Tito's state, a variety of extremist groups have mushroomed over the terrain of what remains of Yugoslavia – that is, throughout rump Yugoslavia, or what is now known as the Federal Republic of Yugoslavia (FRY), consisting of the republics of Serbia and Montenegro. Tito and a series of successors, after the Partisan leader's death in 1980, presided over a centralized state that proved unable to overcome the forces of nationalist sentiment, cultivated and unleashed initially by Serbia's president Slobodan Milošević, who became the president of FRY on 15 July 1997. When Milošević 'played the nationalist card', leaders in the neighbouring republics, and notably Croatia's President Franjo Tuđman, also proved able and willing to following suit (Silber and Little, 1995: 87–97).

The particular variant of Marxism–Leninism dominant in Tito's Yugoslavia, largely cobbled together by the main ideologue, Edvard Kardelj, buttressed a political structure that had merely managed to conceal and submerge ultra-rightist nationalist tendencies. But that tradition of Marxist socialism, as far as Serbia is concerned, was also never explicitly rejected, and has in recent years experienced a striking revival, thereby making no study of right-wing extremism in Serbia complete without discussion of socialism's lingering and symbiotic impact. Furthermore, socialism's recent and continuing resurrection by no means signals an end to extremist politics, or even anything approximating the smallest steps towards a society grounded in the tenets of liberal democracy, defined by a political consensus respectful of individual rights and traditions, and characterized by freedom of the press and freedom of expression (Tepevac, 1994: 83–7). Developments point, in fact, to a retrenchment of ultra-nationalist doctrine.

Today, and for at least the immediate future, Milošević's governing party, the Socialist Party of Serbia (SPS), is subservient to the political machinations of its leader, who in turn has ruled Serbia-Montenegro virtually unchecked, certainly until recently. At times, this reality was lost on observers, who became diverted by Milošević's *prima facie* deference to democratic principles, including the holding of periodic elections and, at least, toleration of opposition parties. The tearing apart of socialist Yugoslavia was undertaken, then, as the means to obtain and preserve authority over one specific jurisdiction. For Milošević, in other words, becoming the uncontested political authority within rump Yugoslavia (including Kosovo, or as much of it as possible) was more important than seeking yet another compromise solution for socialist Yugoslavia's territorial integrity: the latter course ultimately would have meant Milošević contenting himself with being but one of a group of key political players (Silber and Little, 1995: 139–44).

Searching for ideological roots

Milošević's political extremism is partly rooted in tenets of Serbian nationalism. This was particularly evident during the earliest stages of the Milošević regime, and during the period of the President's rise to power, beginning in 1987. Subsequently, though, Milošević's rhetoric dropped its blatant nationalistic overtones, incorporating instead a return to the trappings of communism. Milošević's wife, Mirjana Marković, who headed her own political organization – the Yugoslav United Left (JUL) – became the main conduit for this restoration of seemingly anti-nationalist extremism (*Montena-fax*, 21 June 1996). On 25 April 1996, for instance, Ms Marković, at a convention of JUL, formally denounced radical nationalism, saying that in 'a society made up of several nations, composed also of many minorities, nationalism is not acceptable, and can produce dangerous, even tragic, consequences' (*Tanjug*, 25 April 1996).

Any exploration of Serbian extremism must appreciate how nationalist appeal and trappings came to dominate the political agenda. Conventional interpretations of the Serbian polity include the hypothesis, alluded to above, that Serbian nationalism is rooted in a collective historical self-depiction of Serbs as victims. This interpretation of Serbian extremism, as defined through nationalism, maintains that it was through their historic defeat at the Battle of Kosovo in 1389, at the hands of invading Ottoman forces, that Serbs began their evolution towards embracing a national consciousness. According to one author, therefore, 'Serbian nationalism is rooted in the historic traditions of Serbia as the torch-bearer of Slavism against the Turks' (Singleton, 1976: 229).

A second key ingredient may be summed up under the banner of 'Greater Serbia', conventionally defined as the goal of Serbian state expansionism. A fundamental element of Serbian national goals, the argument proceeds, is the drawing together of all Serb-populated lands under one administration. This quest for a Greater Serbia, or an enlarged Serbian state, has its own extremist qualities and has advocates dating back at least to the nineteenth century. Stojan Protić (1857–1923), a prominent member of the National Radical Party, was among those who may be seen as a precursor of the ethnic cleansing campaigns that have taken place in the recent wars throughout the former Yugoslavia. Among his policy planks was advocacy of the destruction of a Bosnian Muslim identity. He reportedly said, 'As soon as our army crosses the Drina, it will give the Turks [that is, Bosnian Muslims] twenty-four – perhaps forty-eight – hours to return to the faith of their forefathers [Orthodoxy] and then slay those who resist, as we did in Serbia in the past' (Banac, 1984: 107).

Other significant ingredients of Serbian nationalist movements include elements of linguistic and cultural identity. The origins of a common national heritage may be traced back to the theories of Vuk Stefanović

Karadžić (1787–1864) who, arguably more than any other figure, contributed to the standardization of the Serbian language based on the *štokavian* dialect. Likewise, the modern impulse towards state expansion may be traced back to the territorial aggrandizement and balance-of-power objectives of Ilija Garašanin, Serbia's internal affairs minister in the mid-nineteenth century and the author of the 1844 *Nacertanije*, or blueprint for what lands ought to be contained within the borders of a Serbian state (Čubrilović, 1958: 176).

Differences

What makes Serbian radical nationalism, and the ideological impulses that drive it, nearly impossible to define is that they have never been codified with any degree of rigour or precision. Also, many Serb nationalist writings and advocates have expressed their ideas in ways that are not readily comprehended by the mass of the peasant population, therefore making broad popular consensus or understanding of such nationalism nearly impossible. Among the most prominent champions of nationalist doctrines are novelists and poets, whose thinking is targeted at an intellectual elite (Ramet, 1996: 28–9).

Second, of critical importance is the fact that, Serbs do not comprise a group with one single defining cultural or political experience (Petrovich, 1976). The Republic of Serbia is best understood in its modern context by reference to its historical ties with the Ottoman Empire. Montenegro, the other remaining republic in rump Yugoslavia, has its cultural roots planted firmly in traditions of opposition to Ottoman conquest and, while this is on the surface a point of commonality, in fact, Montenegrins were never completely subjugated. Up until the twentieth century, Montenegro enjoyed independence, allowing for the formation of its own unique political institutions and traditions, notably a monarchy separate from Serbia's. This particular past continues to flavour Montenegrin politics, and to some extent balances other political opinion, at its most extreme embodied in the contemporary Serbian Radical Party (SRS). This organization maintains that Montenegrins are purely and simply Serbs, and it advocates the eradication of all borders, physical and otherwise, that divide Serbia and Montenegro.

Complicating matters further, the Republic of Serbia comprises at least three distinct regions. Excluding Serbia proper, its once autonomous Vojvodina province has roots in the Hansburgs' Austro-Hungarian Empire. Thus Vojvodina is that part of the Federal Republic of Yugoslavia whose cultural and political development is not best understood with reference to Ottoman history. Meanwhile, the other once-autonomous province, Kosovo, was populated mainly by ethnic Albanians, who suffered under Belgrade's police-state control and demanded autonomy, if not independence, for themselves. While Kosovo remains in Serb imagining an integral component of the national heartland, the region had all but lost its ethnic Serb character (Brown, 1992: 67–9). Considerations such as these lay behind recent upheavals in this territory.

In summary, what Serbs lack is a common historical and cultural evolution that would predispose them to a single view of nationalism. Nevertheless, political developments which serve to underscore and promote extremist political solutions stem from high political authorities and functionaries, who have sought to rally and manipulate public opinion. In other words, through radical right-wing extremism and ultra-nationalism the political elite (very often, in fact, single individuals) has mobilized public opinion to serve their own political or military objectives. It is this penchant for top-down manipulation that Milošević has inherited from other pioneers of Serbian state expansion.

A presidential career

Slobodan Milošević is at the centre of any understanding or analysis of political extremism in rump Yugoslavia today. In his earlier days, he showed almost no signs of having any political acumen. Born on 29 August 1941 to Montenegrin parents, in the town of Požarevac, he went on to study law at Belgrade University, graduating in 1964. Although he had joined the League of Communists of Yugoslavia (LCY) in 1959, he did not devote himself to politics full-time until 1984, when he went on to become chair of the LCY in Belgrade. It was not until 1989 that he began his meteoric rise to political prominence. On 28 June of that year, six weeks after being elected President of Serbia by the Serbian National Assembly, Milošević seized the opportunity afforded by the six hundredth anniversary of the Battle of Kosovo. Even though it was not Milošević's most fiery speech, it did stress that Kosovo was an integral part of Serbia, and thereby accomplished two key things: the rekindling of Serbian nationalism on a broad public scale, and the introduction of a policy that revoked Kosovo's autonomous status. Both before and subsequently, Milošević has relied on repression, manipulation and force, which are the hallmarks of his governing style. In 1987, his mentor, Ivan Stambolić, had been forced out of the Serbian presidency by his protégé, as Milošević used the pretext that Stambolić, a convinced nationalist, had gone soft on nationalism. Again in 1990, Milošević resorted to legalistic chicanery to pass a new Serbian constitution which effectively revoked the last shreds of autonomy accorded to Vojvodina and Kosovo. Significantly, too, he maintained in control of the Serbian police, his main tool of physical repression.

Broadly speaking, Milošević's accomplishments have been twofold. On the one hand, and as suggested earlier, he has moulded himself in the pattern of Garašanin and other Serbian politicians who had won or assumed office in order to promote an ethnic Serbian nation-state. But the content or substance of any specific accompanying ideology has remained secondary, if not tertiary, so far as Milošević is concerned (Milošević, 1989: 264–9). Staying in power has been of prime consideration for the Serbian president, and at times this has entailed promoting a volatile ultra-right nationalism that supported, when it did not expressly endorse, goals such as genocide and the partition of socialist Yugoslavia.

On the other hand, Milošević's promotion of ultra-nationalism triggered the creation and revival of radical nationalist political parties, both within Serbia-Montenegro and in Serb-populated areas of the other republics of the former Yugoslavia. Many such organizations either were or remain characterized by a paramilitary wing. The most notorious of these continued to be the SRS, led by Vojislav Šešelj, who also headed the paramilitary *Četniks*. In addition, the leader of the notorious Tigers, Željko Raznatović, alias Arkan, has been linked to some of the fiercest ethnic cleansing campaigns in Bosnia and Herzegovina, and he continues to head the Serbian Party of Unity (SSJ) (Silber and Little, 1995: 247). More recently, Arkan and his militia were reported widely as operating in Kosovo in 1999, as the process of ethnic cleansing accelerated.*

Whether or not such radical nationalist political parties can continue to flourish remains an open question. When courting the ultra-nationalist vote and seeking to establish himself as the embodiment of Serbian nationalism, Milošević promoted such political organizations, particularly the SRS. These parties, based on platforms and policies which may be described as backward-looking, peddle antiquated ideals which include appeals to Serbian past military glories. They are very xenophobic, a quality which has led them in effect to justify and participate in ethnic cleansing (*NIN*, 12 February 1993 and 20 August 1993), while they also extol the virtues of ancient and peasant patriarchal social arrangements, known as *zadruga* (Halpern, 1958: 134–50).

As Milošević emerged as Serbian nationalist leader *par excellence*, his tactic for ruling included incorporating ultra-nationalists directly into government. Following Serbia's 1992 parliamentary elections, the SPS emerged with 101 seats, gaining the support of Šešelj's 73 deputies in order to form a government. By May 1993, relations between Šešelj and Milošević had soured, prompting a split and forcing elections in December of that same year (*Borba*, 7 October 1993; Markotich, 1993: 15–20). The basis on which the two parties were able to form a working relationship to begin with was itself a case study of Milošević's manipulation of extreme nationalism, via an effective and indirect appeal to leaders such as Šešelj. Flattery and pandering were key weapons in Milošević's arsenal: Šešelj was hailed publicly as his 'favourite opposition leader', at least until their split became evident. For Šešelj, Milošević represented the only political leader whom he could work with. Following the elections of 20 December 1992, Šešelj had stated that he would refuse to work with all but the SPS, consciously distancing himself from other opposition leaders, and specifically from Vuk Drašković (leader of the Serbian Renewal Movement), by declaring that his SRS 'would never enter into a coalition with the reformers' (*Politika*, 28 December 1992).

At that time, Milošević's ultra-nationalist pedigree was unquestionable. Certainly not lost on Šešelj were the (then) recent political machinations of the Serbian president. Most particularly, and as already noted above, on the occasion of the six hundredth anniversary of the Battle of Kosovo, Milošević gave the speech which may remain in the history books as his most famous. Delivered in Serbia's Kosovo province, which then boasted a 90 per cent ethnic Albanian population, it consisted of a direct appeal to Serbian nationalism through the declaration that Kosovo was, is, and always would remain an integral part of Serbia (Silber and Little, 1995: 75–7). That intervention, more than any single event, stirred public sentiment in favour of Serbia's quest for a Greater Serbian state. It was this kind of discourse that marked Milošević's rise to power: from about 1987, he delivered a series of emotive speeches, some even more robust than the above remarks, that served to spur separatist and independentist demands in Slovenia, Croatia, Bosnia and Herzegovina, and Kosovo.

However, rhetoric was far from Milošević's only link to ultra-nationalism. The notorious *SANU Memorandum*, originating from the Serbian Academy of Sciences and Arts (SANU) in 1986, recalled the alleged grievances and sufferings Serbs had endured in a united socialist Yugoslavia and spelled out the demand for a Greater Serbia as a cure-all for Serbs' political ills. Milošević adopted the document as a blueprint for his politics (*Večernje novosti*, 24 September 1986). Yet, the *SANU Memorandum* was only one step in Milošević's securing of the support of Serbia's intellectual community. Promoting Dobrica Ćosić to the rump Yugoslav federal presidency also enhanced Milošević's public image and his claim to be the defender of Serbia's, as opposed to Yugoslavia's, national interest (Ramet, 1996: 199–200). Significantly, Ćosić had risen to prominence as a nationalist author and, notably, as one of the guiding lights behind the *Memorandum*.

Intellectuals in politics

Milošević's alliance with the intellectuals did not stop with Ćosić. When Milošević needed socially credible defenders for his policy of creating a Greater Serbia, he sponsored conferences in which intellectuals lined up to confer support on expansionist aims, ethnic cleansing and other aspects of the nationalist cause. Just how much weight intellectuals carry in Balkan societies, and in a Serbia where, well into the twentieth century, most people still remained peasants almost totally isolated from emerging political and intellectual trends (Lederer, 1969: 406), was summed up by one author:

> Where the ability to obtain an education has long been associated with freedom from the oppressive rule of a foreign tyranny, attending school and learning to read and write have been regarded as privileges to be cherished, not obligations to be endured. Writers, teachers, and professors [in Serbia] have enjoyed a prestige not always bestowed on their colleagues in other countries . . . Professors have been leaders in the political and economic life of the country (Turosienski, 1949: 230–1).

On 28 March 1992, Milošević's aim to determine the course of Bosnian politics became unequivocally clear as, in Sarajevo, some five hundred delegates attended what is now known as the First Congress of Serbian Intellectuals, with a mandate to find a solution to what was called 'the Yugoslav crisis' (*Borba*, 30 March 1992). In reality, the conference was no neutral gathering of intellectuals, but a carefully orchestrated political affair meant to signal to Bosnian Serb leader Radovan Karadžić that Belgrade was offering its support for his refusal, and all that it implied, to recognize the government of Bosnia and Herzegovina's declaration of independence from what was left of Yugoslavia by March 1992. In short, Milošević was unambiguously and publicly committed now to incorporating Serb-populated areas in Croatia and Bosnia and Herzegovina into a highly centralized Serbia proper.

In addition to winning the support of ultra-nationalist politicians such as Šešelj within Serbia and Karadžić in Bosnia, and of their followers, and of intellectuals as well, Milošević also exerted media control. This enabled him to portray the emerging conflict in such a way as undoubtedly to influence the views of ordinary followers of Serbian media, whether they resided in rump Yugoslavia or on territory held by rebel Serb forces in Croatia or Bosnia. Invariably, the Serbian state-controlled media depicted ethnic Serbs, throughout the territories of the former Yugoslavia, as the passive and wholly innocent victims of aggression and of genocidal ethnic groups. In media campaigns, constant repetition of terms such as *Ustaša*, a pejorative label describing Croats and harking back to the (again) genocidal, fascist Croatian puppet regime of World War II, distorted the real picture but undoubtedly served to reproduce a sense of victimization in the collective Serbian psyche. That such propaganda had the dual effect of winning over public support for ethnic cleansing, and in such a way that at least some of those who carried it out at the very lowest rungs thought it justifiable, is suggested by personal testimony. In one account of the Serbian attack on the Croatian city of Vukovar, it was reported that there was at least 'one very young lady in a military uniform, the mother of two children, also [among the] volunteers, who answered, when asked about why she decided to go to war: "Well now, when I watch television I see what's going on and I want to help, and that's worth making sacrifices for ... [since] this, our Serbia, is [worth] my life" ' (Lalić, 1995: 82).

Breaking alliances

By mid-1993, however, Milošević began putting the brake on his unqualified support for the regional war effort, and distanced himself from his ultra-nationalist allies. By becoming the advocate and most powerful supporter of the Serbs and their aggression throughout former Yugoslavia, Milošević had earned criticism and condemnation from the international community – a pattern repeated in 1999 over ethnic cleansing in Kosovo – and had made Serbia an international pariah subjected to an economic sanctions regime, imposed in May 1992.

As regards political allies, it was the relationship with the SRS that had to be jettisoned. By October 1993, relations between the SRS and the SPS had deteriorated to the point where the former was on the verge of mustering enough votes in the *skupština* (legislature) to win a no confidence vote. In Šešelj's view, Milošević had neglected his duty to defend the ideal of a Greater Serbia. Milošević, though, almost effortlessly defused what appeared to be a political crisis. Debate on the relevant motion began on 7 October but was suspended on 18 October, owing to a parliamentary recess, and was to resume a week later. Milošević, however, used the time afforded by the recess to dissolve parliament and call for elections for December. Throughout the course of the subsequent electoral campaign, Milošević attempted to remake his image. The break with the ultra-nationalists, specifically the SRS, allowed the Serbian president to shift attention from his involvement in the atrocities in the war-torn former Yugoslavia. Seemingly overnight, the SRS went, at the hands of the Belgrade propaganda machine, from being a reliable ally to a haven for war criminals. During the election campaign, Serbian government media reports began stressing that Šešelj was involved in war atrocities. One correspondent working with the Yugoslav Army, Mirko Jovicević, told *Borba* that Šešelj's *Četniks* were answerable for the 'slaughter' of numerous civilians and plundering from defenceless villagers in Bosnia and Herzegovina (*Borba*, 11 November 1993).

Milošević's *de facto* abandonment of ultra-nationalist ideology was accompanied by some quick concrete action. In a letter to the Bosnian Serb leadership, dated 2 August 1994, Milošević warned Radovan Karadžić that Belgrade would withdraw all material support for the Bosnian Serbs in the event that they failed to accept an internationally mediated peace accord which effectively granted them jurisdiction of 49 per cent of Bosnia and Herzegovina (*Politika*, 3 August 1994). Only two days later, Milošević announced sanctions, saying that the River Drina border separating the *Republika Srpska* (RS) from rump Yugoslavia would be closed to everything but humanitarian aid (*Tanjug*, 4 August 1994). While the blockade was far from airtight, Milošević now did very little to retreat from his newly projected image as regional peace broker.

In the summer of 1995, Croatia launched operations Blitz and Storm to reclaim territory held by rebel Serbs once staunchly backed by Belgrade. But, Milošević refused to respond to calls from extremists who insisted that Belgrade's 'national interest' dictated that rump Yugoslavia provide total support to the Serbs in Croatia – including going so far as to bomb Zagreb – in defence of the Croatian Serbs' state, the so-called Republic of Serbian Krajina (*Beta*, 4 August 1995). Faced by Croatia's military offensive, Milošević therefore offered no significant military aid to his former Serb clients (Reuters and *Politika*, 3 August 1995).

That the tide of Milošević's policies had turned against them became apparent to the ultra-nationalists. Speaking on behalf of the SSJ on 10 June 1996, its deputy vice-president, Borislav Pelević, conceded therefore that relations between rump Yugoslavia and Croatia ought to be normalized. As regards the 1995 losses of the Croatian Serbs, Pelević said that all nationalist Serbs everywhere had to face the reality that, 'The war is over. The Serbs have lost.' While recognizing that the ultra-nationalist dream of retaining all the territory that had been conquered had to be forsaken, Pelević also hinted, in not so subtle terms, that it was a reality that did not have to be accepted with any degree of decorum or pleasure: 'We are not happy to have the Croats as neighbours ... but as things are we must co-operate with them' (*Pursuing Balkan Peace*, 18 June 1996).

Even the SRS now accepted that the main objective of the party had to be amended to accommodate and reflect new realities. The independent Belgrade daily *Naša Borba* reported that, while the party had not abandoned the aim of a Greater Serbia, it would for the time being advocate policies which could help consolidate Belgrade's control over the Bosnian Serb entity, the *Republika Srpska*, as defined in the Dayton Peace Accord. The SRS resolved that,

> in these times it is of utmost importance to protect what's left; and as for the return of ... lost parts of the *Republika Srpska* and Serbian Krajina, that will have to wait for a change of regime in Serbia and for a change in the balance of power ... in the international community (*Naša Borba*, 25 March 1996).

Dual ideologies

Clearly, for Milošević, staying in power means more than defining and refining his identity in accordance with the tenets of one specific ideology. For him, the tactics of maintaining power mean that different times and circumstances necessitate emphasizing different ideologies, but never expressly renouncing one or the other. Speech-making and politicking which play up apparently incompatible objectives have, therefore, been characteristic of the Milošević leadership.

Milošević has had no better ally in this respect than the intellectuals. On 22 April 1994, an estimated 1400 intellectuals and prominent political figures met in Belgrade for a two-day conference dubbed the Second Congress of Serbian Intellectuals. According to the propaganda outlining the purpose of the gathering, the event was not intended to be a forum for discussion of politics in the region. Instead, it was supposed to be a meeting in which individuals could outline their personal opinions regarding 'the situation of the Serbian nation in the world today' (*Borba*, 22 April 1994). As expected, many prominent intellectuals ignored the injunction, and the proceedings became a showcase for promulgating ultra-nationalist sentiments. For his part, Mihailo Marković, one-time chief SPS ideologue, contended that the question of political unity was paramount, stressing that 'the first and most important principle of national politics must be the complete union of all ethnic Serbs' (*Politika*, 22 April 1994).

Most intellectuals joined in the chorus, avowing their ideological sympathies and defending the idea of a Greater Serbia. Besides the nationalist rhetoric, there was intolerance towards anyone who dared argue to the contrary. Vuk Drašković, leader of the Serbian Renewal Movement (SPO) opposition, was at one point nearly physically dragged off the speakers' podium for attempting to address the issue of Serb-backed ethnic cleansing in Bosnia (*Süddeutsche Zeitung*, 26 April 1994). Nevertheless, several innocuous press statements emerged, suggesting that the influence of the ultra-nationalists was being rejected, despite their enthusiasm for the nationalist cause at the gathering. According to state-run press coverage of the affair, the congress afforded 'no opportunities for national politics or [formulation] of a national programme, which are rightly in the domain of political and parliamentary institutions' (*Borba*, 22 April 1994).

The intellectuals, however, did not seem quite to gauge how the regime was restructuring its policies. Nearly two years later, though, it became clear that the Second Congress had served as the platform through which the intellectuals were discredited, and this must have eventually dawned on the conference participants. The political influence they wielded was now relegated to the margins. The one-time Milošević stalwarts were restricted to voicing their support for the international pariah and indicted war criminal, but self-proclaimed defender of a Greater Serbia, Bosnian Serb leader Radovan Karadžić. The intellectuals were swiftly marginalized and, for their lack of vision, must shoulder much of the blame for this development. On 10 June 1996, *Naša Borba* published a copy of a manifesto signed by twenty intellectuals, many of whom were prominent organizers of the Second Congress. Under the headline, 'There Is No Peace without the

Leader of All the Serbs', the signatories underscored both their rupture with official Belgrade policy and their disapproval of the terms of the Dayton Peace Accord, the agreement which effectively brought a halt to the Bosnian conflict at the end of 1995, but which the Serb side still maintains provides for the existence of a Bosnian Serb state within Bosnia. According to the manifesto statement, 'President of *Republika Srpska*, Dr Radovan Karadžić, did not during the course of the civil war on ... the territory of Bosnia and Herzegovina issue a single decree ... [calling for] the genocide or ethnic cleansing of Muslim and Croat enemies.' The intellectuals also insisted that Karadžić, and not Milošević, was the genuine architect of a real and lasting peace, noting that 'on 17 December 1992 the assembly of the *Republika Srpska* issued a statement, calling for an end to war, which contained the genuine aspirations of the Serbian people for an end to hostilities and for co-operation with the international community'. Mihailo Marković was among the signatories, as well as the internationally known Serbian historian Milorad Ekmečić.

Among Milošević's main accomplishments was the alienation of the intellectuals, from the time of the Second Congress, from the public policy sphere. In effect, Milošević signalled his intention early on, using the state media to deliver the message, subtly at first, that the intellectuals' defence of nationalistic ideology was *passé*. Thus, even though much of the congress was dedicated to displays of extremist rhetoric, the gathering's underlying purpose, in so far as the regime was concerned, was to begin the public discrediting of the ultra-nationalist faithful.

Clouding the message

Milošević has at times muddied his own rhetoric, infusing it with mixed slogans or old ideological baggage. Thus throughout 1994, the regime continued sending out unambiguous signals that it intended to redress its image as a bastion of ultra-nationalism. This was clear from Milošević's announced break with Karadžić, who continued to defend both ethnic cleansing and a Greater Serbia. At the same time, 1994 was a notable year for contradictory Serbian propaganda; while the regime disavowed its connections to the unsavoury cultural residue from the recent ultra-nationalist past, it almost simultaneously promoted the idea of national pride. Billed as 'Serbia's Year of Culture', 1994 witnessed officialdom rejecting the xenophobic lyrics and music clogging up the radio airwaves. So-called turbo-folk, a blend of popular music and Balkan beats, was dying, if not dead, and Belgrade expended resources on classical concerts and advertising campaigns designed to encourage visits to museums.

Campaigns to present Serbia in the most favourable light as a bastion of multiculturalism and ethnic harmony were now the order of the day. On

23–24 June 1994, for example, SPS deputy chairman Goran Perčević and the deputy leader of the largest political authority of the so-called Shadow State of Kosovo, Fehmi Agani of the Democratic League of Kosovo, met for dialogue. It was here that an opportunity presented itself for Perčević to flaunt the assertion that Serbia was 'a civil society' (*Beta*, 29 June 1994).

But what also marked the summer of 1994 was a spirited and short-lived revival of Milošević as leader of the ultra-nationalist cause. One event was the dedication of a major construction project, and the timing was impeccable. On 7 July, coinciding with Serbia's Uprising Day, commemorating the republic's revolt against World War II Nazi occupation, Milošević opened the Vukov Spomenik metro station. The Serbian president consciously revived national pride, declaring the monument doubly impressive as it represented,

> the fact that our country has realised such a project at a time when it was under a complete international blockade and unprecedented pressure from outside. [All that] proves that [nothing] could prevent Belgrade getting this most beautiful and most modern underground station in Europe ... I am certain that all this and all these projects being realised throughout Serbia ... show a picture of a future, modern, developed, democratic, prosperous Serbia as it will undoubtedly be very soon (Reuters, 7 July 1995).

However, Milošević's flamboyant propaganda and rhetoric faded into the background with the year. By the following year, and certainly by 1996, he refocused on a toned-down rhetoric stressing the country's commitment to reform and democracy. Concerned to underwrite his image as a moderate, Milošević backed legislation that in effect pardoned draft dodgers. The federal parliament approved an amnesty law for about 12,500 conscripts, covering those who had deserted or failed to serve in the wars in Croatia and Bosnia and Herzegovina from 1991 to 1995 (*Naša Borba* and *Politika*, 19 June 1996). Only professional soldiers and officers who fled were exempted from the amnesty, and they could be punished by imprisonment for up to ten years, if convicted of desertion.

Milošević continued with his own image remoulding, signalling that he was prepared to become a player in the international community by recognizing Macedonia. That decision came on 8 April 1996, when federal Foreign Minister Milan Milutinović met his Macedonian counterpart Ljubomir Frckovski in Belgrade and signed an accord on normalizing relations and facilitating bilateral trade. The move was evidently the prerequisite for Belgrade to be extended diplomatic recognition, which was quickly conferred by a number of European Union states. On 22 April, Finland became the tenth country to extend recognition, following France, Britain, Sweden, Denmark, Norway, the Netherlands, Portugal, Italy and Germany (Krause and Markotich, 1996: 54–7). In a related set of developments, on 7 August

1996, Milošević and Tuđman met in Greece, their first official face-to-face meeting since Croatia's independence in 1991. Only two weeks later, on 23 August, the Croatian and Yugoslav foreign ministers, Mate Granić and Milan Milutinović, met to sign a normalization accord. Already, in October 1994, Milošević had been rewarded with the partial lifting of sanctions against Belgrade, following his professed rupture of relations with the Bosnian Serb leadership.

Perhaps the starkest testament to his commitment to abandoning ultra-nationalist rhetoric and ideology was Milošević's ever-closer alliance with the political organization headed by his wife, Mirjana. In the federal and Montenegrin elections held on 3 November 1996, JUL and the SPS ran in coalition federally, along with the support of a minor third party, New Democracy (ND). Formed after the previous elections, JUL had held no parliamentary seats, but the coalition of the three now picked up 64 of the 138 federal seats. Milošević's main Montenegrin allies, the Democratic Socialist Party, won 20 seats. The leading opposition coalition *Zajedno* (Together), made up of Zoran Đinđić's Democratic Party (DS), Drašković's SPO and Vesna Pesić's Serbian Civic Alliance (GSS), won 22 seats. The remaining seats were divided among six other minor parties and coalitions (*Borba*, 7 November 1996).

Even earlier, JUL was placed in a position where it could influence government decision-making. On 28 May 1996, Serbian premier Mirko Marjanović announced a cabinet shuffle. Nedeljko Šipovac replaced Ivko Đonović as Minister of Agriculture and Deputy Premier. Dušan Kanazir replaced Slobodan Unković as Minister of Science, while Milivoje Stamatović took over Labour and Veterans' Affairs from Jovan Radić. Svetolik Kostadinović replaced Aleksa Jokić in Transportation and Communication and, finally, Aleksandar Tijanić replaced Ratomir Vico as Minister of Information. All cabinet newcomers, and Tijanić especially, maintained ties with, if not direct membership of, Marković's JUL (*Naša Borba*, 28 and 29 May 1996).

Milošević's reversion to promoting socialist values and paying homage to Tito's regime in no way suggested that he was, rhetoric notwithstanding, committed to democratization or to reform. While nationalist rhetoric was in abeyance, it had not been disavowed, and certainly what had not been changed were Milošević's authoritarian methods of governing. On 17 November 1996, local elections were held across Serbia. The opposition *Zajedno* coalition won outright majorities in Serbia's twelve largest municipalities, but the regime reacted to this by at first refusing to recognize the returns, an act triggering a show of public disaffection. Beginning on 18 November, a series of mass protests were launched, with demonstrators initially demanding that the authorities recognize the municipal returns, and later calling for Milošević to resign.

At first, Milošević's main attack against the protests came through the mass media, with the authorities striving to depict the demonstrators as subversive, and a dangerous threat to public order (Radio and Television Serbia, 18 November 1996). Milošević also attempted to prove how destabilizing the marches and protests were, but ultimately such tactics failed to win over public sympathy. On 20 January 1997, for example, he sought to demonstrate the threat to law and order by using Belgrade and republican police to attack protesters (Radio B 92, 20 January 1997). But with peaceful and orderly marches a daily occurrence, and with international and local independent media providing timely and accurate information about developments, he seemingly overplayed his hand this time. Rather than succumbing to the intimidation, protesters continued to fill the streets, with at least 200,000 people marching in the Serbian capital on each of several days. Finally, in mid-February, the regime backed off, recognizing opposition wins in fourteen municipalities and attempting to show deference to the public wish for political reform by demoting or ousting politicians advocating a hard line against the demonstrators, including Minister of Information Tijanić. For his part, Đinđić became mayor of Belgrade, the first non-communist to hold that post in just over fifty years. Subsequently, even Vuk Drašković (see above) became a deputy premier in Milošević's regime, only to fall out over strategy in Kosovo in 1999.

Conclusion: Serbian extremism and the Kosovo tragedy

Serbian extremism, in whatever incarnation, is the product of strong top-down political leadership, and the type of political currency which can most effectively be invoked in societies where social groups may have little, if any, protection against political norms being defined and disseminated from above (Gruenwald, 1983: 285). Serbian and Balkan societies, in general, are open to such phenomena, since there is no overriding or unifying social consensus which might immunize the body politic against leaders who infuse their political agendas with extremist radicalism. Serbian right-wing extremism may certainly have some superficial resemblance to other regional forms of political extremism. However, the home-grown Serbian variant is fluid and constantly mutating. Its ideological content is flexible – as an examination of the evolution of Milošević's political manoeuvring shows. From his early career beginning in 1987 to perhaps late 1993, Milošević was the guiding force behind Serbian expansionist nationalism. He then set aside ultra-rightist ideology in favour of a return to a socialist brand of intolerance harking back to the days of Tito's Yugoslavia. In July 1997, although constitutionally barred from seeking a third term as Serbian president, he managed to secure a lease on his political career by having the federal parliament elect him to the post of the federal presidency. Reports concerning this development also said that the federal parliament did not approve Milošević's efforts to secure constitutional amendments granting the presidency virtually unlimited powers (Radio and Television Serbia, 15 and 16 July 1997).

In March 1999, NATO began its air campaign against the regime of Yugoslav president Slobodan Milošević. At issue was the safety of the ethnic Albanian population of Kosovo. Talks in Rambouillet in February 1999 and in Paris in March did not persuade Milošević to give in to the international community's demand for a troop presence, regarded as the guarantee for regional peace and the mechanism that would bring a measure of safety to the ethnic Albanian population in the once autonomous province. Hindsight now suggests that Milošević even welcomed the air attacks, using them as the pretext for launching the worst ethnic cleansing campaign in contemporary Balkan history. With the war six weeks old, an estimated 88 per cent of Kosovo's population had been displaced,[1] with the bulk forced to seek refuge in neighbouring Albania and Macedonia. From the very start of the war, and indeed throughout the year of its buildup, the Milošević regime was careful to use its propaganda machinery to inform the Serbian public that Belgrade was by no means anti-Albanian. Rather, the problem that needed to be addressed was that of the Kosovo Liberation Army (KLA), an alleged group of terrorists aiming to wrench Kosovo out of the rightful boundaries of the Federal Republic of Yugoslavia. The Serbian public, fed countless reports of the terrorist KLA, was conditioned to equate the term 'Albanian' with 'terrorist'. Milošević's chilling Kosovo campaign is colossal testimony to his two-track approach of incorporating ethnic hatred and nationalism alongside multiculturalism, as planks in his ethnic nationalism. On 22 May 1999, the United Nations' Tribunal for War Crimes in Former Yugoslavia charged Milošević and four of his top aides with human rights atrocities: planning, organizing and carrying out, since the beginning of the year, the mass deportation of Kosovo Albanians and the killings of hundreds of defenceless civilians. This was the first time that a sitting head of state had been formally indicted as a war criminal.

Notes

1. Estimate made by former deputy premier and leader of the Serbian Renewal Movement (SPO) Vuk Drašković, reported by Radio M (Sarajevo), 22 April 1999.

References

Banac, I. (1984) *The National Question in Yugoslavia: Origins, History, Politics.* Ithaca, NY: Cornell University Press.

Bennett, C. (1995) *Yugoslavia's Bloody Collapse: Causes, Course and Consequences.* New York: New York University Press.

Brown, J. F. (1992) *Nationalism, Democracy, and Security in the Balkans*. Brookfield, VT: Dartmouth.

Burg, S. L. and Berbaum, M. L. (1984) 'Community, Stability and Integration in Multinational Yugoslavia', *American Political Science Review* 83(2), 536–54.

Cohen, L. J. (1995) *Broken Bonds: The Disintegration of Yugoslavia*, 2nd edition. Boulder, CO: Westview Press.

Čubrilović, V. (1958) *Istorija politicke misli u Srbiji XIX veka*. Belgrade: Prosveta.

Glenny, M. (1992) *The Fall of Yugoslavia: The Third Balkan War*. London: Penguin.

Glenny, M. (1999) 'Slobodan's basic instinct', *Observer* (London), 18 April.

Gruenwald, O. (1983) *The Yugoslav Search for Man*. South Hadley, MA: J.F. Bergin.

Halpern, J. M. (1958) *A Serbian Village*. New York: Columbia University Press.

Jelavich, B. (1983) *A History of the Balkans*, Vol. 2. Cambridge: Cambridge University Press.

Krause, S. (1995) 'Greece: Redefining Neighbourly Relations', *Transition* 1(21), 17 November.

Krause, S. and Markotich, S. (1996) 'Rump Yugoslavia and Macedonia Deal the Cards of Mutual Recognition', *Transition* 2(11), 31 May.

Lalić, L. (1995) *Tri TV Godine u Srbiji*. Belgrade: Nezavisni Sindikat Medija.

Lederer, I. J. (1969) 'Nationalism and the Yugoslavs', in Sugar, P. F. and Lederer, I. J. (eds) *Nationalism in Eastern Europe*. Seattle: University of Washington Press.

Markotich, S. (1993) 'Serbia Prepares for Elections', *RFE/RL Research Report* 2(49), 10 December.

Milošević, S. (1989) *Godine raspleta*, 5th edition. Balgrade: Beogradski izdavačko-graficki zavod.

Petrovich, M. B. (1976) *A History of Modern Serbia*. New York: Harcourt Brace Jovanovich.

Ramet, S. P. (1996) *Balkan Babel: The Disintegration of Yugoslavia from the Death of Tito to Ethnic War*, 2nd edition. Boulder, CO: Westview Press.

Silber, L. and Little, A. (1995) *The Death of Yugoslavia*. London: Penguin.

Singleton, F. (1976) *Twentieth Century Yugoslavia*. New York: Columbia University Press.

Tepevac, M. (1994) *Demokratija ili despotija*. Belgrade: CIP Štampa.

Thompson, M. (1992) *A Paper House: The Ending of Yugoslavia*. New York: Pantheon.

Turosienski, S.K. (1949) 'Education', in Kerner, R. J. (ed.) *Yugoslavia*. Berkeley: University of California Press.

Woodward, S. (1995) *Balkan Tragedy: Chaos and Dissolution after the Cold War*. Washington, DC: Brookings Institution.

Press and media (various dates)

Beta news agency
Borba (daily)
Montena-fax news agency

Naša Borba (daily)
NIN (weekly)
Politika (daily)
Pursuing Balkan Peace: Open Media Research Institute (OMRI) Special Report (weekly)
Radio and Television Serbia
Reuters news agency
Süddeutsche Zeitung (daily)
Tanjug news agency
Večernje novosti (daily)

*Editor's postscript: In January 2000, Arkan was shot and killed by an assassin in a Belgrade hotel.

CHAPTER THIRTEEN

The politics of anger: the extreme right in the United States

Michael Cox and Martin Durham

Introduction

In recent years, the term 'extreme right' has been applied to a considerable array of American political phenomena. For example, Pat Buchanan, who ran for the Republican nomination as president in 1992 and 1996 and is shaping to run again in 2000, has been described by many as an extreme rightist. His call for an 'America First' foreign policy has been compared with the America First Committee, which in 1941 tried to keep America from going to war against Nazi Germany. Similarly, his pronouncements on immigration controls and 'Western civilization' vividly express nativist impulses that have surfaced time and again in American politics for over a century. The Christian Right in the United States has also been viewed as being on the extreme right. Vehemently opposed to abortion, feminism and gay rights, organizations such as Christian Coalition have achieved a prominent position in the Republican Party, and much publicity has been generated by the writings of its leading figure, the religious broadcaster Pat Robertson, who claims that the United States is under attack from a conspiracy involving secret societies and international financiers. The notion of a huge conspiracy and the belief that the true values of the nation are being undermined (either from without or from within) are an equally important component part of the ideology of those paramilitary formations known generically as the Militias. Active in a number of states since 1994 and propelled into the limelight by the horrific bombing of an Oklahoma federal building in 1995, the Militias, it is argued, represent the most brutal face of the extreme right in the United States today.

Our brief list alerts us to an obvious definitional problem – namely, who or what should be included under the umbrella term, the American 'extreme right'? Historically, the concept has been applied to a multitude of rather different political parties, groups and individuals. Thus, in the 1930s, it was used to describe the populist and anti-semitic demagogue Father Coughlin (Cremoni, 1998); in the 1950s, the anti-communist Joseph McCarthy; and a decade later, Senator Goldwater and his ill-fated and ill-timed 1964 campaign for the presidency. The term has also been applied to the once influential John Birch Society, the American neo-Nazi movement, as well as the Ku Klux Klan. In this chapter, we will certainly not apply the term to every right-wing manifestation. In our opinion, some sections of the American right are best seen as conservative; others as ultra-conservative or 'radical' in their views. Only for some should we reserve the term extreme right. Not always easily distinguishable from the other strands on the right, the American extreme right rarely calls for the imposition of a dictatorship; and though often anti-semitic, some on the right today seem less hostile to what many have traditionally seen as the 'Zionist occupation of America' than they are to the federal government itself. Furthermore, while many extremists define themselves as militant Christians (hardly surprising in a country where organized Christianity has been and remains so central to American identity), it would be wrong to assume that Christian theology motivates them. A distorted form of Christianity may provide some extremists with a vocabulary. Christianity, however, is not their driving ideology. By the same token, it would be quite misleading to assume that all those who manipulate race for political purposes are extreme rightists. If this were the case, then we would have to place Richard Nixon, Ronald Reagan and George Bush in the extremist camp. That said, race is central to the worldview of the extreme right, who believe that the United States was and should remain a white man's land; that white people are biologically superior; and that what they call 'white civilization' is under threat and has to be defended by all means necessary. Paranoid in style and often violent by inclination, the extreme right today clearly stands on the margins of American politics. However, this should not lead us to underestimate this sometimes heavily armed and occasionally very dangerous movement. Nor should we ignore its ability to exploit the anxieties of those in the white community who feel increasingly alienated from the political system and marginalized by irreversible social changes which are leaving many in society without purpose or meaning.

Basically, three groupings or strands will receive the greater part of our attention here. One, which straddles the boundary between radical right and the extreme right, is the Patriot movement – of which the Militias are a part. Another is National Socialism. A third, which we shall now go on to discuss in some historical detail, is the oldest and best-known form of the extreme right: the Ku Klux Klan. Born out of the calamity of the American Civil War, it has persisted over time and even today forms an important core of the violent right in the United States.

The origins of the Ku Klux Klan

One aspect of what has been termed American exceptionalism was the persistence of the institution of slavery, that peculiarly pre-capitalist social form adapted to capitalist purposes following the development of tobacco-growing in Virginia during the seventeenth century, and cotton in the states south of the Mason–Dixon line. Tragically, the abolition of slavery left the South economically shredded and morally bruised, and its white inhabitants determined to reassert their dominance over the newly emancipated black population. The Ku Klux Klan was to be a key instrument in this process of reassertion (Trelease, 1972).

The original Klan was not simply some quaint, rather oddly dressed group of nightriders standing on the edge of southern society – even less the romantic defenders of a misunderstood oppressed civilization portrayed in D. W. Griffith's 'rampantly racist' film *Birth of a Nation* (Wright, 1976: 28). Rather, it was an organized conspiracy whose primary objective was to restore white supremacy after the Civil War (Horn, 1939). First established in 1865 when six ex-confederate soldiers met in their home town of Pulaski, Tennessee, the aims of the Klan were never in doubt: to force reforming northerners out of the Confederacy and to destroy every vestige of nascent black political power in the southern states. The ideology of the Klan was explicitly supremacist. As stated in 1867, the 'maintenance of the supremacy of the White Race in this Republic' was its 'main and fundamental objective'. Moreover, only those who were opposed to 'social and political equality for Negroes' and who fought 'Congressional advocates of harsh Reconstruction measures' would be considered for membership of the organization (Anti-Defamation League [ADL] 1988a: 75).

In the pursuit of these goals between 1867 and 1871, the Klan instituted a relentless reign of terror throughout all the states of the former Confederacy. In 1871, a Joint Congressional Committee conducted an extensive investigation of Klan violence. It revealed that in the four-year period, the Klan had been responsible for hundreds, possibly thousands, of black deaths. According to one estimate, in a single county of northern Florida alone, over 150 black men had been murdered by Klansmen in a few months. The commanding general of federal troops in Texas reported that 'murders of negroes' were so common 'as to render it impossible to keep accurate accounts of them' (ADL, 1988a: 75).

The results achieved by the Klan and other secret organizations such as the Knights of the White Camelia, the Society of the White Rose and the '76 Association should not be underestimated (Carman and Syrett, 1952: 32; Brogan, 1986: 378). First, white terror almost completely aborted reform in the South. It also frightened a large number of blacks away from the polls and in this way guaranteed a white political monopoly. Finally, over the longer term, it created a violent pattern for regulating relations between the races in the United States that was to persist for nearly a century (Mecklin, 1924; Lowe, 1967; Rice, 1962; Fisher, 1980; Wade, 1987).

The rise and fall of the 'second' Klan

After lying dormant and inactive following its first bout of frenzied activity, the Klan was reborn in 1915 'under a blazing fiery torch' on top of Stone Mountain, near Atlanta. Colonel William Joseph Simmons, the founder of the new Klan, had for a long time given serious thought to the creation of an order standing for 'comprehensive Americanism' throughout the Republic. Fascinated from boyhood by the romantic story of the old Klan of Reconstruction days, he called his order the Knights of the Ku Klux Klan. The new Klan was as uncompromisingly racist as its predecessor. As one of its booklets, *Ideals of the Knights of the Ku Klux Klan*, made clear, 'this is a White man's organization ... teaching the doctrine of White Supremacy'. The booklet even invoked Christ in the holy cause, insisting that 'all of Christian Civilization depends upon the preservation and up-building of the White Race' (ADL, 1988a: 76).

The reactivated Klan was different from its predecessor, however, in at least two important ways. First, it extended its range of targets. Jews, Catholics, non-Aryan foreigners and socialists were now regarded as enemies by the Klan. Expressing and in turn attempting to fan the nativist reaction to mass Catholic and Jewish immigration into the country before 1914, the Klan thus became as anti-semitic, anti-Catholic and anti-foreigner as it had always been anti-black. The Klan also attacked people considered immoral or traitors to the white race. Indeed, all those who deviated from a strict conservative norm were regarded as legitimate targets (MacLean, 1994). Second, the new Klan managed to extend its influence outside the South – and by the mid-1920s had become a national organization, a reflection of the unsettled conditions in America following World War I, during which a conservative, xenophobic reaction swept the country. Although estimates vary, at the peak of its power in 1925, Klan membership may have reached as high as 5 million. In certain northern states such as Indiana and Ohio, Klan membership was actually larger than in any single state in the South (Jackson, 1967).

In the first half of the 1920s at least, the Klan's impact upon US political life was considerable. Many communities fell directly under Klan control. In 1922, Texas voters even sent Klansman Earl Mayfield to the US Senate. Klan campaigns also helped defeat two Jewish congressmen who had headed an inquiry into Klan activities in 1921. Klan efforts were credited with helping to elect governors in Georgia, Alabama, California, Indiana and Oregon. In Colorado, Arkansas, Oklahoma and Ohio, too, the Klan acquired influence. During the 1924 presidential campaign, the Klan was particularly active, and its leader, Hiram Wesley Evans, later claimed that it had helped secure the re-election of Calvin Coolidge. He even boasted that the Klan had been instrumental in forcing a tightening-up in US immigration laws when the quota allowing 'minorities' into the country was lowered to a mere 2 per cent (Miller, 1958: 355). Yet the new Klan, 'which in 1924 seemed to be sweeping all before it', quickly faded as a real force in the land (Brogan, 1986: 519). By 1926, membership had dropped by nearly 60 per cent, to slightly more than 2 million. A year later it had fallen again, this time quite catastrophically to 350,000. By 1930, the organization had little more than 35,000 members. Throughout the 1930s, Klan numbers then fell annually until, in 1941, membership stood at less than 10,000.

There were several reasons for this decline. In part it was due to the outbreak of schismatic divisions within the organization, which in turn led to damaging revelations about the Klan's violent activities. Friends in high (and low) office, fearful of being associated with the Klan, then began to desert their old ally, hence removing its respectable cover. Equally importantly, during the 1920s, immigration declined significantly, thus undermining the Klan's message that the United States was being swamped by foreigners. There is some indication too that the continuing economic boom of the 1920s did much to weaken its appeal. The Depression, it is true, did lead to a certain resurgence on the extreme right, though ironically for the anti-Catholic Klan, much of this was centred on the radio broadcasts of a Michigan Catholic priest, Father Charles E. Coughlin. Coughlin indeed managed to build up a substantial following with his attacks on the machinations of international finance and the inadequacies (or worse) of Franklin Roosevelt, denunciations that were increasingly laced with anti-semitism (Cremoni, 1998). A considerably smaller following gathered around the strange figure of William Dudley Pelley, who in 1933 formed the Silver Shirts, which sought to emulate Germany's storm-troopers. The Silver Shirts had the somewhat unusual feature of receiving – Pelley claimed – a message of support from Christ himself. Other such organizations surfaced, and in 1940 the Klan even held a joint camp with the German–American Bund, the official face of National Socialism in the United States.

The war against the Axis after 1941 inevitably did great damage to the cause of right-wing extremism. Indeed, following the United States' entry into the war, the Catholic Church finally silenced Coughlin. Pelley and others like him were prosecuted as Nazi sympathizers, and the Ku Klux Klan was temporarily dissolved following the demand that it pay a massive tax bill dating back to its heyday. The extreme right was thus checked and was not to re-emerge again until the 1950s – in response to the rise of its ancient foe: the demand for black equality in the South.

The Klan and the civil rights movement

The history of the rise of the civil rights movement in the United States after World War II is one which has been told many times before. The story is one of political frustration and betrayal by Congress which finally impelled the main civil rights organization – the National Association for the Advancement of Colored People (NAACP) – to turn to the courts for redress. This resulted in the landmark decision by the US Supreme Court in May 1954, *Brown v. Board of Education*. In this, the court declared against separate, ostensibly equal, educational facilities. A year later, the court then ruled that segregated school districts in seventeen states and the District of Columbia should implement desegregation programmes. From the point of view of the old South, these moves were tantamount to a revolution from above. What made the situation all the more threatening was the parallel rise of a mass civil rights campaign (O'Neill, 1971).

In this highly charged atmosphere, where southern whites felt squeezed between, on the one hand, an establishment in Washington increasingly unsympathetic to their cause and, on the other, demands for black equality, opposition took on mass proportions. The main expression of this, the Citizens' Councils, achieved a membership of perhaps 250,000 by 1957. The Klan, too, had no difficulty in attracting new members (McMillen, 1994: 153; Zanden, 1960: 454–62). By the end of 1960, membership had grown four- or fivefold to 40,000 or 50,000. It then remained steady for the next five years (in 1965 the Klan had 42,000 members), but during the 'long hot summer' of 1967, membership rose to 55,000.

Accompanying the growth in membership was an inevitable escalation in Klan activities against the civil rights movement in particular, and blacks in general. Significantly, whereas only six people had been slain by racists before 1960 (four in Mississippi alone), 34 died during the next eight years, including Martin Luther King. In addition, there were the 'normal' beatings, cross-burnings and floggings that bore the hallmark of the Klan. Between 1956 and 1966, the Klan and other racists were responsible for more than 1000 documented violent incidents, including the murder of civil rights activists James Cheney, Andrew Goodman and Michael Schwerner in Mississippi in June 1964 (Klanwatch, 1988: 23).

The third Klan renaissance, however, began to fade during the late 1960s. The most obvious reason for this decline was its failure to turn the tide of history. The civil rights movement was simply too strong for the forces of white reaction in the South. Many were no doubt alienated, too, by the increasing violence displayed by some of the Klan's more dangerous members. Moreover, while hostile to the civil rights movement and to the left, the FBI (Federal Bureau of Investigation) was also actively involved in efforts to disrupt the Klan (Ungar, 1976: 405–21; O'Reilly, 1989; George and Wilcox, 1992: 399–401). Indeed, as a result of its efforts (of the estimated

10,000 active Klan members in 1967, some 2000 were relaying information to the government), many key activists in the Klan were arrested and jailed, including Robert Shelton, the leader of the biggest faction. The Johnson administration also contributed to the decline of the Klan by calling upon the House Committee on Un-American Activities to investigate the organization. Its final report, *The Present Day Ku Klux Klan Movement*, released on 11 December 1967, did much to weaken the credibility of the Klan. The fact that the investigation was conducted by the House Committee on Un-American Activities made the attack all the more effective, for it clearly implied that the Klan was not just 'a hooded society of bigots' – to use Johnson's own words – but also disloyal to the American way of life.

Finally, as a result of post-war public spending and inflows of capital, the South was experiencing an economic transformation after the war. This was now threatened by the instability caused by white supremacist resistance to black demands. Herein perhaps was the biggest problem of all for the Klan. As an organization, it may indeed have expressed what many whites felt about blacks. However, the overt championing of white supremacy was increasingly out of step with the new economic and political realities.

The radical right

If the late 1950s and 1960s were to witness a short-lived resurgence for the Klan, the period was also propitious for others on the right. Conservatism, which had been effectively sidelined during World War II, experienced a resurgence during the early years of the Cold War. Motivated less by racial prejudice than by anti-communism, many of the more militant conservatives agreed with Senator McCarthy's denunciations in the early 1950s of Democrats as fellow-travellers of communism. Writers in the highly conservative *National Review* saw McCarthy as an instrument of Western will in the war against communism; the very essence of Western civilization; a freedom fighter for the truth 'that man has the free will to choose between good and evil' (Latham, 1966: 408). They also shared with him the oft-expressed and, by the early 1950s, popular view that the United States was confronted with some vast conspiracy based in Moscow but organized at all levels of American life, and that the only way to root out this insidious disease was by total ideological vigilance supported by radical political surgery on the home front. The inclination to view the world through a lens of paranoia was taken to its logical conclusion by the then dominant force on the radical right: the John Birch Society. Founded by former National Association of Manufacturers vice-president Robert H. W. Welch in 1958 (and named after an American army captain killed by Chinese Communists shortly after the end of World War II), by 1962 it had over 60,000 members, over 75 full-time workers and an annual payroll of $625,000. Prominently involved in the defeat of Nelson Rockefeller and the success of Barry Goldwater in the fight for the 1964 Republican nomination for president, the society achieved considerable notoriety, both for its conspiratorial methods and for its even more conspiratorial beliefs. Welch, like many Americans at the time, was both fascinated and repelled by communism. But, he asked, if the United States was the strongest and best country in the world, why was communism gaining ground? The answer, he concluded, was obvious: treason within the US government. Communists and their agents were everywhere. Indeed, as he proclaimed in 1961, 'communist influences were now in almost complete control of our Federal Government'. Increasingly, however, Welch was convinced that communism was not the only enemy. 'For two centuries', he came to believe, a sinister grouping, the Insiders, had been pursuing a 'strategy of world conquest'. Among its 'diabolic ... far-reaching and ... all-inclusive' tactics, he wrote, were 'the promotion of racial turmoil and riots ... the deliberate undermining of the American dollar ... the creation of the "hippie" mentality on our campuses', and the 'protection of criminals' by the Supreme Court (Mintz, 1985: 142–4; Lipset and Raab, 1978: 250–1).

The John Birch Society represented only one segment of a much wider movement. According to one source, there were over 3000 right-wing groups and publications in existence in the United States in 1965, most of them warning of the dangers of liberalism, communism in high places and social engineering of any kind (Thayer, 1967: 147). Encouraged by the atmosphere of the times to see the world as a dangerous and menacing place, these groups were (in electoral terms, at least) almost insignificant. Nonetheless, what they lacked in numbers they made up for in terms of frenetic activity. Later viewed as a genuine threat to democracy by academics of a liberal persuasion, they were in their own way a classical manifestation of a deep populist tendency in US political life. Though this expressed itself in what, to outsiders, must have seemed like an almost pathological preoccupation with a menace that was almost non-existent in the United States, the radical right's attacks on communism were in some respects only a cover which allowed the 'small man' to vent his anger against those in power, who had failed (in their opinion) to resolve the world's and the United States' problems. And though only loosely connected to the extreme right – and in the majority of cases not at all – those of a 'radical' right persuasion did create an environment that encouraged those of a more violent and racist nature to express themselves publicly.

Racist right

Three groups in particular deserve mention here, each giving rather different answers to one of the most pressing questions for racist activists –

namely, what was the relationship between their beliefs and those of National Socialism?

For the first group, the American Nazi Party, the answer was self-evident. Founded in 1958 by George Lincoln Rockwell, the party secured massive publicity by a succession of attention-grabbing stunts. (In his autobiography, the optimistically titled *This Time the World*, Rockwell had declared that by displaying the swastika and calling for gas chambers, he would make it impossible to ignore his movement.) Troubled by splits during Rockwell's lifetime, the American Nazi Party was to suffer yet more after his murder in 1967 by a dissident ex-member. The result was a splintering of a never strong movement. The largest group, the National Socialist White People's Party (NSWPP), changed its name in 1982 to the New Order, and in 1988 was estimated to have about a hundred members (ADL, 1988b: 26).

If for the American Nazi Party and its successor organizations, the racist message was openly National Socialist, another product of the 1950s, the National States Rights Party was (marginally) more cautious. Originating, as its name suggests, in the southern fight against segregation, the party's founders, J. B. Stoner and Edward R. Fields, had already long been active in white supremacist politics. Stoner, for instance, had originally been a Klan organizer and had later run as an Anti-Jewish Party candidate in the 1948 Congressional elections. Under their leadership, the National States Rights Party would persist into the 1980s, while Stoner and Fields have continued to be active (separately) since. The party, whose paper revelled in such headlines as 'Scientists Say Negro Still in Ape Stage' and 'Jews Behind Race Mixing', distributed the infamous 'Jewish Ritual Murder' edition of the 1930s Nazi paper *Der Stürmer*. But, unlike the American Nazi Party, the party did not call itself National Socialist, preferring instead to act as a hybrid between those who wanted to identify wholly with the Third Reich and those who thought that a militant American racism meant keeping a distance from its German counterpart.

The third of the groups which deserve further comment, Liberty Lobby, emerged in 1957 and appeared, at first sight, to be part of the radical right. Urging the Republican Party to take up the demands of southern whites, it cultivated links with members of Congress and gave testimony to hearings on proposed legislation. Supporting Goldwater in 1964, it suggested that the party should champion immigration controls, economic protectionism and, a pointer to its deeper concerns, the separate development of the races. But it was also drawn to a candidate who had entered a number of Democratic primaries, Alabama governor George Wallace, and in 1965 it produced *Stand Up for America*, a sympathetic portrayal which argued that, instead of running as a Democrat or an independent in 1968, Wallace should run as a Republican and bring to the party the white working-class support that Goldwater had been unable to attract. In 1968, Wallace would indeed run again. The result, however, would not only demonstrate the drawing power of his racial populist politics, but also bring to light the inner dynamics of Liberty Lobby, a group which would exert considerable influence within the extreme right in the years that followed.

Wallace and beyond

George Wallace was that most southern of American political phenomena: a genuine populist who was not in the classical sense conservative. Indeed, while at the same time attacking all manner of liberals, racial integrationists and elitist interlopers from the North, he was pushing hard for a larger public sector to improve the economic lot of white working people (Edsall and Edsall, 1992; Carter, 1995). Wallace's appeal was thus not simply to race. Nonetheless, race was critical in his campaign of 1968, and his ability to gain nearly 10 million votes as a third-party candidate in the presidential contest has been interpreted as crucial in eroding the link between the Democratic Party and much of its traditional white constituency, both in the South and elsewhere. Yet if the Republicans' incorporation of Wallace's issues and his constituency was to be damaging to the Democrats over the longer term, it was also to the detriment of the extreme right. In 1964, Goldwater had been supported by a myriad of rightist groups. But it was not the same line-up that supported the maverick Democrat governor four years later. Goldwater had been supported by the nascent conservative movement and the radical right. Wallace, running against Richard Nixon, could not expect to retain the same degree of conservative support, even if he had shared Goldwater's opposition to public spending (which he did not). Goldwater, moreover, had been wary of racial issues. Wallace, on the other hand, had been made by racial politics and was running in the aftermath of widespread riots and spiralling racial conflict. Effectively, he preached nationally what he had long practised in his home state. In these circumstances, even if he had not had associations with the Klan (one of whose leading activists was his chief speechwriter), it was all but inevitable that he would draw racist militants into his campaign. The Wallace campaign thus gave the extreme right an experience of mass politics. The subsequent disintegration of any effective vehicle to retain that support, however, would prove to be a major setback.

One attempt to retain that support, Youth for Wallace, is particularly illuminating in this regard. Formed in May 1968, it transmuted later that year into the National Youth Alliance. Urging the formation of a movement of the 'white American middle class' that would take on and destroy both the campus left and the black power movement, the group would not survive for long and, having purged those who expressed alarm at a fondness for Nazi regalia, it then broke in two. One section remained loyal to the central figure in Liberty Lobby, Willis Carto; the other, later renamed the National Alliance, supported instead a former officer in the National Socialist White People's Party, William Pierce. The National Youth Alliance was bitterly critical of mainstream conservatism and, amid its internal disarray, *National Review* was to strike back against its tormentors. Publishing extracts from correspondence in which Carto attacked 'organized Jewry' and called for the repatriating of black people to Africa, the magazine made a series of allegations that was permanently to damage his standing on more respectable sections of the right. Later, Carto would stir up yet more controversy with his central role in efforts to deny the existence of the Holocaust. He would also be a crucial figure in what would turn out to be the most important component of the American extreme right: the Patriot movement. But before we turn to the rise of the Patriots, we must briefly return to the Klan.

The Klan's last stand?

The main Klan group of the 1960s, the United Klans of America (UKA), continued as an organization into the 1970s. But when the Klan experienced a new resurgence, growing from around 5000 members to 10,000 by the end of the decade, two new groupings were to be the beneficiaries: the Knights of the Ku Klux Klan and the Invisible Empire. The former, led by David Duke, was to receive considerable publicity as the articulate and media-conscious Duke appeared on television programmes and before student audiences declaring that the new Klan was not bigoted and violent but merely wanted 'equal rights for whites'. Consciously pursuing not only a moderate but a modernizing image, by disavowing both the Klan's past anti-Catholicism and the secondary role it had usually assigned to women, Duke was ultimately to resign from the Klan in search of a more successful strategy, a quest to which we will return. The organization he left, led first by Don Black, then by Thom Robb, would prove to be the longest-lasting of the larger Klan groupings, even though Robb's attempts to eschew the Klan's violent image cost him some of his more hard-line members.

The other beneficiary of Klan resurgence in the late 1980s, the Invisible Empire, preferred to cultivate a paramilitary image and was initially to benefit from Duke's departure. Soon afterwards, however, this was cast into doubt by the revelation that its leader, Bill Wilkinson, had for some time been giving information on the Klan to the FBI. Klan membership in general began to fall by 1982, and the subsequent emergence of a new leader, James Farrands, rather than resulting in the Invisible Empire's revival, was to lead to its demise. Faced with a lawsuit for a 1987 attack on civil rights marchers in Forsyth County, Georgia, he agreed to dissolve the organization. The Invisible Empire's destruction, furthermore, had already been preceded by the demise of the United Klans of America. In 1987, the mother of one of its murder victims, Michael Donald, was awarded $7m damages because of the involvement of two of its members in his slaying. To add political insult to financial injury, the anti-Klan Southern Poverty Law Center (the architect too of the Invisible Empire's downfall) was granted possession of the UKA's Alabama headquarters as part of the final settlement.

Beyond the Klan?

The groups we have discussed are only the most prominent of a considerable and ever-changing array of Klan organizations. Former Klan activists have also attempted to create similar organizations without the disadvantages of the name. In 1979, in Greensboro, North Carolina, an alliance of Klan and Nazi activists opened fire on an anti-Klan rally, killing five left-wing demonstrators. One of those there that day, Glenn Miller, a former Special Forces master sergeant, would later turn his Carolina Knights of the Ku Klux Klan into the White Patriot Party. Similarly, in California, the state organizer for the Knights of the Ku Klux Klan, Tom Metzger, who in the late 1970s had organized a border patrol to capture Mexican immigrants trying to enter the country, left shortly afterwards to create the White American Political Association, subsequently White Aryan Resistance (WAR). The White Patriot Party was to prove short-lived, Miller himself testifying against other racist leaders at a trial in the late 1980s. Metzger would prove a more significant figure, not least for his taking up of a new constituency for organized racism: skinheads.

Like their British counterparts, American racist skinheads were responsible for a good deal of vandalism and acts of racial violence. Many of these attacks have been in southern California, but incidents have also been reported in a number of other states, including one in Wisconsin in 1988, when the Skinhead Army of Milwaukee (SHAM) set upon a group of non-racist skinheads. Nearly all the extreme right-wing groups have made a concerted effort to recruit among the 'skins', but Metzger was particularly successful. His association with them was largely driven by a belief that the 'skins' (whom he called his 'frontline warriors') had already demonstrated a willingness to use violence. His enthusiasm for them was also a function of his own political strategy. Two decades of working within the system, he maintained, had finally convinced him that the only way forward was a white revolution leading to the overthrow of a 'totally corrupt capitalist system'. The skinheads, he believed, were the natural storm-troopers for such an uprising, for they already stood outside the system.

In 1989, however, three skinheads were imprisoned, one for murder, the other two for manslaughter, following the beating to death of an Ethiopian man with a baseball bat in Portland, Oregon. The Southern Poverty Law Center and Jewish Anti-Defamation League subsequently filed a lawsuit against Metzger on the basis that the Portland group had been organized by WAR. The jury's decision to award damages of $12.5 million dollars, while it did not result in anywhere near that amount being taken from Metzger, was to cause both him and WAR serious problems in the years that followed. For WAR, as for the United Klans and the Invisible Empire, a reputation for violence had in the short term attracted recruits. In the longer term, however, it has hampered or even completely crippled their ability to propagate their racist message.

Patriots

Yet if the Klan and groups that have emerged from it have declined, another strand on the far right has emerged. More diffuse in character, the Patriot movement is particularly based in the western states but, as with the Klan and its southern roots, exists across the nation. Fuelled by resentment towards taxation and insistent that attempts to restrict gun ownership are not only un-American but sinister in intent, Patriots have created a host of organizations, some of which have engendered considerable publicity. Posse Comitatus, created at the end of the 1960s by a former Silver Shirt, Mike Beach, has been one such organization.

The name Posse Comitatus is Latin for 'power of the county', and the Posse literally believes that all government power should be rooted at the county level and that the best form of justice is the vigilante kind which used to be meted out to wrongdoers by true Christian Americans in the nineteenth century. This reflects not only a hankering for a return to the days of the old frontier when there was no central or state authority, but a suspicion that the government itself is controlled by enemies (usually Jewish). As an organization, Posse attracted nation-wide attention when in 1983 Gordon Kahl, an active Posse member, killed two federal marshals in North Dakota. Kahl later died in a shoot-out with Arkansas law officers, in which a local sheriff was also killed. Kahl, however, went on to become a hero and martyr to many in the Patriot movement. Posse Comitatus, a decentralized and shadowy organization, needs to be understood in the broader context of a turn towards a millenarian conspiracy theory on the part of many on the extreme right. The social system, they believe, is about to succumb to a cataclysm. Those who wish to survive thus have to prepare themselves. This vision of Armageddon – partly religious in inspiration and partly derived from an almost Marxist-like reading of the contemporary contradictions of modern capitalism – is crucial to understanding the movement.

Two groups centrally associated with preparing for the 'end times' have been The Covenant, the Sword and the Arm of the Lord (CSA), and the

Christian Patriot's Defense League (CPDL). The CSA is (or at least was) a paramilitary survivalist organization operating a 'Christian' communal settlement called Zarepath-Horeb on 224 acres of secluded land near the Arkansas–Missouri border. Composed of about 100 people, they believed US society to be approaching civil war and that it was essential to prepare for this by stockpiling arms, food and wilderness survival gear. The CSA ran a training school offering courses in urban warfare and military tactics. Its leader, Jim Ellison, a former San Antonio fundamentalist, also conducted seminars throughout the South and Mid-West in which he not only demonstrated what weapons were available for 'self-protection', but also distributed such literature as the Protocols of the Elders of Zion, *The Negro and the World Crisis* and *Who's Who in the Zionist Conspiracy*. Following a raid by federal authorities in 1985, Ellison and others were imprisoned and the compound disbanded. (Ellison, like the White Patriot Party's Glenn Miller, was later to testify for the government in court proceedings against his former comrades.)

Like the CSA, the CPDL also preaches a conspiracy theory of history, using Christianity as the basis of its bigotry. It is also heavily involved in paramilitarism. Formed in 1977 by John R. Harrell, an Illinois millionaire involved in extremism since the 1950s, one of its chief activities has been the organization of a 'Freedom Festival', held twice annually at his 55 acres estate in Louisville, Illinois. In 1980, over a thousand people attended the festival, which included classes in weapons and combat, and discussion of the group's anti-semitic and racist literature. No doubt encouraged by his early success, Harrell announced the opening of a 90-acre 'permanent base' in Missouri's Ozark region, and another survival base in West Virginia. Fears of experiencing the same fate as the CSA have, however, helped diminish the size of the Freedom Festivals, and caused the CPDL to drop weapons training as part of its programme. Nevertheless, the group still continues to operate (ADL, 1988c; Ridgeway, 1990; Barkun, 1994).

The Patriot movement is remarkably diverse and contains many who are not motivated by racism or likely to engage in violence. Nonetheless, amid the fear of hidden enemies who would destroy America, they have secured a following. In the eyewitness account of left-wing writer Sara Diamond, at one California meeting in 1995 about two hundred gathered to share ideas on federal government conspiracies and how best to avoid the attentions of the Internal Revenue Service. But, she notes, 'there was a gap between the content of formal, on-the-record presentations and the materials spread out on the literature tables'. Thus, alongside the information on how to file a form declaring oneself a state citizen, and therefore, it was claimed, ineligible for federal taxation, one could also find material on the Zionist conspiracy and a book list from a virulently racist organization, the Sons of Liberty (Diamond, 1995b).

One reason for the existence of racism among Patriots is the popularity of a peculiar religious doctrine known as Christian Identity, currently held to be 'the ideology most widespread among white supremacists' (Zeskind, 1999: 12). Derived from an earlier belief-system known as Anglo-Israelism, Identity adherents believe that people of Northern European stock are the true descendants of the ten 'Lost Tribes' of Israel. In its original form, the argument saw Britain as God's chosen nation. Later modified to include the United States, Christian Identity prioritized the claims of the latter and linked it with an astonishingly virulent anti-semitism. In this teaching, Jews were not reduced to a mere segment of the Chosen, but expelled from that category altogether. Whites, it was held, were the children of God; Jews, the literal children of Satan's seduction of Eve. Like fundamentalists, whom they despise as teaching a racially naive Judaeo-Christianity, they believe in a Second Coming of Christ. Unlike most fundamentalists, however, they do not think that the saved will be lifted to the heavens before the earth goes through the tribulation of a cosmic battle between good and evil. Instead, they will remain as the cities go up in flames, creating a new Israel in America (Zeskind, 1986; Kaplan, 1993).

The central figure in the early development of Christian Identity was Wesley Swift, a former Ku Klux Klan organizer who, in the aftermath of World War II, established an Anglo-Saxon Christian Congregation in Lancaster, California. Following Swift's death in 1970, his mantle was claimed by Richard Girnt Butler, whose own Identity church was based in Hayden Lake, Idaho, along with its political wing, Aryan Nations. Just as there were different congregations (and, to a degree, different interpretations of the doctrine) in Swift's lifetime, different groupings have continued to emerge in recent years. One of the most important, Scriptures for America, is headed by Colorado-based Pete Peters, while other groupings are to be found in Oregon, Washington State and elsewhere.

If one indicator of sympathy for racism within the Patriot movement is the existence of Christian Identity, another is to be seen when we look at Patriot activity in the 1980s. During this period, Patriots were particularly active among small farmers in the West and Midwest, struggling to survive, often unsuccessfully, in an increasingly harsh economic environment. A number of groups were active, including Posse Comitatus, whose pamphlet *The American Farmer: Twentieth Century Slave* apparently received wide distribution in the West. ('The Jew-run banks and federal loan agencies', it declared, were 'working hand in hand, foreclosing on thousands of farms. They are, in essence, nationalizing farms for the Jews'.) One group that emerged in the mid-1980s, the Populist Party, was linked with the most widely circulated publication on the extreme right, the weekly paper *The Spotlight*. The Populists, who consciously modelled themselves on the agrarian protest movement of that name in the latter part of the nineteenth century, were initially chaired by a former Klan leader, Robert Weems, but the most important figure on its national executive (and in the editorial policy of *The Spotlight*) was Willis Carto.

The existence of Christian Identity and the popularity of anti-semitic economic theories do not, it needs to be emphasized, define the Patriot movement as a whole as part of the extreme right. The John Birch Society and other radical right organizations are also an influence on many Patriots. To a large degree, the movement can best be seen as a meeting point and a ground for political competition between different forms of the right. What is not to be doubted, however, is the opportunities it presents. *The Spotlight* was reportedly selling some 75,000 issues per week in the early 1990s (McLemee, 1994). On a smaller scale, the annual gatherings of Aryan Nations bring together members of the Klan, National Socialists, skinheads and Identity believers. Within these different, but overlapping, circles, tensions and rivalries are evident. How the cause can best be advanced is a matter of dispute, and two competing approaches have been among the most visible in recent years. One, which we will discuss shortly, is electoral. The other, which we will turn to first, is that of physical force.

The armed road

Paramilitary organization has long been favoured by sections of the extreme right. At the beginning of the 1980s, for instance, one state organizer for the Knights of the Ku Klux Klan, Louis Beam, organized the paramilitary Texas Emergency Reserve, while the Invisible Empire in Alabama engaged in weapons training in Camp My Lai, named provocatively after the site of an infamous massacre of civilians by American soldiers during the Vietnam War. In the 1960s, a much-publicized group, called the Minutemen sought to organize a guerrilla army in the event of a Russian invasion, while another group, the California Rangers, was founded by Colonel William Gale, who became later a central figure in Posse Comitatus. In our concluding discussion, we will turn our attention to the contentious question of the recent rise of militia groups and their relationship to the extreme right. The most important paramilitary grouping of the previous decade will first be considered here.

In September 1983, Robert Mathews, a member of the National Alliance and an attendee of Richard Butler's Church of Jesus Christ Christian, brought together other activists to create an underground organization, The Order. Soon after, the group not only started to counterfeit money on the Aryan Nations printing press, but began a series of armed robberies which included two of armoured cars (the first netting over $500,000, the second over $3.6 million). An over-talkative sympathizer, Walter West, was murdered by members and, in June 1984, an assassination team followed home a controversial Jewish talk radio show host, Alan Berg, and machine-gunned him to death. Ultimately, federal authorities were able to break up the group, and 23 members were convicted in subsequent court proceedings. A twenty-fourth, David Tate, was sentenced to life imprisonment for the killing of a state trooper while seeking to evade arrest. Mathews was not among those apprehended. After wounding an FBI agent while escaping from a Portland hotel, he was traced to a house on Whidbey Island, Washington State, and was killed in the resulting gun battle.

This turn to terrorism was in large part prompted by frustration felt by activists unable to reverse changes they hated. Behind it all, they were sure, was the Zionist conspiracy, and unless 'white men rose and turned the tide', Mathews wrote shortly before his death, then his son would grow up to 'be a stranger in his own land, a blond-haired, blue-eyed Aryan in a country populated mainly by mexicans, mulattos, blacks and asians' (Ridgeway, 1990: 96). Underpinning this feverish vision was a book written by the National Alliance's founder, William Pierce. Published in 1978, *The Turner Diaries* was the story of a future white guerrilla army which engages in gun battles, the bombing of a federal building, the mass hanging of 'race traitors' along the streets of Los Angeles and, ultimately, the unleashing of nuclear war. The name of the secret organization behind this genocide was The Order.

As with the case of Gordon Kahl, Robert Mathews's death fed the martyrology of the American extreme right. For one prominent militant, the former state leader of the United Klans in Michigan, Robert Miles, an 'armed party' was 'being born'. These 'dragons of God' would have no time for pamphlets or speeches but would take up the methods of an underground army in another land. 'Out of the North, out of the frozen lands, once again the giants gather. Soon, America becomes Ireland recreated.' His evocation of 'the pattern of operations of the IRA' would be a potent image in such circles, as the emergence of another armed group, the Aryan Republican Army, would demonstrate in the mid-1990s (ADL, 1985a: 6; *Searchlight*, 1996). But, as with Irish republicanism, for American extreme rightists there always remained a tension between the gun and the election campaign.

Duke with three Ks

Extreme rightists have sought election on a number of occasions in recent years. In 1980, for instance, Harold Covington, the leader of the main rival Nazi grouping to the NSWPP, the National Socialist Party of America, gained nearly 43 per cent in the Republican primary for state attorney general of North Carolina. In the same year a former member of the Klan and other supremacist groups gained the Republican nomination for a Congressional district in Michigan, achieving 32 per cent of the vote in the subsequent contest. On most occasions, however, extreme right candidates have been spectacularly unsuccessful, and the electoral road's disappointments have undoubtedly been important in generating support for the armed struggle, for the building of racist communities and for other non-electoral strategies. One activist, though, has been successful in pursuing elected office, former Knights of the Ku Klux Klan leader David Duke.

Duke was first brought into racial politics through the Citizens' Councils. He subsequently became an active National Socialist before becoming the most prominent racist activist of the late 1970s. After leaving the Klan to form his own National Association for the Advancement of White People (NAAWP), he was to play a prominent part in the 1987 demonstrations against the civil rights movement in Forsyth County, Georgia. The following year, he entered the presidential contest, first gaining 22,000 votes in selected Democrat primaries, then running as the Populist candidate and achieving some 150,000 votes. But his real breakthrough came in 1989, when he was elected as a Republican to the Louisiana House of Representatives. His candidacy and its success generated massive publicity, and later the same year he made an equally well-publicized bid to capture a seat in the US Senate. To the surprise and horror of many, in the final vote in October 1990, he managed to capture 44 per cent of the total vote and a majority of the white vote.

The most important question to ask here is why Duke did so well. The superficial answer is that he 'cleaned up his act', changed his image and repeatedly apologized for past 'misdemeanours'. But there was more to it than that. Basically, Duke won votes because he identified a number of white fears and frustrations and directed them against a number of specific targets (Ferguson, 1990: 16–18). The first of these, not surprisingly, was the 'establishment' in Washington. According to Duke, its members had consistently ignored the interests of hard-working white Americans while lining their own pockets. Not surprisingly, again this populist argument went down particularly well in Louisiana, a state where unemployment was higher than the national average and where living standards were either stagnant or in decline for the white majority. His second target was foreign economic competition, which, he declared, was robbing honest Americans of their livelihoods. But Duke's populist economic nationalist message was only the icing on the cake. In meeting after meeting around Louisiana he repeated the same simple, alarming message: that all the United States' problems from crime, education and drugs stemmed from the welfare system and the burgeoning, predominantly black, underclass. 'Working families', he declared at one rally in Baton Rouge, 'are paying for [their] illegitimate kids'. These people, he went on, 'are having children faster than they can raise your taxes to pay for them' (Barber, 1990). This oft-repeated message undoubtedly struck a chord with many whites, especially those who felt that social programmes such as affirmative action and welfare had given blacks an undeserved advantage. Duke, indeed, claimed that whites had actually become second-class citizens in their own country. 'We demand equal rights for whites', he proclaimed at his meetings, skilfully manipulating the slogan traditionally associated with the civil rights movement in order to advance his own racist cause (Powell, 1990).

Having made real headway in the Senate race of 1990, Duke decided to run for governor in 1991. If anything, his well-publicized campaign in October and November received even more media attention than his earlier bid for power. Again he was extremely successful in mobilizing the white vote behind his banner. In the first ballot, he received 32 per cent of the total vote and between 42 and 44 per cent of the white vote. In the run-off, he obtained 39 per cent of the total and 55 per cent of the white vote. The Democrat, Edwin Edwards, had won. But as Duke pointed out, while white voters 'may have rejected' him, they had not rejected his 'message'. And the message was that white people wanted equal rights, rejected welfare dependency and affirmative action programmes favouring minorities, and demanded that the government ensure economic prosperity while fighting drugs and crime effectively.

The extreme right in the 1990s

Following David Duke's 1989 election victory, Pat Buchanan wrote that the Republican Party should 'deal with Duke' the way it had 'dealt with the far more formidable challenge of George Wallace'. The issues Duke had won on, he argued, should be expropriated wherever they did not conflict with Republican values (*Monitor*, 1989) As his comment suggests, the relationship between mainstream conservatism and the extreme right might be seen as two-way traffic. Duke's issues and his constituency are available to Republicans – not least, of course, to Buchanan himself. Duke, in attempting to repackage the extreme right and broaden its appeal, may, in the end, only be delivering his supporters to the mainstream right. (Indeed, we might note here his failure to regain the Republican nomination to the US Senate in the 1996 Louisiana primaries.) But, conversely, Buchanan's positioning as a nationalist and populist was to give yet more opportunities to extreme right militants to leave the margins and enter a campaign with greater popular support than they are ever likely to gain alone. Thus the Populist Party, before dissolving in 1995, was to declare its support for Buchanan, while extreme right publications were full of speculation about the opportunities presented by his candidacy. Other changes too are happening within the mainstream right which encourage racist activists. A bitter dispute in the late 1980s between two conservative groupings, neo-conservatives and palaeo-conservatives, had already brought to light a divide between those who favour a globalist foreign policy and those who identify themselves with the isolationism of the pre-war right. This conflict, with its accusations of anti-semitism and nativism, has overlapped both with a rising argument about immigration controls and with the emergence of groupings, such as the Southern League and the Council of Conservative Citizens, which consciously identify with what they see as the heroic values of the Confederacy (Diamond, 1995a; Zeskind, 1996; Prague, 1996). In this atmosphere, sections of the extreme right can be found alongside mainstream conservatives, each pursuing their own agenda.

This picture of a mainstreaming of parts of the extreme right is only one aspect of recent developments. The enthusiastic promotion of racist rock music has made Detroit-based Resistance Records a major force within the skinhead movement (a movement which even exists within the armed forces). Among the scattered Nazi groupings, the attempt by the veteran racist Harold Covington to re-create the NSWPP represents yet another manoeuvre in the unending battle for Lincoln Rockwell's succession (Talty, 1996; Sapsted, 1987; *Searchlight*, 1994b). It appears unlikely, however, that such initiatives will generate a breakthrough for the American extreme right, any more than will the activities of the Klan. Skinheads make up a tiny section of white American youth, let alone the white population in general, and like much of the extreme right are drawn to behaviour more likely to result in attempting to organize in prison than attempting to organize in the outside world. Nor will seeking to build an openly Nazi party fare any better. While Rockwell was right that a provocative appearance draws attention, this does not mean that it draws mass support. Furthermore, unlike the Klan, with its roots in native soil, groups like the NSWPP have the grave disadvantage of looking distinctly un-American. As for the Klan, it has not only declined in numbers but also changed its nature in many ways. In the 1860s, as in the 1960s, its main goal was the preservation of white privilege in the South. In the 1920s, it sought to defend an endangered small-town and rural Protestant hegemony. Now the Klan frequently espouses a biological racism that has brought it ideologically ever closer to other strands of the extreme right. Moreover, through its manipulation of symbol and ritual, the Klan has been able to provide its members with something which many other groups on the extreme right cannot: a sense of collective identity and mystery. But none of this is enough to make it a likely vehicle for a mass movement.

What of the Patriot movement? Here, considerable attention has been given in recent years to the rise of a new generation of armed organizations, the citizen Militias. The subject of wildly differing estimates of support (from 10,000 to 40,000 and even higher still in some accounts), the Militias emerged in the aftermath of the 1993 siege in Waco, Texas, of a religious cult, the Branch Davidians, whose leader, David Koresh, was wanted for firearms law violations. The culmination of the siege, in which fire spread through the buildings, killing 75 members of the group, was seen by Patriots as final proof of their belief about a government that sought to take away people's guns and would stop at nothing to crush any resistance. US history, they held, had shown that the only way to stop tyranny was a willingness to use force; and the following year armed Militias appeared in a number of states including, most importantly, Montana and Michigan.

The subject of considerable comment, the Militias have not been well understood. The Oklahoma bombing, apparently the work of an extreme right Patriot cell, may well, as has been suggested, have been partly inspired by the description of a similar bombing in William Pierce's *The Turner Diaries*. But rather than applaud the action, let alone initiate it, Militias disavowed it, claiming the attack was a 'Reichstag '95', an attempt to frame them by an unscrupulous government. Conspiracy theories involving mysterious black helicopters, UN plans to invade the United States and the deliberate creation of deadly viruses abound in such circles, fed by radical right and extreme right alike, and certainly the latter has not been slow to recognize a new chance to extend its constituency. The Montana group, probably the most important, was founded by an Identity believer, John Trochmann – and another siege one year before Waco, in which the son and wife of Idaho white supremacist Randy Weaver had been shot dead, had been a crucial factor in laying the ground for the new movement. But while militants from an earlier generation of racist militancy, notably former Klansman Louis Beam and Posse Comitatus leader James Wickstrom, are involved in this new mobilization, the Militias are not in themselves a force for white supremacy. As with the Patriots as a whole, rather than being the racist right's base, the Militias represent a potential constituency for which it must compete not only with the radical right but with mainstream conservatism's formidable capacity to appropriate anger and channel discontent (Durham, 1996; Dees and Corcoran, 1996; Stern, 1996).

In the 1960s, *National Review* had sought to secure the borders of official conservatism by denouncing the John Birch Society's paranoid conspiratorialism. In the 1970s, as we have seen, Liberty Lobby was to be attacked as comprising anti-semites disguised as conservatives. Despite occasional tremors, the national populism encapsulated by Pat Buchanan has not been excluded from conservative orthodoxy. Like the Wallace movement before it, it represents both an opportunity for the extreme right and also a danger. If conservative strategists are successful, the issues and the constituency that Buchanan has championed will not be lost to forces to their right. Instead, the American extreme right will once again, at best, be foot soldiers in someone else's army.

MICHAEL COX AND MARTIN DURHAM

References and further reading

Abanes, R. (1996) *American Militias*. Downers Grove: InterVarsity Press.

Aho, J. A. (1990) *The Politics of Righteousness: Idaho Christian Patriotism*. Seattle: University of Washington Press.

Alexander, C. C. (1965) *The Ku Klux Klan in the Southwest*. Lexington: University of Kentucky Press.

Anti-Defamation League (1983) *The 'Identity Churches': A Theology of Hate*. Spring, New York.

Anti-Defamation League (1985a) *Computerized Networks of Hate*. January, New York.

Anti-Defamation League (1985b) *The Populist Party: The Politics of Right-Wing Extremism*. Autumn, New York.

Anti-Defamation League (1986a) *Extremism Targets the Prisons*. Special report, June.

Anti-Defamation League (1986b) *Extremist Group Outreach to Rural Americans*. Special edition, October.

Anti-Defamation League (1987a) *The Liberty Lobby Network*. Special edition, October.

Anti-Defamation League (1987b) *'Shaved for Battle': Skinheads Target America's Youth*. New York.

Anti-Defamation League (1988a) *The Murder of Alan Berg*. Special edition, June.

Anti-Defamation League (1988b) *Young and Violent: The Growing Menace of America's Neo-Nazi Skinheads*. New York.

Anti-Defamation League (1988c) *Hate Groups in America: A Record of Bigotry and Violence*. New York.

Anti-Defamation League (1994) *Armed and Dangerous: Militias Take Aim at the Federal Government*. New York.

Anti-Defamation League (1995) *Beyond the Bombing: The Militia Menace Grows*. New York.

Anti-Defamation League (1996) *Extremists Exploit the Internet*. New York.

Barber, L. (1990) 'Former Klansman Puts a New Face on Racist Past', *Financial Times* (London), 5 October.

Barkun, M. (1994) *Religion and the Racist Right: The Origins of the Christian Identity Movement*. Chapel Hill: University of North Carolina Press.

Barkun, M. (1996) 'Religion, Militias and Oklahoma City: The Mind of Conspiratorialists', *Terrorism and Political Violence*, Spring.

Bennett, D. H. (1988) *The Party of Fear: From Nativist Movements to the New Right in American History*. Chapel Hill: University of North Carolina Press.

Berlet, C. (ed.) (1995) *Eyes Right! Challenging the Right Wing Backlash*. Boston: South End Press.

Blee, K. M. (1991) *Women of the Klan: Racism and Gender in the 1920s*. Berkeley: University of California Press.

Brogan, H. (1986) *The Pelican History of the United States of America*. Harmondsworth: Penguin.

Carman, H. J. and Syrett, H. C. (1952) *A History of the American People since 1865*, Vol. 2. New York: Columbia University Press.

Carter, D. T. (1995) *The Politics of Rage: George Wallace, the Origins of the New Conservatism, and the Transformation of American Politics*. New York: Simon & Schuster.

Center for Democratic Renewal (1981) *Violence, the Ku Klux Klan and the Struggle for Equality*. Atlanta.

Center for Democratic Renewal (1985) *Racist Anti-Semitic Intervention in the Farm Protest Movement*. September, Atlanta.

Center for Democratic Renewal (1996) *Militias Exploit the Mainstream*. March, Atlanta.

Center for Democratic Renewal (n.d.) *It's not Populism – America's New Populist Party: A Fraud by Racists and Anti-Semites*. Atlanta.

Chalmers, D. M. (1981) *Hooded Americanism*. New York: Franklin Watts.

Coates, J. (1987) *Armed and Dangerous: The Rise of the Survivalist Right*. New York: Hill & Wang.

Corcoran, J. (1991) *Bitter Harvest – Gordon Kahl and the Posse Comitatus: Murder in the Heartland*. New York: Viking Penguin.

Crawford, R., Gardner, S. L., Mozzochi, J. and Taylor, R. L. (1994) *The Northwest Imperative: Documenting a Decade of Hate*. Portland: Coalition for Human Dignity.

Cremoni, L. (1998) 'Anti-semitism and Populism in the United States in the 1930s: The Case of Father Coughlin', *Patterns of Prejudice* 32(1).

Davies, H. (1996) 'Ex-Klansman Seeks Senate Seat', *Daily Telegraph* (London), 12 July.

Dees, M. and Corcoran, J. (1996) *Gathering Storm: America's Militia Threat*. New York: HarperCollins.

Diamond, S. (1995a) *Roads to Dominion: Right-wing Movements and Political Power in the United States*. New York: Guilford Press.

Diamond, S. (1995b) 'Patriot Games', *The Progressive*, September.

Durham, M. (1996) 'Preparing for Armageddon: Citizen Militias, the Patriot Movement and the Oklahoma City Bombing', *Terrorism and Political Violence*, Spring.

Edsall, T. B. and Edsall, M. D. (1992) *Chain Reaction: The Impact of Race, Rights and Taxes on American Politics*. New York: W.W. Norton.

Ferguson, A. (1990) 'The Wizardry of David Duke', *The American Spectator*, October.

Fisher, W. H. (1980) *The Invisible Empire*. Metuchen, NJ: Scarecrow Press.

Flynn, K. and Gerhardt, G. (1989) *The Silent Brotherhood: Inside America's Racist Underground*. New York: Free Press.

George, J. and Wilcox, L. (1992) *Nazis, Communists, Klansmen and Others on the Fringe: Political Extremism in America*. Buffalo: Prometheus Books.

Horn, S. F. (1939, [1969]) *Invisible Empire: The Story of the Ku Klux Klan, 1866–1871*. New Jersey: Patterson Smith.

Jackson, K. T. (1967) *The Ku Klux Klan in the City, 1915–1930*. New York: Oxford University Press.

Jeansonne, G. (1988) *Gerald L. K. Smith: A Minister of Hate*. New Haven, CT: Yale University Press.

Kaplan, J. (1993) 'The Context of American Millenarian Revolutionary Theology: The Case of the "Identity Christian" Church of Israel', *Terrorism and Political Violence*, Spring.

Kaplan, J. (1995) 'Right-Wing Violence in North America', in Björgo, T. (ed.) *Terror from the Extreme Right*. London: Frank Cass.

Katz, W. L. (n.d.) *The Invisible Empire: The Ku Klux Klan's Impact on History*. Seattle: Open Hand.

Klanwatch, (1988) *The Ku Klux Klan: A History of Racism and Violence*, 3rd edition. Montgomery, AL: Klanwatch.

Latham, E. (1996) *The Communist Controversy in Washington*. Cambridge, MA: Harvard University Press.

Lester, J.C. (1971) *Ku Klux Klan: Its Origin, Growth and Disbandment*. New York: AMS Press.

Lipset, S. M. and Raab, E. (1978) *The Politics of Unreason: Right-Wing Extremism in America, 1790–1977*. Chicago: University of Chicago Press.

Louks, E. H. (1936) *The Ku Klux Klan in Pennsylvania: A Study in Nativism*. Harrisburg, PA: Telegraph Press.

Lowe, D. (1967) *The Ku Klux Klan: The Invisible Empire*. New York: W.W. Norton.

Lutz, C. *They Don't All Wear Sheets: A Chronology of Racist and Far Right Violence, 1980–1986*. Atlanta: Center for Democratic Renewal.

MacLean, N. (1994) *Behind the Mask of Chivalry: The Making of the Second Ku Klux Klan*. New York: Oxford University Press.

McLemee, S. (1994) 'Spotlight on the Liberty Lobby', *Covert Action Quarterly*, Fall.

McLennan, P., McLennan, T. and Chalmers, D. (1985) *The True Story of the Ku Klux Klan vs Organized Labor*. Atlanta: Center for Democratic Renewal.

McMillen, N. R. (1994) *The Citizens' Council: Organized Resistance to the Second Reconstruction, 1954–64*. Urbana: University of Illinois Press.

Mecklin, J. M. (1924 [1963]) *The Ku Klux Klan: A Study of the American Mind*. New York: Russell & Russell.

Miller, W. (1958) *A New History of the United States*. New York: George Braziller.

Mintz, F. P. (1985) *The Liberty Lobby and the American Right: Race, Conspiracy and Culture*. Westport, CT: Greenwood Press.

Monitor, The (1989) 'David Duke's Louisiana Victory Is Reflection of a National Strategy', May.

Moore, J. B. (1993) *Skinheads Shaved for Battle: A Cultural History of American Skinheads*. Bowling Green, OH: Bowling Green State University Popular Press.

Novick, M. (1995) *White Lies White Power: The Fight against White Supremacy and Reactionary Violence*. Monroe: Common Courage Press.

O'Neill, W. L. (1971) *Coming Apart: An Informal History of America in the 1960s*. New York: Times Books.

O'Reilly, K. (1989) *'Racial Matters': The FBI's Secret file on Black America: 1960–1972*. New York: Free Press.

Powell, L. N. (1990) 'Read My Liposuction', *New Republic*, 15 October.

Prague, E. G. (1996) 'The Neo-Confederate Movement', *Turning the Tide*, Summer.

Ribuffo, L. P. (1983) *The Old Christian Right: The Protestant Far Right from the Great Depression to the Cold War*. Philadelphia: Temple University Press.

Rice, A. S. (1962) *The Ku Klux Klan in American Politics*. Washington, DC: Public Affairs Press.

Ridgeway, J. (1990) *Blood in the Face: The Ku Klux Klan, Aryan Nations, Nazi Skinheads, and the Rise of a New White Culture*. New York: Thunder's Mouth Press.

Rose, D. D. (ed.) (1992) *The Emergence of David Duke and the Politics of Race*. Chapel Hill: University of North Carolina Press.

Sapsted, D. (1997) 'Race Killers May Face Death Penalty', *Daily Telegraph* (London), 1 March.

Sargent, L. T. (1995) *Extremism in America: A Reader*. New York: New York University Press.

Searchlight (1994a) *State of the Union*, February.

Searchlight (1994b) *Covington Stages Takeover Bid*, October.

Searchlight (1996) 'New Bank Robbers Imitate Old "Order" ', May.

Seymour, C. (1991) *Committee of the States: Inside the Radical Right*. Mariposa: Camden Place Communications.

Stanton, B. (1992) *Klanwatch: Bringing the Ku Klux Klan to Justice*. New York: Mentor.

Stern, K. S. (1996) *A Force upon the Plain: The American Militia Movement and the Politics of Hate*. New York: Simon & Schuster.

Stone, B. A. (1974) 'The John Birch Society: A Profile' *Journal of Politics* 36.

Talty, S. (1996) 'The Method of a Neo-Nazi Mogul', *New York Times Magazine*, 25 February.

Thayer, G. (1967) *The Farther Shore of Politics: The American Political Fringe Today*. New York: Simon & Schuster.

Trelease, A. W. (1972) *White Terror: The Ku Klux Klan Conspiracy and Southern Reconstruction*. London: Secker & Warburg.

Ungar, S. J. (1976) *FBI: An Uncensored Look behind the Walls*. Boston: Little, Brown.

Wade, W. C. (1987) *The Fiery Cross: The Ku Klux Klan in America*. New York: Simon & Schuster.

Weinberg, L. (1993) 'The American Radical Right: Exit, Voice, and Violence', in Merkl, P. H. and Weinberg, L. (eds) *Encounters with the Contemporary Radical Right*. Boulder, CO: Westview.

Wheaton, E. (1987) *Codename GREENKIL: The 1979 Greensboro Killings*. Athens, GA: University of Georgia Press.

Wright, B. (1976) *The Long View: An International History of the Cinema*. London: Paladin.

Zanden, J. W. V. (1960) 'The Klan Revival', *American Journal of Sociology* 65.

Zatarin, M. (1990) *David Duke: Evolution of a Klansman*. New York: Pelican.

Zeskind, L. (1986) *The 'Christian Identity Movement'*. Atlanta: Center for Democratic Renewal.

Zeskind, L. (1996) 'White-Shoed Supremacy', *The Nation*, 10 June.

Zeskind, L. (1999) 'Christian Identity: White Nationalism's Theology', *Searchlight* 287 (May), p. 12.

Index